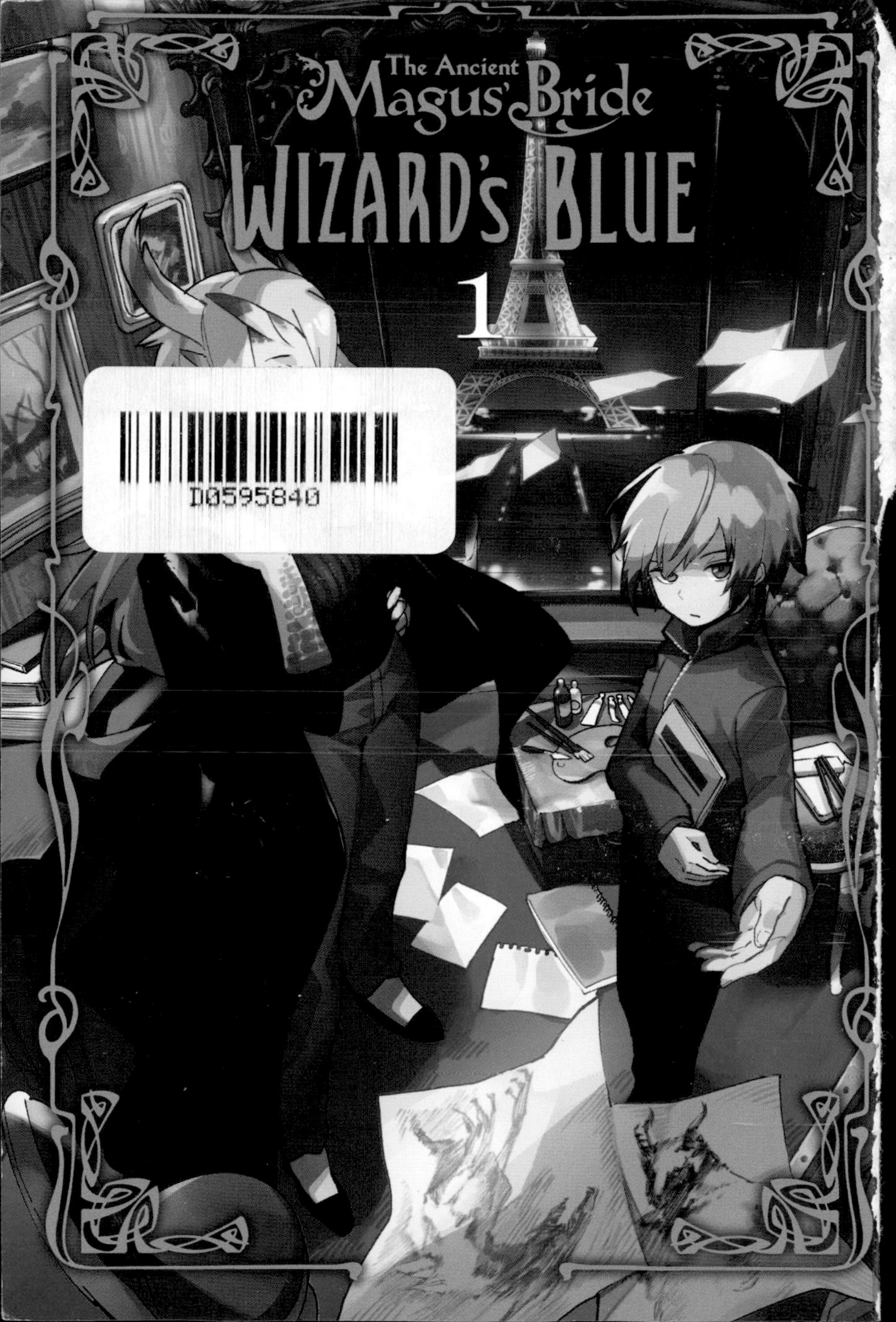
The Ancient
Magus' Bride
WIZARD's BLUE
1

The Ancient Magus' Bride
WIZARD's BLUE
1

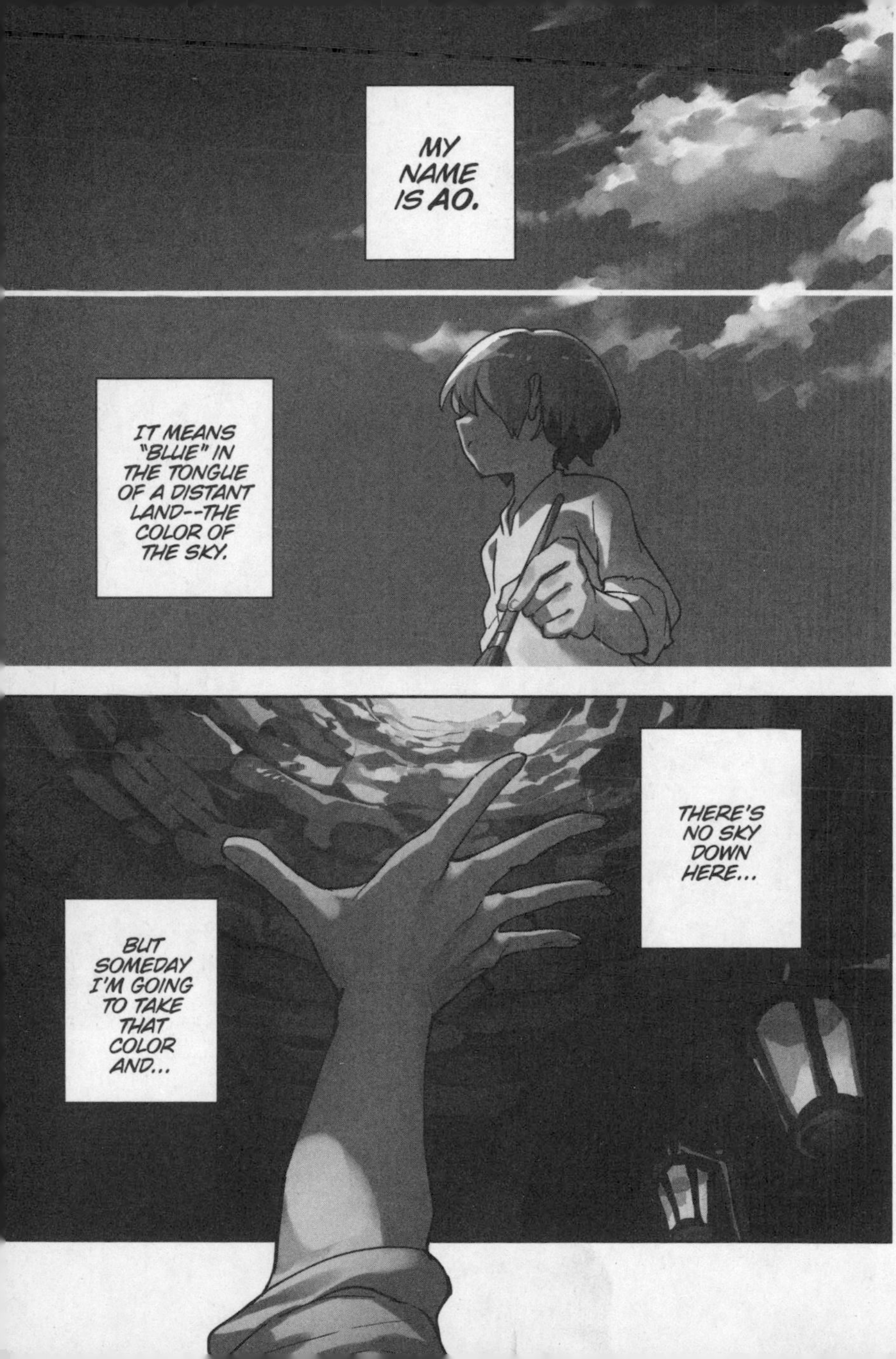
MY NAME IS AO.
IT MEANS "BLUE" IN THE TONGUE OF A DISTANT LAND--THE COLOR OF THE SKY.
THERE'S NO SKY DOWN HERE...
BUT SOMEDAY I'M GOING TO TAKE THAT COLOR AND...

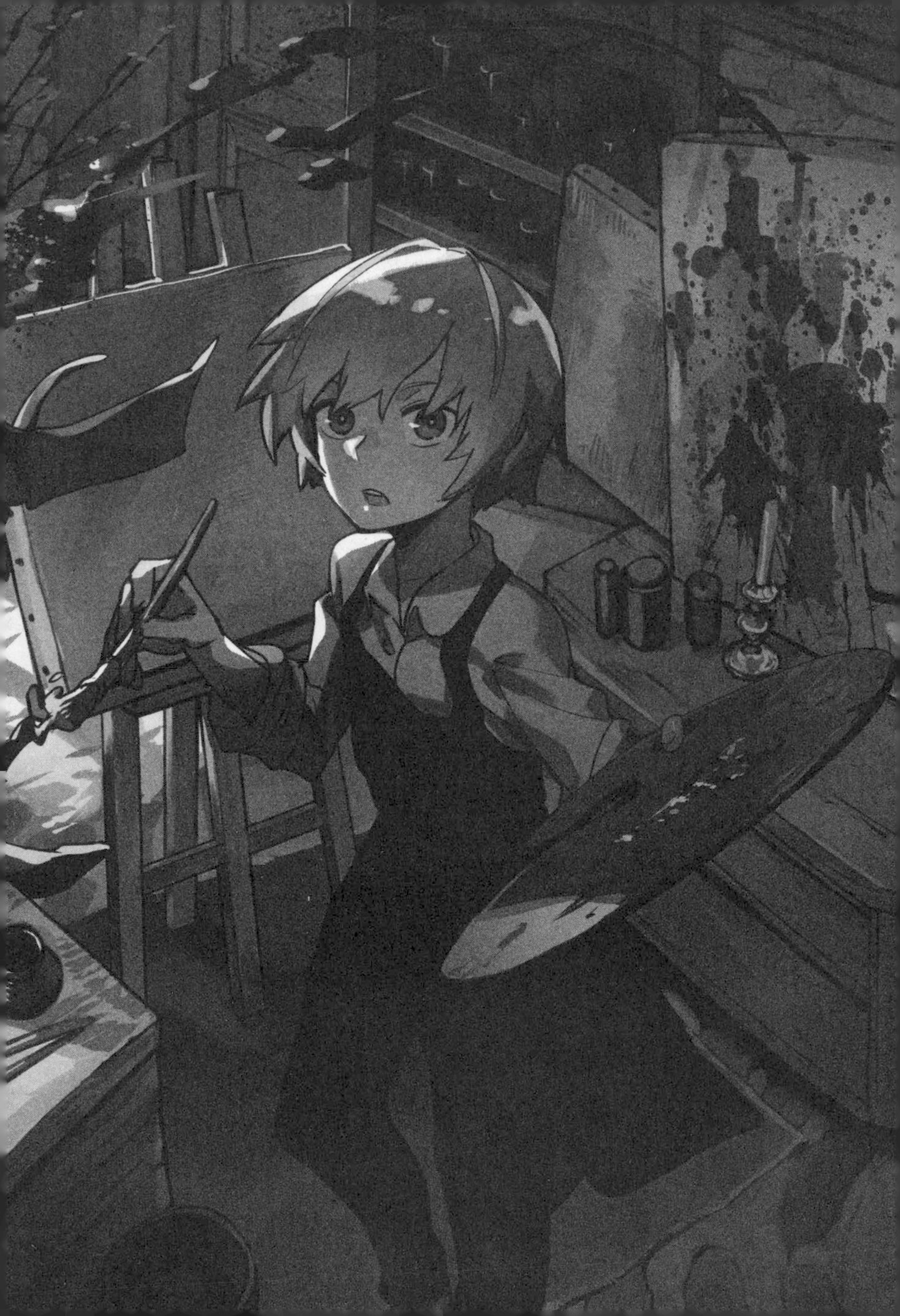

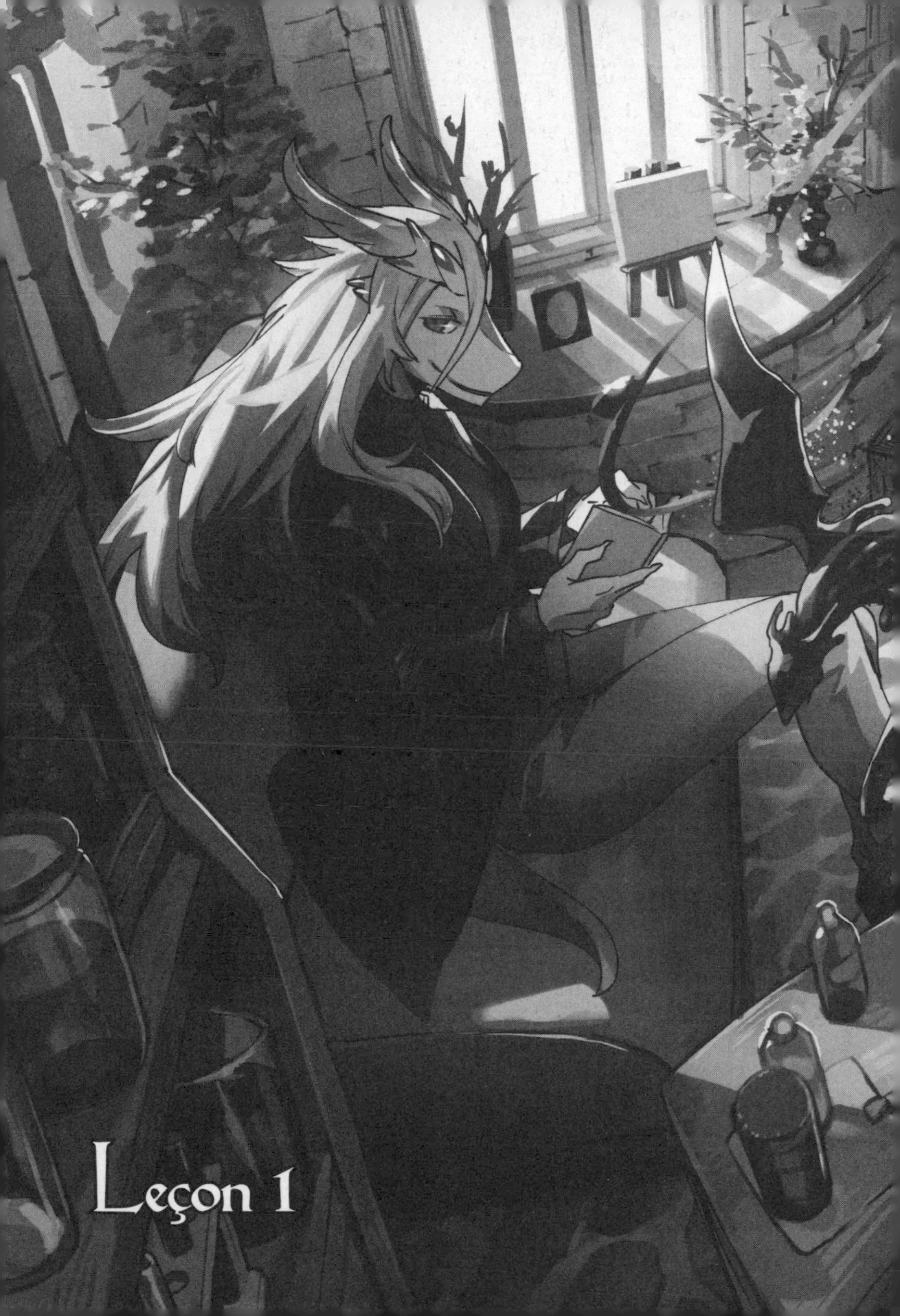

Leçon 1

The Ancient Magus' Bride

WIZARD's BLUE

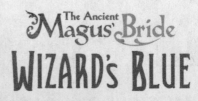

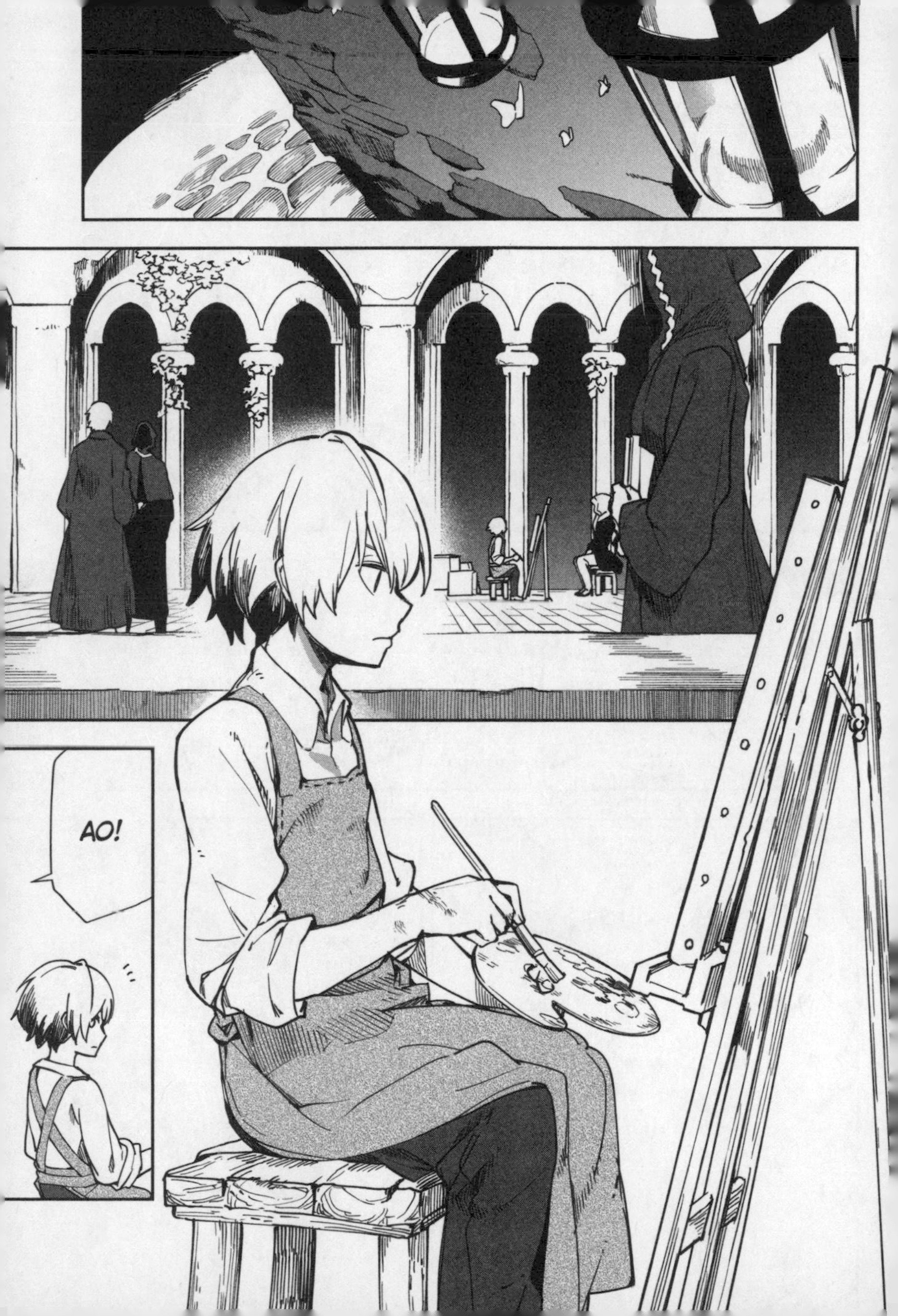
AO!

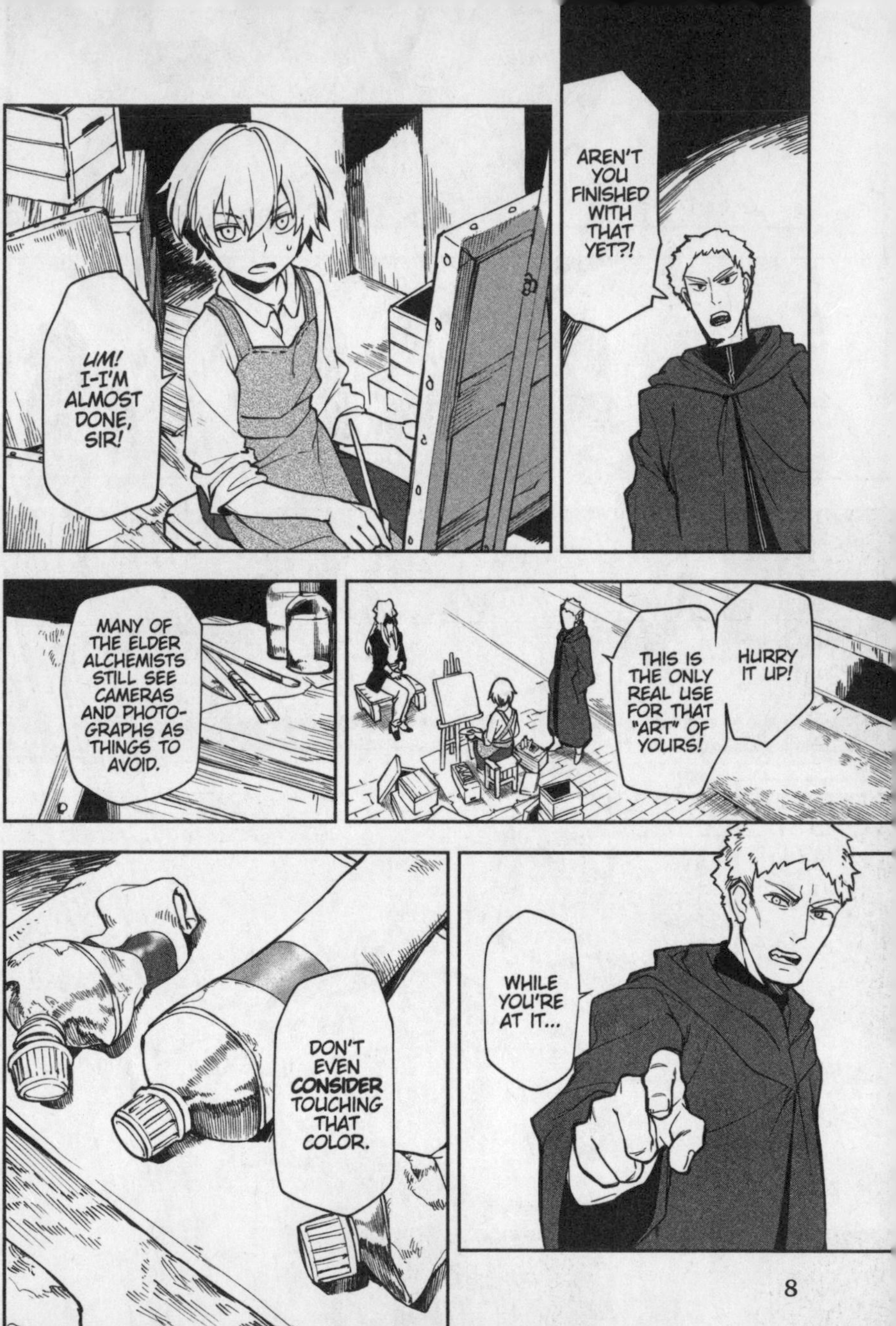
AREN'T YOU FINISHED WITH THAT YET?!
UM! I-I'M ALMOST DONE, SIR!
HURRY IT UP!
THIS IS THE ONLY REAL USE FOR THAT "ART" OF YOURS!
MANY OF THE ELDER ALCHEMISTS STILL SEE CAMERAS AND PHOTO-GRAPHS AS THINGS TO AVOID.
WHILE YOU'RE AT IT...
DON'T EVEN **CONSIDER** TOUCHING THAT COLOR.

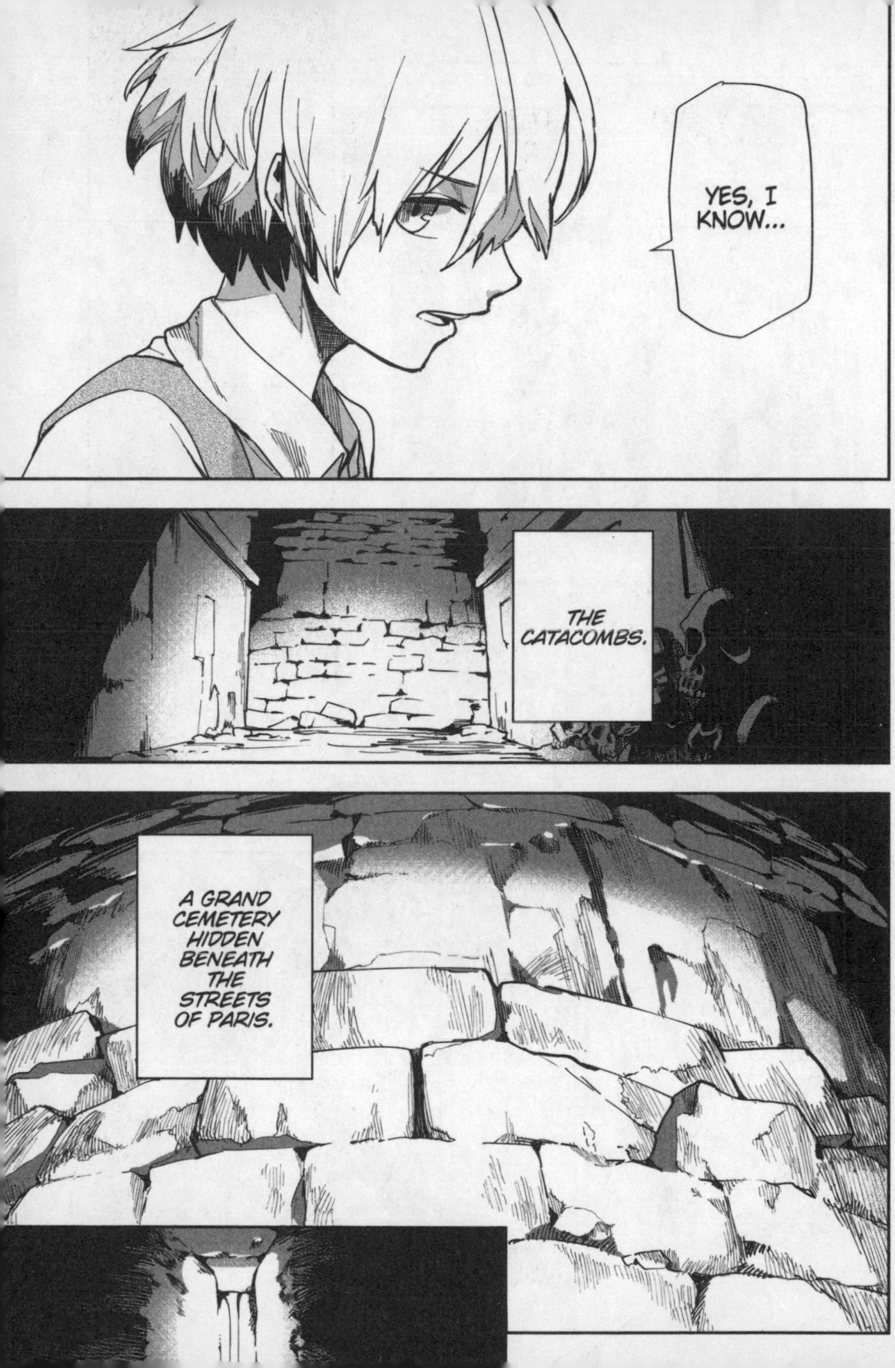
YES, I KNOW...
THE CATACOMBS.
A GRAND CEMETERY HIDDEN BENEATH THE STREETS OF PARIS.

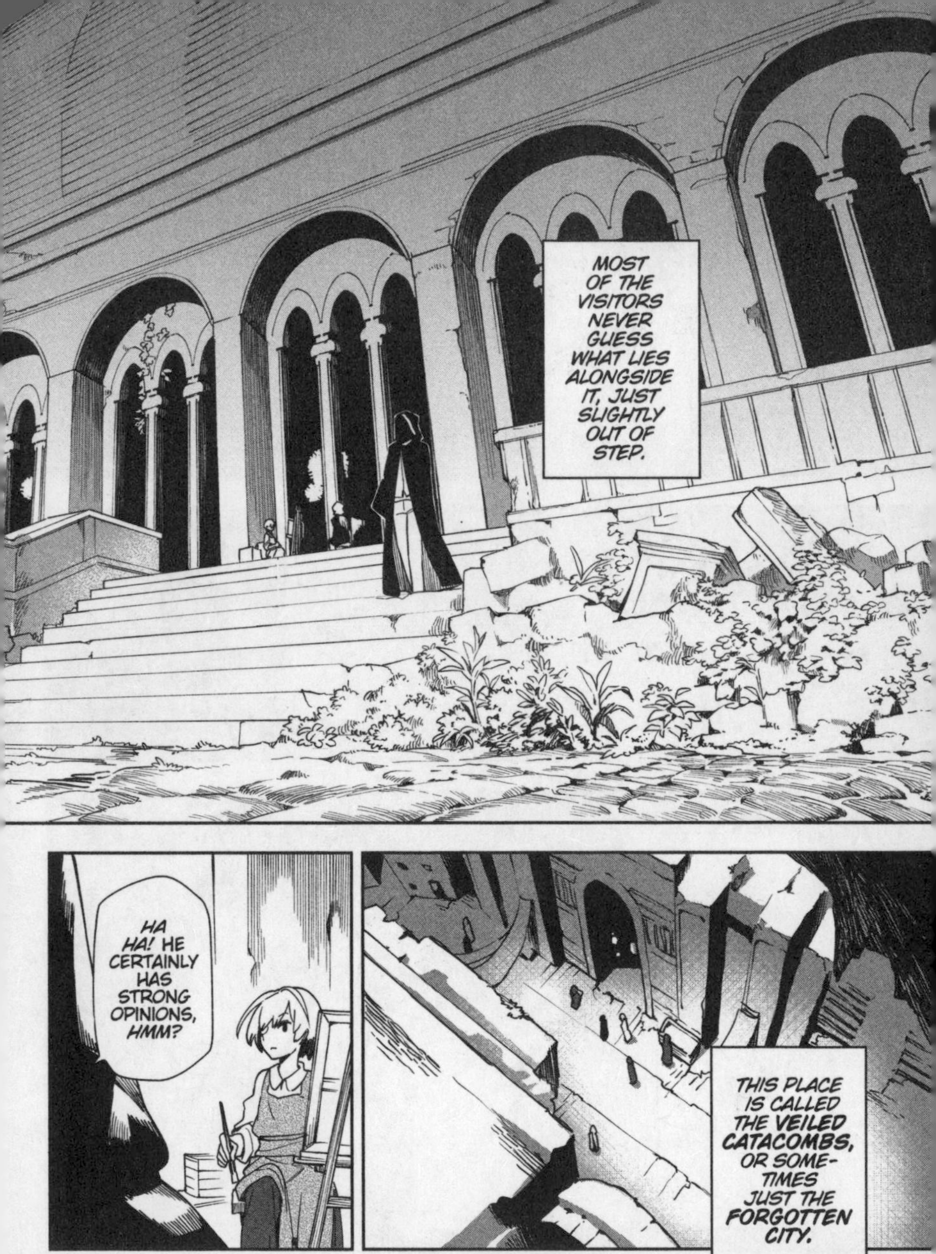
MOST OF THE VISITORS NEVER GUESS WHAT LIES ALONGSIDE IT, JUST SLIGHTLY OUT OF STEP.
THIS PLACE IS CALLED THE VEILED CATACOMBS, OR SOME-TIMES JUST THE FORGOTTEN CITY.
HA HA! HE CERTAINLY HAS STRONG OPINIONS, HMM?

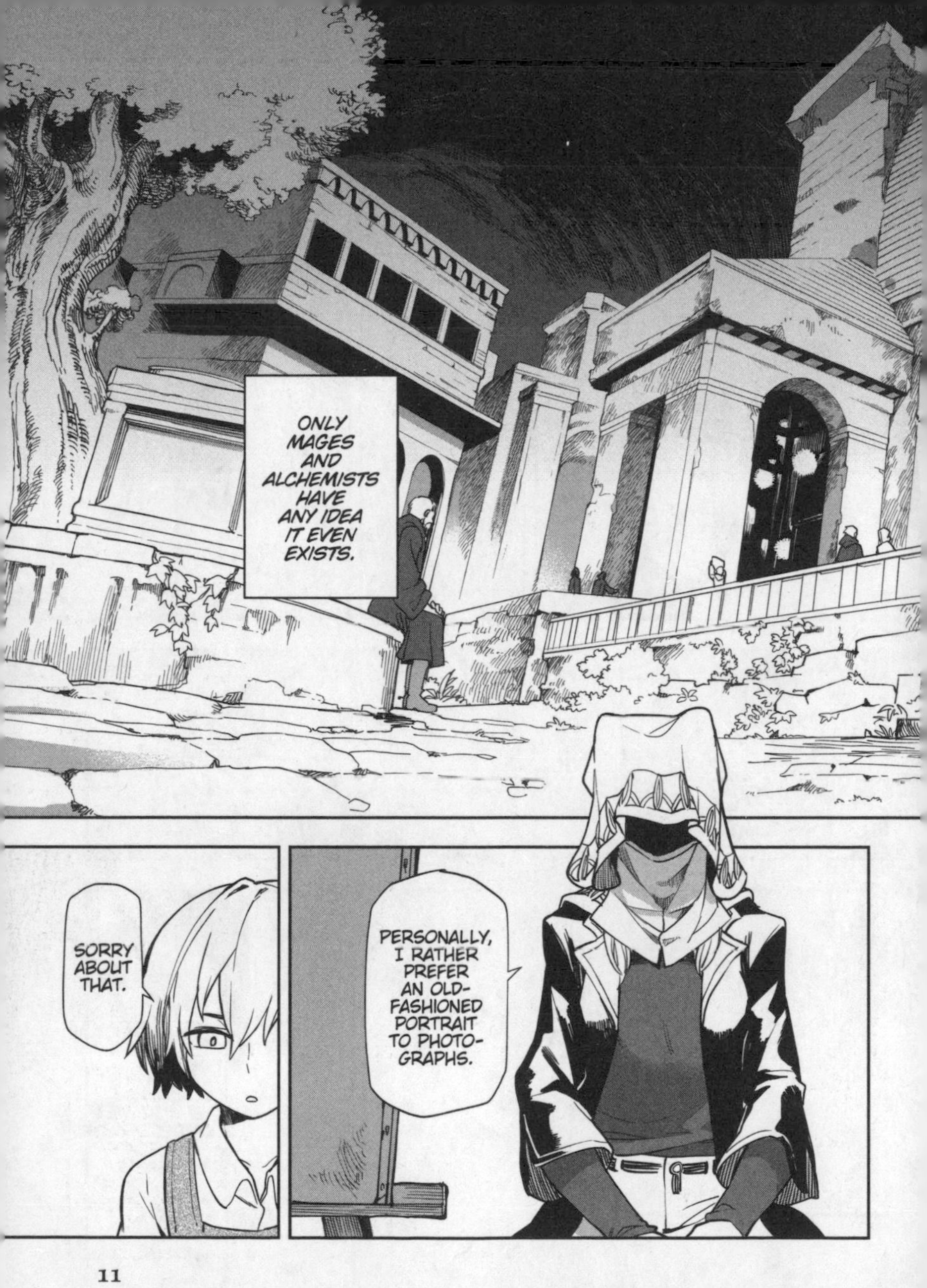
ONLY MAGES AND ALCHEMISTS HAVE ANY IDEA IT EVEN EXISTS.
PERSONALLY, I RATHER PREFER AN OLD-FASHIONED PORTRAIT TO PHOTO-GRAPHS.
SORRY ABOUT THAT.

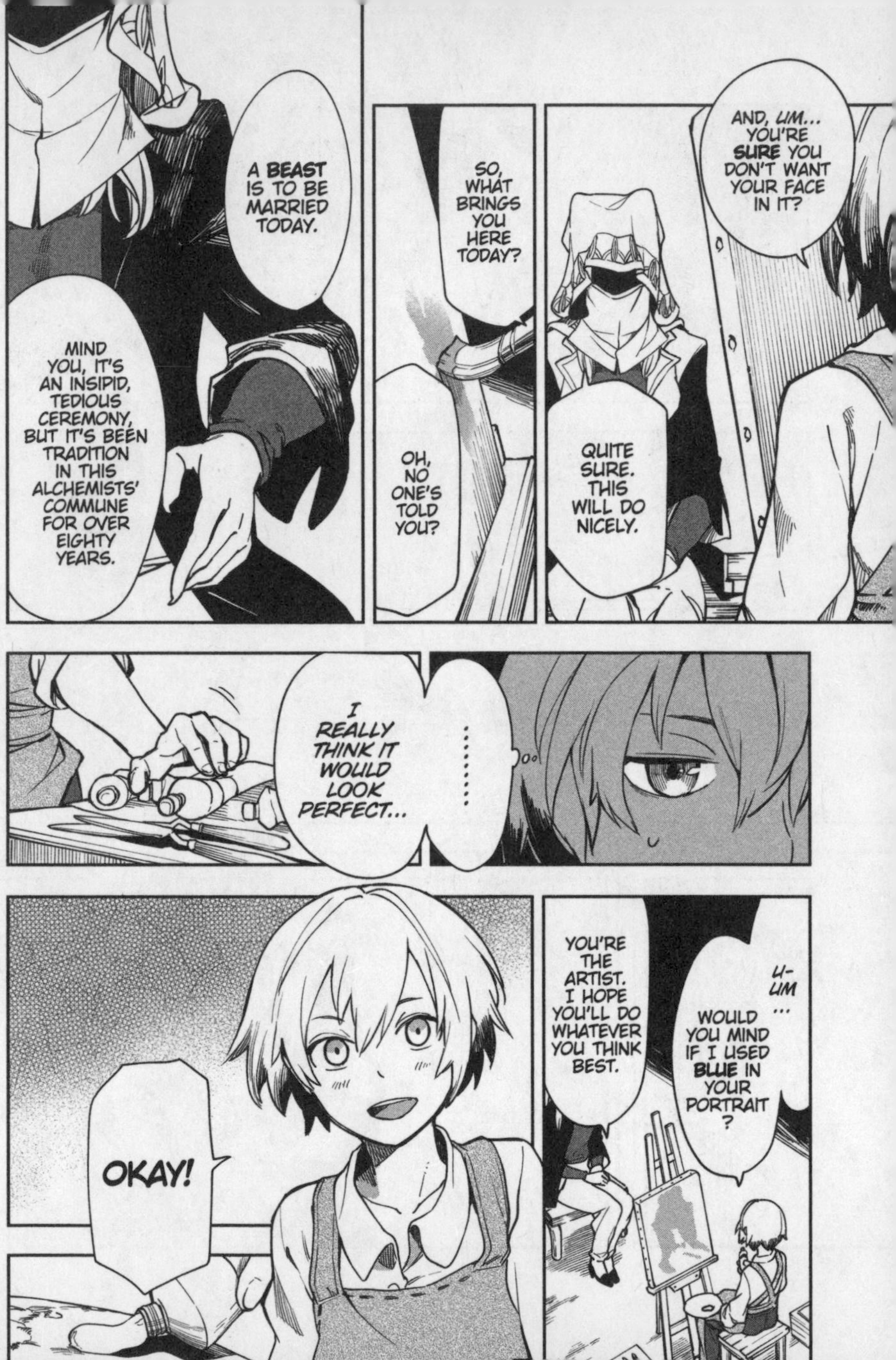
AND, UM... YOU'RE SURE YOU DON'T WANT YOUR FACE IN IT?
QUITE SURE. THIS WILL DO NICELY.
SO, WHAT BRINGS YOU HERE TODAY?
OH, NO ONE'S TOLD YOU?
A BEAST IS TO BE MARRIED TODAY.
MIND YOU, IT'S AN INSIPID, TEDIOUS CEREMONY, BUT IT'S BEEN TRADITION IN THIS ALCHEMISTS' COMMUNE FOR OVER EIGHTY YEARS.
......
I REALLY THINK IT WOULD LOOK PERFECT...
U-UM...
WOULD YOU MIND IF I USED BLUE IN YOUR PORTRAIT?
YOU'RE THE ARTIST. I HOPE YOU'LL DO WHATEVER YOU THINK BEST.
OKAY!

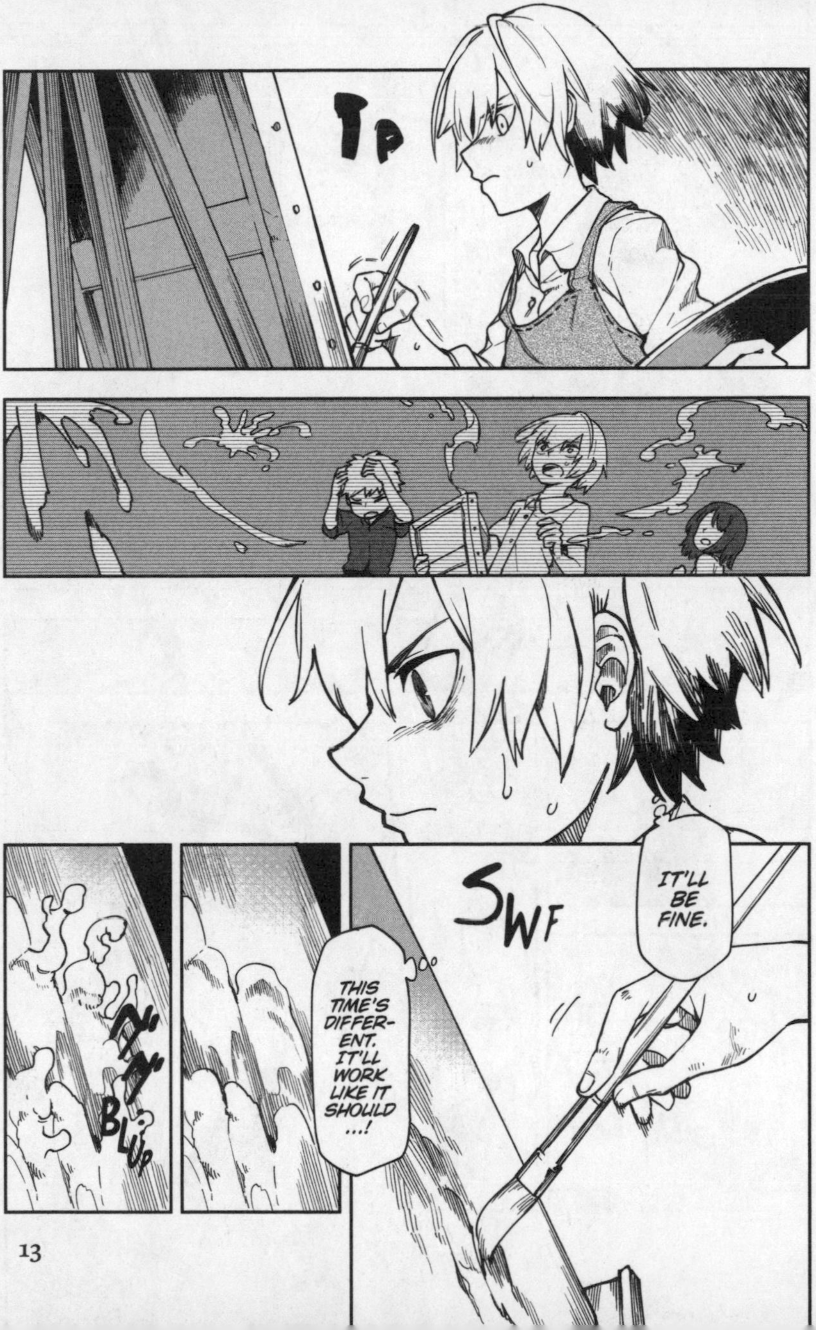
TP
SWF
IT'LL BE FINE.
THIS TIME'S DIFFER-ENT. IT'LL WORK LIKE IT SHOULD ...!
BLUP

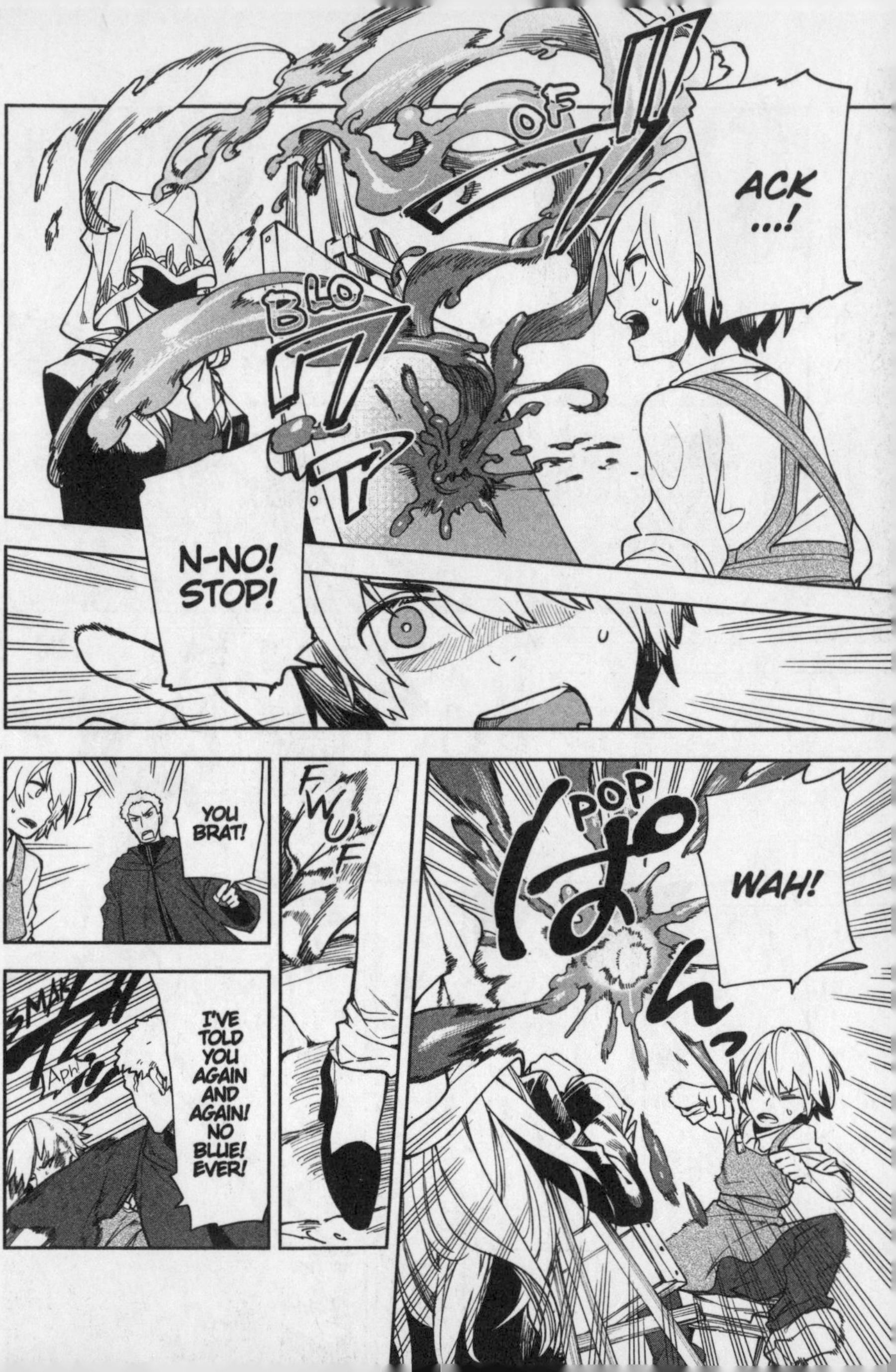
ACK ...!
BLO
OF
N-NO! STOP!
POP
WAH!
FWUF
YOU BRAT!
SMAK
Aph!
I'VE TOLD YOU AGAIN AND AGAIN! NO BLUE! EVER!

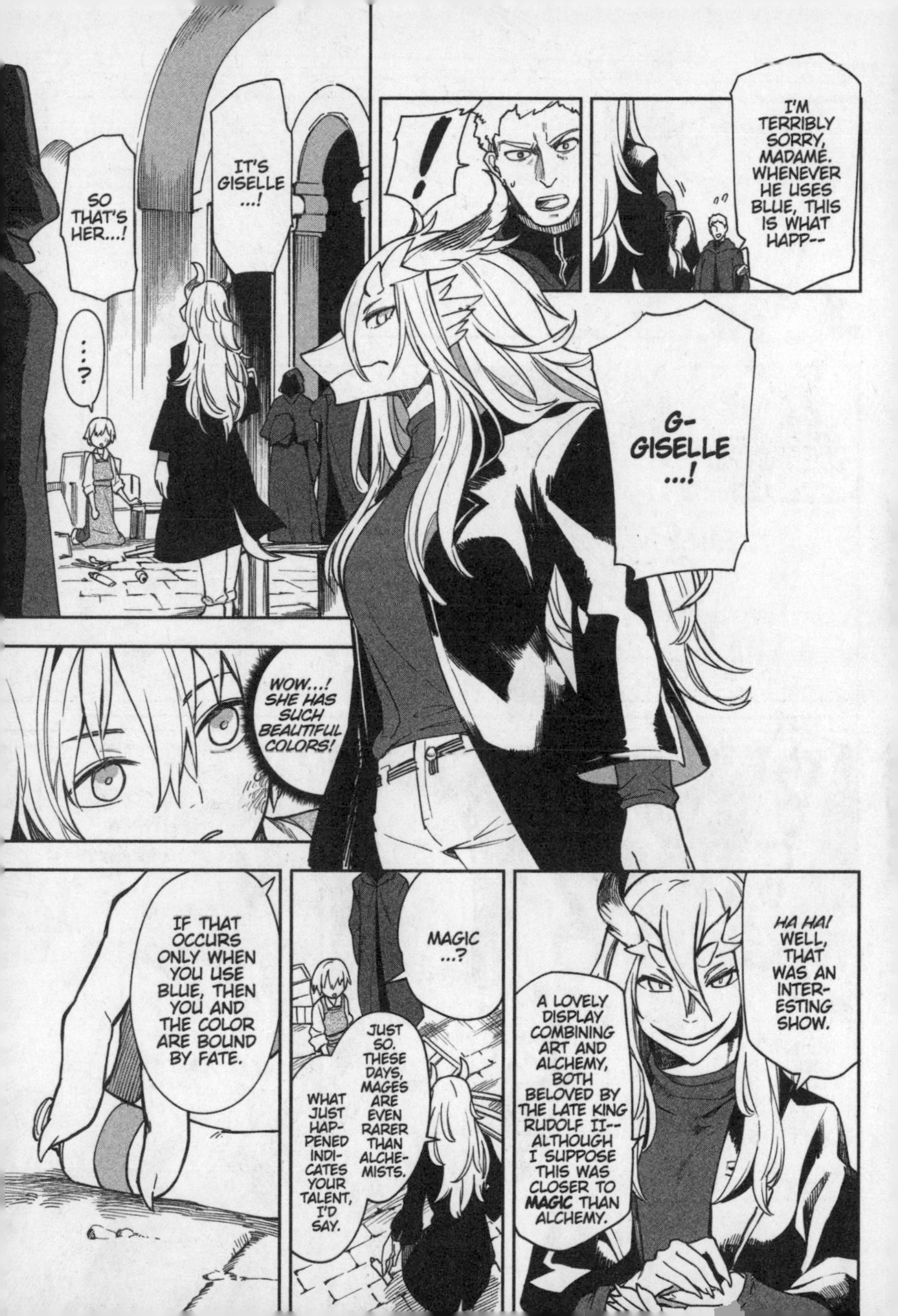
I'M TERRIBLY SORRY, MADAME. WHENEVER HE USES BLUE, THIS IS WHAT HAPP--
!
G-GISELLE ...!
IT'S GISELLE ...!
SO THAT'S HER...!
...?
WOW...! SHE HAS SUCH BEAUTIFUL COLORS!
HA HA! WELL, THAT WAS AN INTER-ESTING SHOW.
A LOVELY DISPLAY COMBINING ART AND ALCHEMY, BOTH BELOVED BY THE LATE KING RUDOLF II-- ALTHOUGH I SUPPOSE THIS WAS CLOSER TO MAGIC THAN ALCHEMY.
MAGIC ...?
JUST SO. THESE DAYS, MAGES ARE EVEN RARER THAN ALCHE-MISTS.
WHAT JUST HAP-PENED INDI-CATES YOUR TALENT, I'D SAY.
IF THAT OCCURS ONLY WHEN YOU USE BLUE, THEN YOU AND THE COLOR ARE BOUND BY FATE.

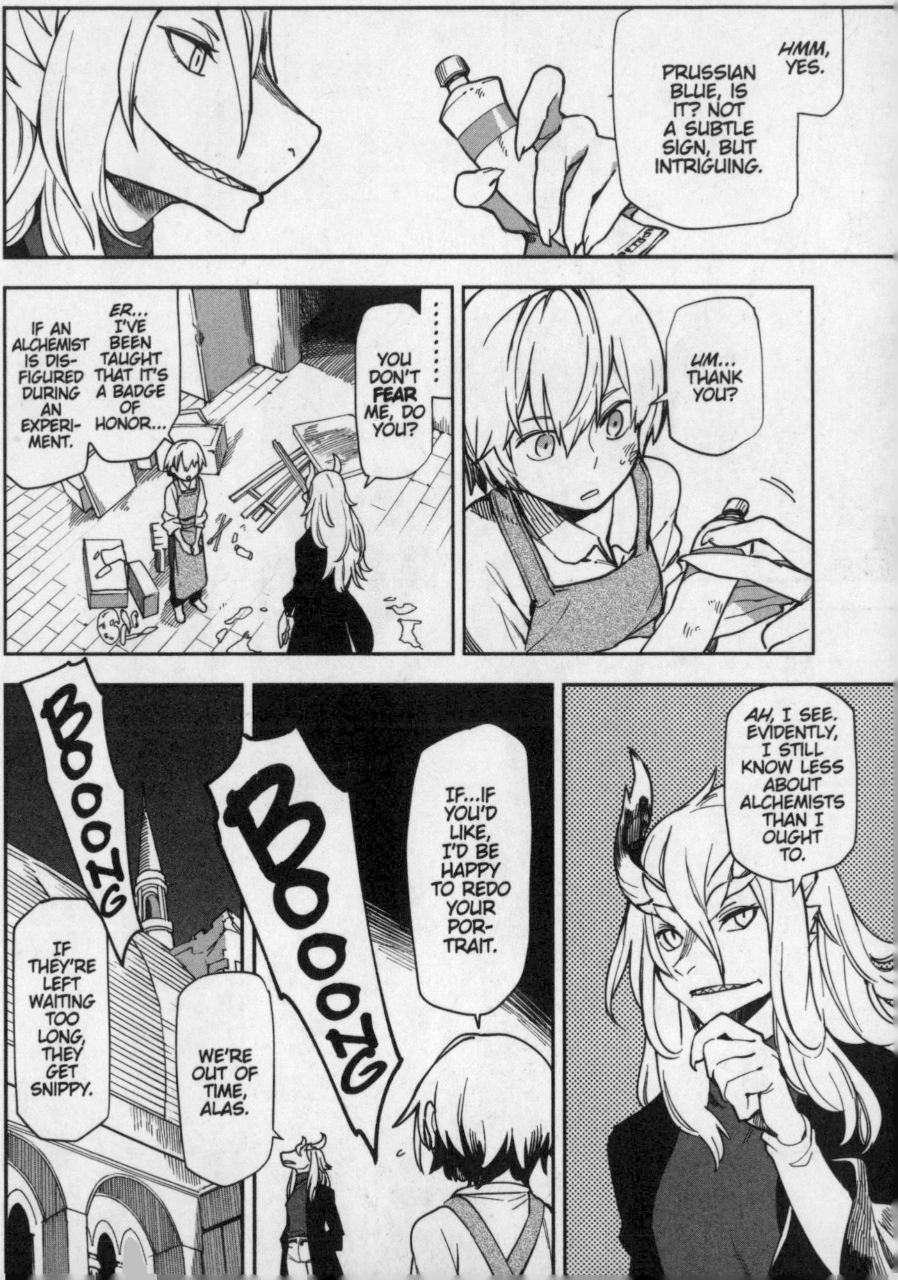
HMM, YES.
PRUSSIAN BLUE, IS IT? NOT A SUBTLE SIGN, BUT INTRIGUING.
UM... THANK YOU?
......
YOU DON'T FEAR ME, DO YOU?
ER... I'VE BEEN TAUGHT THAT IT'S A BADGE OF HONOR...
IF AN ALCHEMIST IS DIS-FIGURED DURING AN EXPERI-MENT.
AH, I SEE. EVIDENTLY, I STILL KNOW LESS ABOUT ALCHEMISTS THAN I OUGHT TO.
IF...IF YOU'D LIKE, I'D BE HAPPY TO REDO YOUR POR-TRAIT.
BOOONG
BOOONG
WE'RE OUT OF TIME, ALAS.
IF THEY'RE LEFT WAITING TOO LONG, THEY GET SNIPPY.

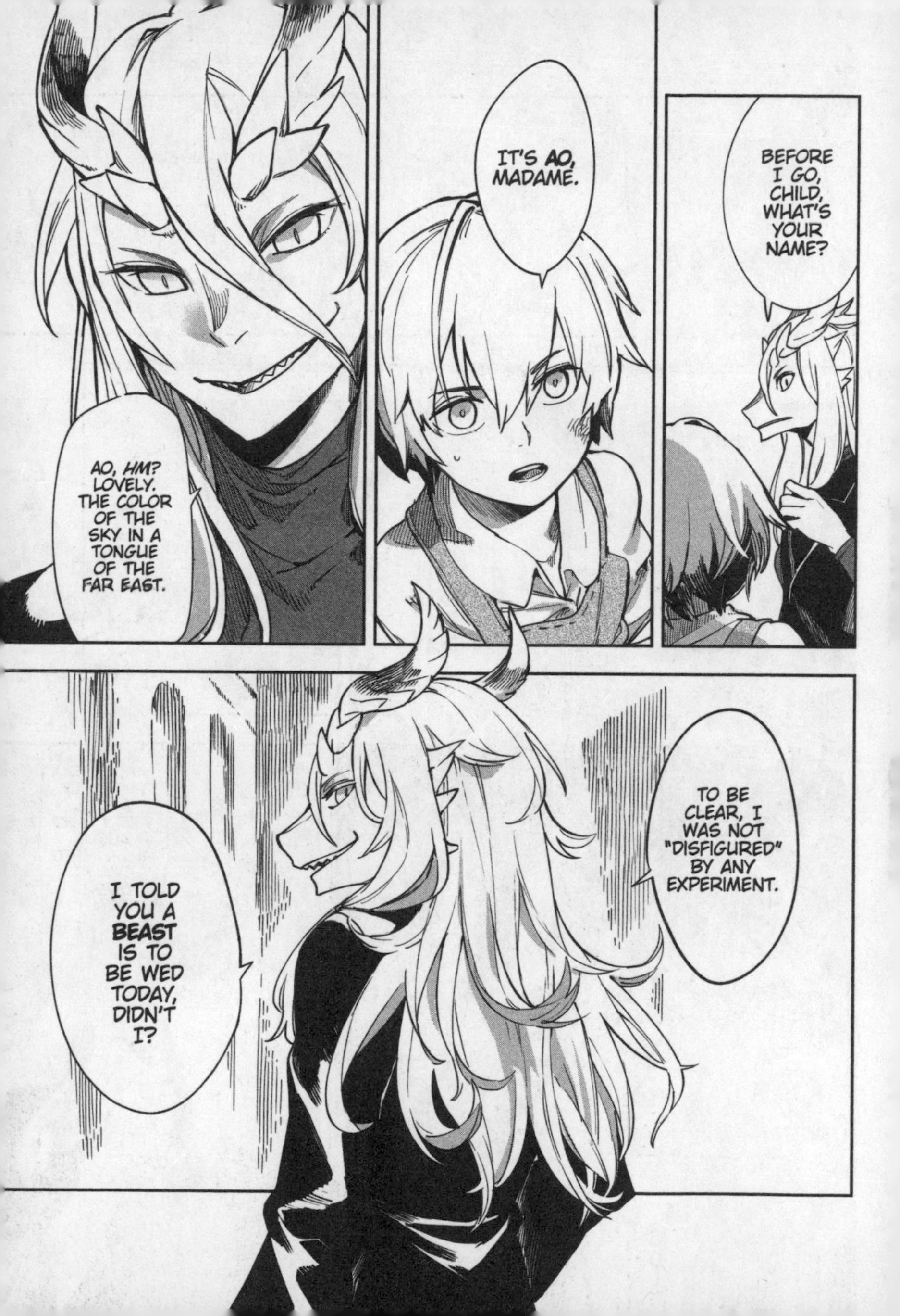
BEFORE I GO, CHILD, WHAT'S YOUR NAME?
IT'S AO, MADAME.
AO, HM? LOVELY. THE COLOR OF THE SKY IN A TONGUE OF THE FAR EAST.
TO BE CLEAR, I WAS NOT "DISFIGURED" BY ANY EXPERIMENT.
I TOLD YOU A BEAST IS TO BE WED TODAY, DIDN'T I?

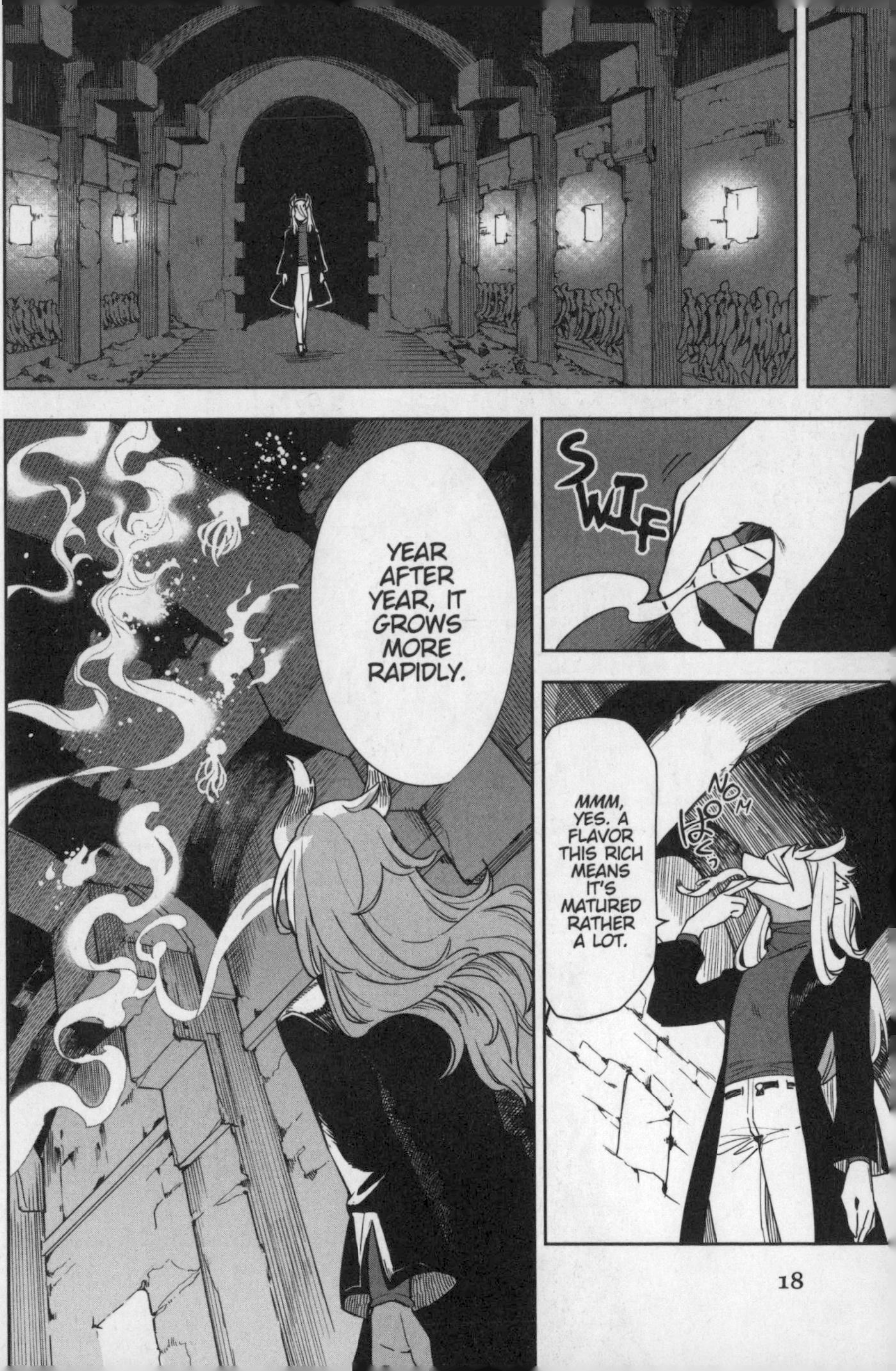
SWIF
MMM, YES. A FLAVOR THIS RICH MEANS IT'S MATURED RATHER A LOT.
YEAR AFTER YEAR, IT GROWS MORE RAPIDLY.

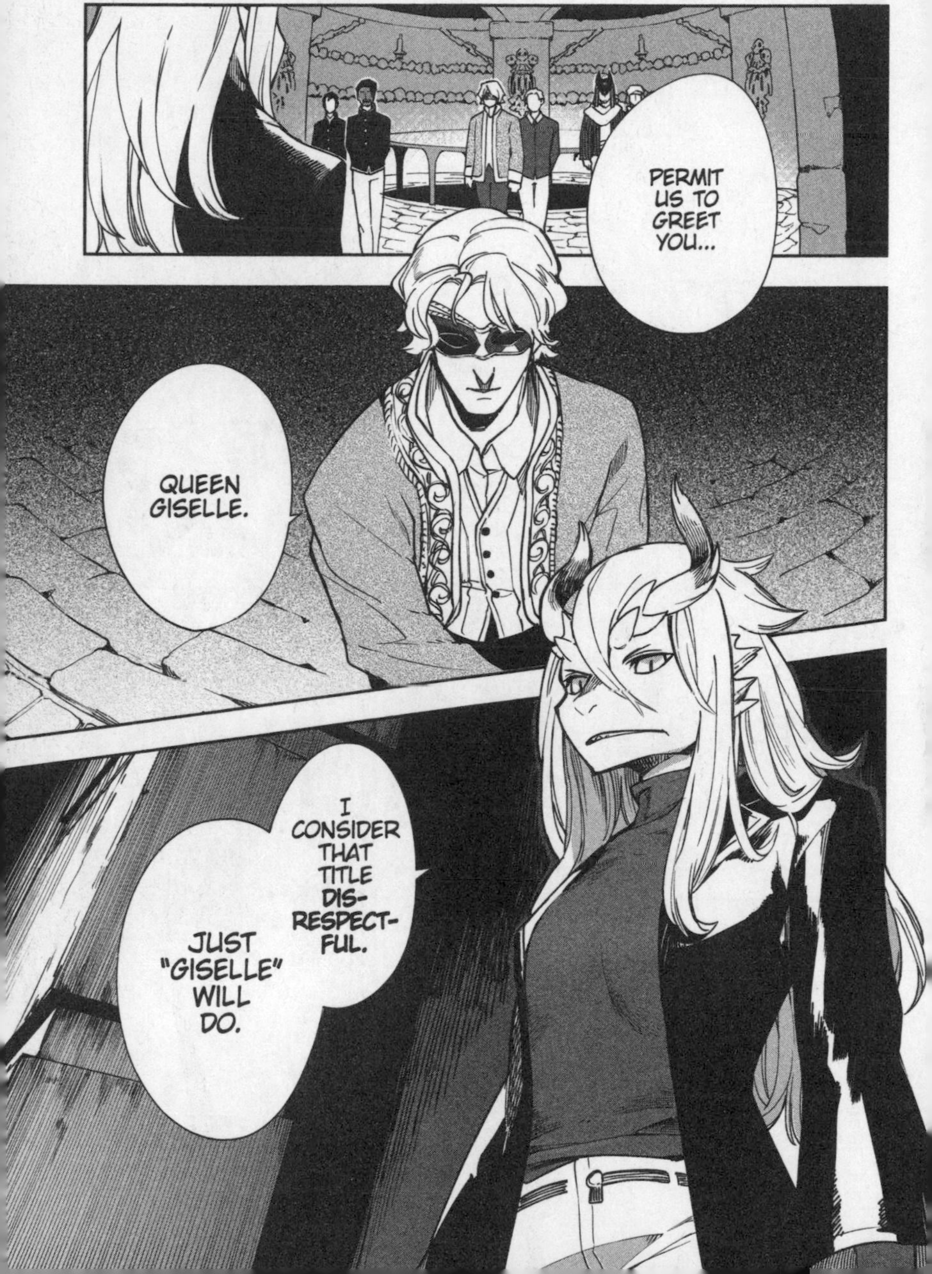
PERMIT US TO GREET YOU...
QUEEN GISELLE.
I CONSIDER THAT TITLE DIS-RESPECT-FUL.
JUST "GISELLE" WILL DO.

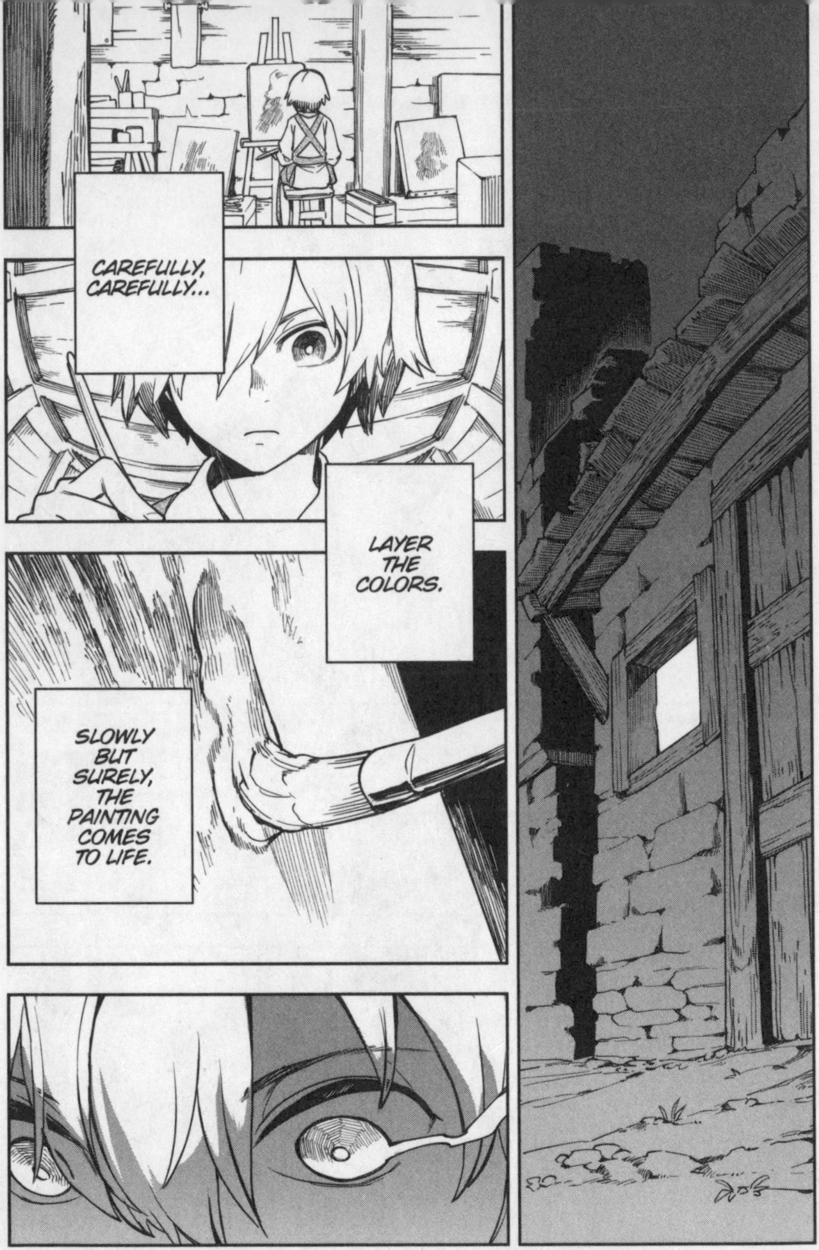
CAREFULLY, CAREFULLY...
LAYER THE COLORS.
SLOWLY BUT SURELY, THE PAINTING COMES TO LIFE.

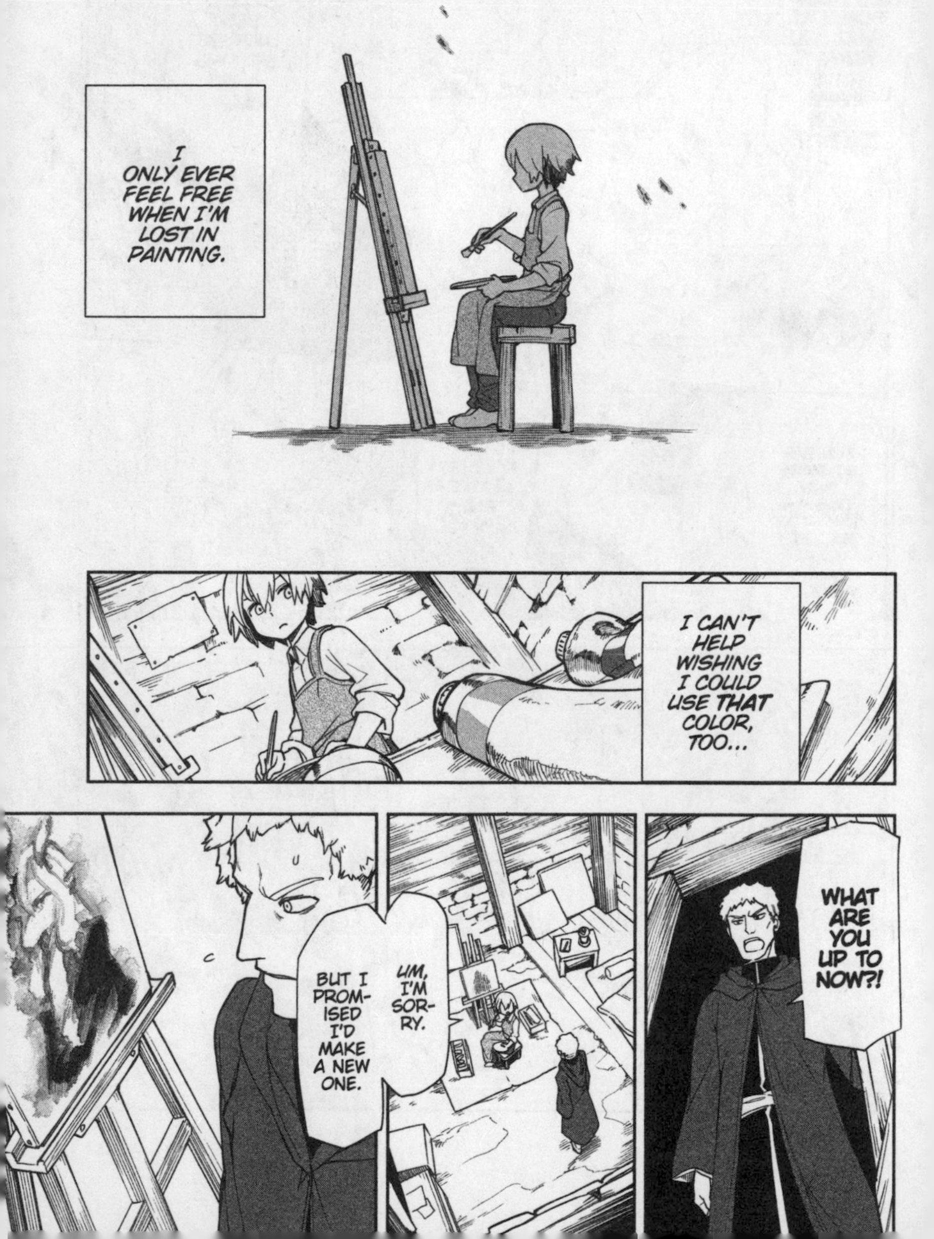

I ONLY EVER FEEL FREE WHEN I'M LOST IN PAINTING.
I CAN'T HELP WISHING I COULD USE THAT COLOR, TOO...
WHAT ARE YOU UP TO NOW?!
UM, I'M SORRY.
BUT I PROMISED I'D MAKE A NEW ONE.

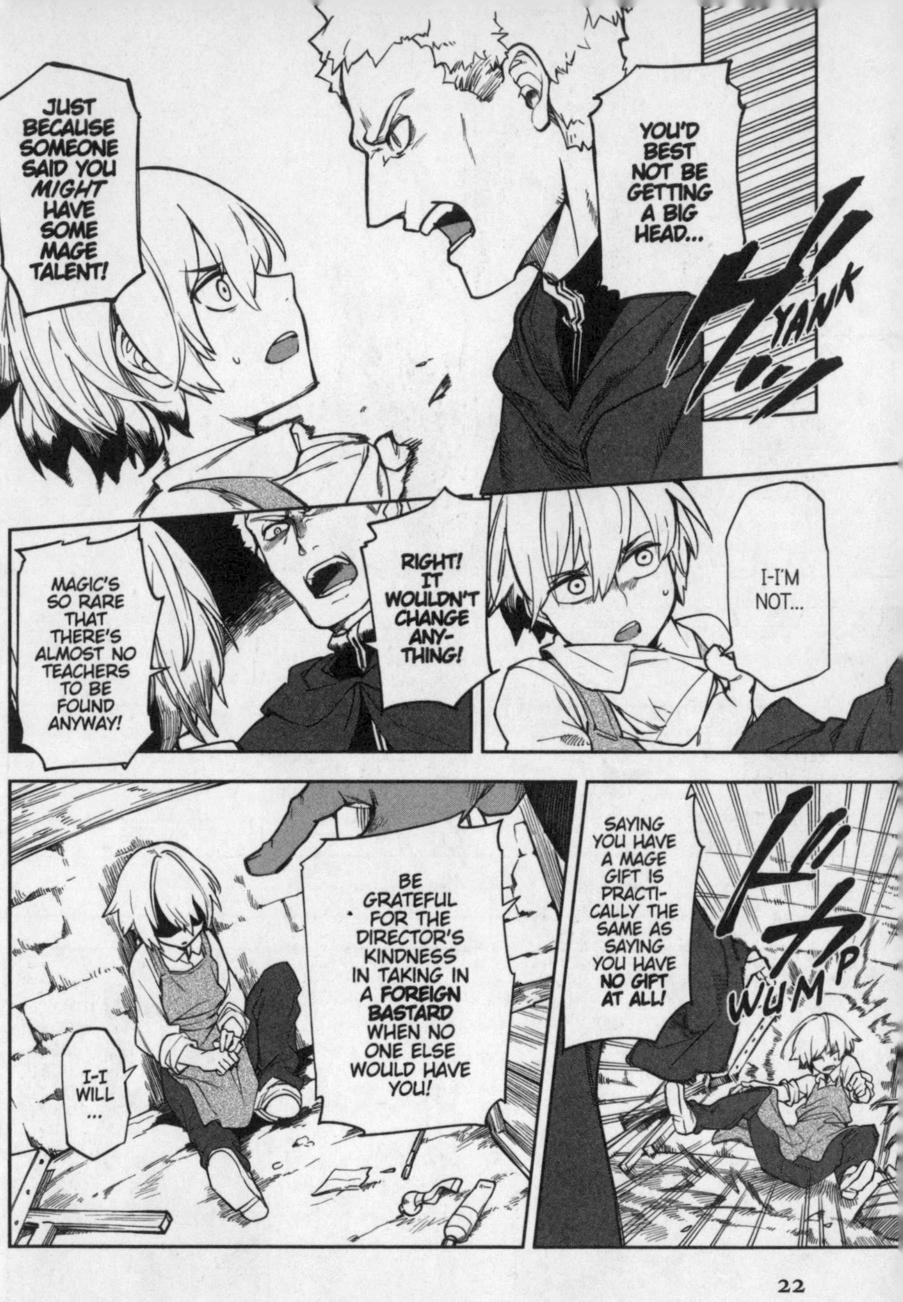
YOU'D BEST NOT BE GETTING A BIG HEAD...
YANK
JUST BECAUSE SOMEONE SAID YOU *MIGHT* HAVE SOME MAGE TALENT!
I-I'M NOT...
RIGHT! IT WOULDN'T CHANGE ANY-THING!
MAGIC'S SO RARE THAT THERE'S ALMOST NO TEACHERS TO BE FOUND ANYWAY!
SAYING YOU HAVE A MAGE GIFT IS PRACTI-CALLY THE SAME AS SAYING YOU HAVE **NO GIFT AT ALL!**
WUMP
BE GRATEFUL FOR THE DIRECTOR'S KINDNESS IN TAKING IN A **FOREIGN BASTARD** WHEN NO ONE ELSE WOULD HAVE YOU!
I-I WILL ...

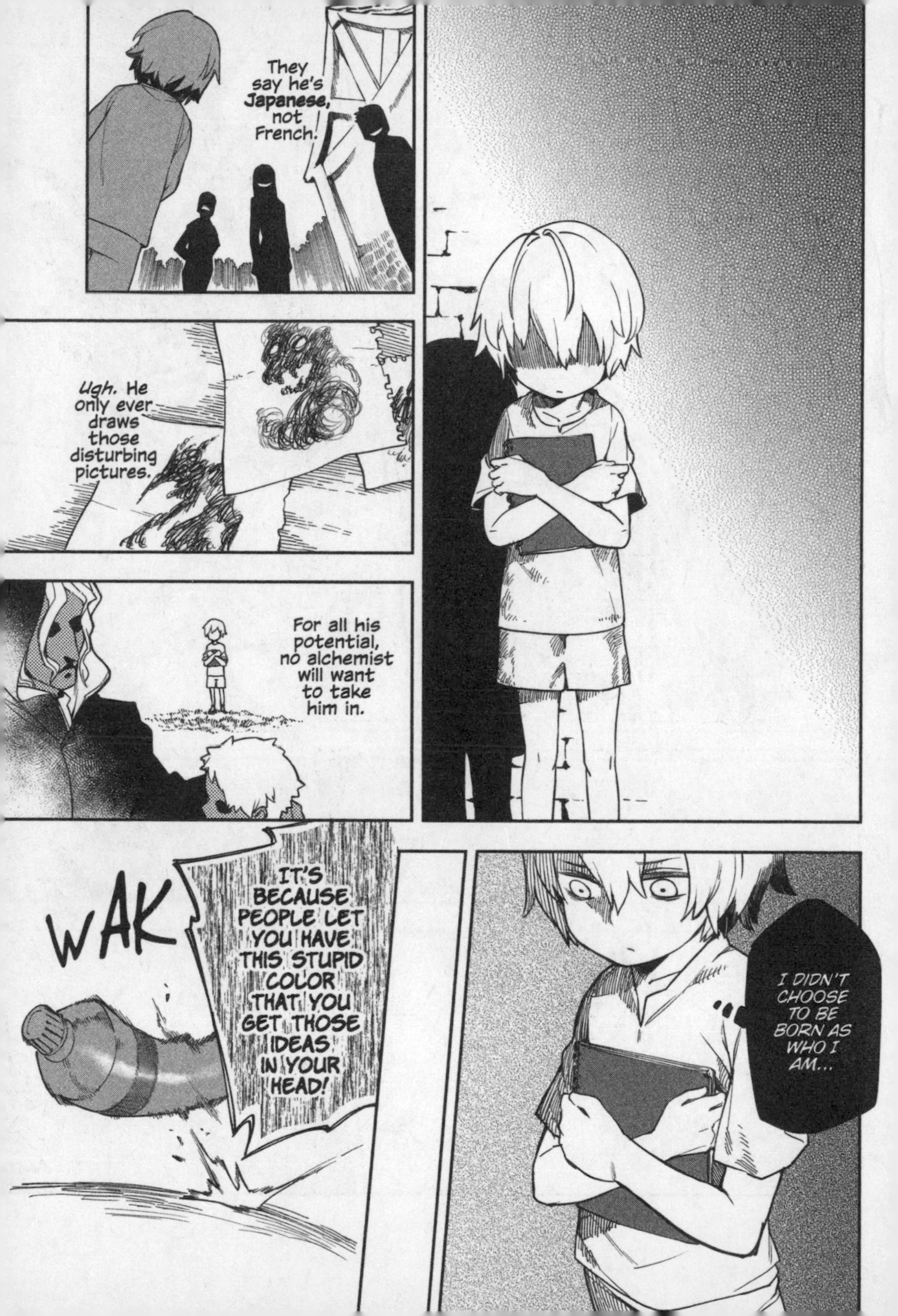
They say he's Japanese, not French.
Ugh. He only ever draws those disturbing pictures.
For all his potential, no alchemist will want to take him in.
I DIDN'T CHOOSE TO BE BORN AS WHO I AM...
...
IT'S BECAUSE PEOPLE LET YOU HAVE THIS STUPID COLOR THAT YOU GET THOSE IDEAS IN YOUR HEAD!
WAK

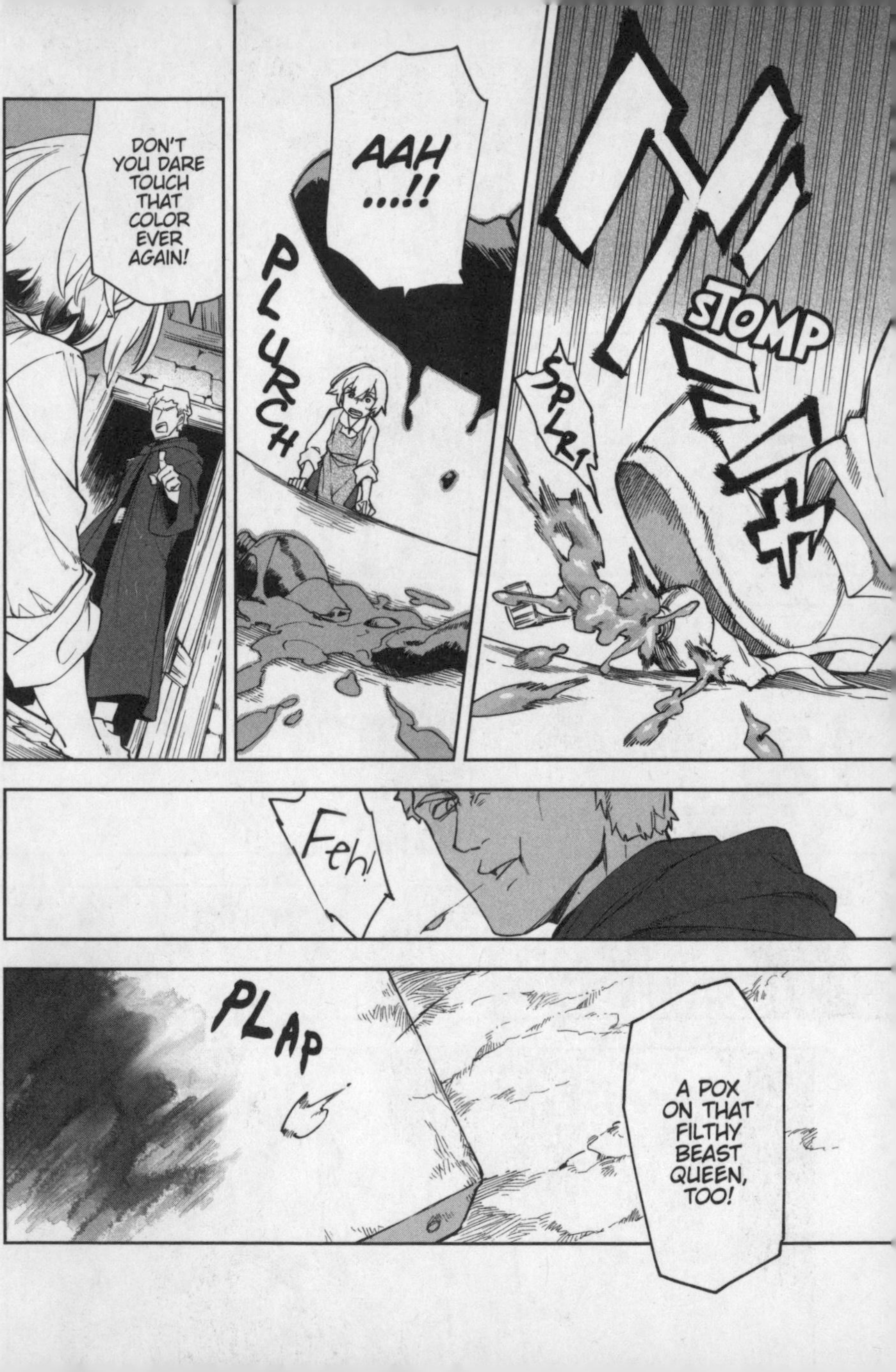
STOMP
SPLRT
AAH ...!!
PLURCH
DON'T YOU DARE TOUCH THAT COLOR EVER AGAIN!
Feh!
A POX ON THAT FILTHY BEAST QUEEN, TOO!
PLAP

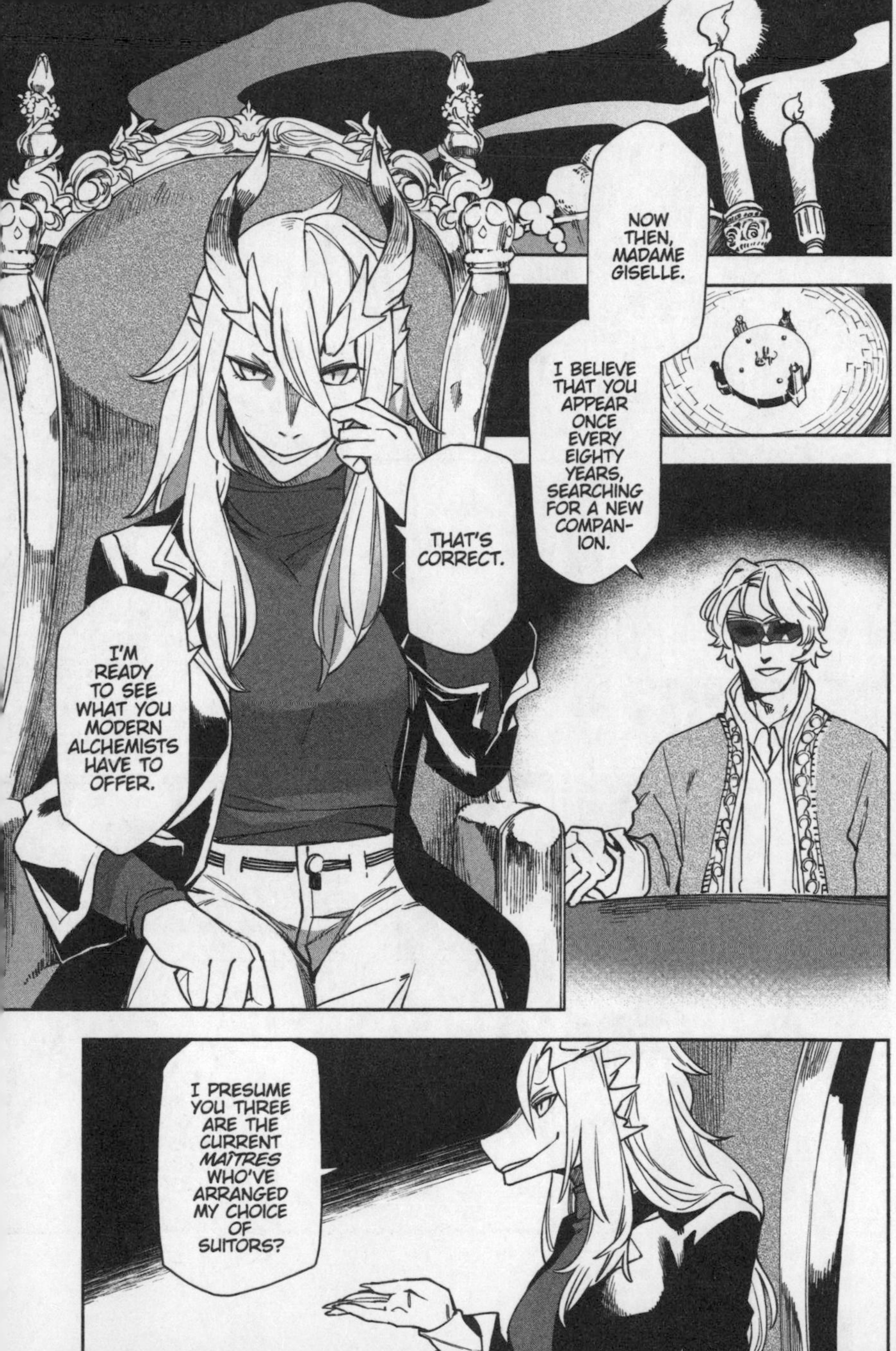
NOW THEN, MADAME GISELLE.
I BELIEVE THAT YOU APPEAR ONCE EVERY EIGHTY YEARS, SEARCHING FOR A NEW COMPAN-ION.
THAT'S CORRECT.
I'M READY TO SEE WHAT YOU MODERN ALCHEMISTS HAVE TO OFFER.
I PRESUME YOU THREE ARE THE CURRENT *MAÎTRES* WHO'VE ARRANGED MY CHOICE OF SUITORS?

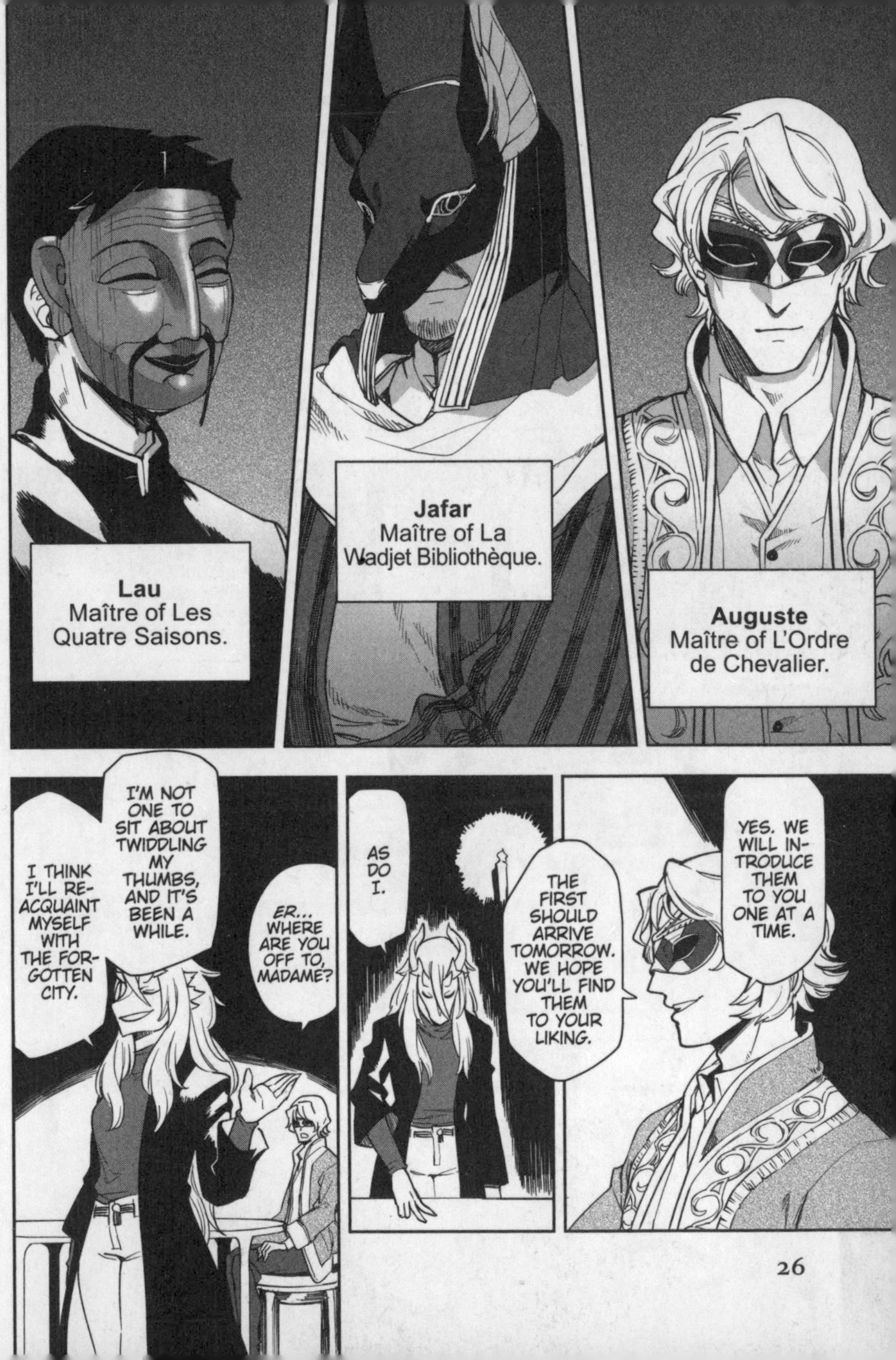
Auguste
Maître of L'Ordre de Chevalier.
Jafar
Maître of La Wadjet Bibliothèque.
Lau
Maître of Les Quatre Saisons.
YES. WE WILL INTRODUCE THEM TO YOU ONE AT A TIME.
THE FIRST SHOULD ARRIVE TOMORROW. WE HOPE YOU'LL FIND THEM TO YOUR LIKING.
AS DO I.
ER... WHERE ARE YOU OFF TO, MADAME?
I'M NOT ONE TO SIT ABOUT TWIDDLING MY THUMBS, AND IT'S BEEN A WHILE.
I THINK I'LL REACQUAINT MYSELF WITH THE FORGOTTEN CITY.

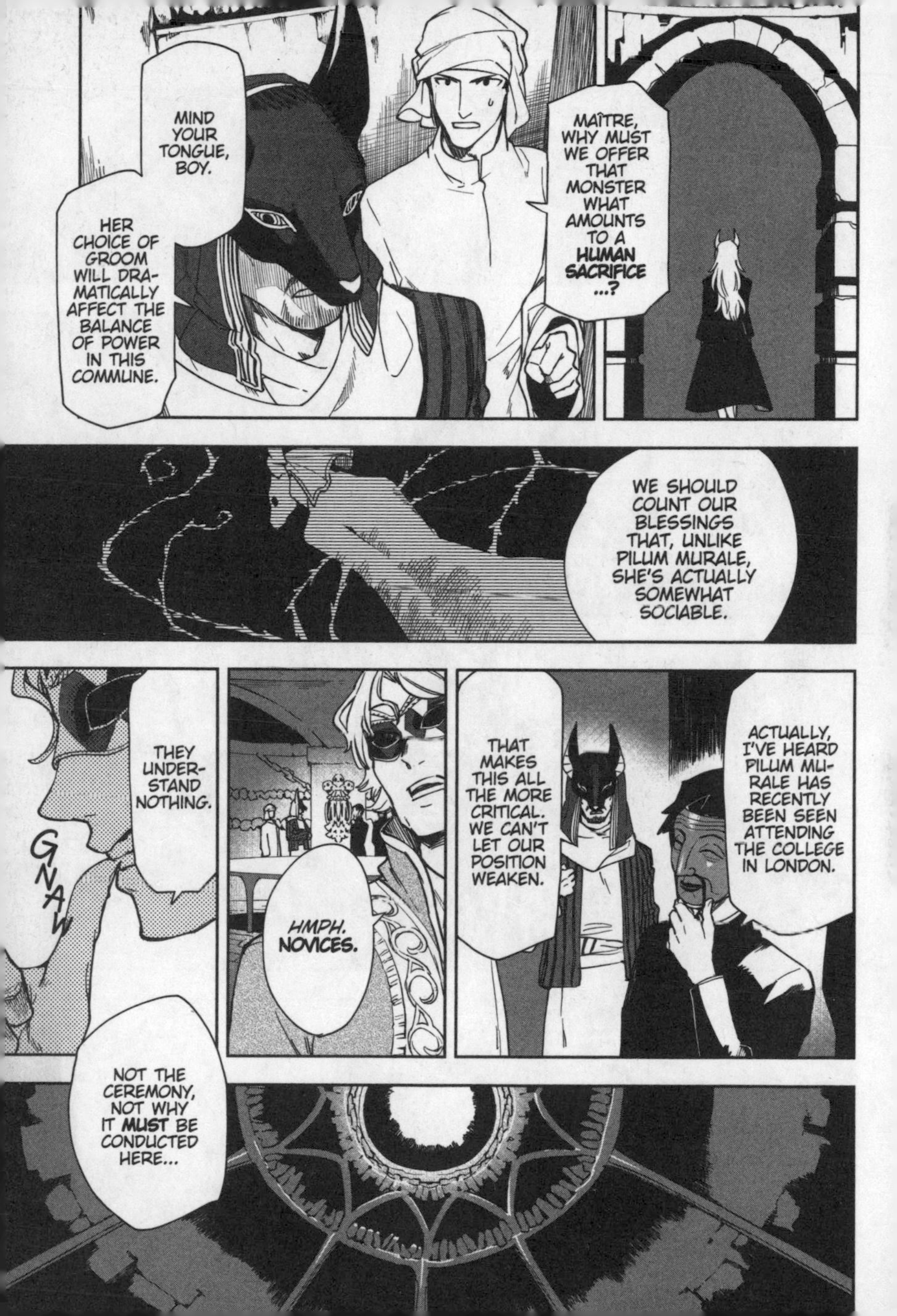
MAÎTRE, WHY MUST WE OFFER THAT MONSTER WHAT AMOUNTS TO A **HUMAN SACRIFICE**...?
MIND YOUR TONGUE, BOY.
HER CHOICE OF GROOM WILL DRAMATICALLY AFFECT THE BALANCE OF POWER IN THIS COMMUNE.
WE SHOULD COUNT OUR BLESSINGS THAT, UNLIKE PILUM MURALE, SHE'S ACTUALLY SOMEWHAT SOCIABLE.
ACTUALLY, I'VE HEARD PILUM MURALE HAS RECENTLY BEEN SEEN ATTENDING THE COLLEGE IN LONDON.
THAT MAKES THIS ALL THE MORE CRITICAL. WE CAN'T LET OUR POSITION WEAKEN.
HMPH. **NOVICES.**
THEY UNDERSTAND NOTHING.
GNAW
NOT THE CEREMONY, NOT WHY IT **MUST** BE CONDUCTED HERE...

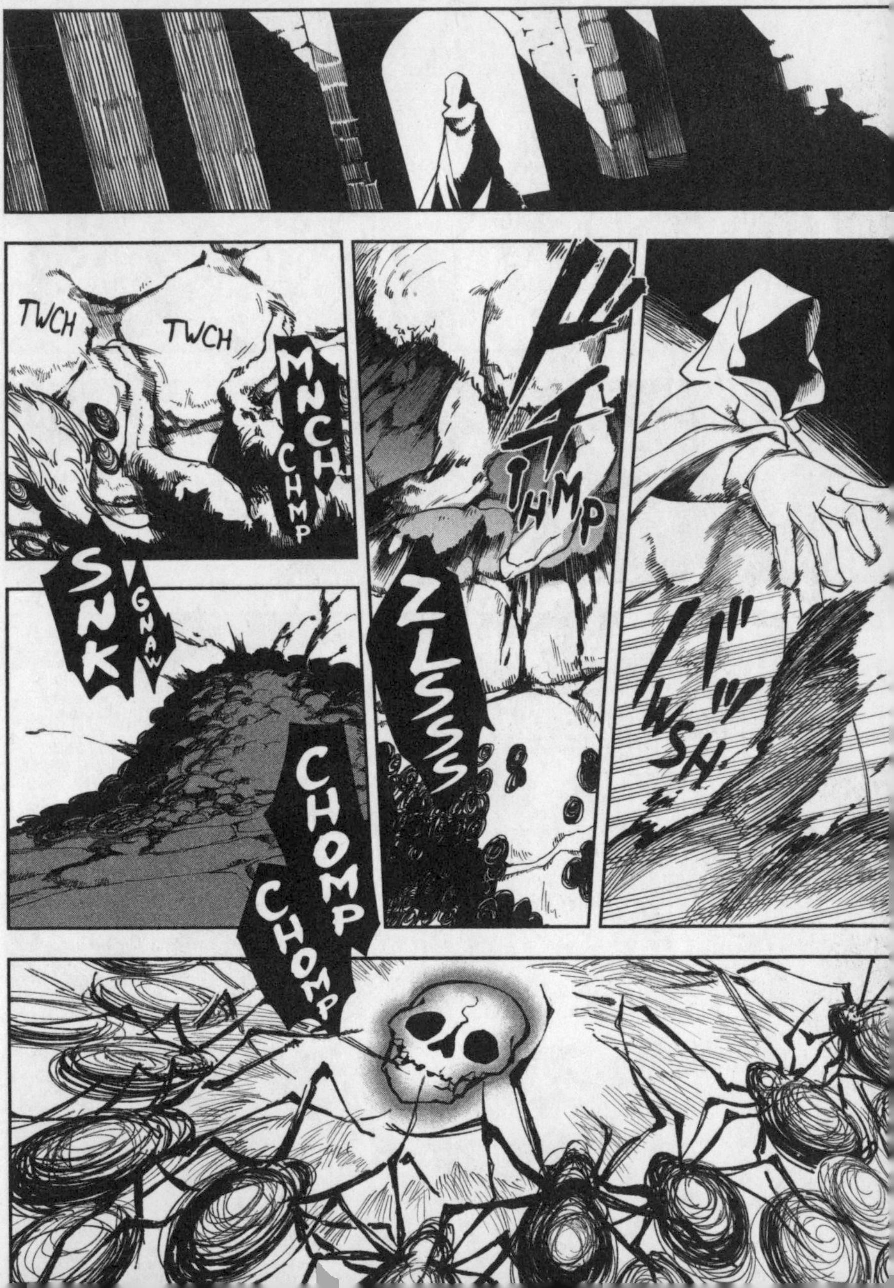
WSH
THMP
ZLSSS
MNCH
CHMP
TWCH
TWCH
SNK
GNAW
CHOMP
CHOMP

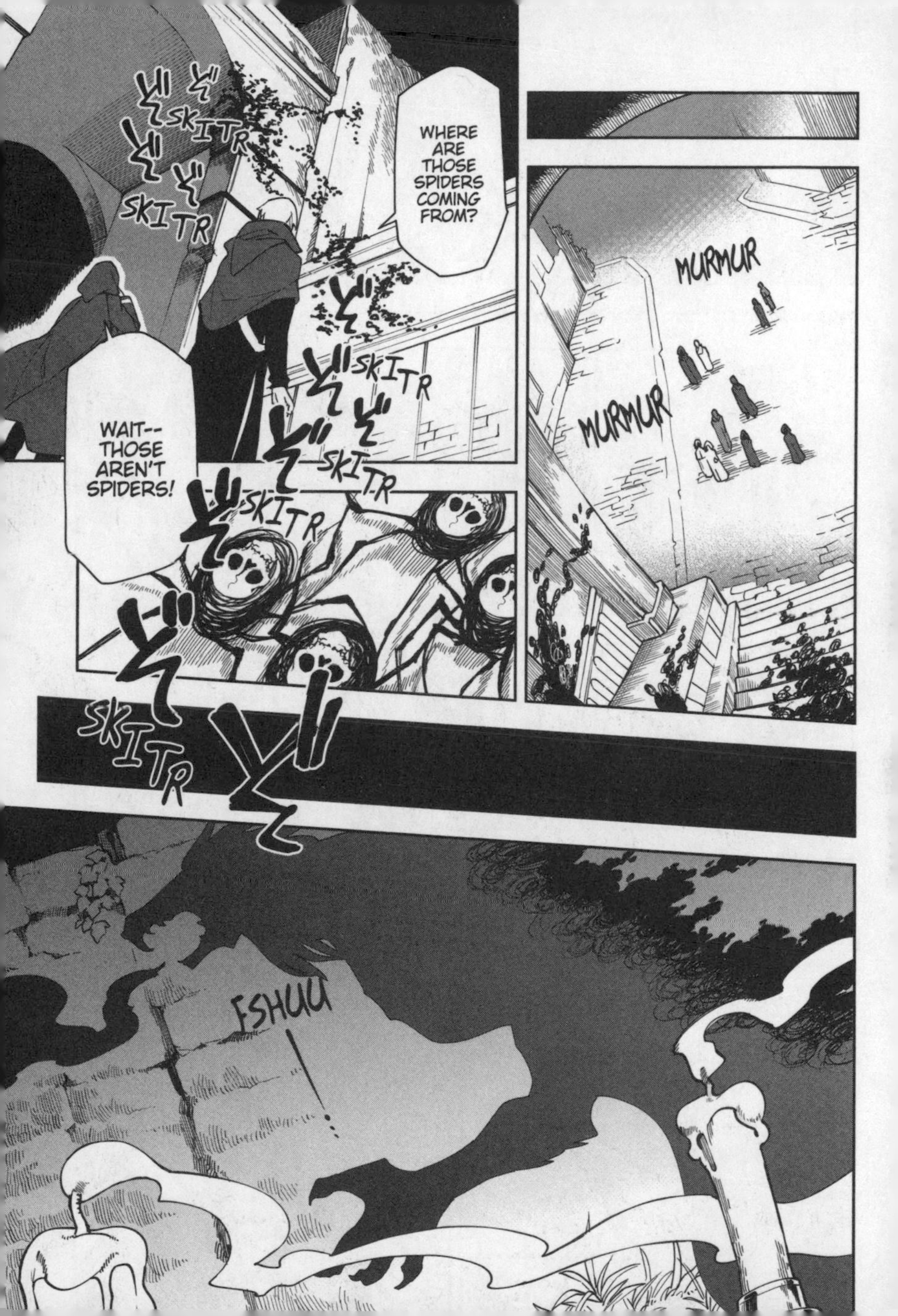
MURMUR
MURMUR
WHERE ARE THOSE SPIDERS COMING FROM?
SKITR
SKITR
SKITR
SKITR
SKITR
WAIT-- THOSE AREN'T SPIDERS!
SKITR
FSHUU

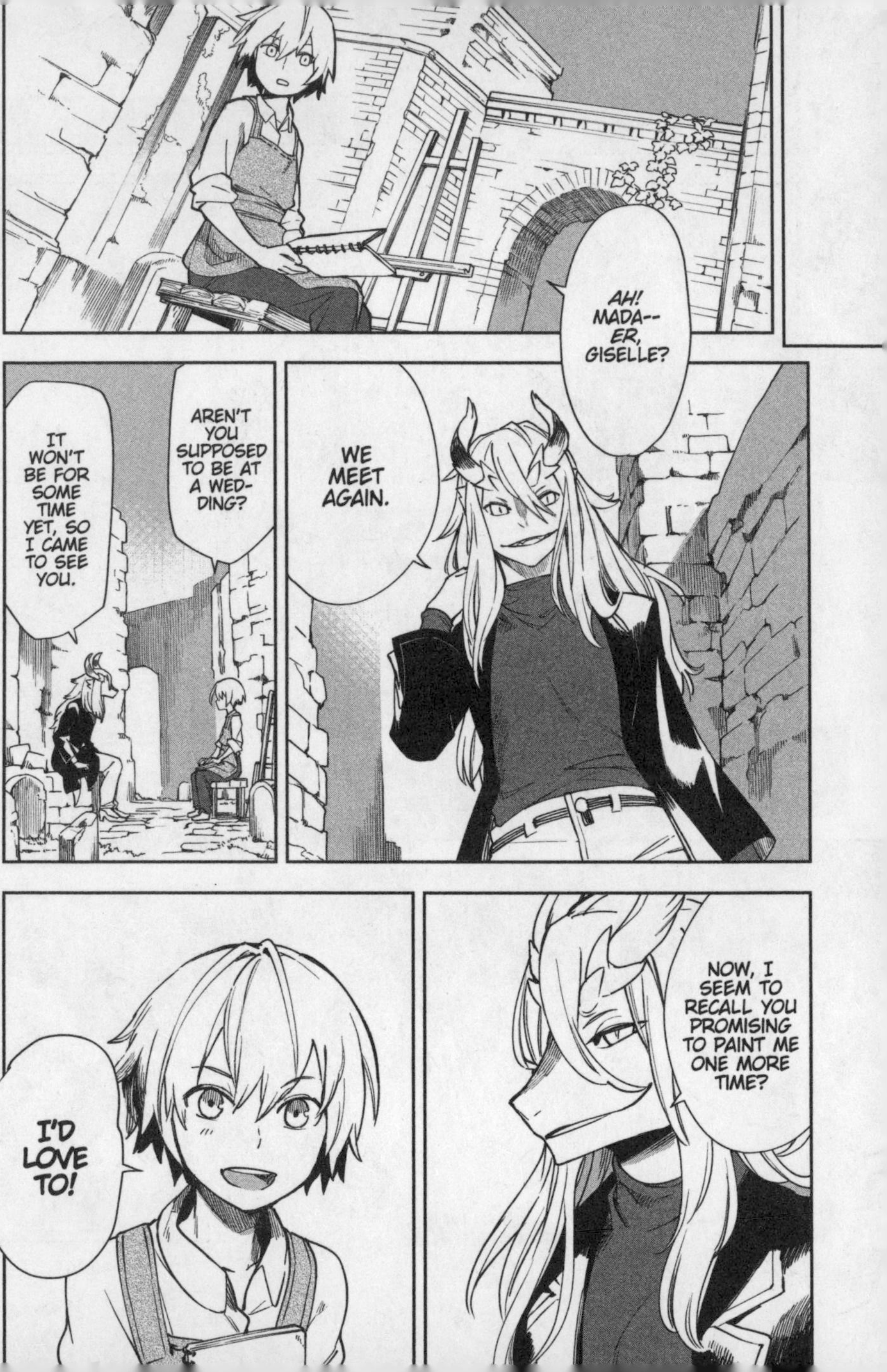
AH! MADA-- ER, GISELLE?
WE MEET AGAIN.
AREN'T YOU SUPPOSED TO BE AT A WED-DING?
IT WON'T BE FOR SOME TIME YET, SO I CAME TO SEE YOU.
NOW, I SEEM TO RECALL YOU PROMISING TO PAINT ME ONE MORE TIME?
I'D LOVE TO!

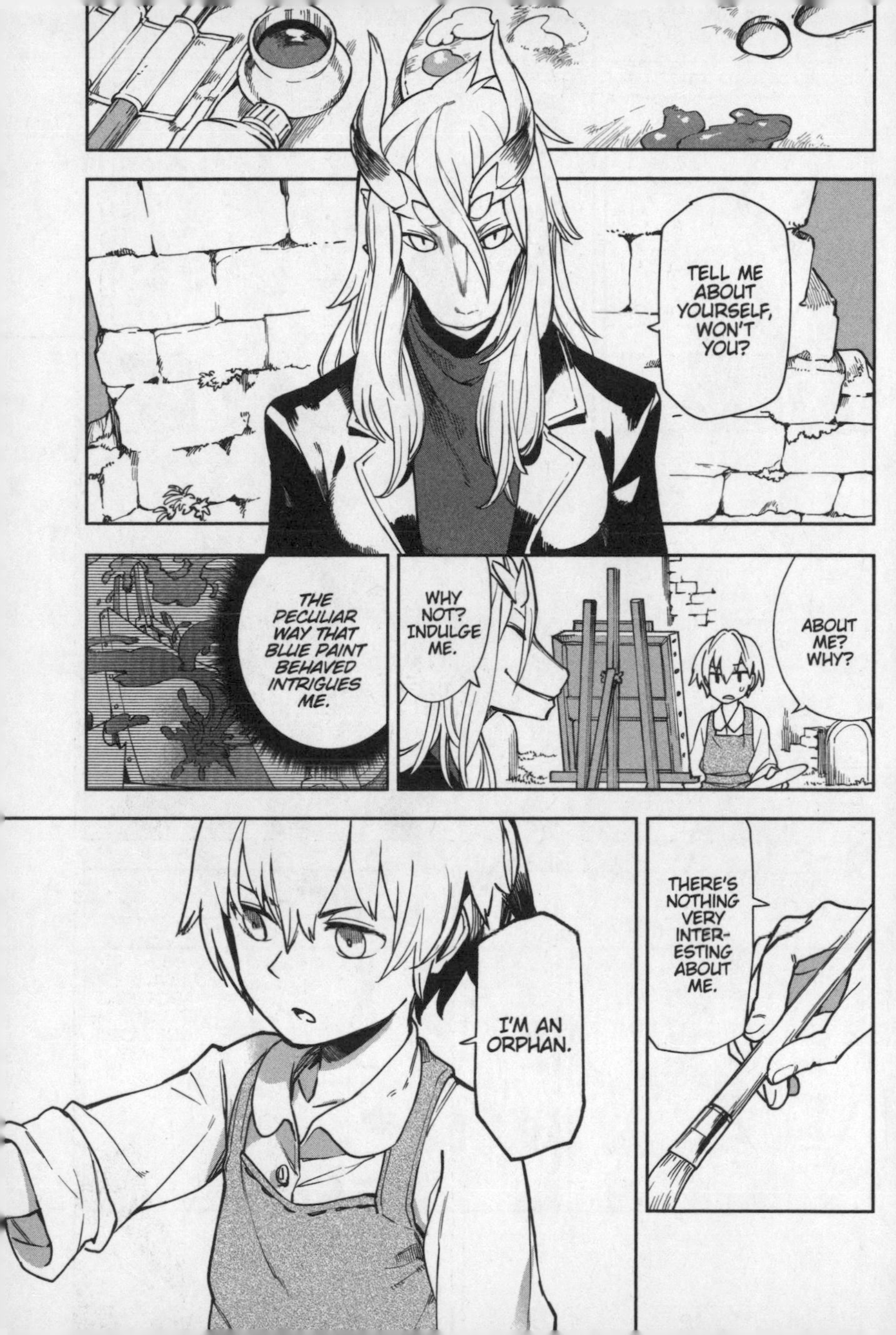
TELL ME ABOUT YOURSELF, WON'T YOU?
ABOUT ME? WHY?
WHY NOT? INDULGE ME.
THE PECULIAR WAY THAT BLUE PAINT BEHAVED INTRIGUES ME.
THERE'S NOTHING VERY INTER-ESTING ABOUT ME.
I'M AN ORPHAN.

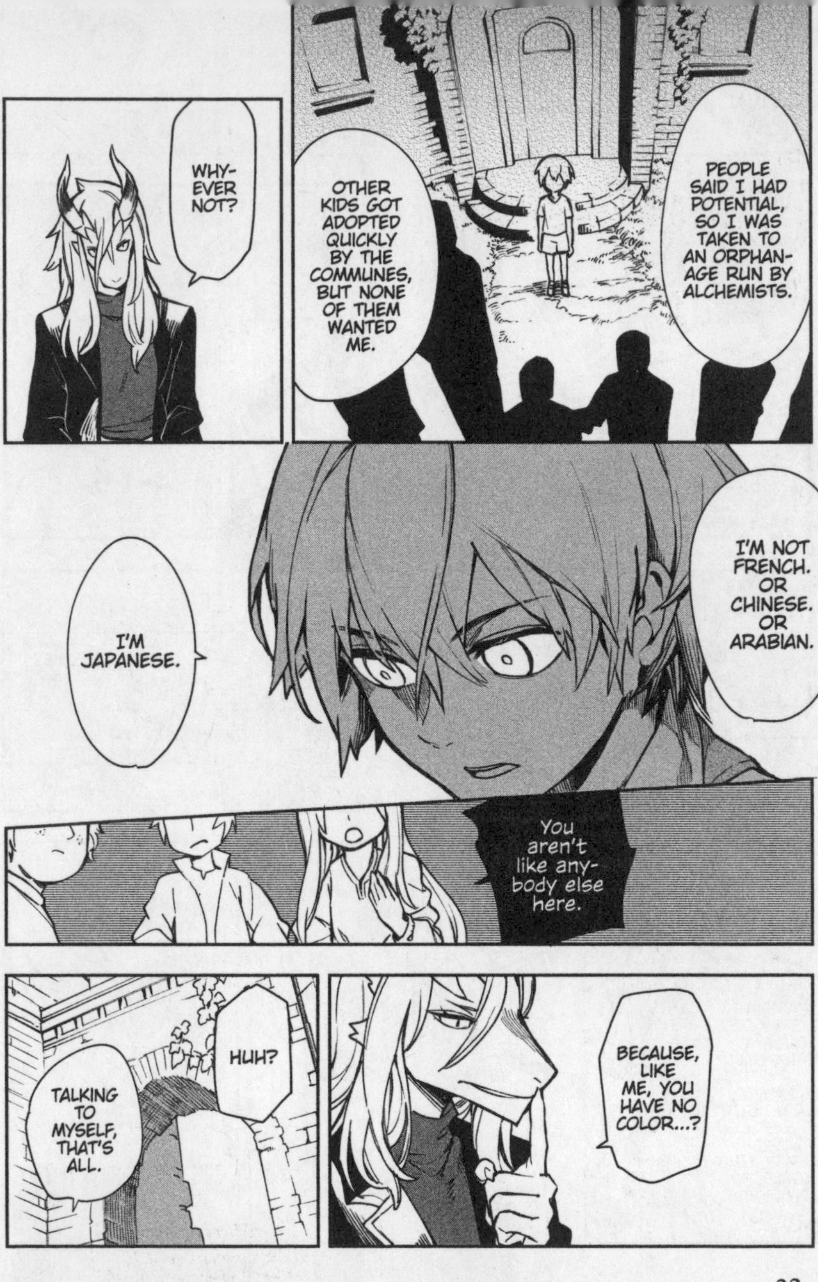
PEOPLE SAID I HAD POTENTIAL, SO I WAS TAKEN TO AN ORPHANAGE RUN BY ALCHEMISTS.
OTHER KIDS GOT ADOPTED QUICKLY BY THE COMMUNES, BUT NONE OF THEM WANTED ME.
WHY-EVER NOT?
I'M NOT FRENCH. OR CHINESE. OR ARABIAN.
I'M JAPANESE.
You aren't like anybody else here.
BECAUSE, LIKE ME, YOU HAVE NO COLOR...?
HUH?
TALKING TO MYSELF, THAT'S ALL.

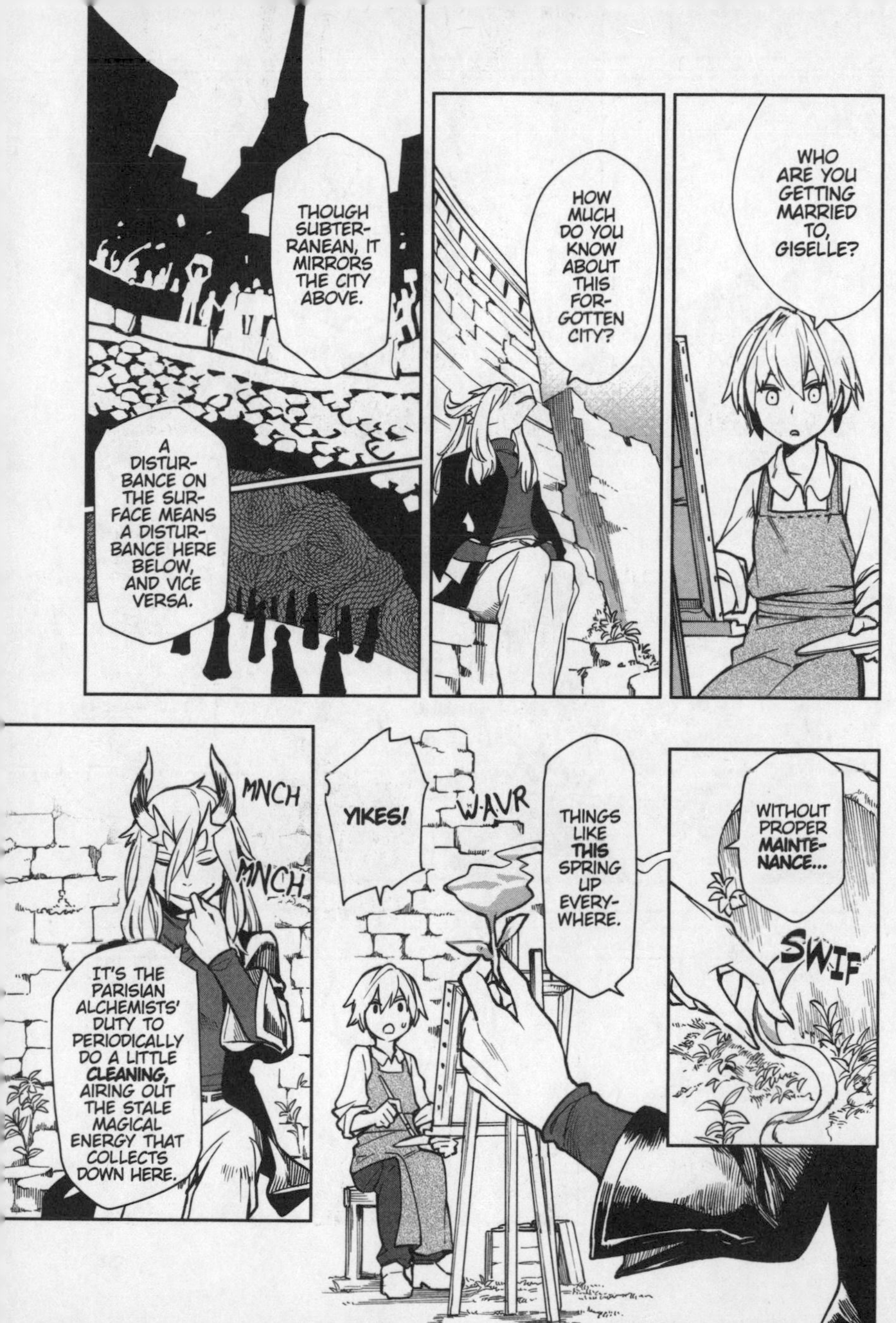
WHO ARE YOU GETTING MARRIED TO, GISELLE?
HOW MUCH DO YOU KNOW ABOUT THIS FORGOTTEN CITY?
THOUGH SUBTERRANEAN, IT MIRRORS THE CITY ABOVE.
A DISTURBANCE ON THE SURFACE MEANS A DISTURBANCE HERE BELOW, AND VICE VERSA.
WITHOUT PROPER MAINTENANCE...
SWIF
THINGS LIKE THIS SPRING UP EVERYWHERE.
W-AVR
YIKES!
MNCH
MNCH
IT'S THE PARISIAN ALCHEMISTS' DUTY TO PERIODICALLY DO A LITTLE CLEANING, AIRING OUT THE STALE MAGICAL ENERGY THAT COLLECTS DOWN HERE.

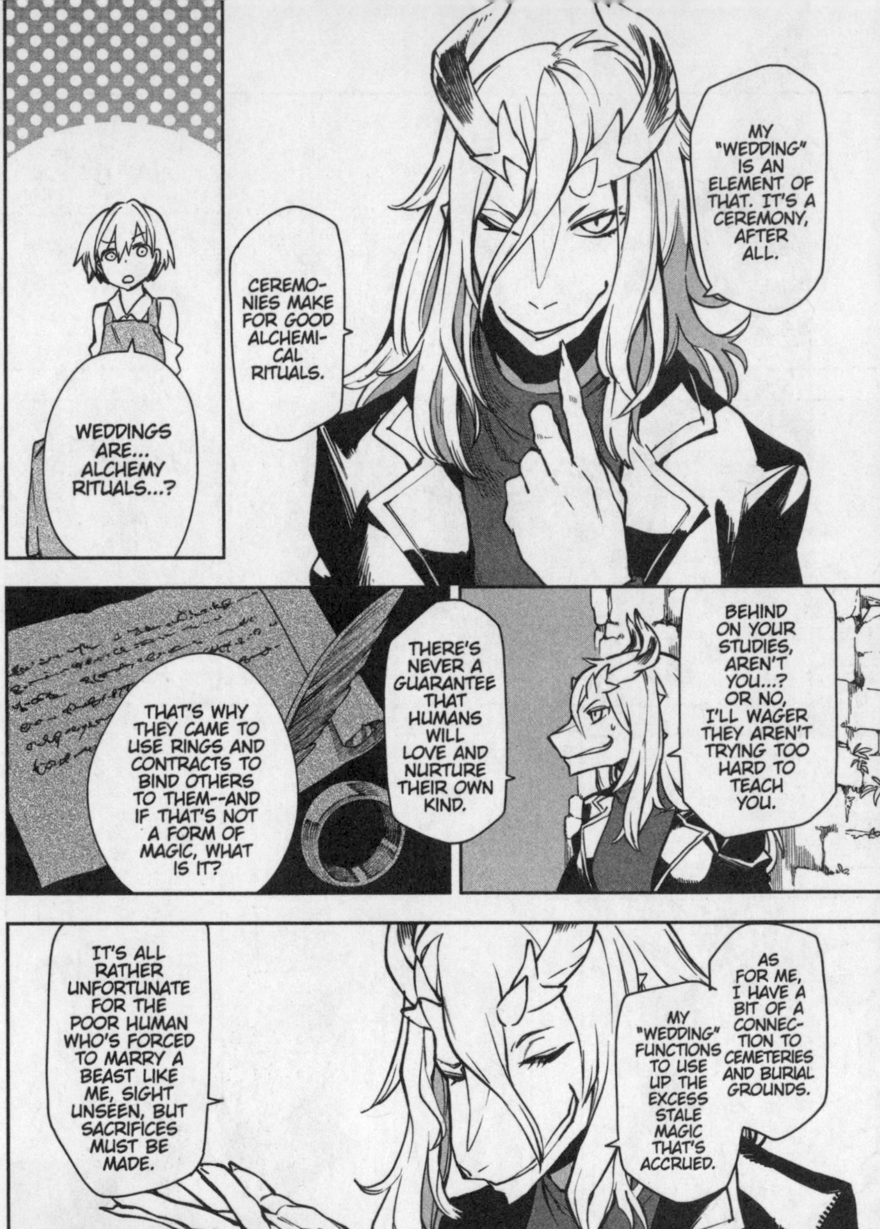
MY "WEDDING" IS AN ELEMENT OF THAT. IT'S A CEREMONY, AFTER ALL.
CEREMONIES MAKE FOR GOOD ALCHEMICAL RITUALS.
WEDDINGS ARE... ALCHEMY RITUALS...?
BEHIND ON YOUR STUDIES, AREN'T YOU...? OR NO, I'LL WAGER THEY AREN'T TRYING TOO HARD TO TEACH YOU.
THERE'S NEVER A GUARANTEE THAT HUMANS WILL LOVE AND NURTURE THEIR OWN KIND.
THAT'S WHY THEY CAME TO USE RINGS AND CONTRACTS TO BIND OTHERS TO THEM--AND IF THAT'S NOT A FORM OF MAGIC, WHAT IS IT?
AS FOR ME, I HAVE A BIT OF A CONNECTION TO CEMETERIES AND BURIAL GROUNDS.
MY "WEDDING" FUNCTIONS TO USE UP THE EXCESS STALE MAGIC THAT'S ACCRUED.
IT'S ALL RATHER UNFORTUNATE FOR THE POOR HUMAN WHO'S FORCED TO MARRY A BEAST LIKE ME, SIGHT UNSEEN, BUT SACRIFICES MUST BE MADE.

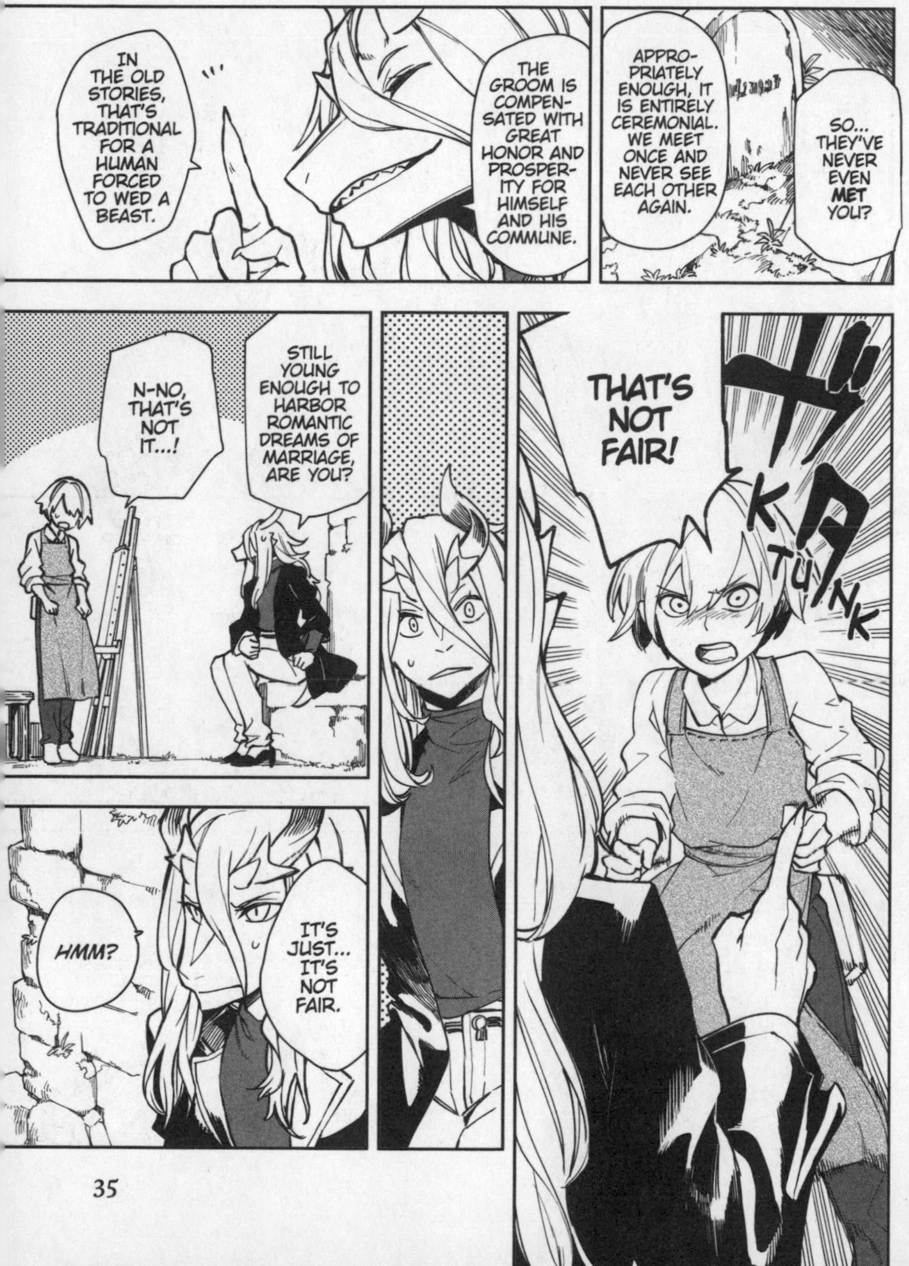
IN THE OLD STORIES, THAT'S TRADITIONAL FOR A HUMAN FORCED TO WED A BEAST.
THE GROOM IS COMPENSATED WITH GREAT HONOR AND PROSPERITY FOR HIMSELF AND HIS COMMUNE.
APPROPRIATELY ENOUGH, IT IS ENTIRELY CEREMONIAL. WE MEET ONCE AND NEVER SEE EACH OTHER AGAIN.
SO... THEY'VE NEVER EVEN MET YOU?
STILL YOUNG ENOUGH TO HARBOR ROMANTIC DREAMS OF MARRIAGE, ARE YOU?
N-NO, THAT'S NOT IT...!
HMM?
IT'S JUST... IT'S NOT FAIR.
THAT'S NOT FAIR!
KATUNK

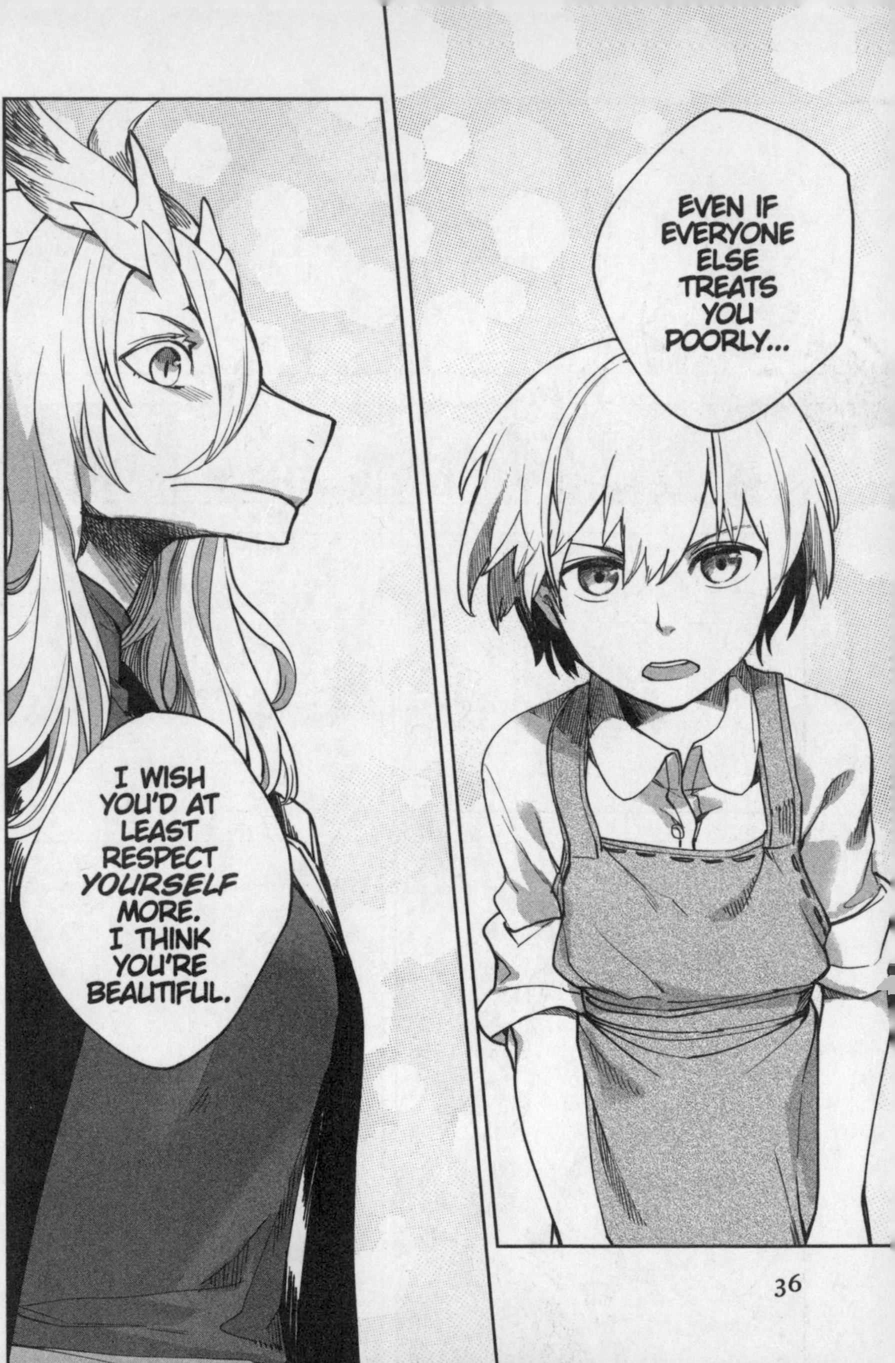
EVEN IF EVERYONE ELSE TREATS YOU POORLY...
I WISH YOU'D AT LEAST RESPECT *YOURSELF* MORE. I THINK YOU'RE BEAUTIFUL.

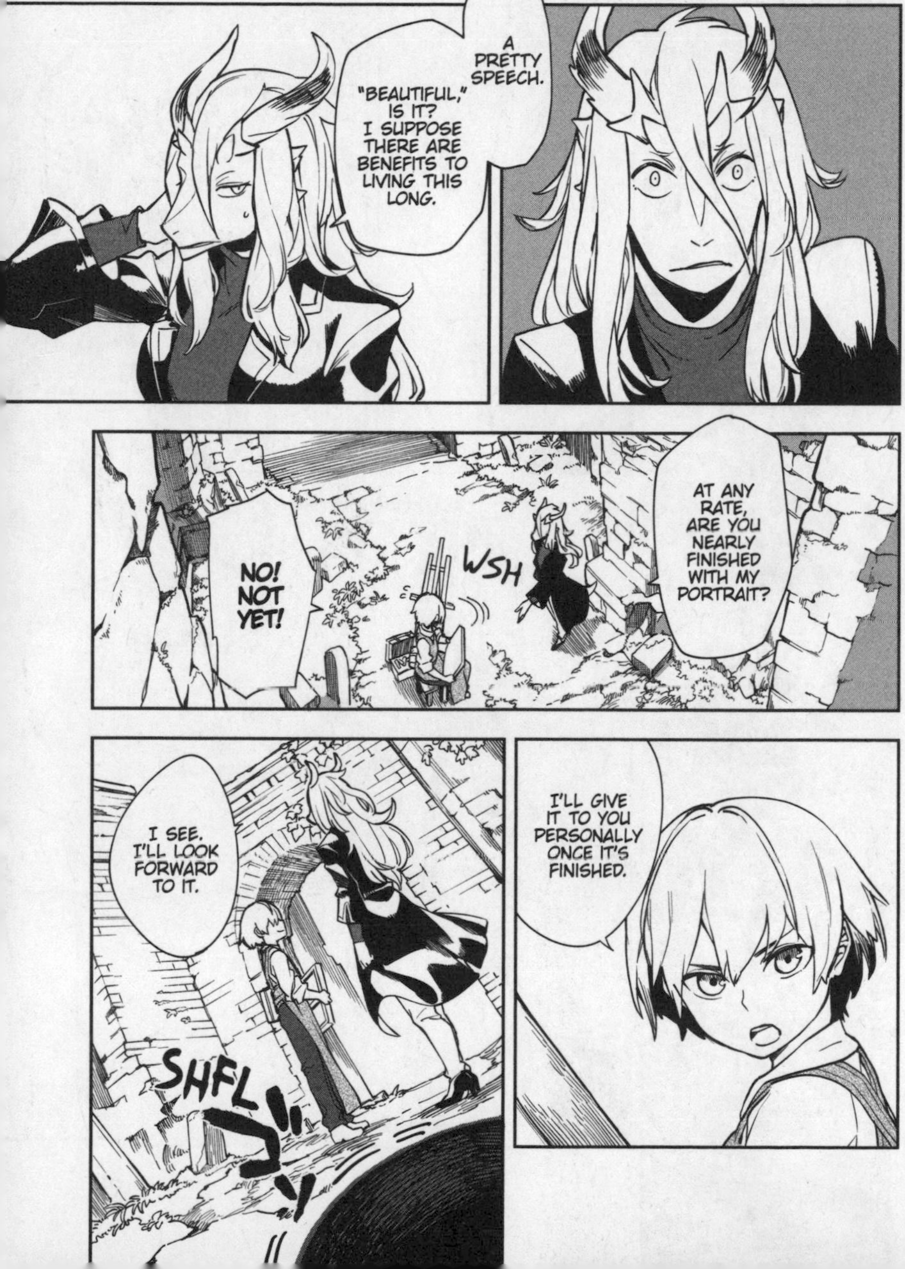
A PRETTY SPEECH. "BEAUTIFUL," IS IT? I SUPPOSE THERE ARE BENEFITS TO LIVING THIS LONG.
AT ANY RATE, ARE YOU NEARLY FINISHED WITH MY PORTRAIT?
WSH
NO! NOT YET!
I'LL GIVE IT TO YOU PERSONALLY ONCE IT'S FINISHED.
I SEE. I'LL LOOK FORWARD TO IT.
SHFL

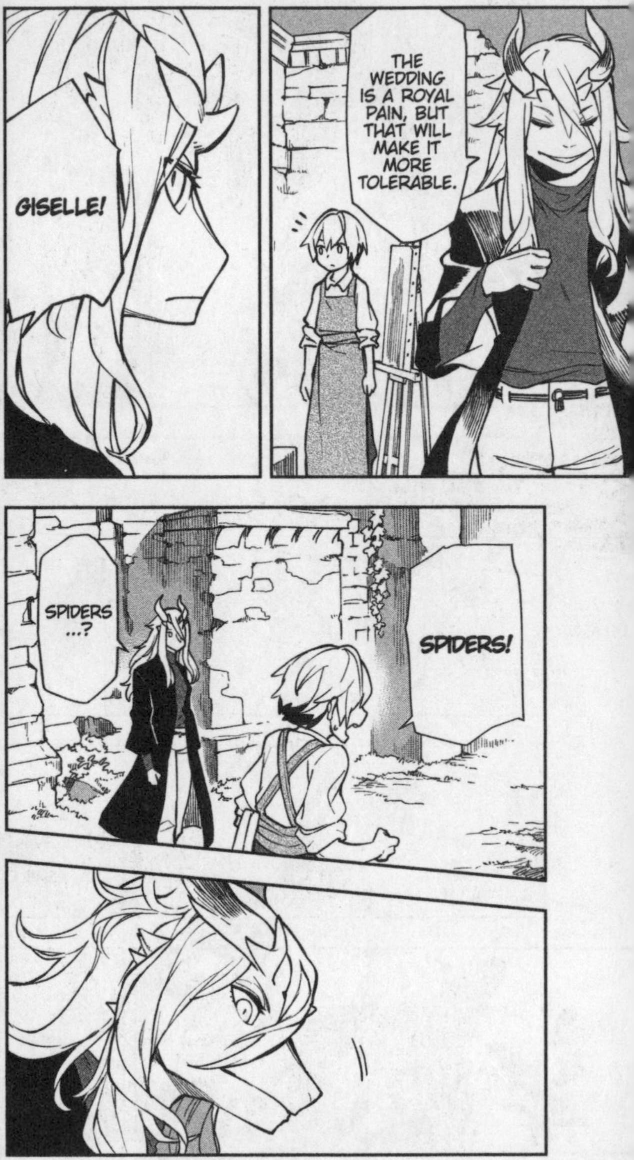
THE WEDDING IS A ROYAL PAIN, BUT THAT WILL MAKE IT MORE TOLERABLE.
GISELLE!
SPIDERS!
SPIDERS ...?

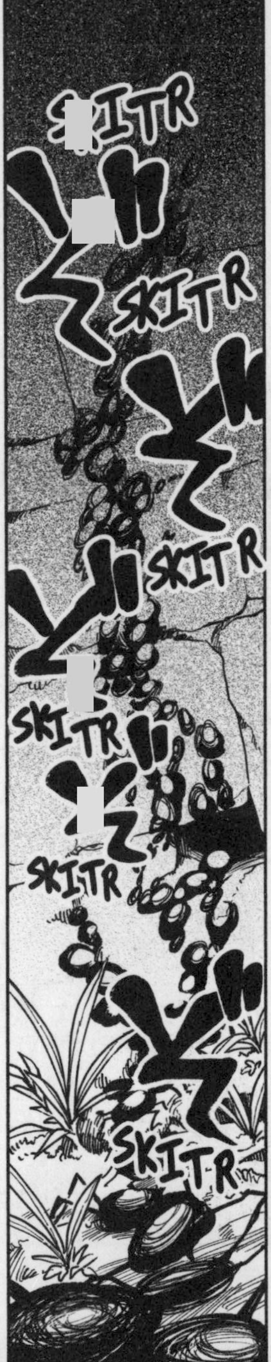
SKITR
SKITR
SKITR
SKITR
SKITR

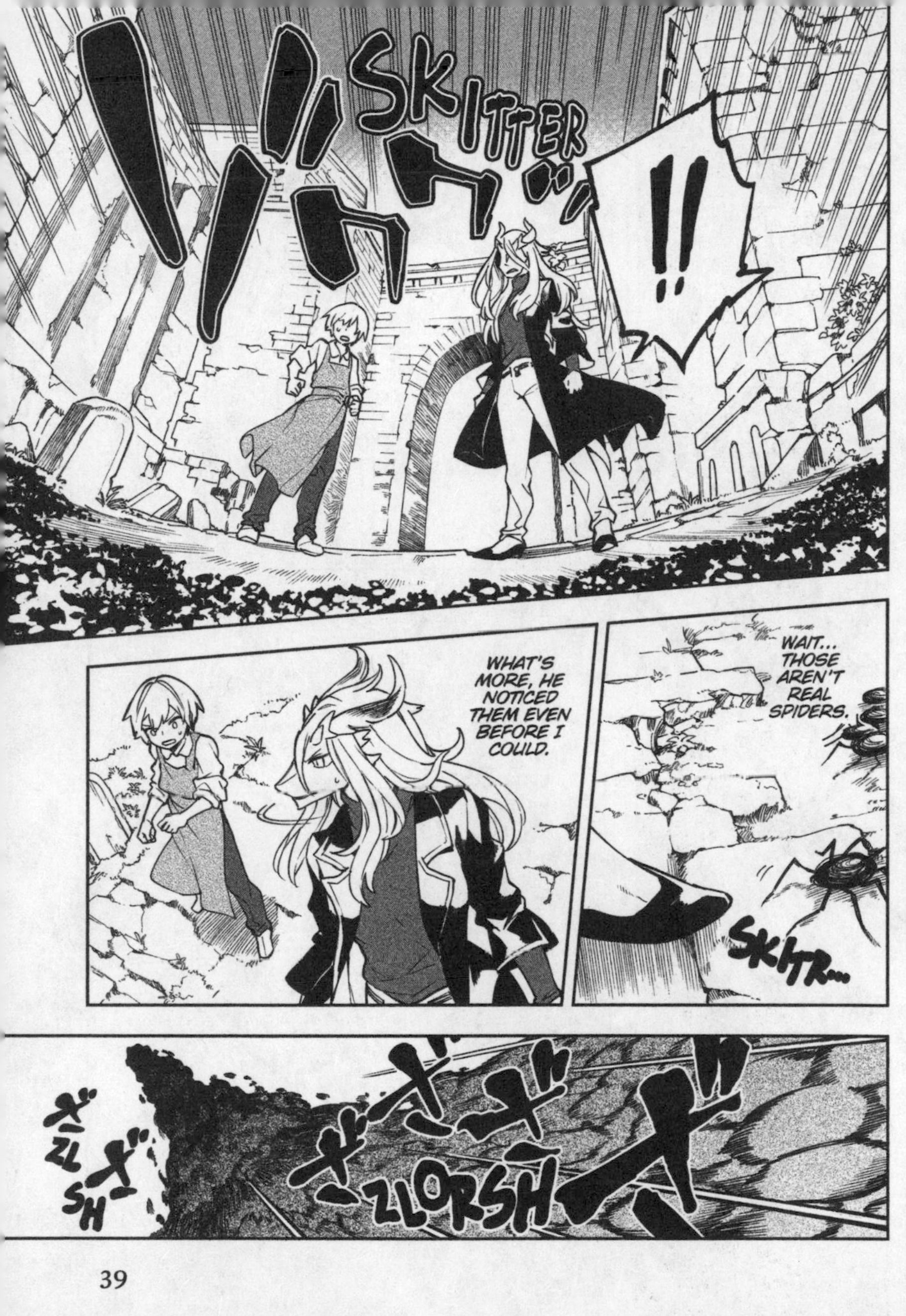
SKITTER
!!
WAIT... THOSE AREN'T REAL SPIDERS.
SKITR...
WHAT'S MORE, HE NOTICED THEM EVEN BEFORE I COULD.
ZZLORSH
ZZLSH

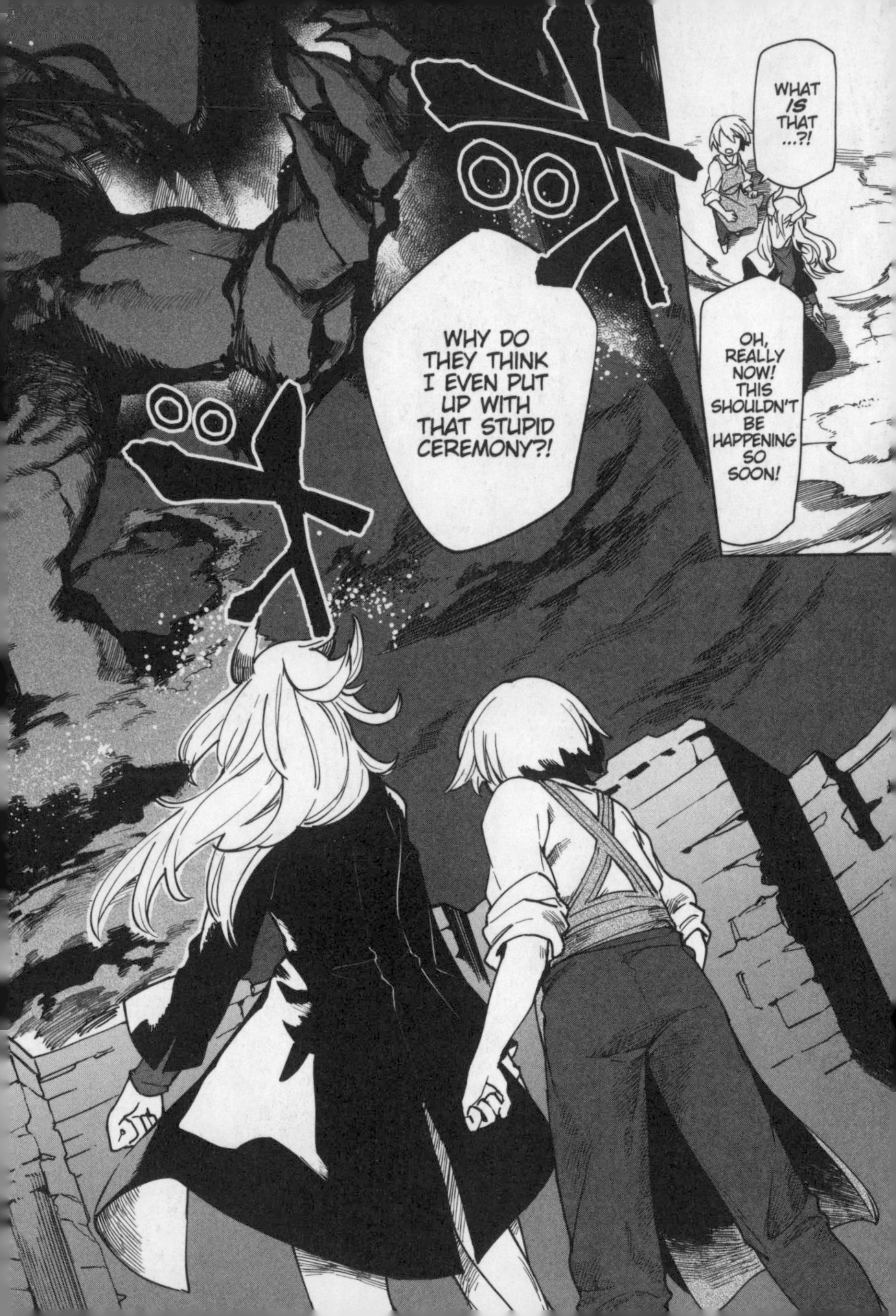
WHAT *IS* THAT ...?!
OH, REALLY NOW! THIS SHOULDN'T BE HAPPENING SO SOON!
WHY DO THEY THINK I EVEN PUT UP WITH THAT STUPID CEREMONY?!

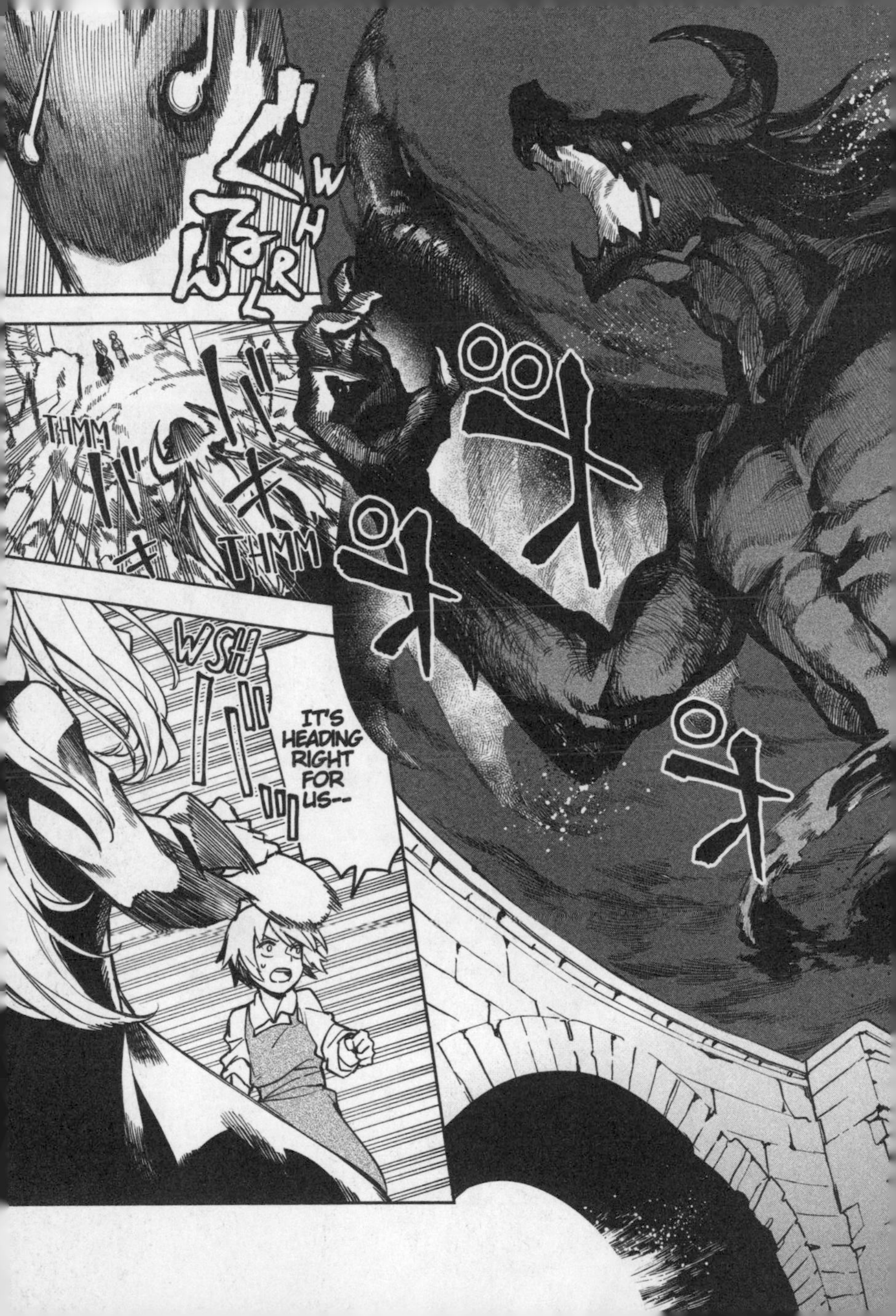
WHRL
THMM
THMM
WSH
IT'S HEADING RIGHT FOR US--

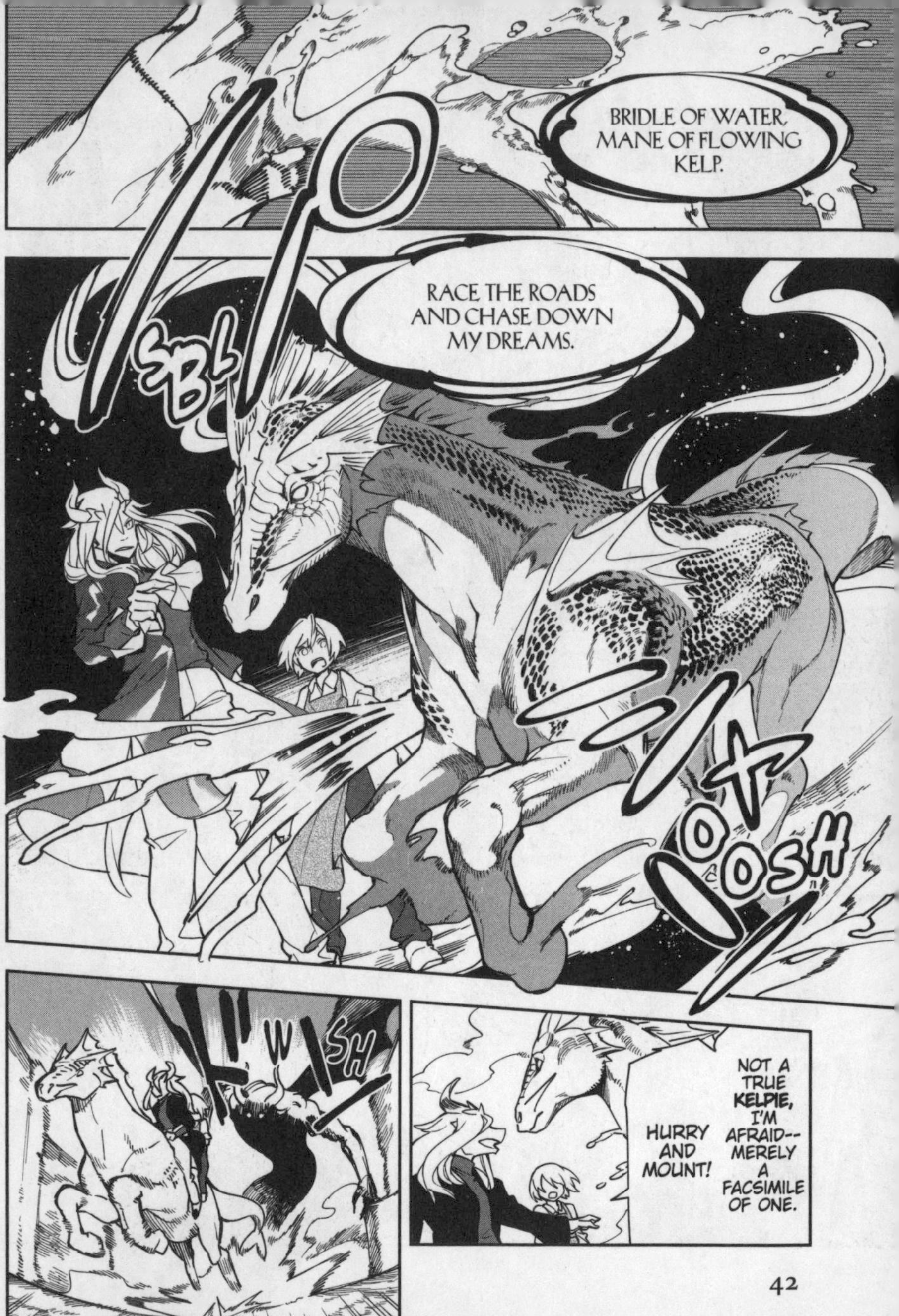
BRIDLE OF WATER, MANE OF FLOWING KELP.
RACE THE ROADS AND CHASE DOWN MY DREAMS.
NOT A TRUE **KELPIE,** I'M AFRAID-- MERELY A FACSIMILE OF ONE.
HURRY AND MOUNT!

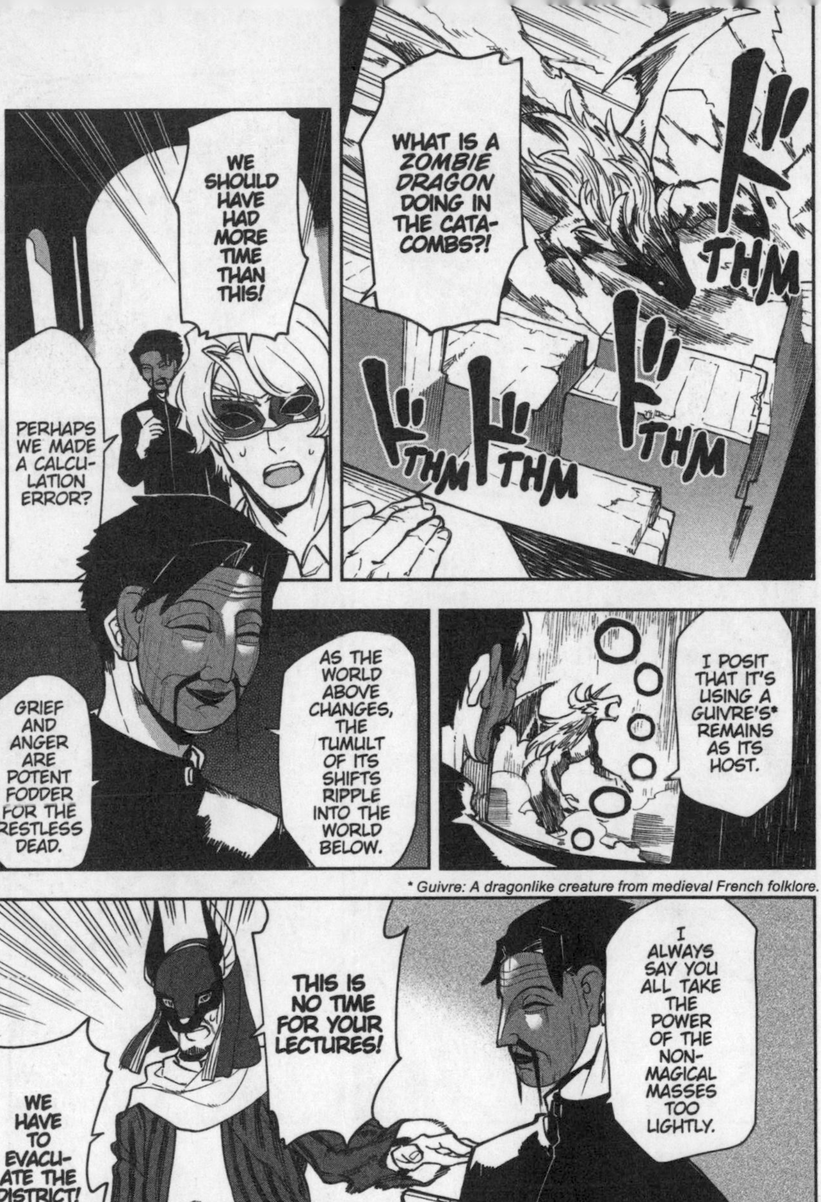
WHAT IS A ZOMBIE DRAGON DOING IN THE CATA-COMBS?!
THM
THM
THM
THM
WE SHOULD HAVE HAD MORE TIME THAN THIS!
PERHAPS WE MADE A CALCU-LATION ERROR?
I POSIT THAT IT'S USING A GUIVRE'S* REMAINS AS ITS HOST.
AS THE WORLD ABOVE CHANGES, THE TUMULT OF ITS SHIFTS RIPPLE INTO THE WORLD BELOW.
GRIEF AND ANGER ARE POTENT FODDER FOR THE RESTLESS DEAD.
I ALWAYS SAY YOU ALL TAKE THE POWER OF THE NON-MAGICAL MASSES TOO LIGHTLY.
THIS IS NO TIME FOR YOUR LECTURES!
WE HAVE TO EVACU-ATE THE DISTRICT!

** Guivre: A dragonlike creature from medieval French folklore.*

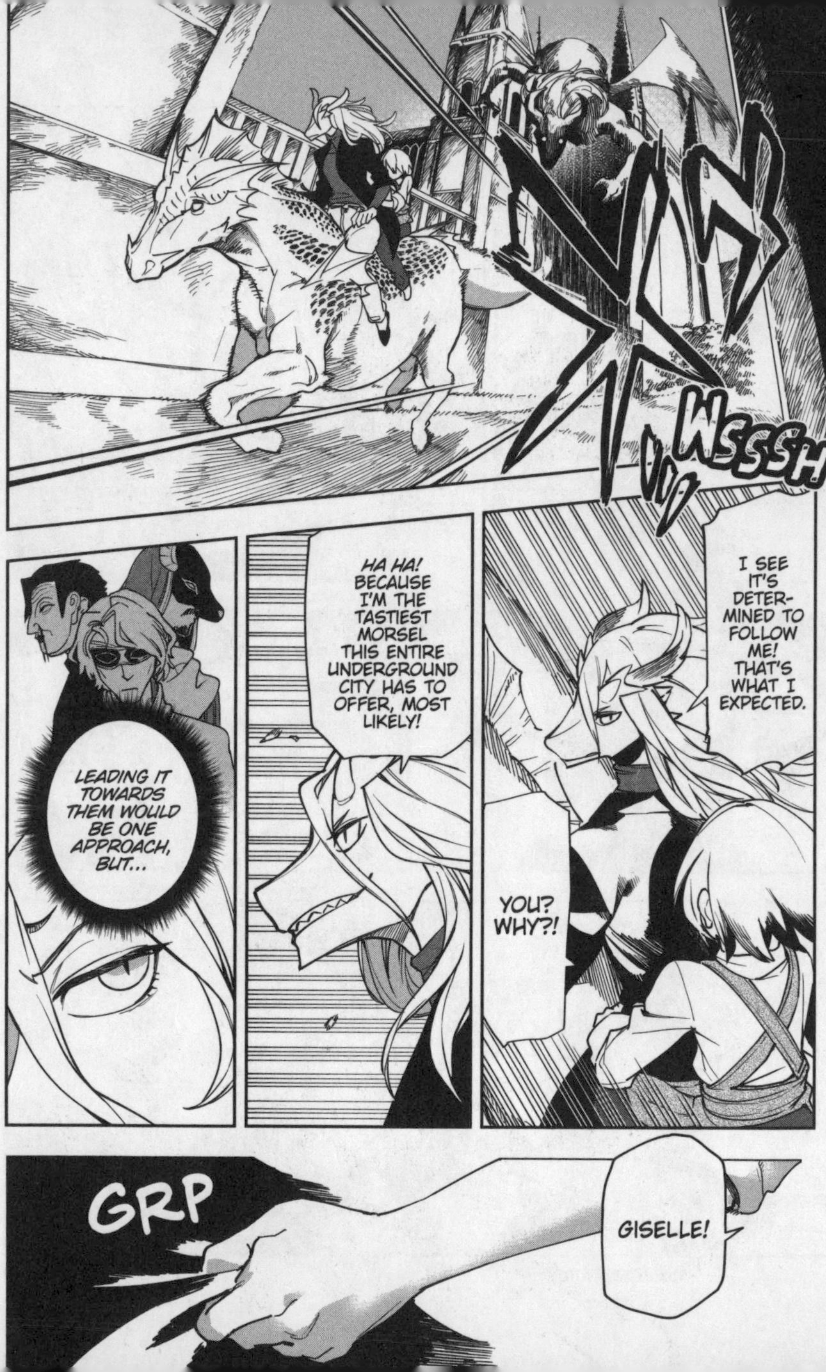
WSSSH
I SEE IT'S DETER-MINED TO FOLLOW ME! THAT'S WHAT I EXPECTED.
YOU? WHY?!
HA HA! BECAUSE I'M THE TASTIEST MORSEL THIS ENTIRE UNDERGROUND CITY HAS TO OFFER, MOST LIKELY!
LEADING IT TOWARDS THEM WOULD BE ONE APPROACH, BUT...
GISELLE!
GRP

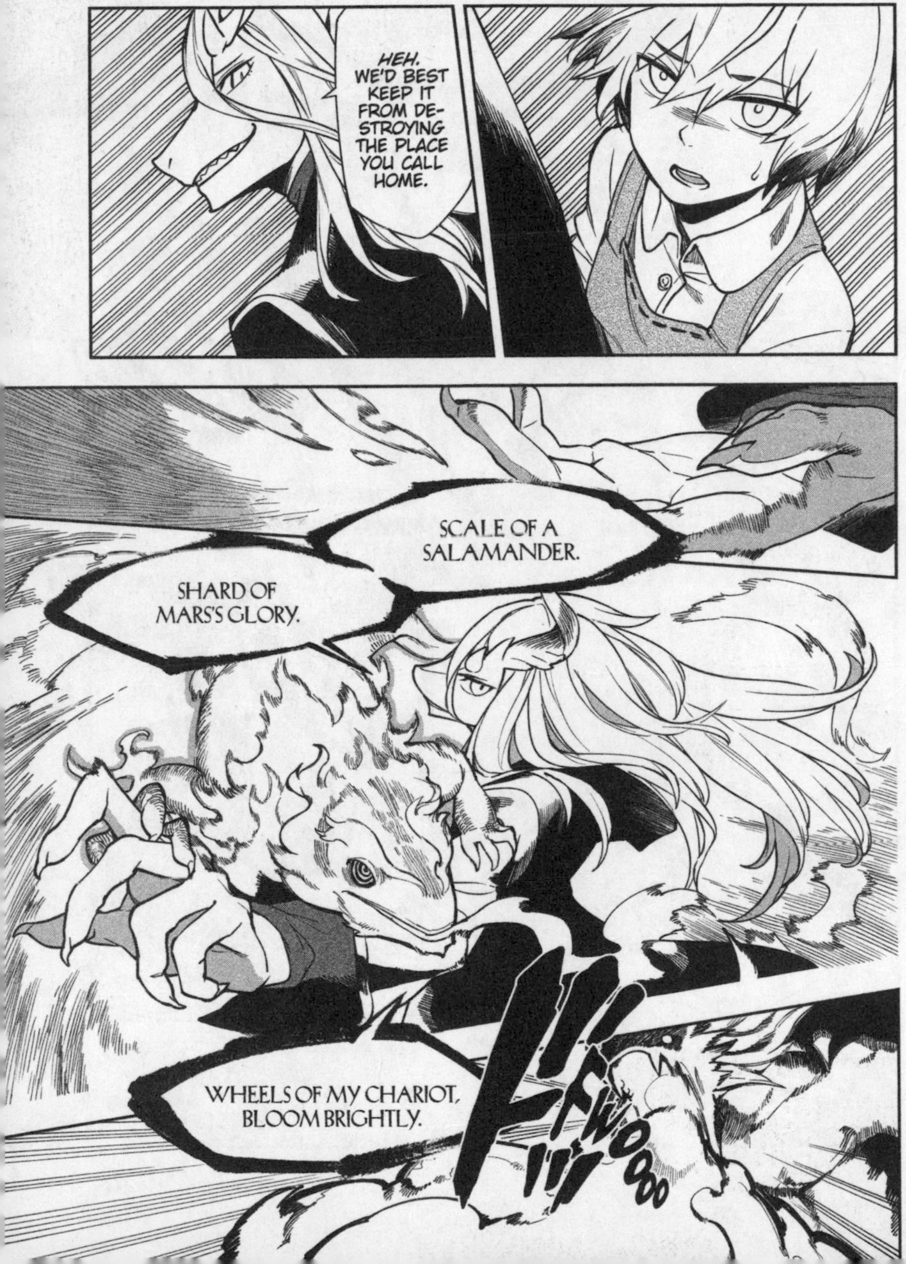
HEH. WE'D BEST KEEP IT FROM DE-STROYING THE PLACE YOU CALL HOME.
SCALE OF A SALAMANDER.
SHARD OF MARS'S GLORY.
WHEELS OF MY CHARIOT, BLOOM BRIGHTLY.
FWOOOO!!!

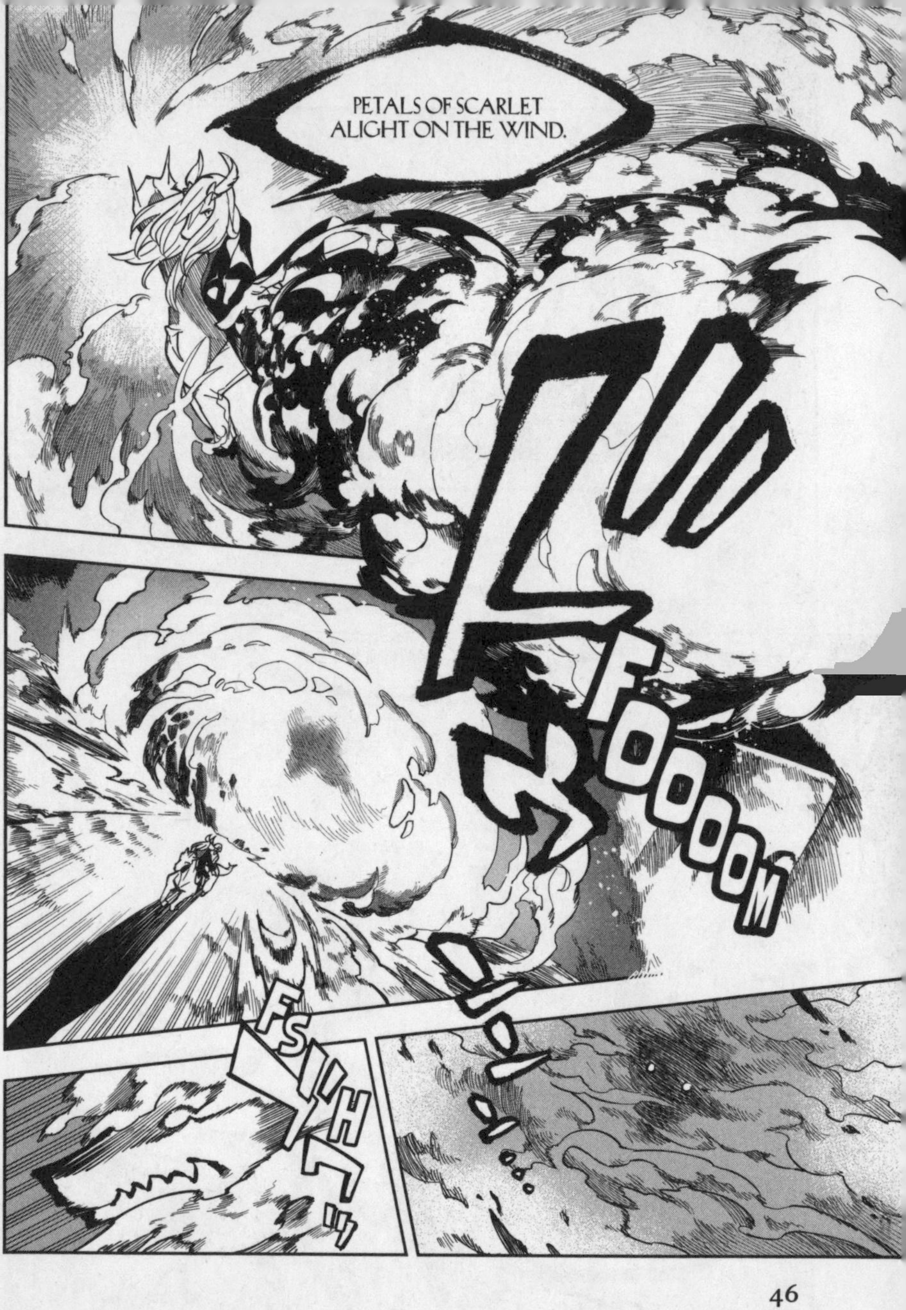
PETALS OF SCARLET
ALIGHT ON THE WIND.
FOOOOM
FSH

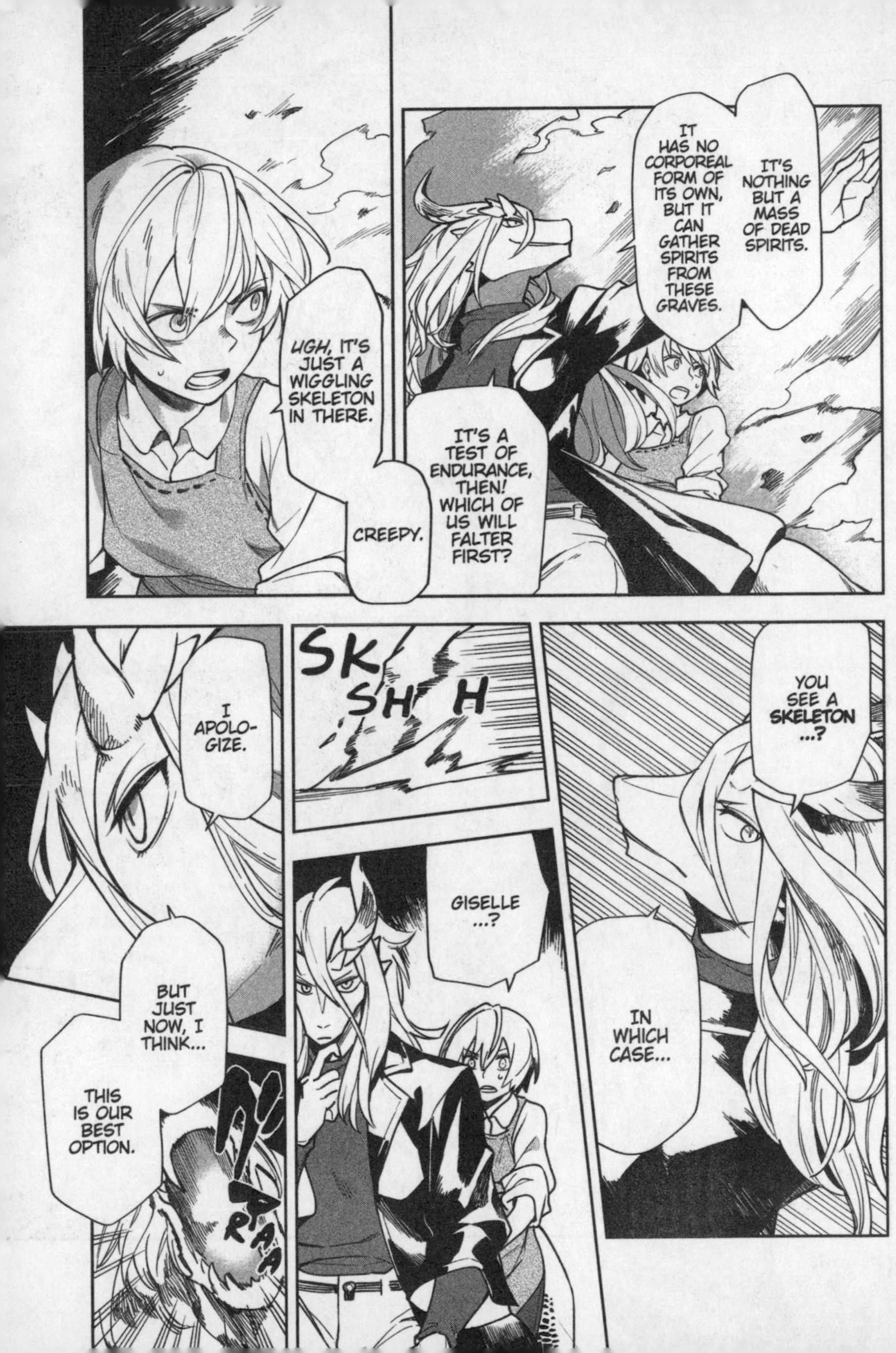

IT'S NOTHING BUT A MASS OF DEAD SPIRITS.
IT HAS NO CORPOREAL FORM OF ITS OWN, BUT IT CAN GATHER SPIRITS FROM THESE GRAVES.
IT'S A TEST OF ENDURANCE, THEN! WHICH OF US WILL FALTER FIRST?
UGH, IT'S JUST A WIGGLING SKELETON IN THERE.
CREEPY.
YOU SEE A SKELETON...?
IN WHICH CASE...
SKSHH
GISELLE...?
I APOLOGIZE.
BUT JUST NOW, I THINK...
THIS IS OUR BEST OPTION.

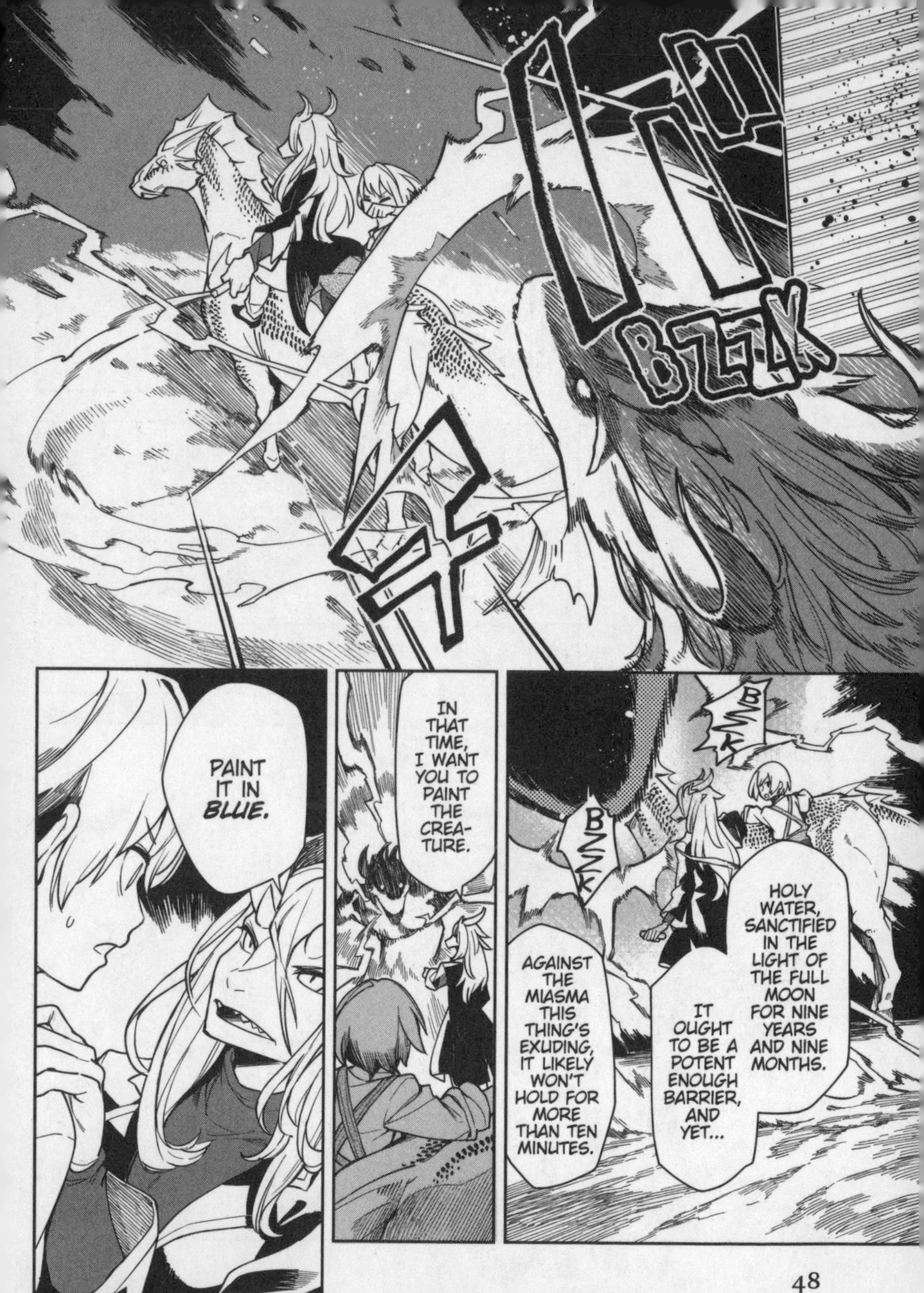
BZZK
BZZK
BZZK
HOLY WATER, SANCTIFIED IN THE LIGHT OF THE FULL MOON FOR NINE YEARS AND NINE MONTHS.
IT OUGHT TO BE A POTENT ENOUGH BARRIER, AND YET...
AGAINST THE MIASMA THIS THING'S EXUDING, IT LIKELY WON'T HOLD FOR MORE THAN TEN MINUTES.
IN THAT TIME, I WANT YOU TO PAINT THE CREATURE.
PAINT IT IN **BLUE.**

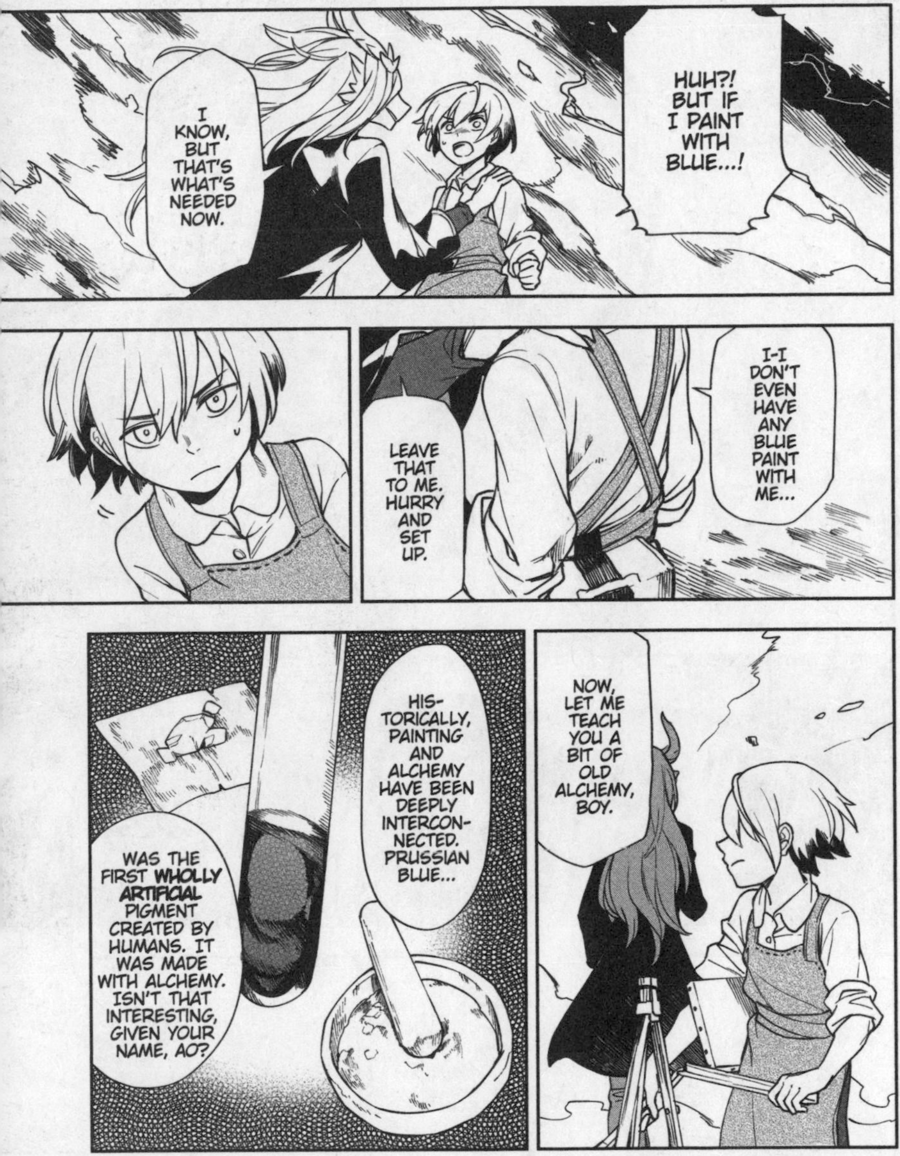
HUH?! BUT IF I PAINT WITH BLUE...!
I KNOW, BUT THAT'S WHAT'S NEEDED NOW.
I-I DON'T EVEN HAVE ANY BLUE PAINT WITH ME...
LEAVE THAT TO ME. HURRY AND SET UP.
NOW, LET ME TEACH YOU A BIT OF OLD ALCHEMY, BOY.
HISTORICALLY, PAINTING AND ALCHEMY HAVE BEEN DEEPLY INTERCONNECTED. PRUSSIAN BLUE...
WAS THE FIRST **WHOLLY ARTIFICIAL** PIGMENT CREATED BY HUMANS. IT WAS MADE WITH ALCHEMY. ISN'T THAT INTERESTING, GIVEN YOUR NAME, AO?

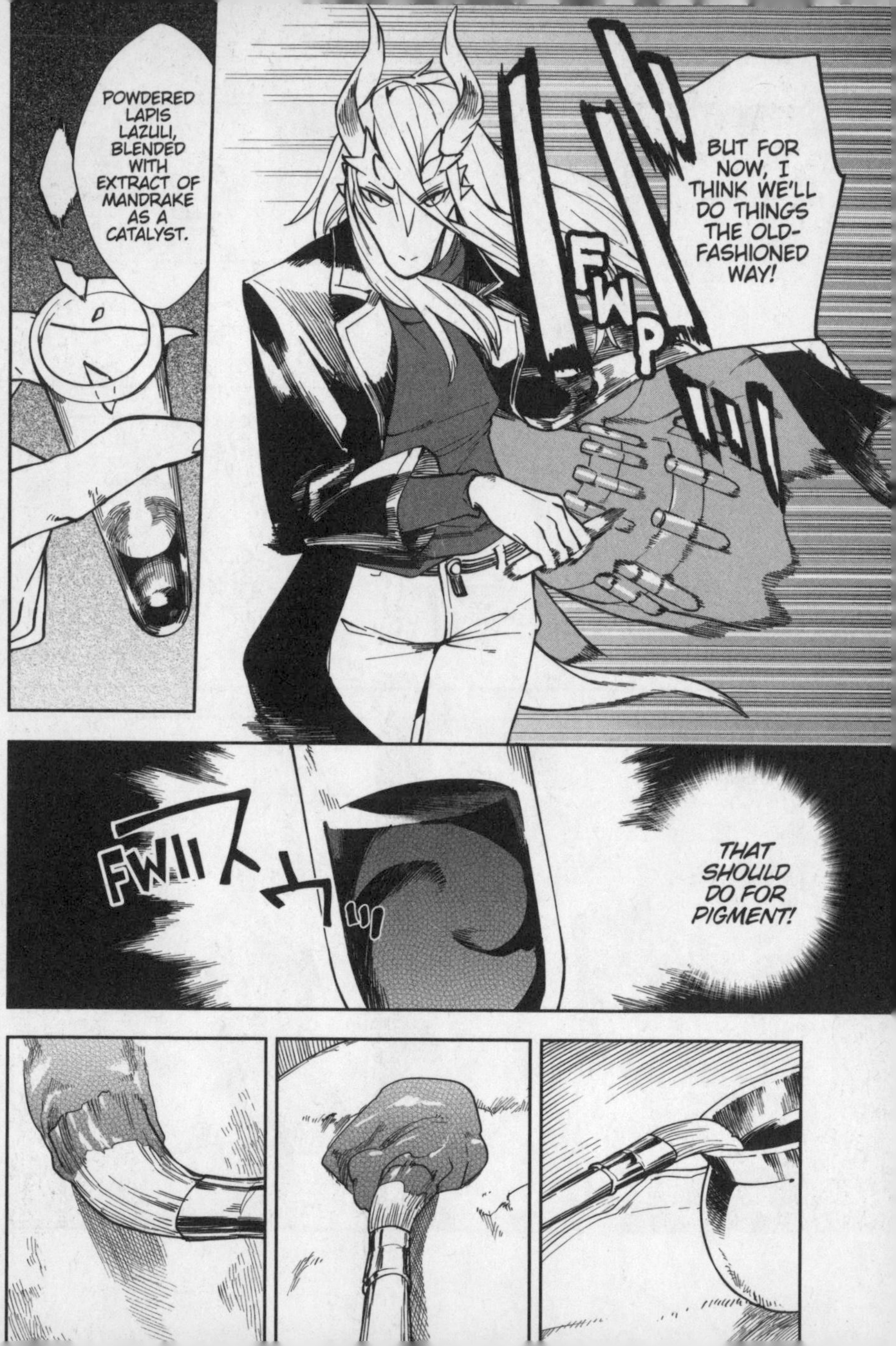
BUT FOR NOW, I THINK WE'LL DO THINGS THE OLD-FASHIONED WAY!
FWP
POWDERED LAPIS LAZULI, BLENDED WITH EXTRACT OF MANDRAKE AS A CATALYST.
THAT SHOULD DO FOR PIGMENT!
FWIII

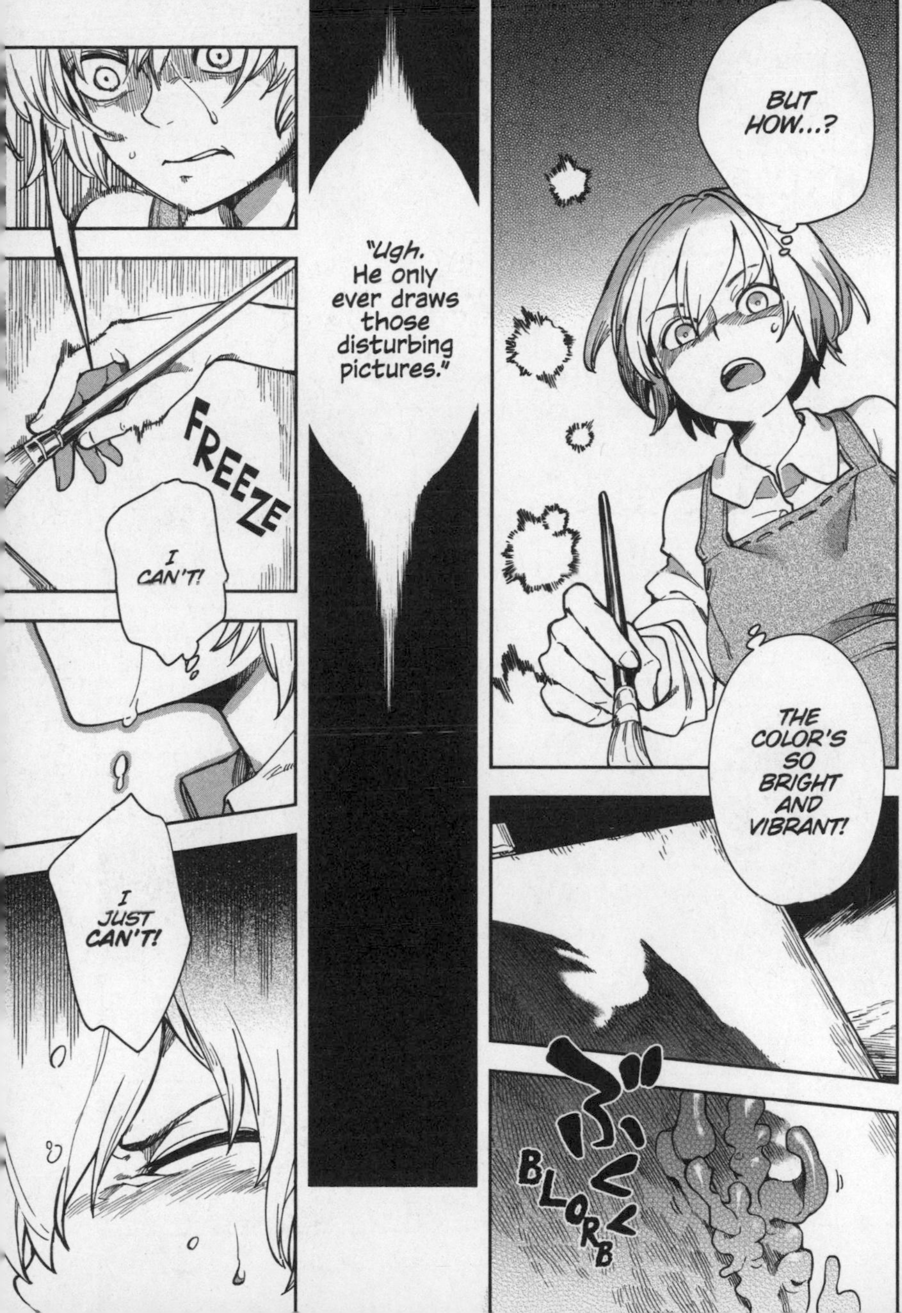
BUT HOW...?
THE COLOR'S SO BRIGHT AND VIBRANT!
ぷくく
BLORB
"Ugh. He only ever draws those disturbing pictures."
FREEZE
I CAN'T!
I JUST CAN'T!

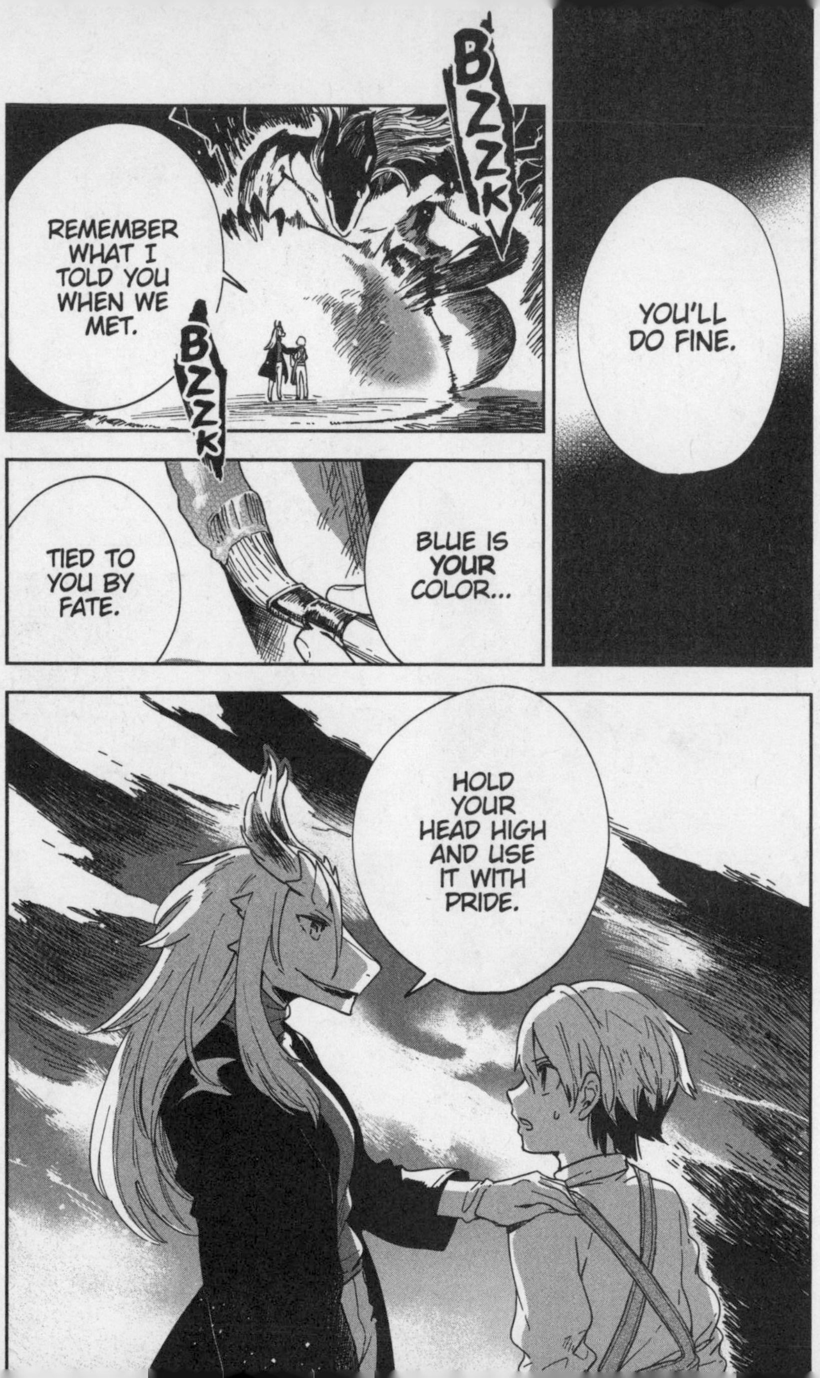
YOU'LL DO FINE.
BZZK
REMEMBER WHAT I TOLD YOU WHEN WE MET.
BZZK
BLUE IS YOUR COLOR...
TIED TO YOU BY FATE.
HOLD YOUR HEAD HIGH AND USE IT WITH PRIDE.

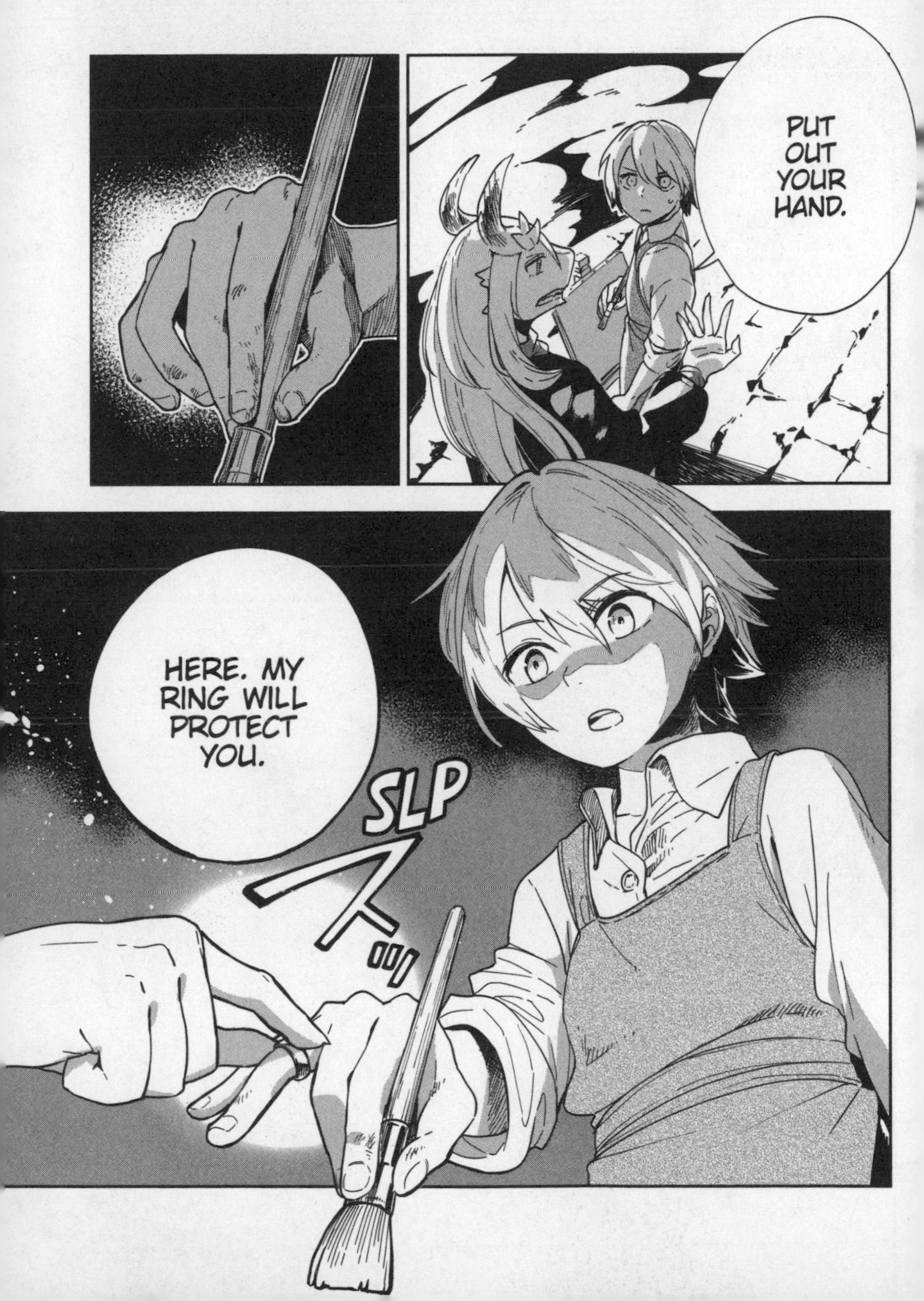
PUT OUT YOUR HAND.
HERE. MY RING WILL PROTECT YOU.
SLP

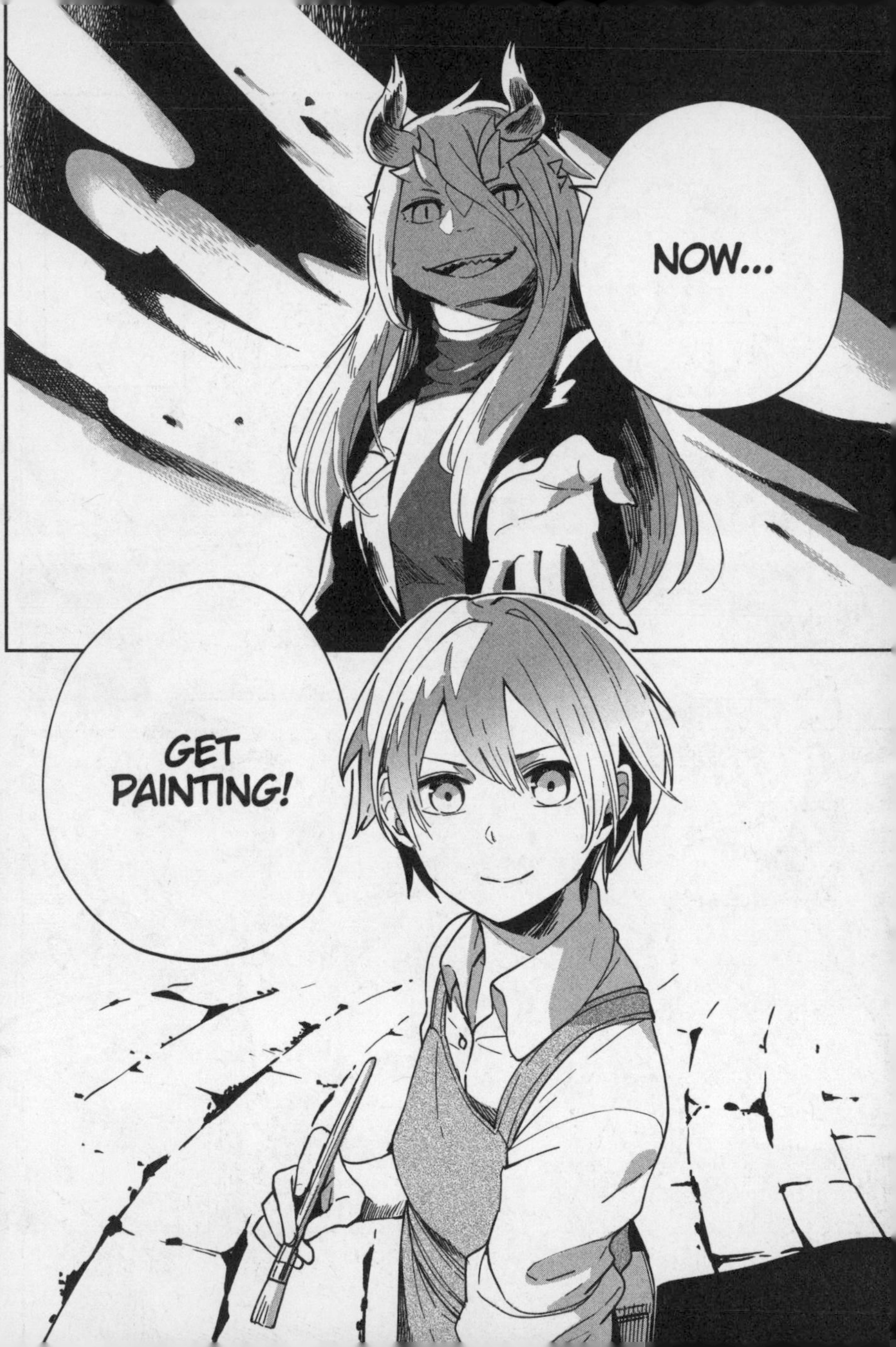
NOW...
GET PAINTING!

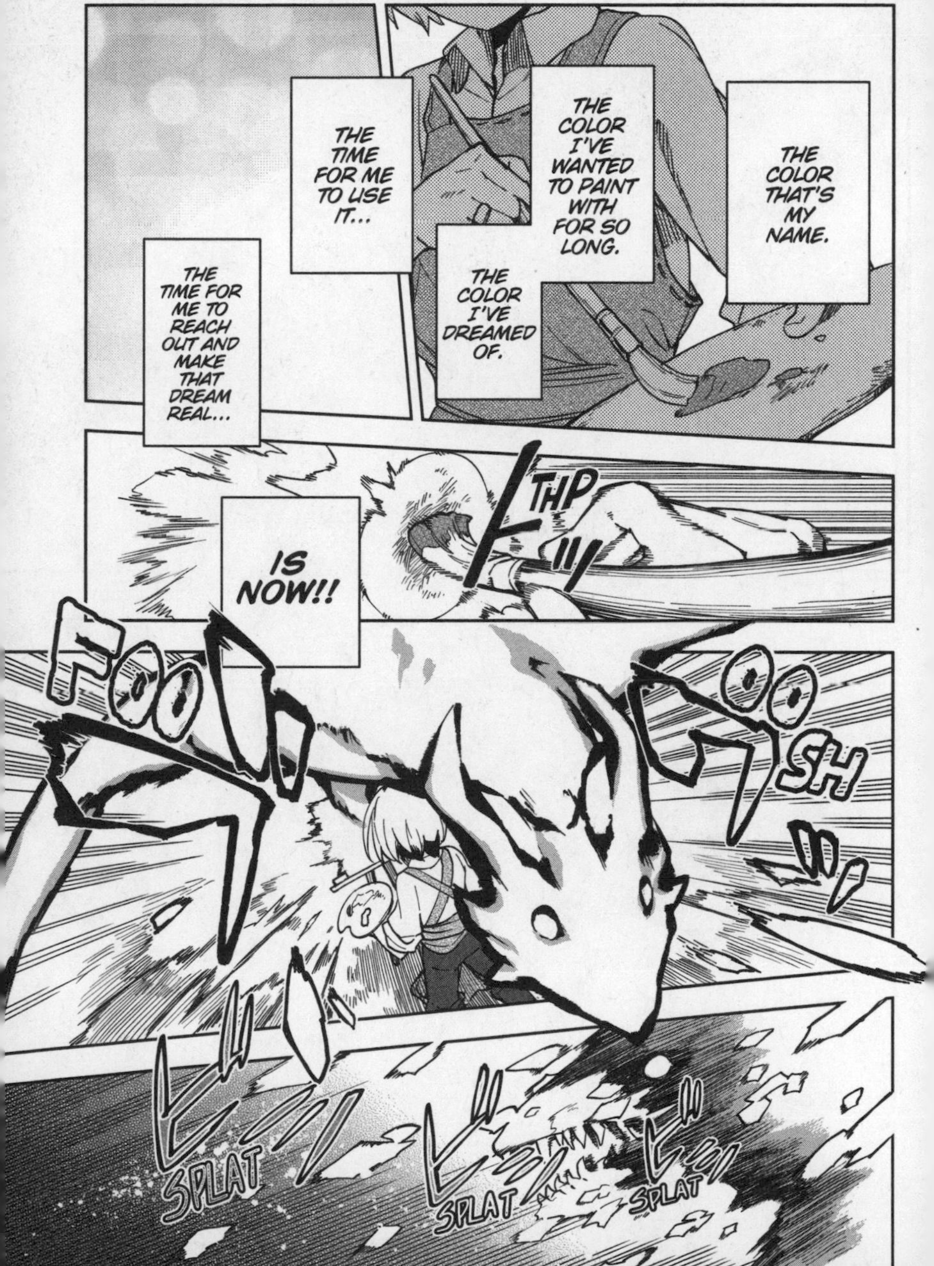
THE COLOR THAT'S MY NAME.
THE COLOR I'VE WANTED TO PAINT WITH FOR SO LONG.
THE COLOR I'VE DREAMED OF.
THE TIME FOR ME TO USE IT...
THE TIME FOR ME TO REACH OUT AND MAKE THAT DREAM REAL...
THP
IS NOW!!
FOOOOOOSH
SPLAT
SPLAT
SPLAT

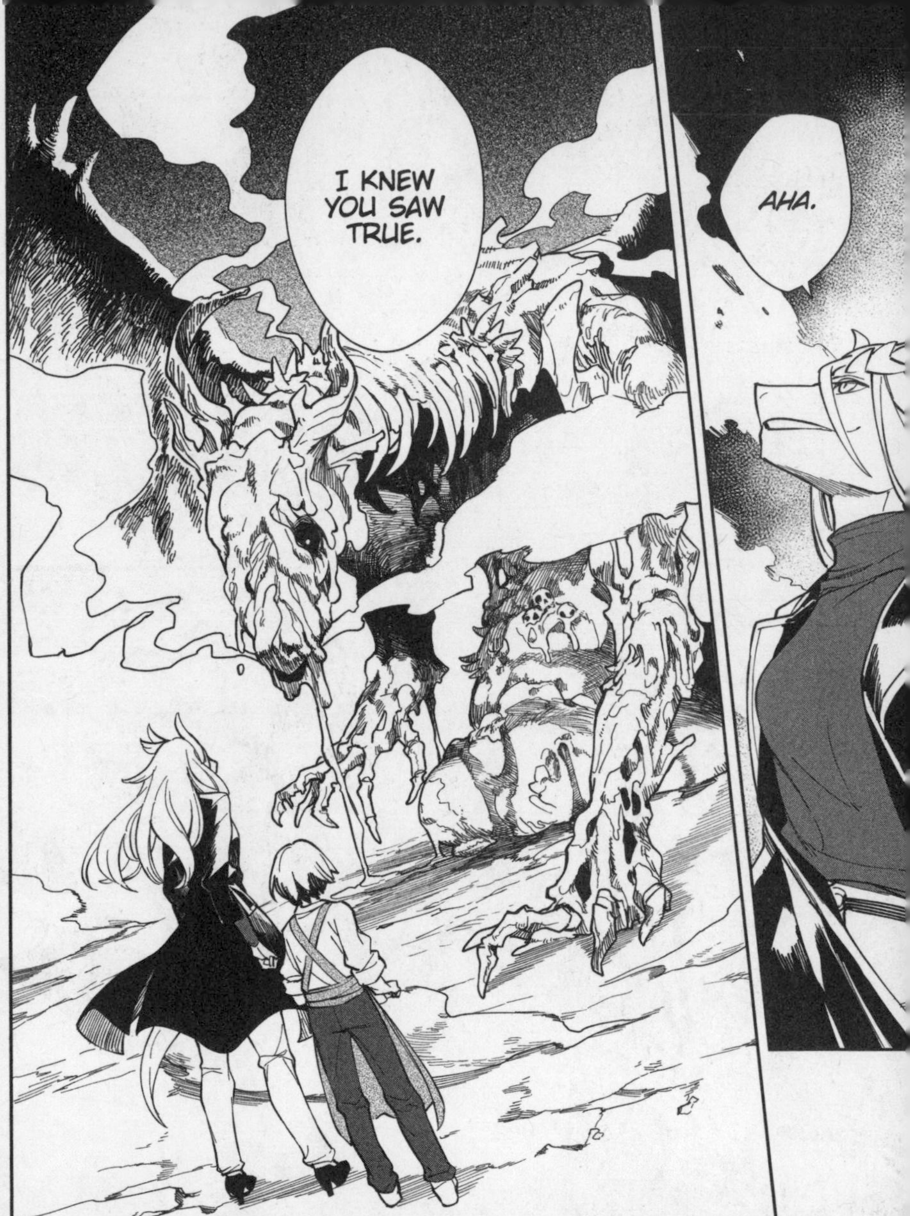
AHA.
I KNEW YOU SAW TRUE.

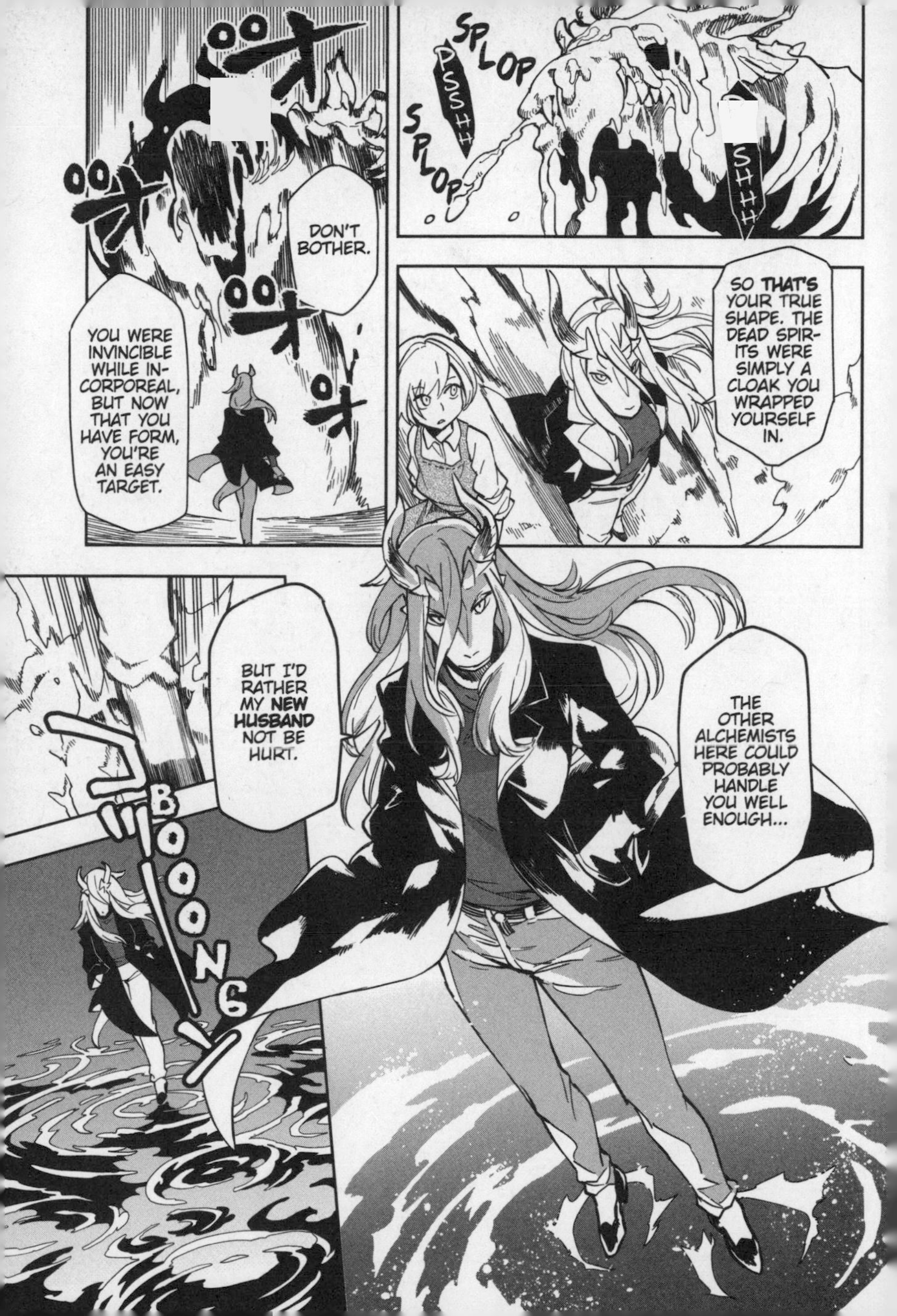
SPLOP
PSSHH
SPLOP
SHHH
SO THAT'S YOUR TRUE SHAPE. THE DEAD SPIRITS WERE SIMPLY A CLOAK YOU WRAPPED YOURSELF IN.
オ
オ
オ
オ
DON'T BOTHER.
YOU WERE INVINCIBLE WHILE INCORPOREAL, BUT NOW THAT YOU HAVE FORM, YOU'RE AN EASY TARGET.
THE OTHER ALCHEMISTS HERE COULD PROBABLY HANDLE YOU WELL ENOUGH...
BUT I'D RATHER MY NEW HUSBAND NOT BE HURT.
BOOONG

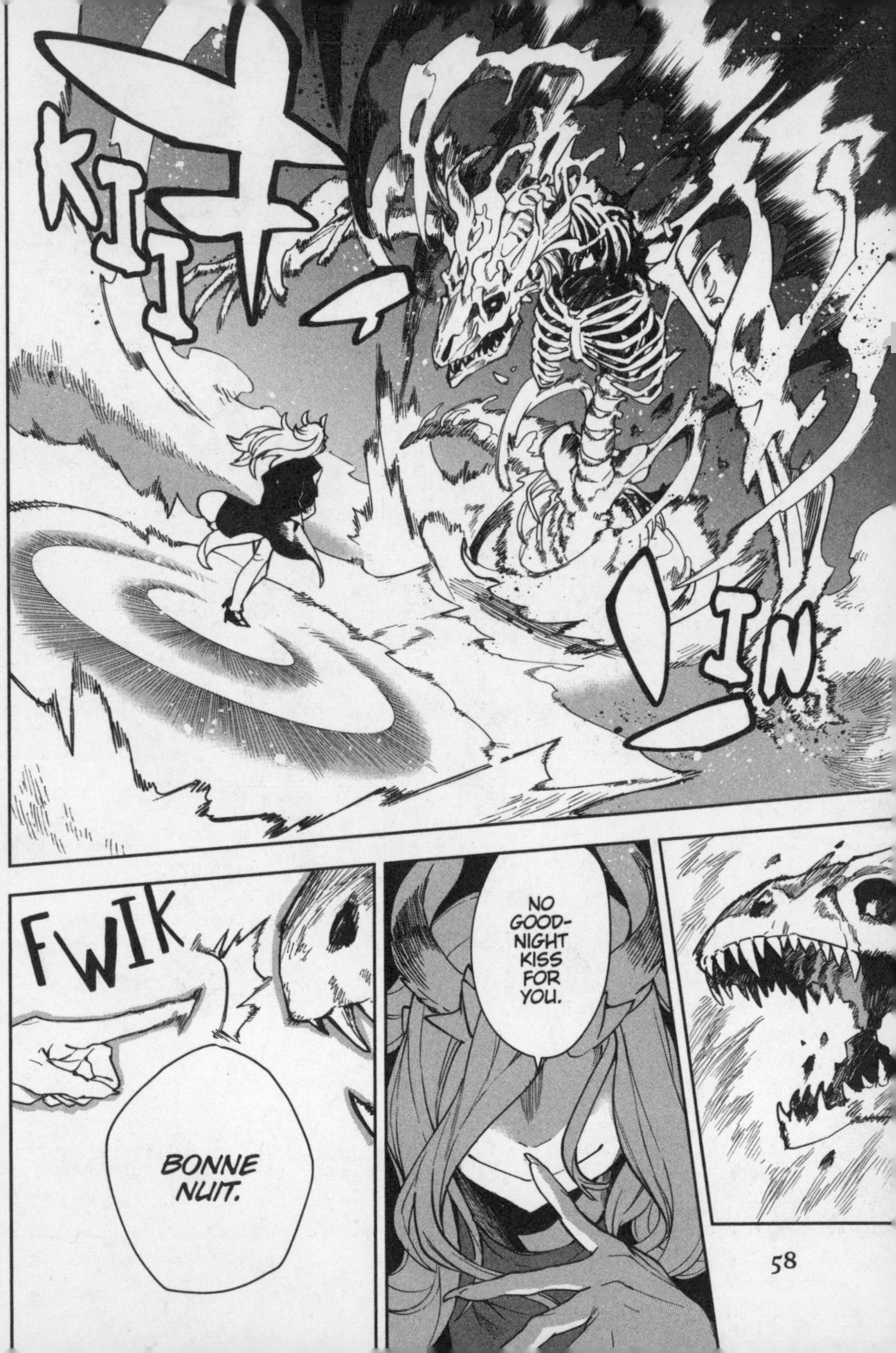
KII
IN
NO GOOD-NIGHT KISS FOR YOU.
FWIK
BONNE NUIT.

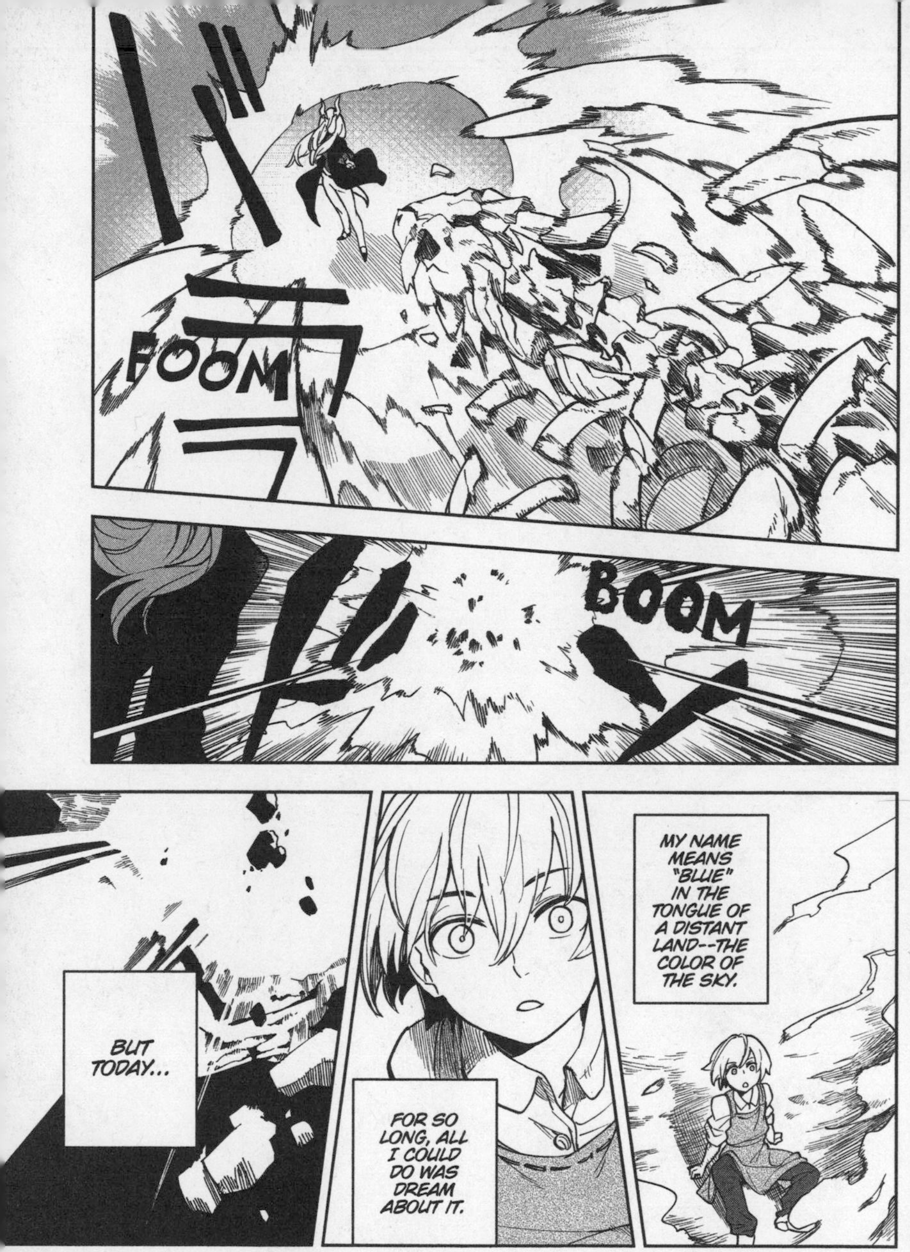
FOOM
BOOM
MY NAME MEANS "BLUE" IN THE TONGUE OF A DISTANT LAND--THE COLOR OF THE SKY.
FOR SO LONG, ALL I COULD DO WAS DREAM ABOUT IT.
BUT TODAY...

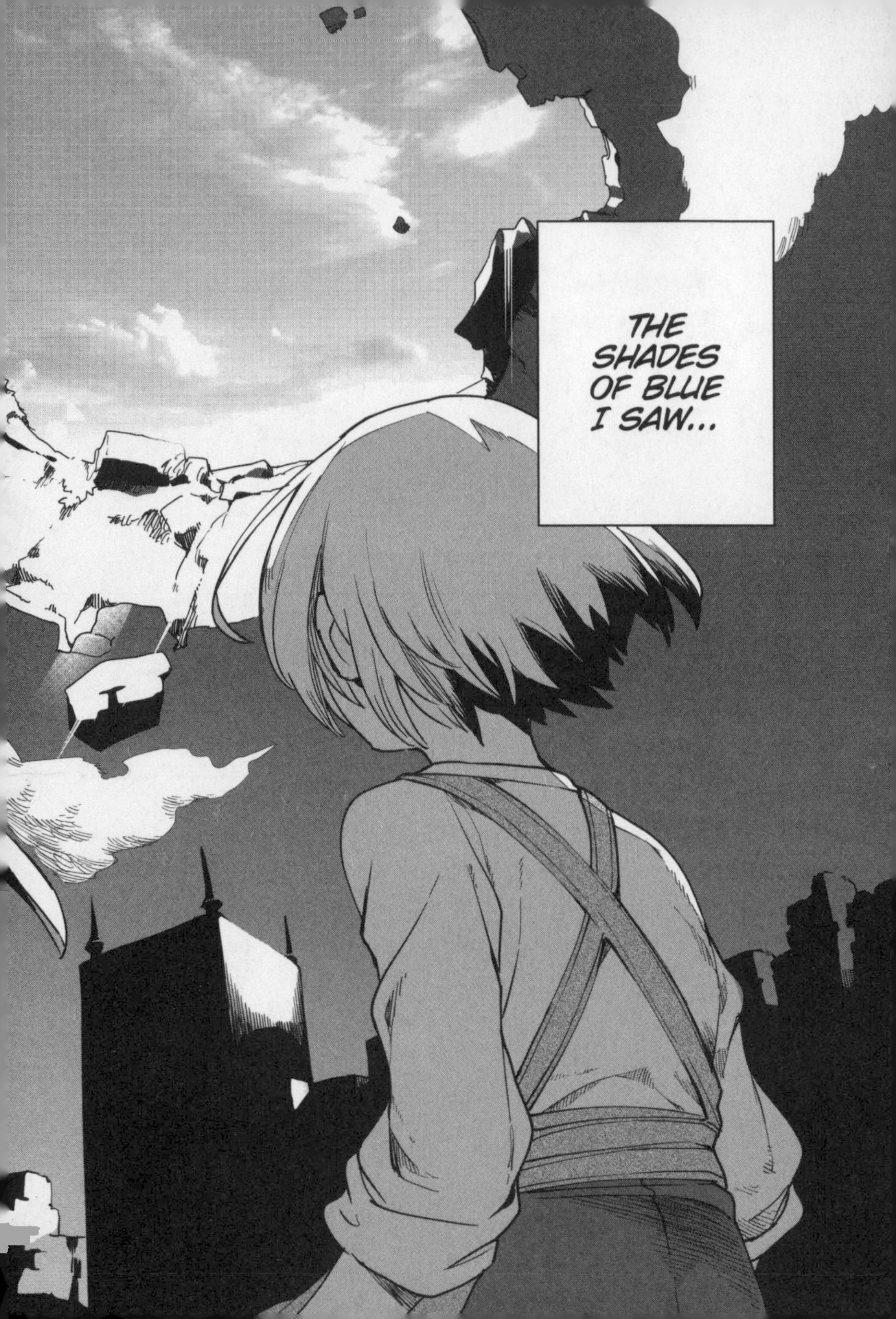
THE SHADES OF BLUE I SAW...

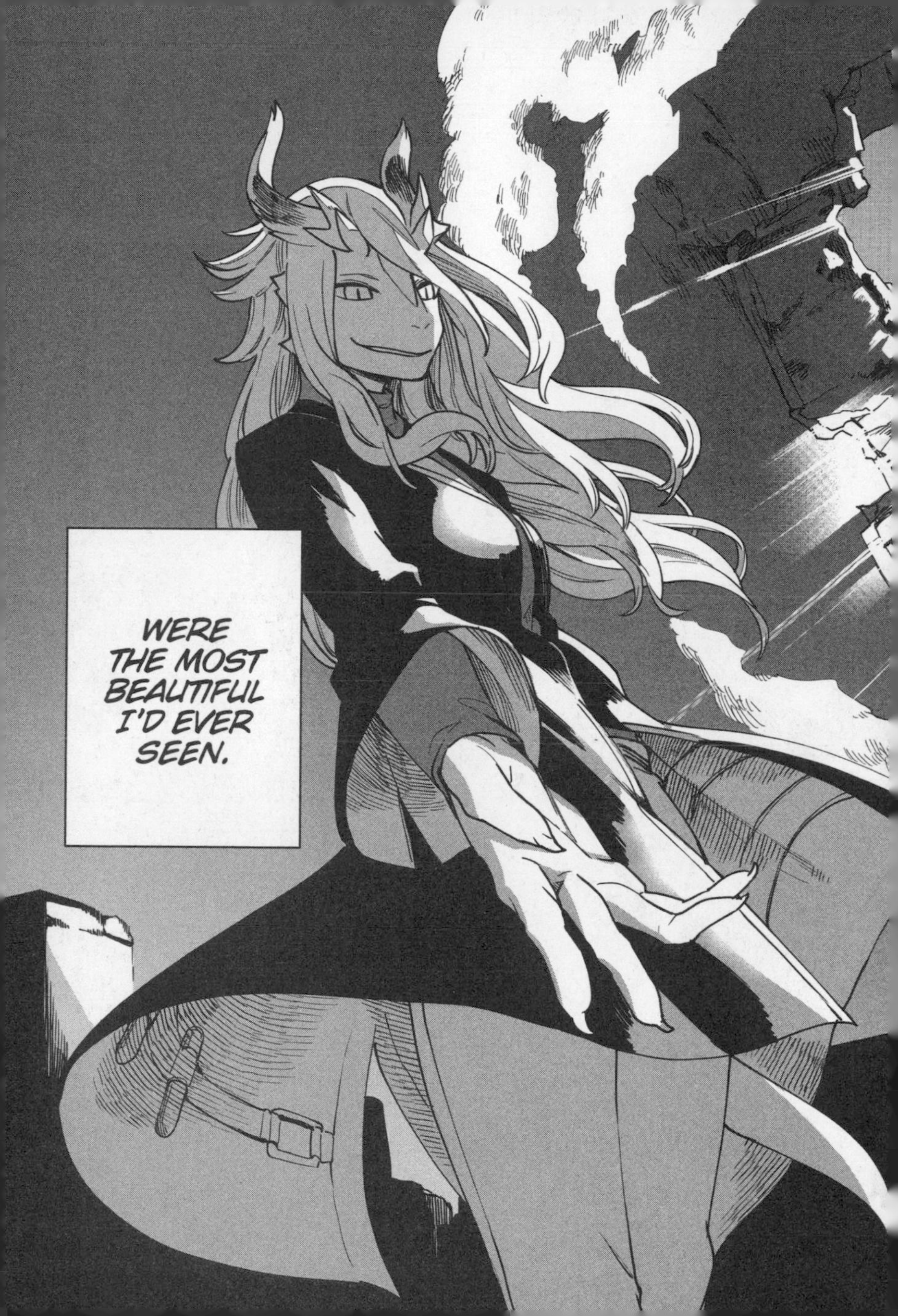
WERE THE MOST BEAUTIFUL I'D EVER SEEN.

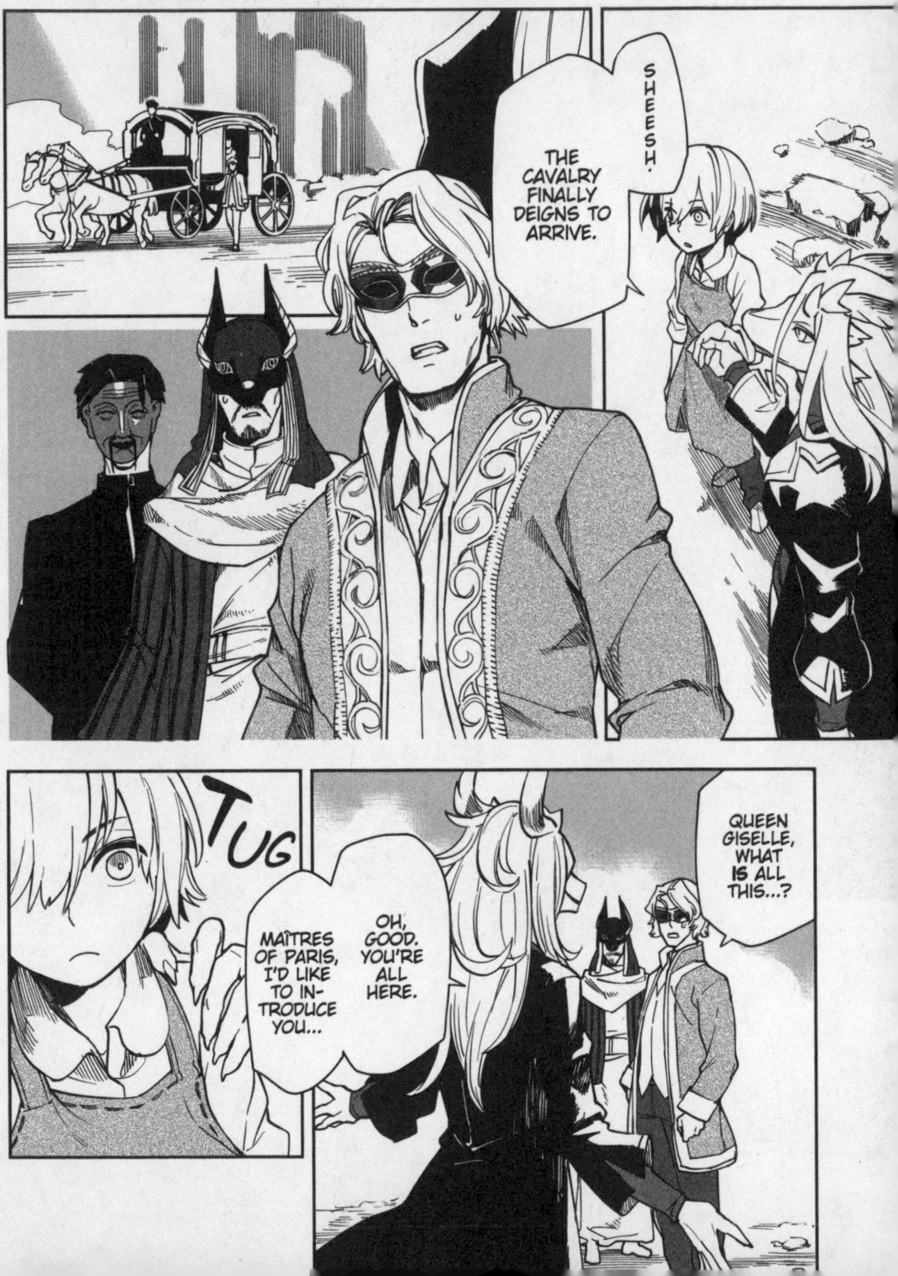
SHEESH.
THE CAVALRY FINALLY DEIGNS TO ARRIVE.
QUEEN GISELLE, WHAT IS ALL THIS...?
OH, GOOD. YOU'RE ALL HERE.
MAÎTRES OF PARIS, I'D LIKE TO IN-TRODUCE YOU...
TUG

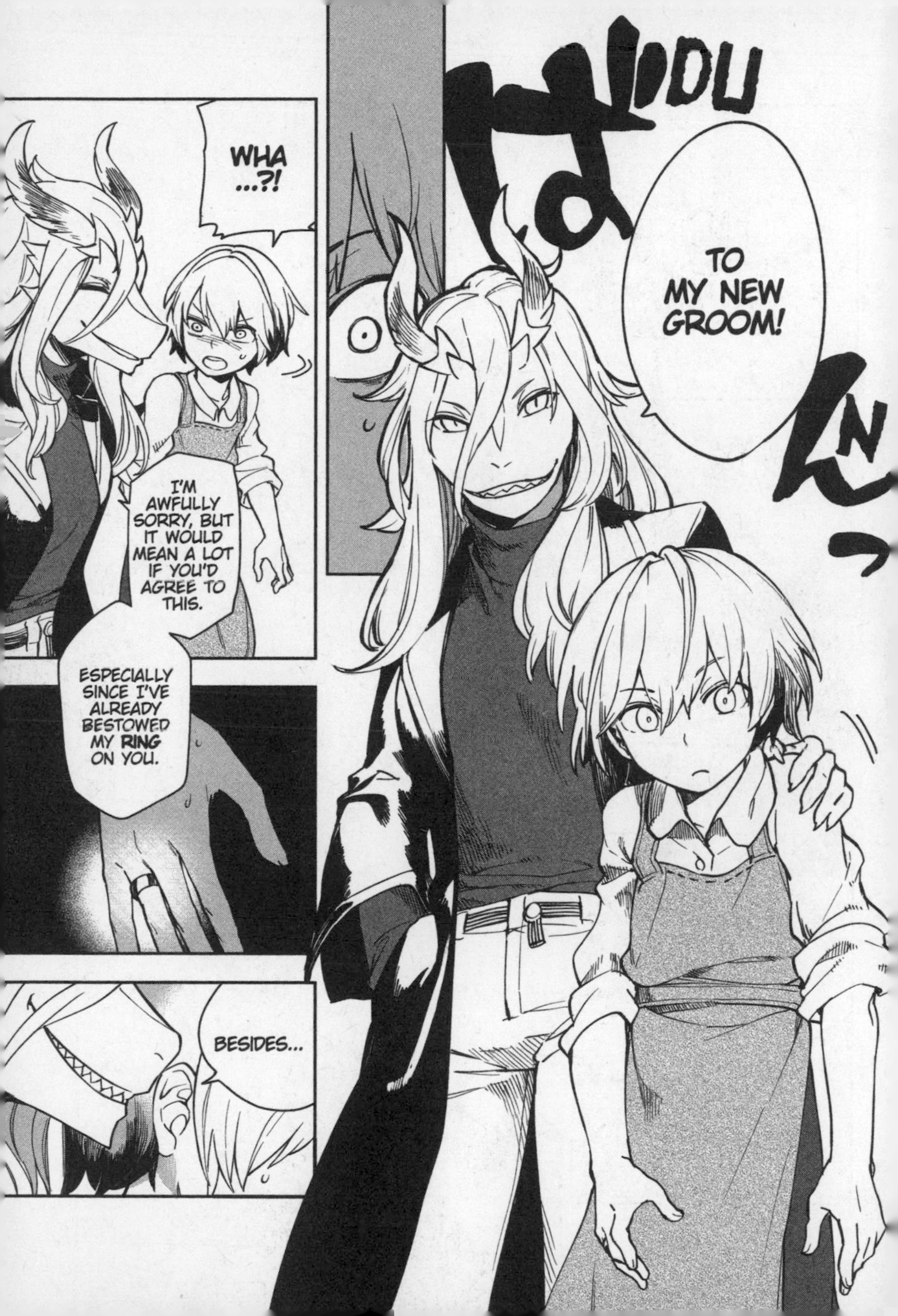
ば DOU
TO MY NEW GROOM!
ん N
WHA ...?!
I'M AWFULLY SORRY, BUT IT WOULD MEAN A LOT IF YOU'D AGREE TO THIS.
ESPECIALLY SINCE I'VE ALREADY BESTOWED MY **RING** ON YOU.
BESIDES...

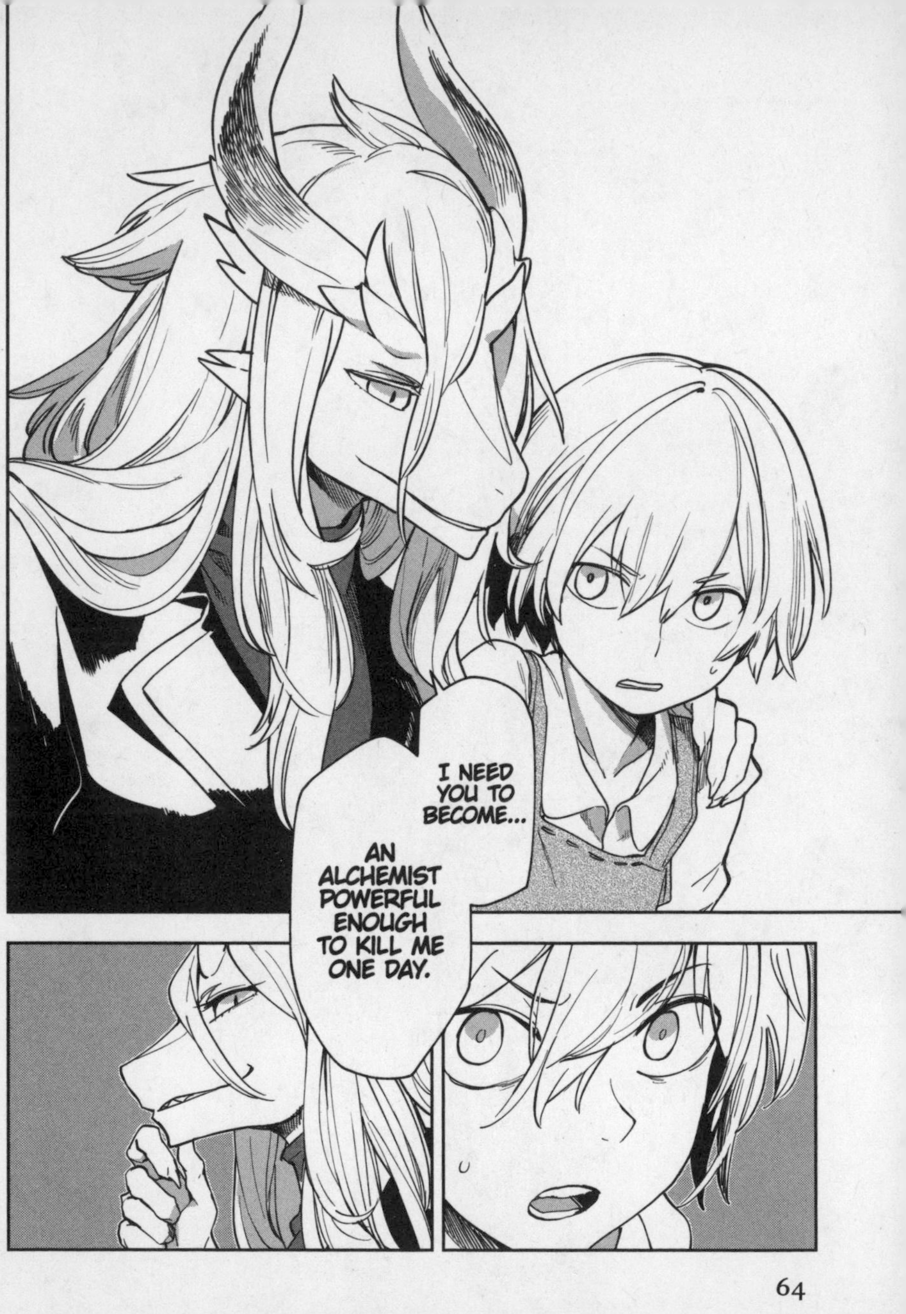
I NEED YOU TO BECOME...
AN ALCHEMIST POWERFUL ENOUGH TO KILL ME ONE DAY.

The Ancient
Magus' Bride

WIZARD's BLUE

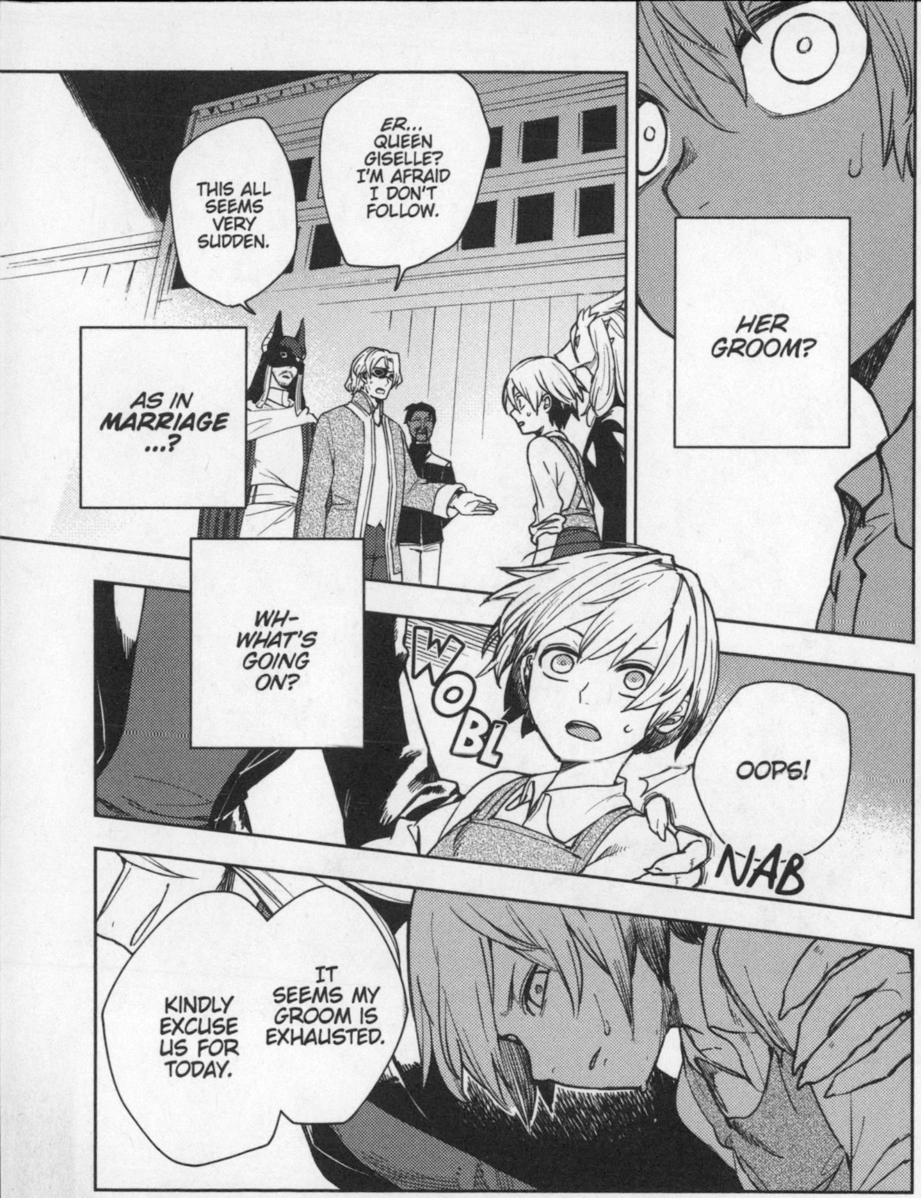
HER GROOM?
ER... QUEEN GISELLE? I'M AFRAID I DON'T FOLLOW.
THIS ALL SEEMS VERY SUDDEN.
AS IN MARRIAGE ...?
WH- WHAT'S GOING ON?
WOBL
OOPS!
NAB
IT SEEMS MY GROOM IS EXHAUSTED.
KINDLY EXCUSE US FOR TODAY.

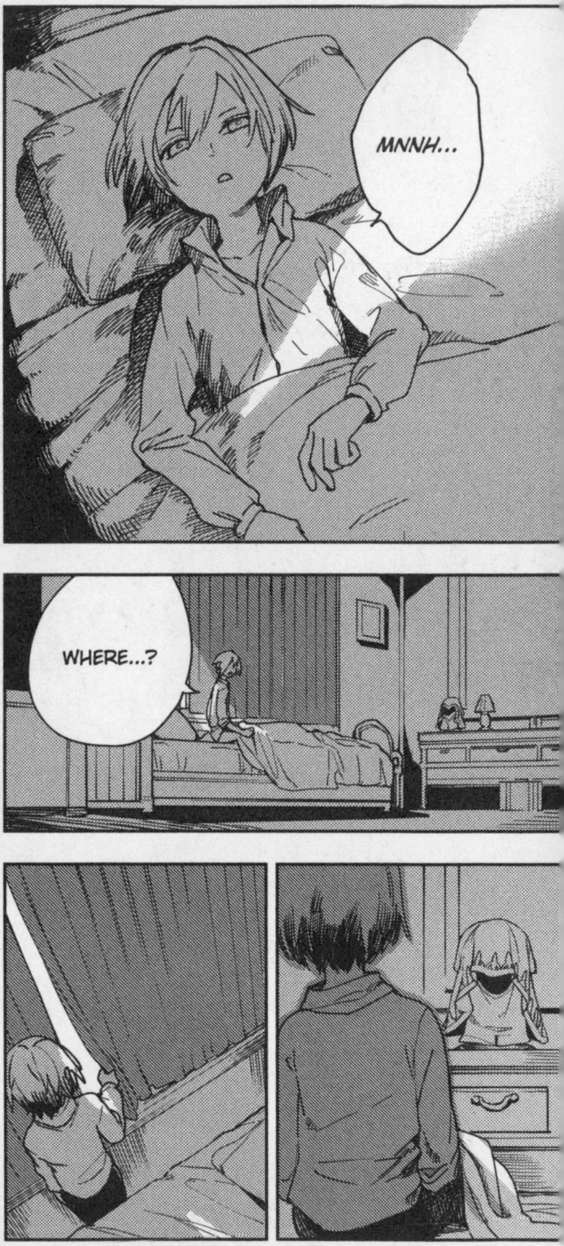
MNNH...
WHERE...?

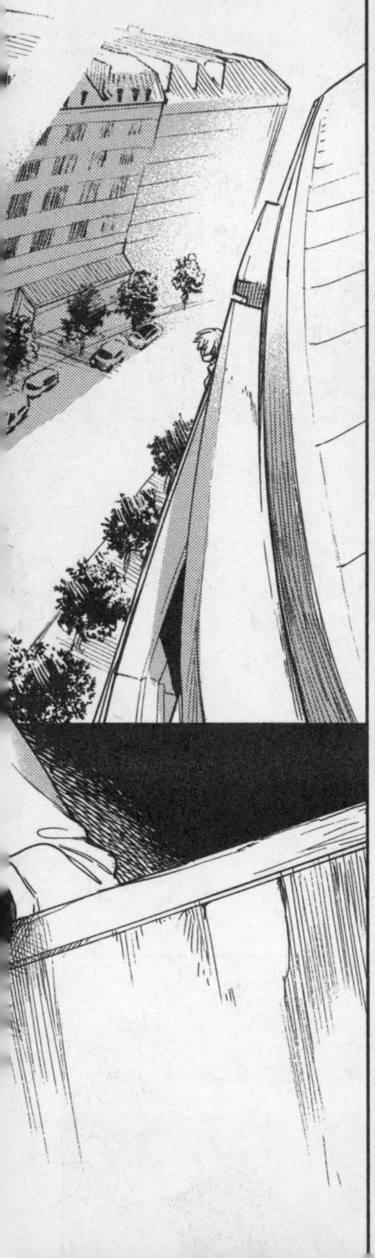

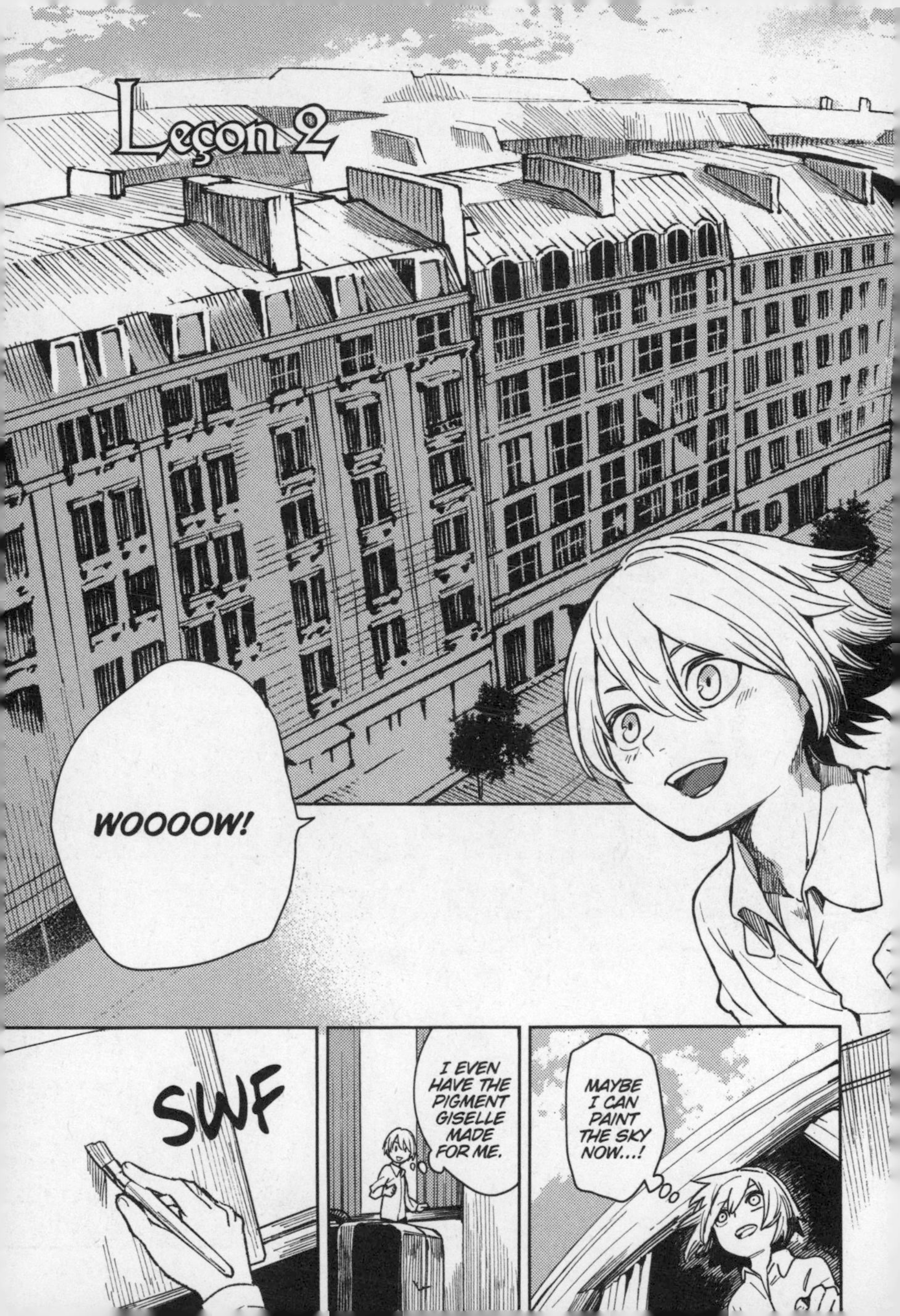
Leçon 2
WOOOOW!
MAYBE I CAN PAINT THE SKY NOW...!
I EVEN HAVE THE PIGMENT GISELLE MADE FOR ME.
SWF

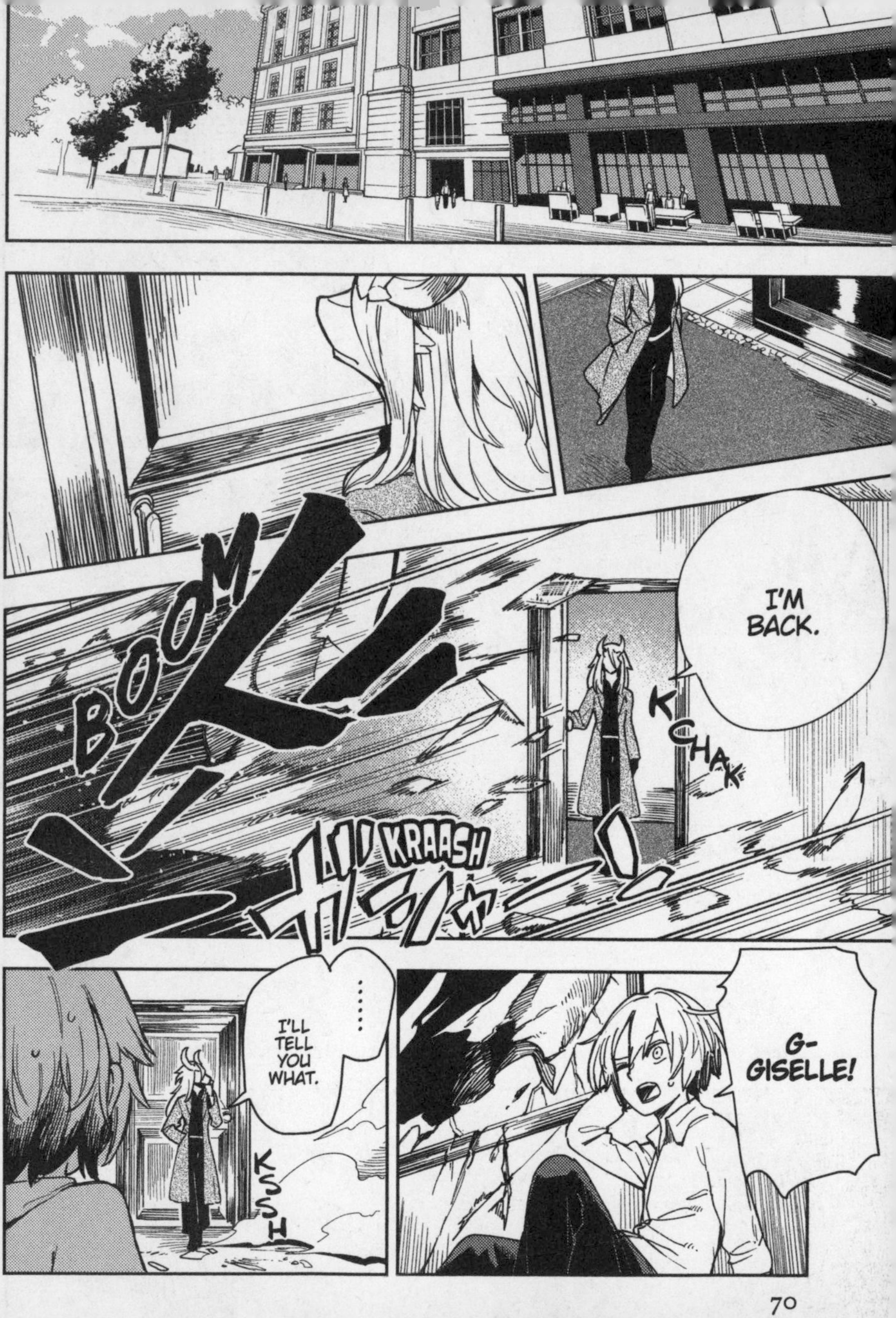
I'M BACK.
KCHAK
BOOM
KRAASH
G-GISELLE!
......
I'LL TELL YOU WHAT.
KSSH

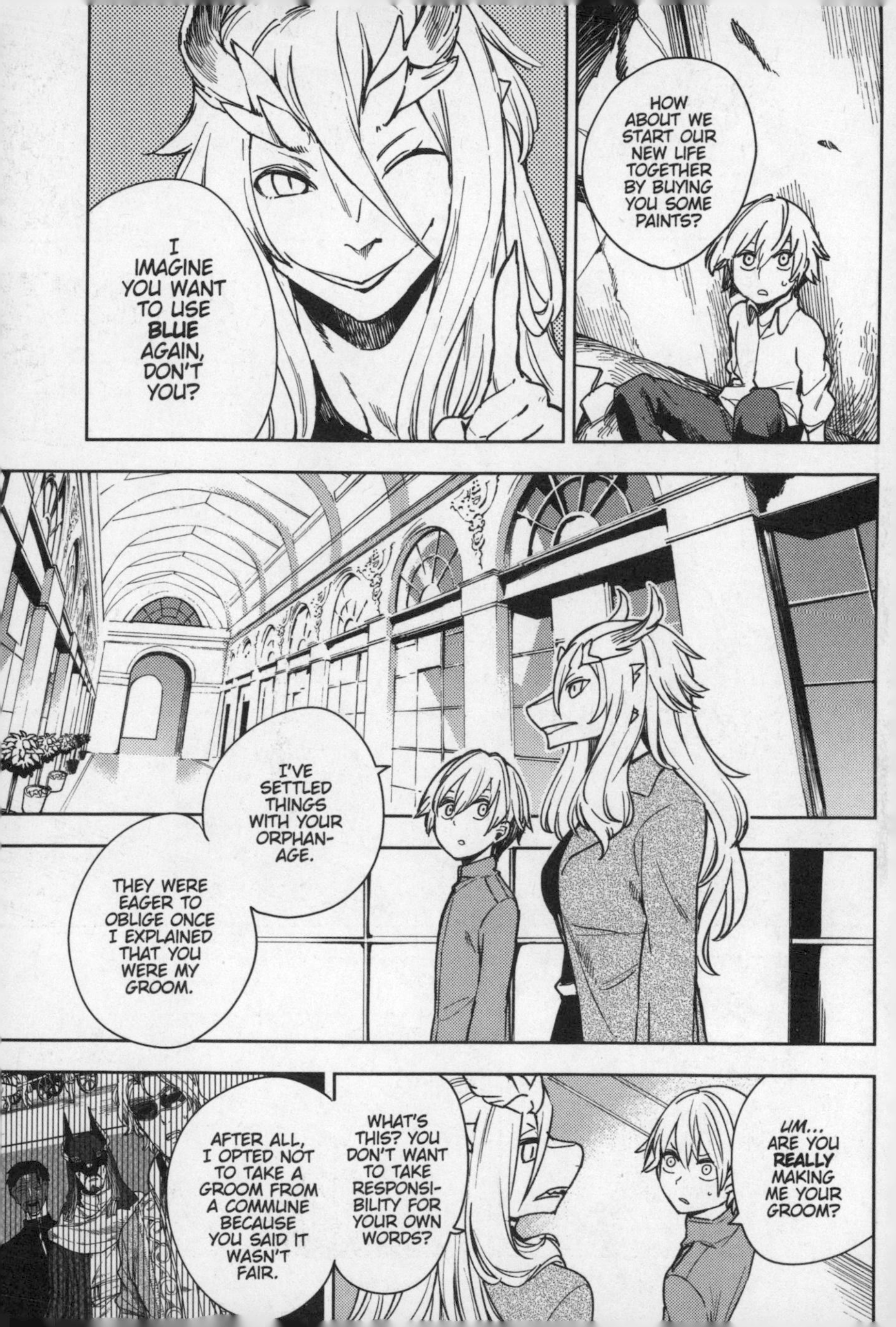
HOW ABOUT WE START OUR NEW LIFE TOGETHER BY BUYING YOU SOME PAINTS?
I IMAGINE YOU WANT TO USE **BLUE** AGAIN, DON'T YOU?
I'VE SETTLED THINGS WITH YOUR ORPHAN-AGE.
THEY WERE EAGER TO OBLIGE ONCE I EXPLAINED THAT YOU WERE MY GROOM.
UM... ARE YOU **REALLY** MAKING ME YOUR GROOM?
WHAT'S THIS? YOU DON'T WANT TO TAKE RESPONSI-BILITY FOR YOUR OWN WORDS?
AFTER ALL, I OPTED NOT TO TAKE A GROOM FROM A COMMUNE BECAUSE YOU SAID IT WASN'T FAIR.

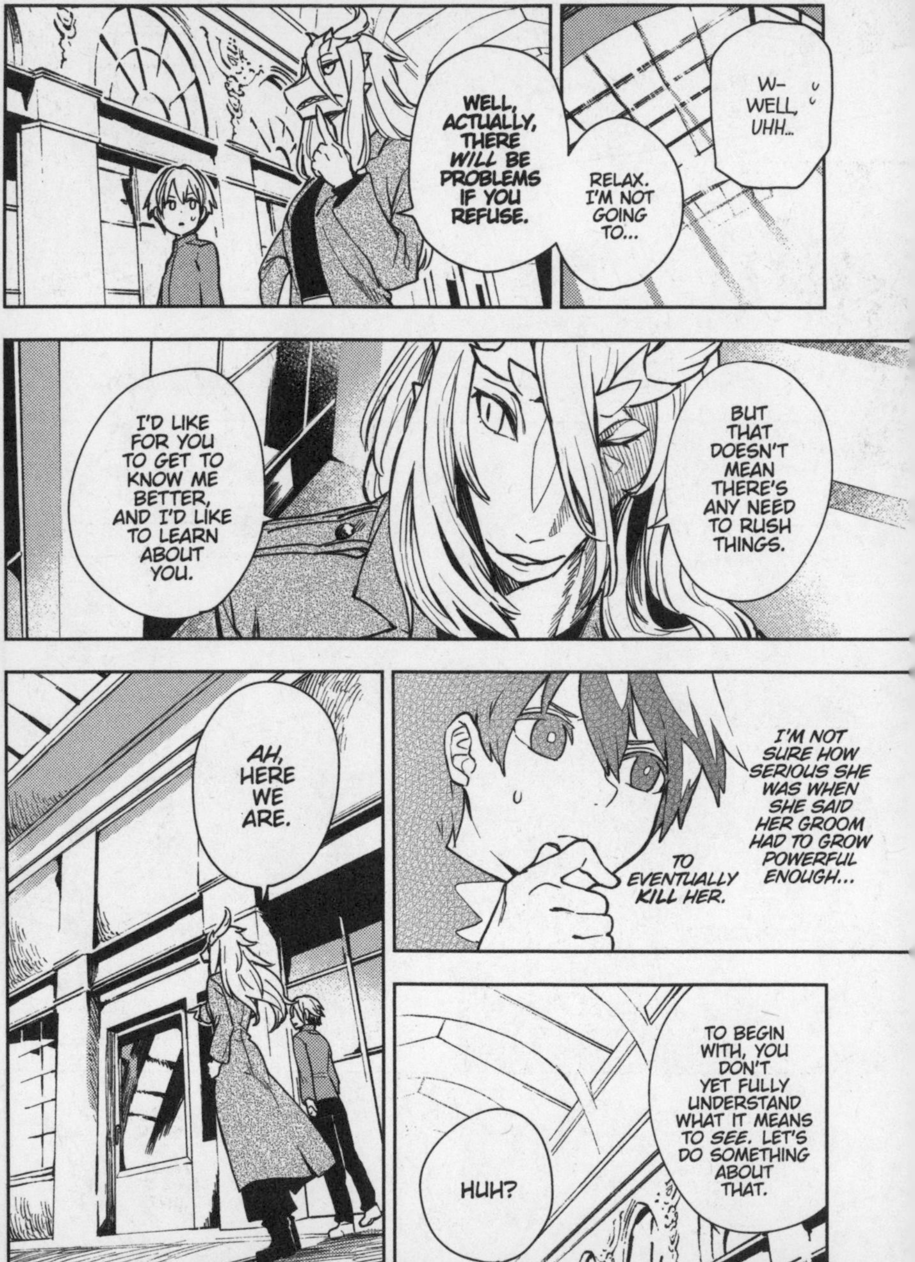
W–
WELL, UHH...
RELAX. I'M NOT GOING TO...
WELL, ACTUALLY, THERE *WILL* BE PROBLEMS IF YOU REFUSE.
BUT THAT DOESN'T MEAN THERE'S ANY NEED TO RUSH THINGS.
I'D LIKE FOR YOU TO GET TO KNOW ME BETTER, AND I'D LIKE TO LEARN ABOUT YOU.
I'M NOT SURE HOW SERIOUS SHE WAS WHEN SHE SAID HER GROOM HAD TO GROW POWERFUL ENOUGH...
TO EVENTUALLY *KILL* HER.
TO BEGIN WITH, YOU DON'T YET FULLY UNDERSTAND WHAT IT MEANS TO SEE. LET'S DO SOMETHING ABOUT THAT.
HUH?
AH, HERE WE ARE.

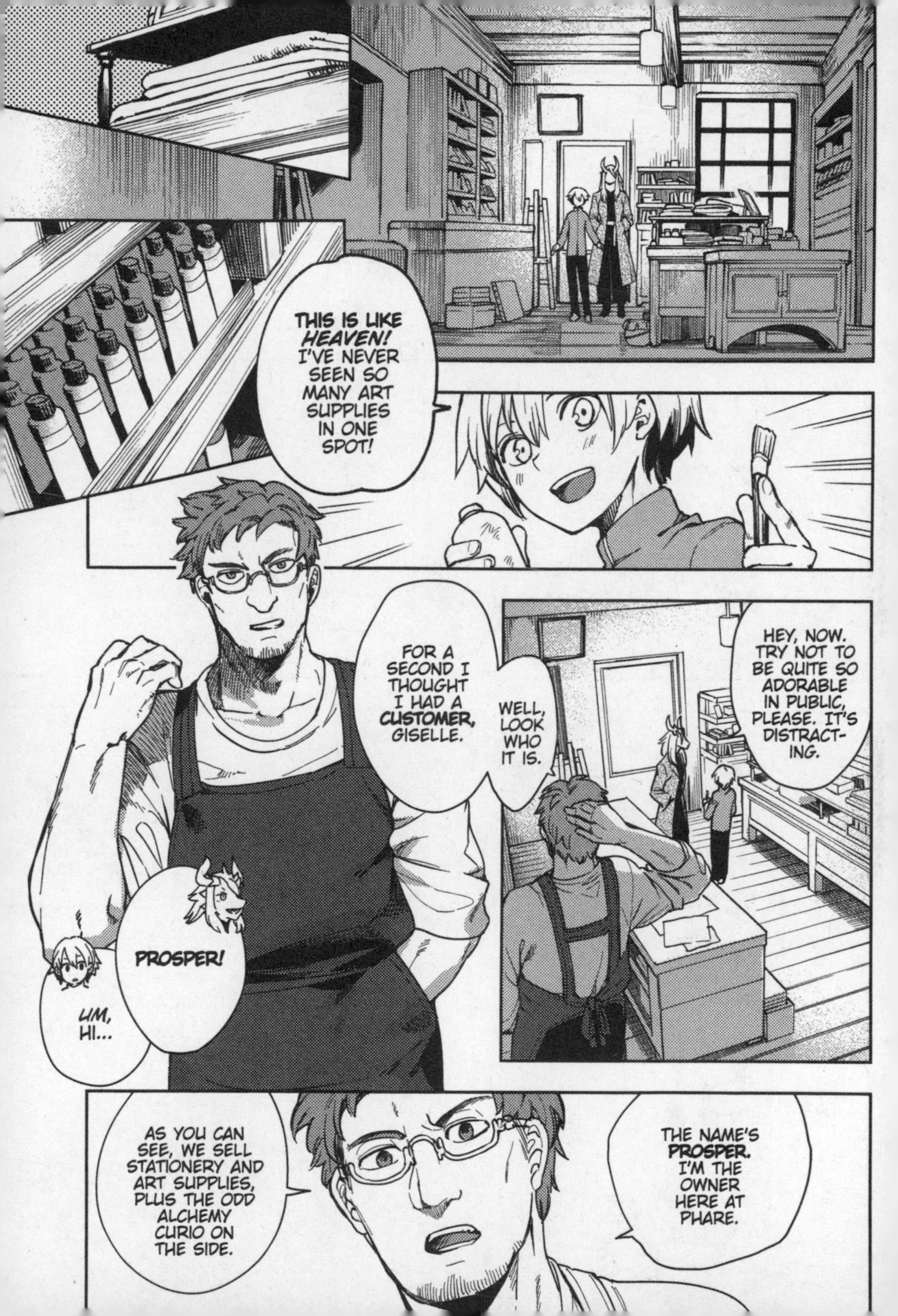

THIS IS LIKE HEAVEN! I'VE NEVER SEEN SO MANY ART SUPPLIES IN ONE SPOT!
HEY, NOW. TRY NOT TO BE QUITE SO ADORABLE IN PUBLIC, PLEASE. IT'S DISTRACT-ING.
WELL, LOOK WHO IT IS.
FOR A SECOND I THOUGHT I HAD A CUSTOMER, GISELLE.
PROSPER!
UM, HI...
THE NAME'S PROSPER. I'M THE OWNER HERE AT PHARE.
AS YOU CAN SEE, WE SELL STATIONERY AND ART SUPPLIES, PLUS THE ODD ALCHEMY CURIO ON THE SIDE.

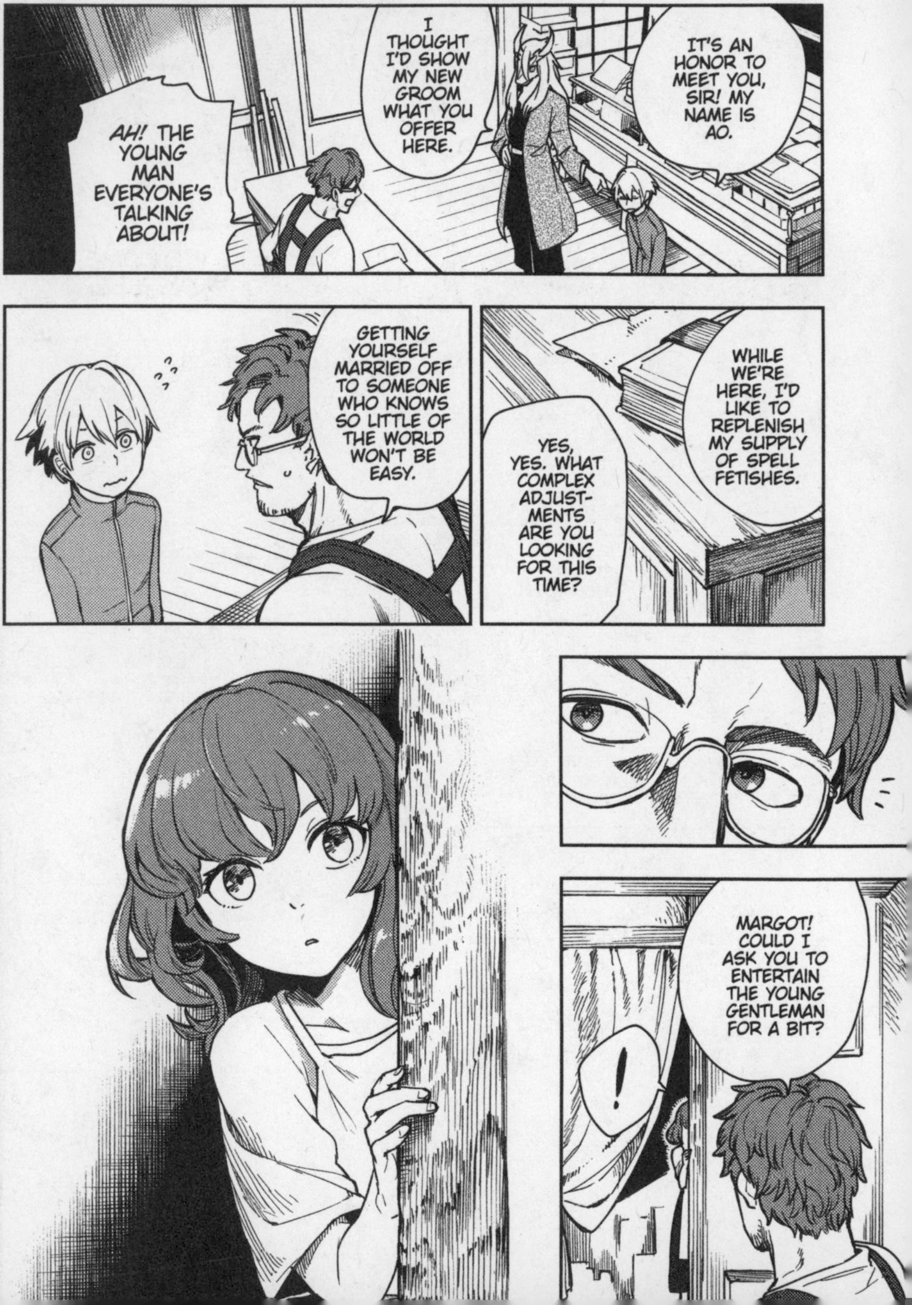
IT'S AN HONOR TO MEET YOU, SIR! MY NAME IS AO.
I THOUGHT I'D SHOW MY NEW GROOM WHAT YOU OFFER HERE.
AH! THE YOUNG MAN EVERYONE'S TALKING ABOUT!
WHILE WE'RE HERE, I'D LIKE TO REPLENISH MY SUPPLY OF SPELL FETISHES.
YES, YES. WHAT COMPLEX ADJUSTMENTS ARE YOU LOOKING FOR THIS TIME?
GETTING YOURSELF MARRIED OFF TO SOMEONE WHO KNOWS SO LITTLE OF THE WORLD WON'T BE EASY.
MARGOT! COULD I ASK YOU TO ENTERTAIN THE YOUNG GENTLEMAN FOR A BIT?
!

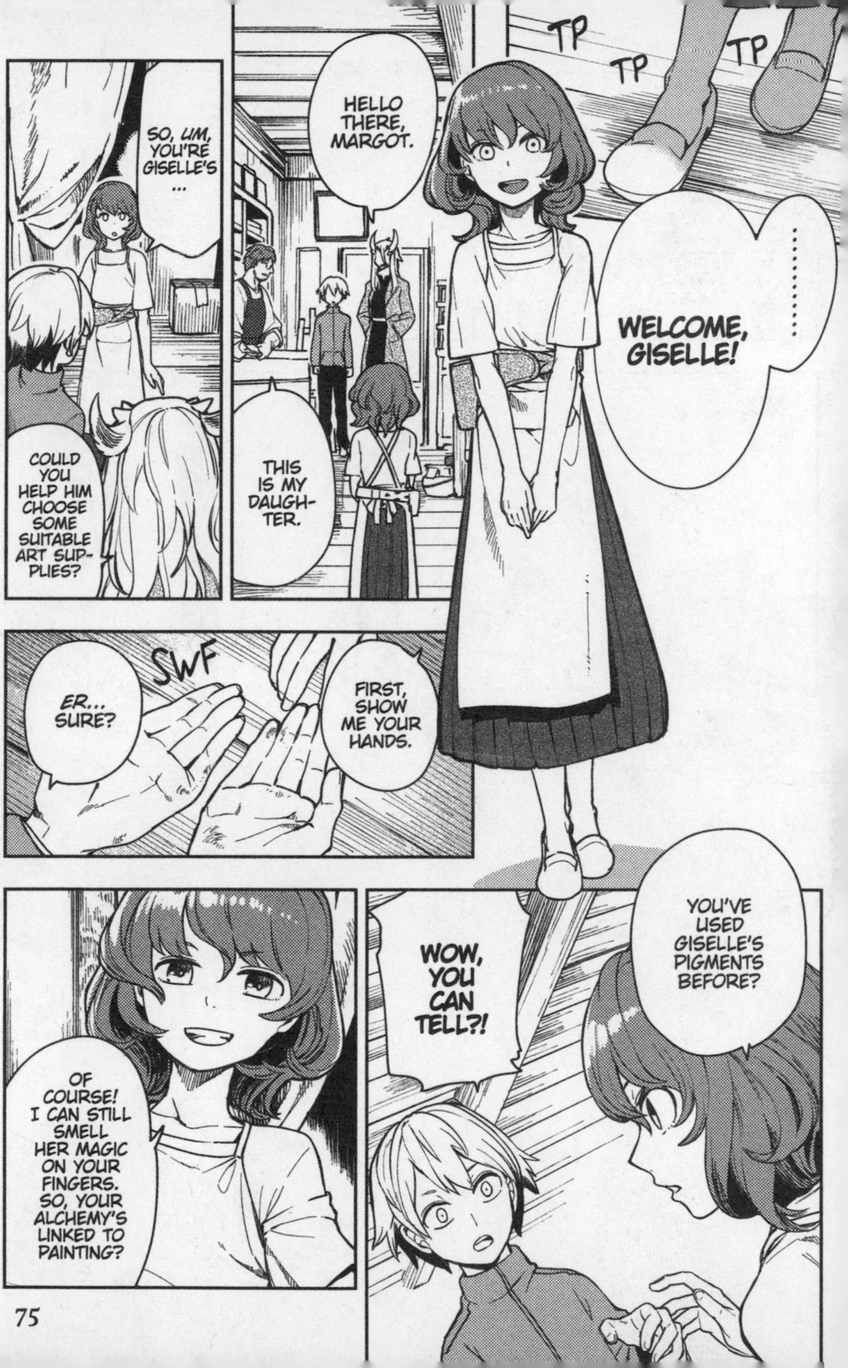
TP
TP
TP
......
WELCOME, GISELLE!
HELLO THERE, MARGOT.
THIS IS MY DAUGHTER.
SO, UM, YOU'RE GISELLE'S ...
COULD YOU HELP HIM CHOOSE SOME SUITABLE ART SUPPLIES?
SWF
FIRST, SHOW ME YOUR HANDS.
ER... SURE?
YOU'VE USED GISELLE'S PIGMENTS BEFORE?
WOW, YOU CAN TELL?!
OF COURSE! I CAN STILL SMELL HER MAGIC ON YOUR FINGERS. SO, YOUR ALCHEMY'S LINKED TO PAINTING?

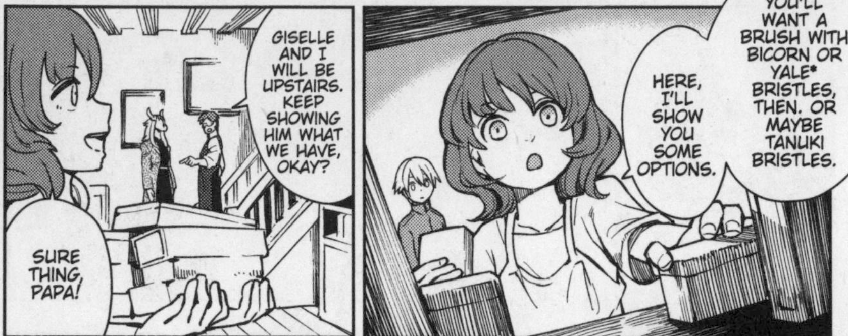
YOU'LL WANT A BRUSH WITH BICORN OR YALE* BRISTLES, THEN. OR MAYBE TANUKI BRISTLES.
HERE, I'LL SHOW YOU SOME OPTIONS.
GISELLE AND I WILL BE UPSTAIRS. KEEP SHOWING HIM WHAT WE HAVE, OKAY?
SURE THING, PAPA!

* *Bicorn and yale: Mythical beasts appearing in medieval European bestiaries and heraldry. Bicorns have various descriptions but always have two horns, and yales are goatlike creatures.*

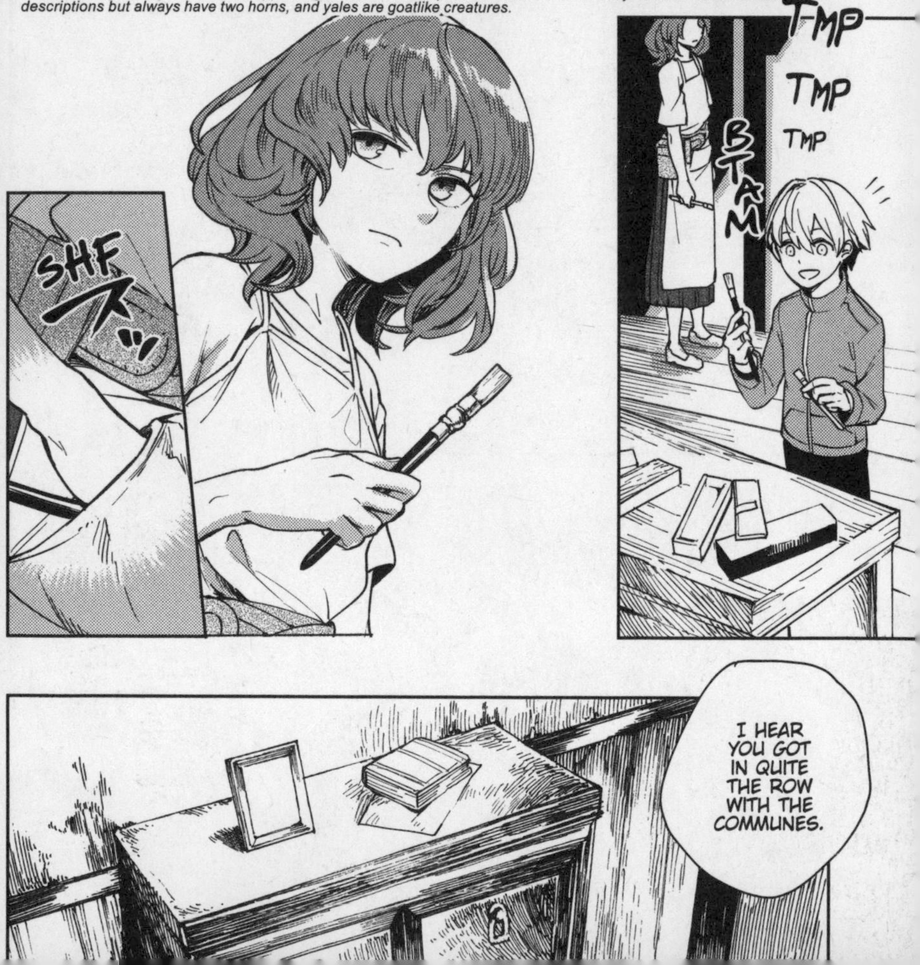
TMP
TMP
TMP
BTAM
SHF
I HEAR YOU GOT IN QUITE THE ROW WITH THE COMMUNES.

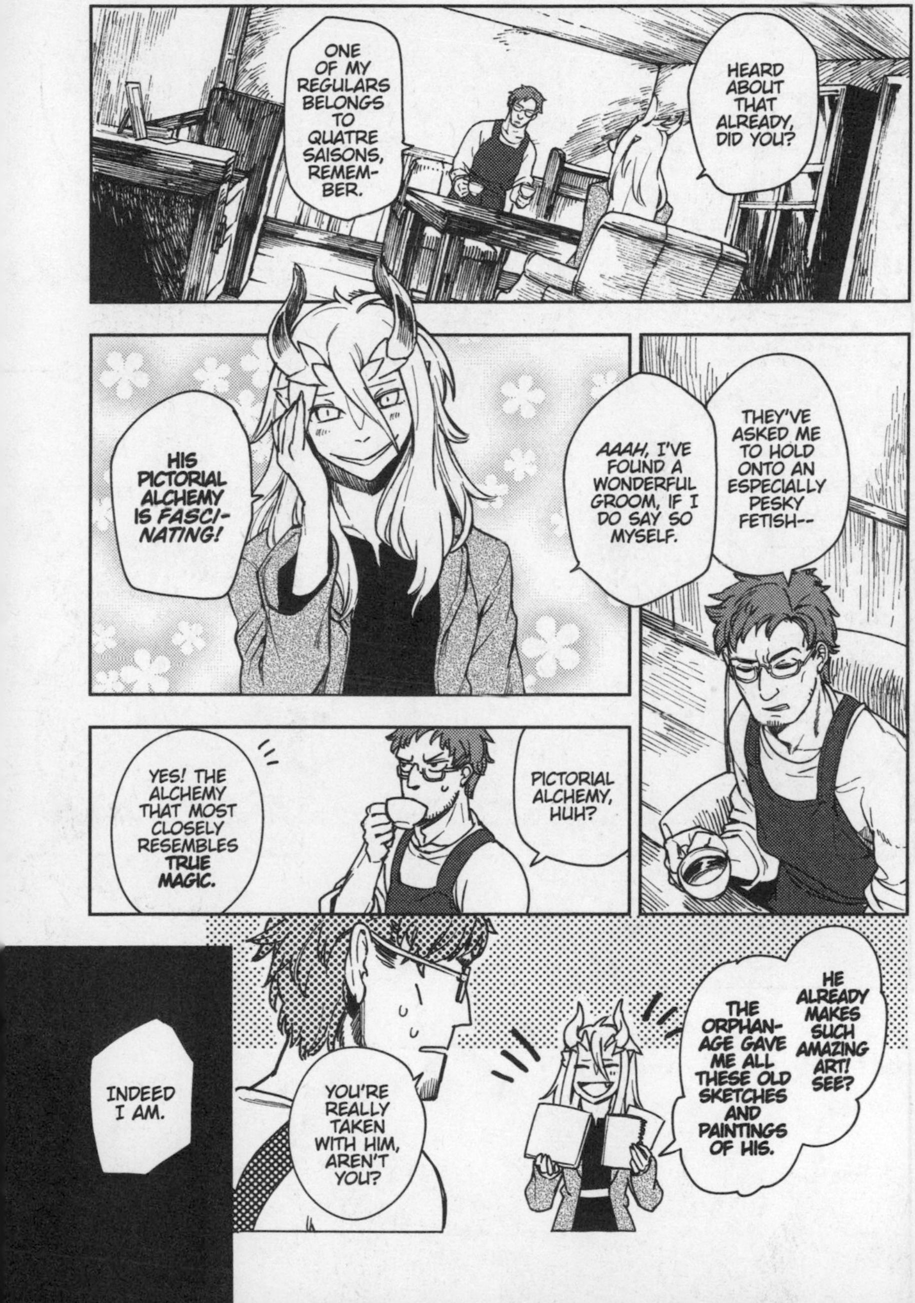
HEARD ABOUT THAT ALREADY, DID YOU?
ONE OF MY REGULARS BELONGS TO QUATRE SAISONS, REMEMBER.
THEY'VE ASKED ME TO HOLD ONTO AN ESPECIALLY PESKY FETISH--
AAAH, I'VE FOUND A WONDERFUL GROOM, IF I DO SAY SO MYSELF.
HIS PICTORIAL ALCHEMY IS *FASCINATING!*
PICTORIAL ALCHEMY, HUH?
YES! THE ALCHEMY THAT MOST CLOSELY RESEMBLES **TRUE MAGIC.**
HE ALREADY MAKES SUCH AMAZING ART! SEE?
THE ORPHANAGE GAVE ME ALL THESE OLD SKETCHES AND PAINTINGS OF HIS.
YOU'RE REALLY TAKEN WITH HIM, AREN'T YOU?
INDEED I AM.

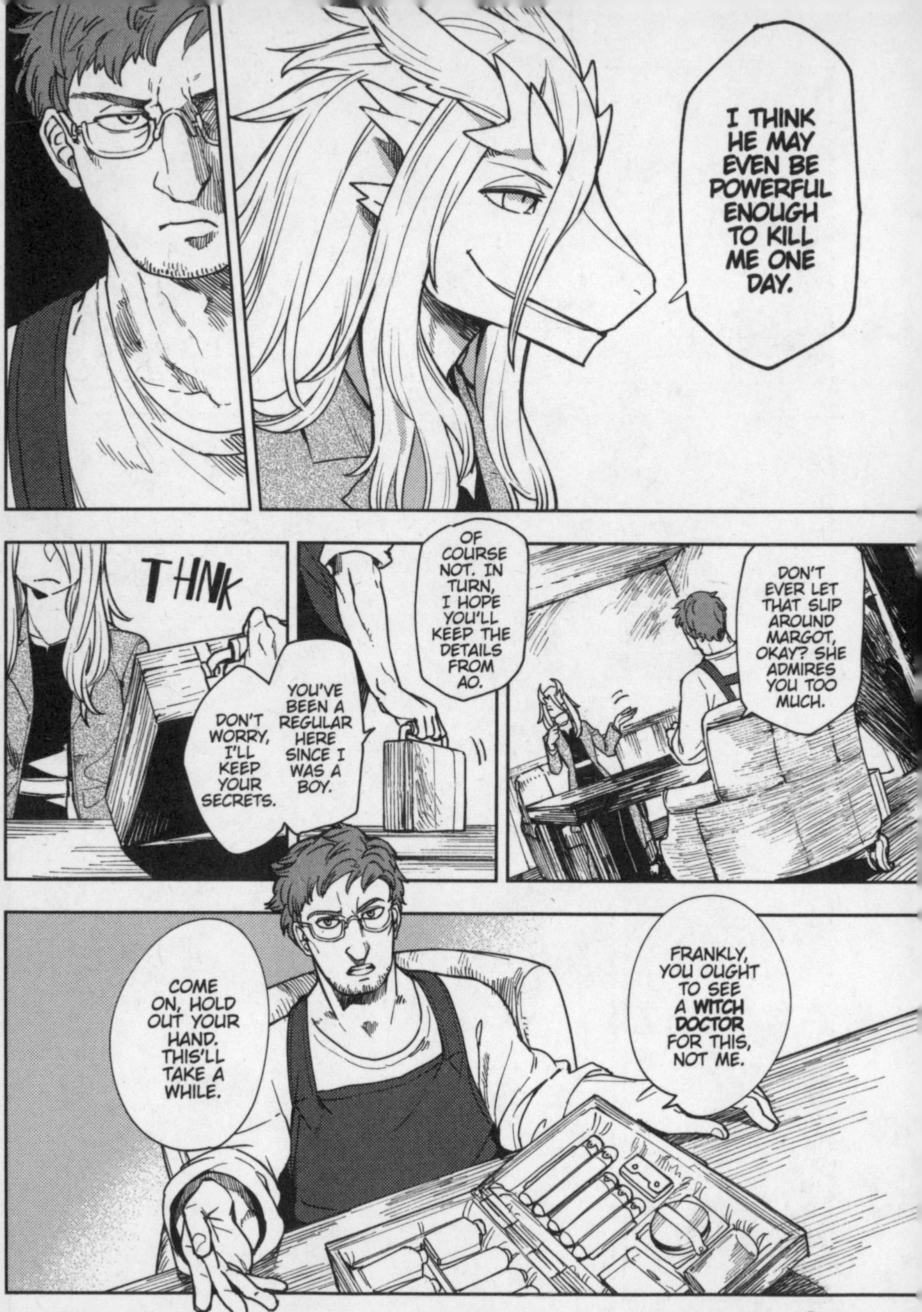

I THINK HE MAY EVEN BE POWERFUL ENOUGH TO KILL ME ONE DAY.
DON'T EVER LET THAT SLIP AROUND MARGOT, OKAY? SHE ADMIRES YOU TOO MUCH.
OF COURSE NOT. IN TURN, I HOPE YOU'LL KEEP THE DETAILS FROM AO.
THNK
YOU'VE BEEN A REGULAR HERE SINCE I WAS A BOY.
DON'T WORRY, I'LL KEEP YOUR SECRETS.
FRANKLY, YOU OUGHT TO SEE A **WITCH DOCTOR** FOR THIS, NOT ME.
COME ON, HOLD OUT YOUR HAND. THIS'LL TAKE A WHILE.

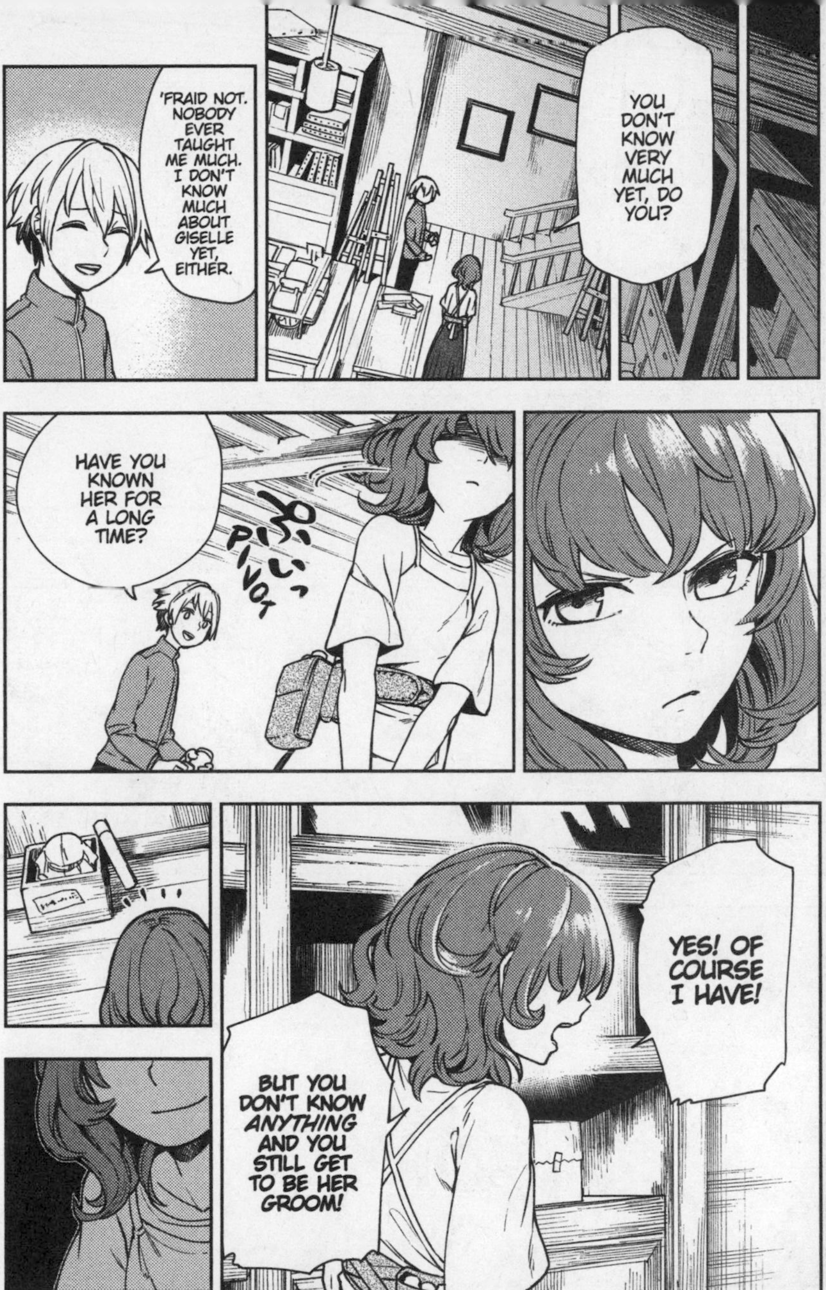
YOU DON'T KNOW VERY MUCH YET, DO YOU?
'FRAID NOT. NOBODY EVER TAUGHT ME MUCH. I DON'T KNOW MUCH ABOUT GISELLE YET, EITHER.
HAVE YOU KNOWN HER FOR A LONG TIME?
PIVOT
YES! OF COURSE I HAVE!
BUT YOU DON'T KNOW *ANYTHING* AND YOU STILL GET TO BE HER GROOM!

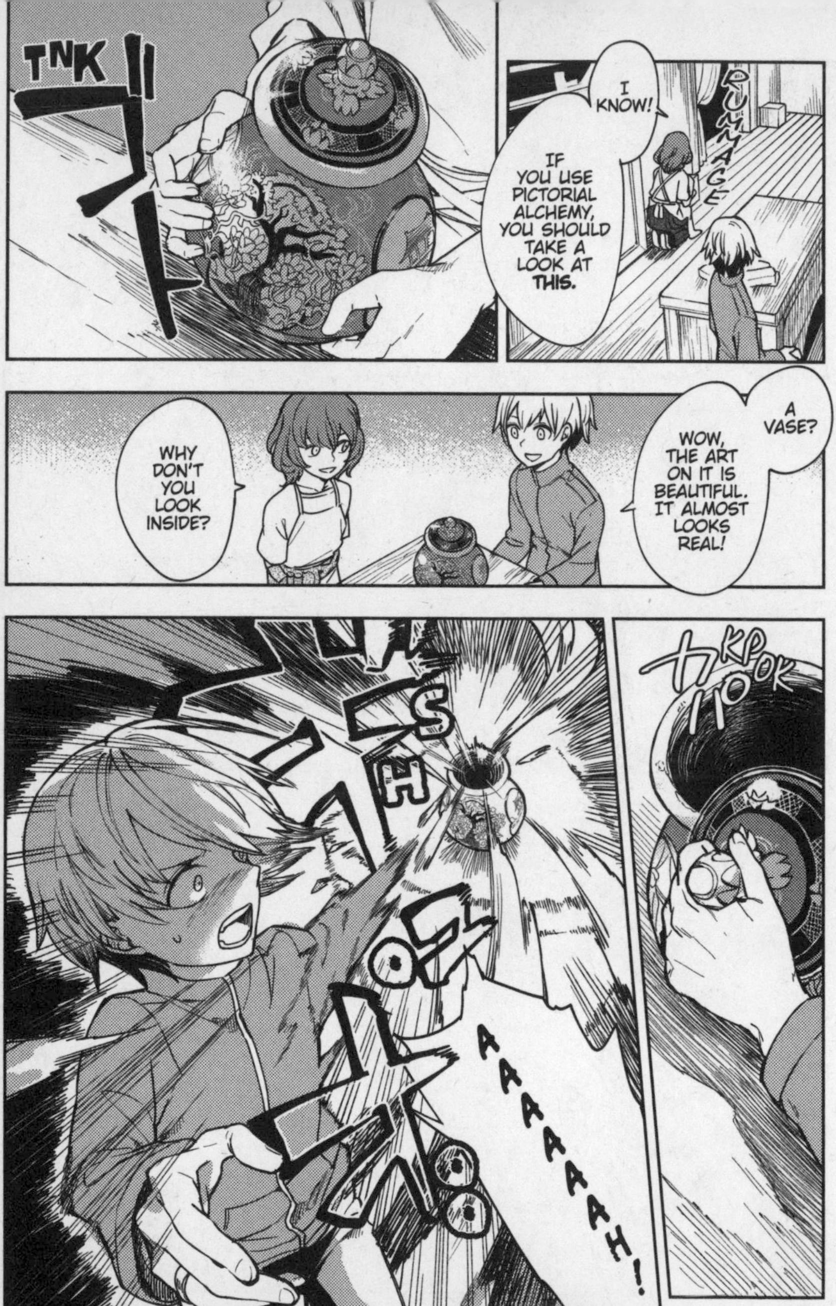
I KNOW!
RUMMAGE
IF YOU USE PICTORIAL ALCHEMY, YOU SHOULD TAKE A LOOK AT **THIS.**
TNK
A VASE?
WOW, THE ART ON IT IS BEAUTIFUL. IT ALMOST LOOKS REAL!
WHY DON'T YOU LOOK INSIDE?
KPOK
AAAAAAAAH!

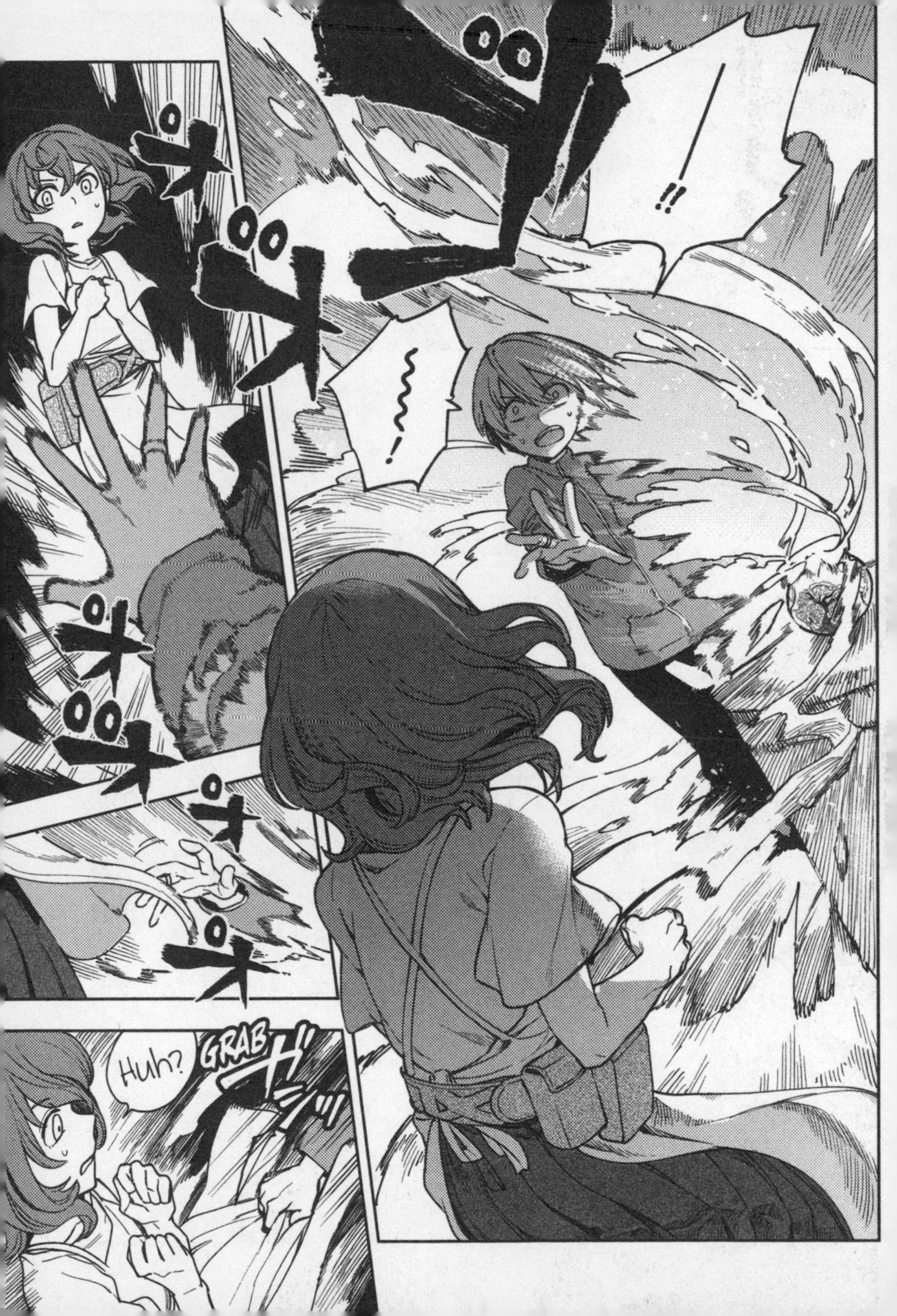

!!
~~~!
Huh?
GRAB
~~~

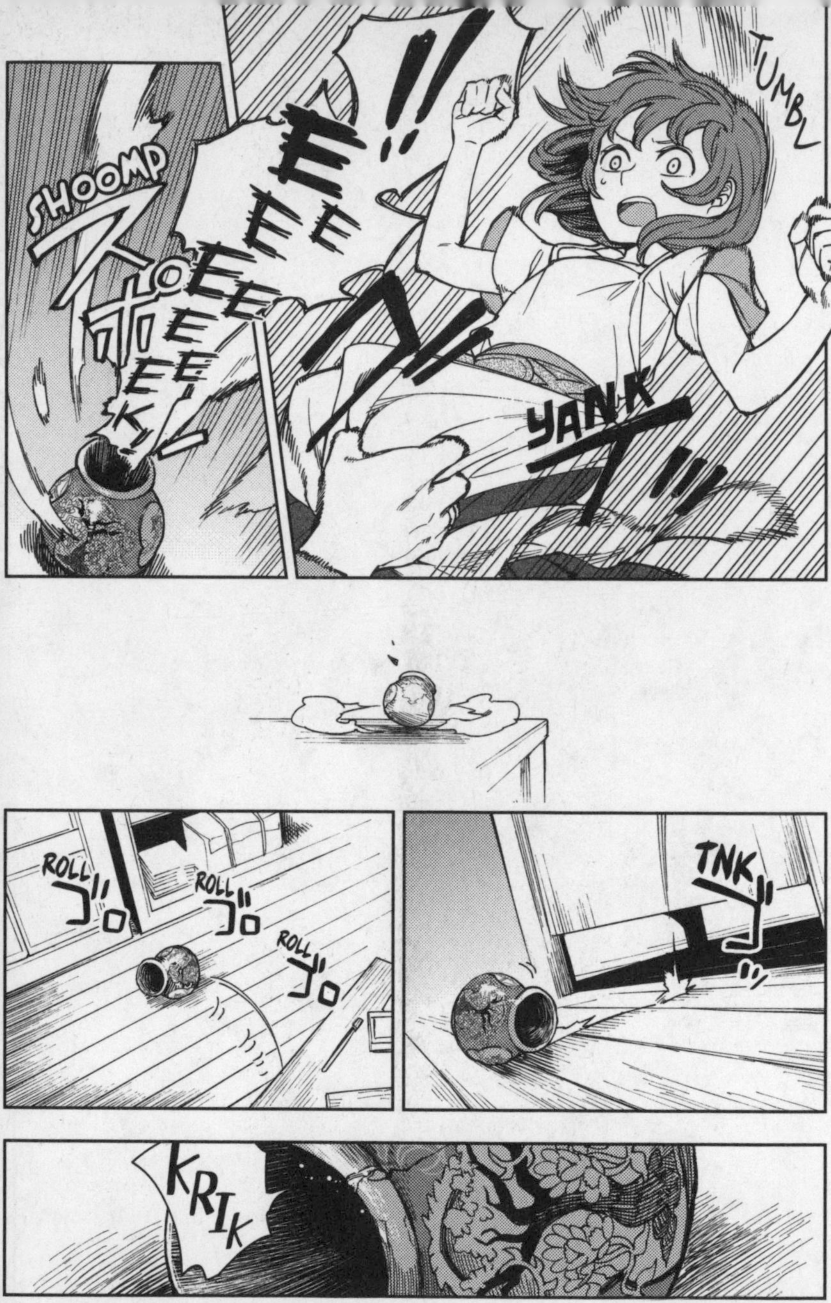
TUMBL
EEEEEEEEK!!
YANK
SHOOMP
TNK
ROLL
ROLL
ROLL
KRIK

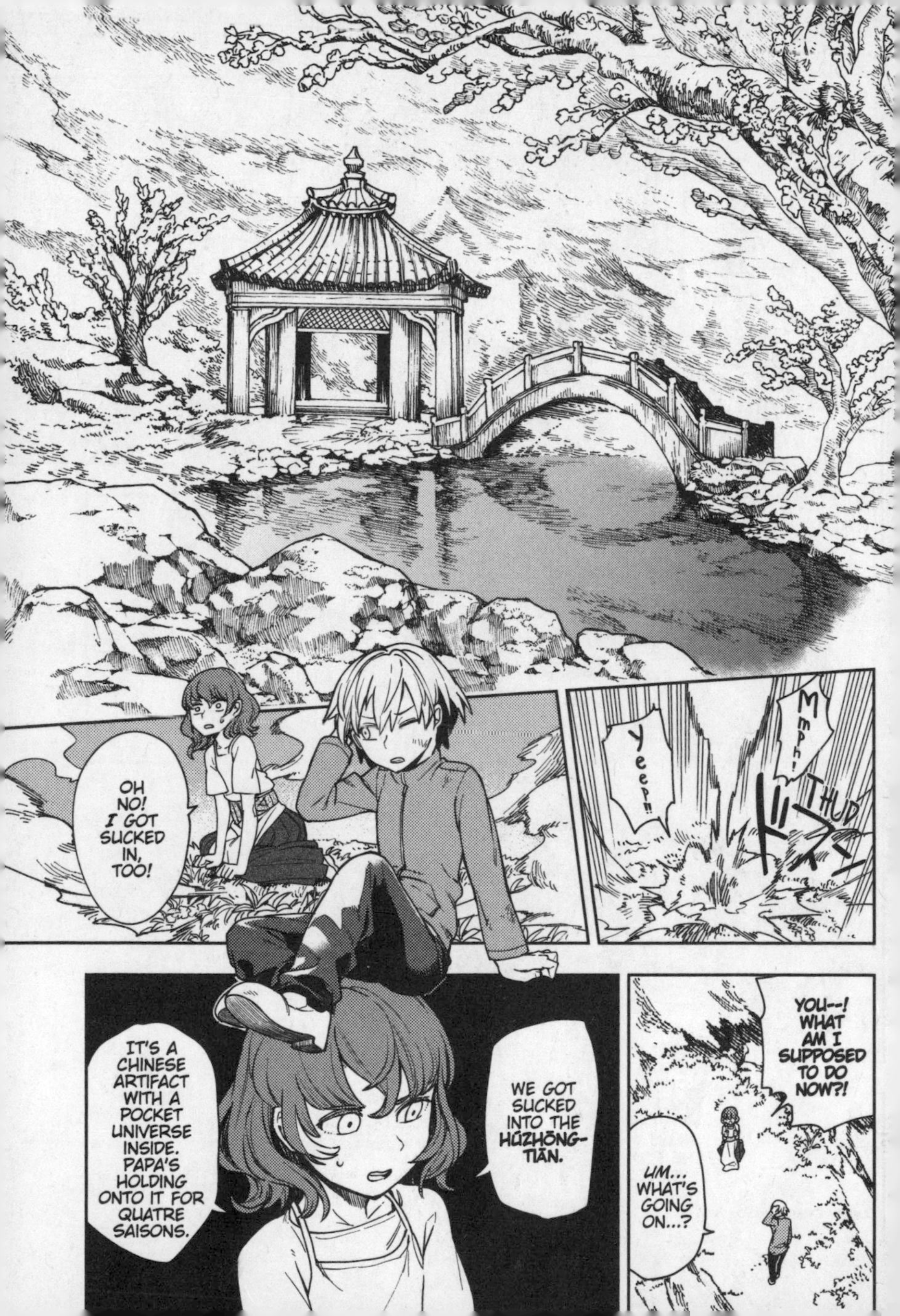
Mmph!
Yeep!!
THUD
OH NO! I GOT SUCKED IN, TOO!
YOU--! WHAT AM I SUPPOSED TO DO NOW?!
UM... WHAT'S GOING ON...?
WE GOT SUCKED INTO THE HÚZHŌNG-TIĀN.
IT'S A CHINESE ARTIFACT WITH A POCKET UNIVERSE INSIDE. PAPA'S HOLDING ONTO IT FOR QUATRE SAISONS.

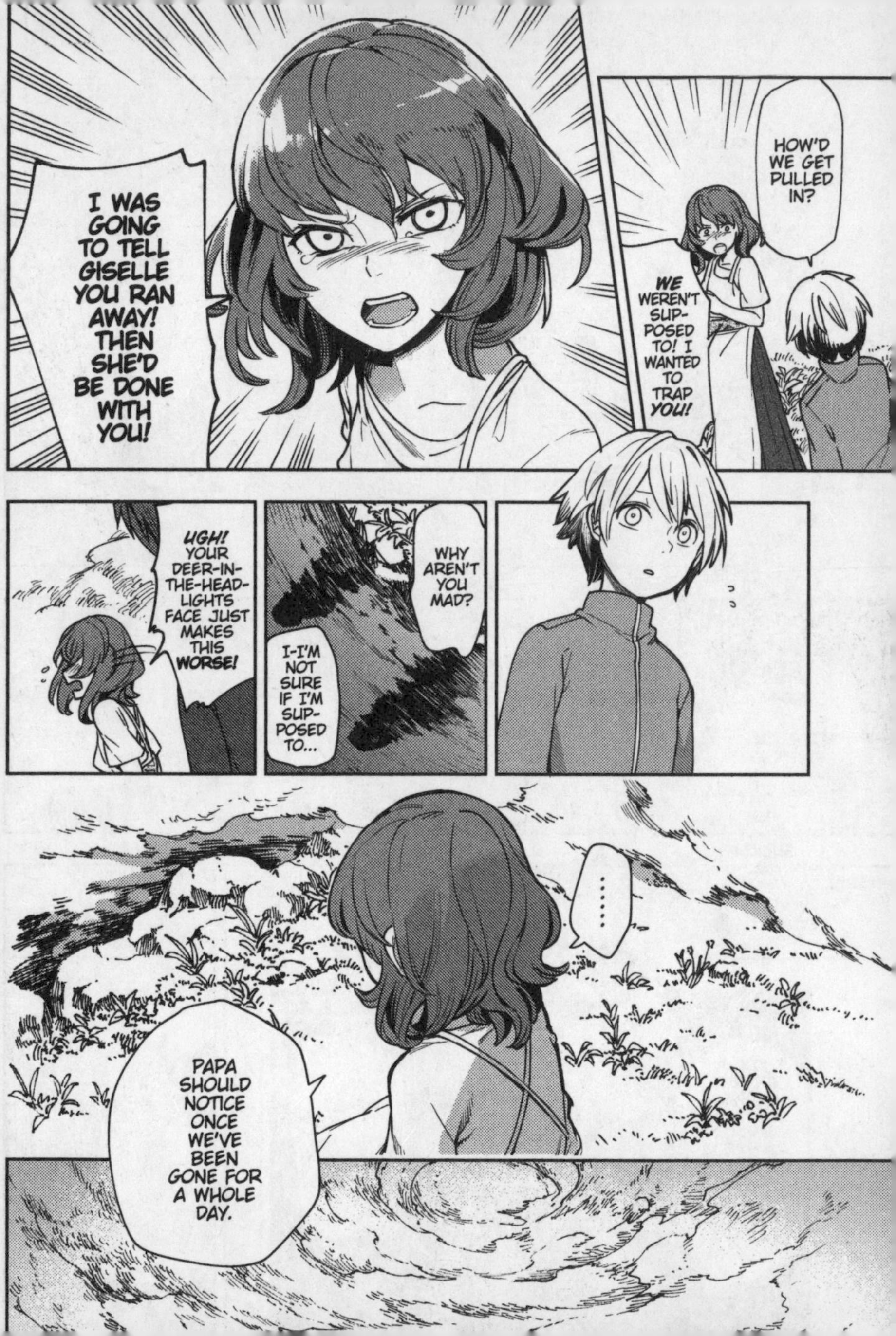
HOW'D WE GET PULLED IN?
WE WEREN'T SUP-POSED TO! I WANTED TO TRAP YOU!
I WAS GOING TO TELL GISELLE YOU RAN AWAY! THEN SHE'D BE DONE WITH YOU!
WHY AREN'T YOU MAD?
I-I'M NOT SURE IF I'M SUP-POSED TO...
UGH! YOUR DEER-IN-THE-HEAD-LIGHTS FACE JUST MAKES THIS WORSE!
......
PAPA SHOULD NOTICE ONCE WE'VE BEEN GONE FOR A WHOLE DAY.

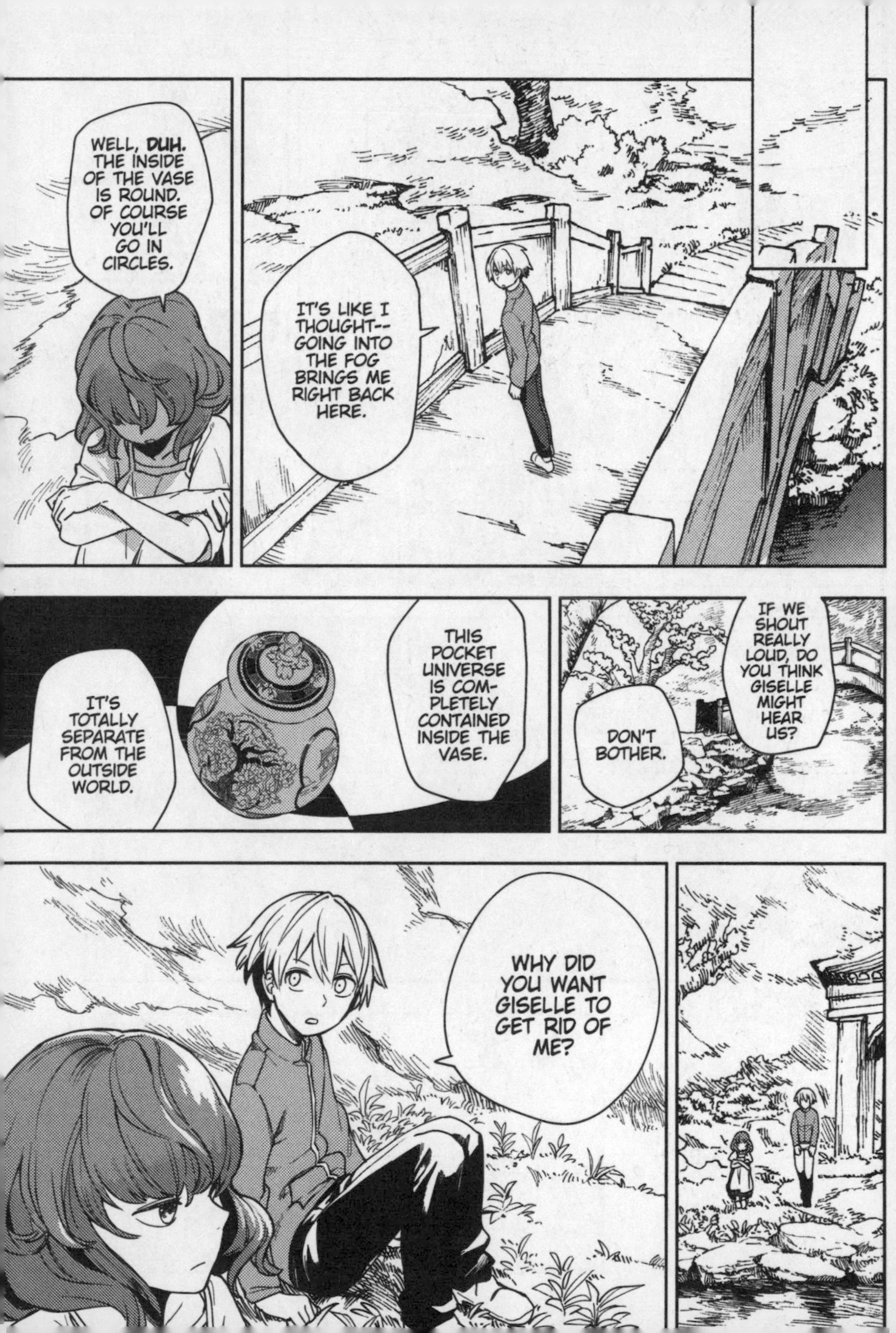
IT'S LIKE I THOUGHT-- GOING INTO THE FOG BRINGS ME RIGHT BACK HERE.
WELL, DUH. THE INSIDE OF THE VASE IS ROUND. OF COURSE YOU'LL GO IN CIRCLES.
IF WE SHOUT REALLY LOUD, DO YOU THINK GISELLE MIGHT HEAR US?
DON'T BOTHER.
THIS POCKET UNIVERSE IS COMPLETELY CONTAINED INSIDE THE VASE.
IT'S TOTALLY SEPARATE FROM THE OUTSIDE WORLD.
WHY DID YOU WANT GISELLE TO GET RID OF ME?

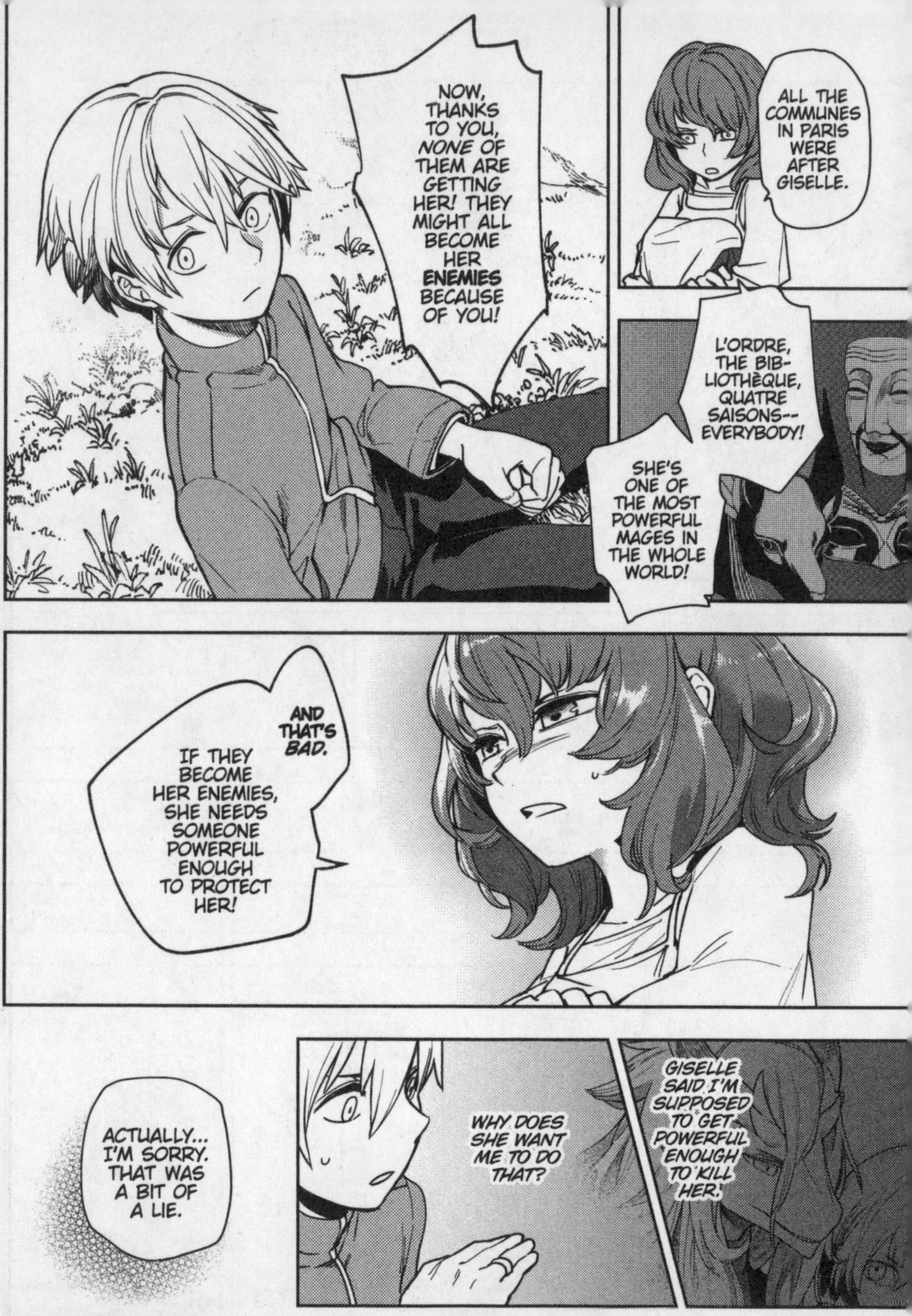
ALL THE COMMUNES IN PARIS WERE AFTER GISELLE.
L'ORDRE, THE BIBLIOTHÈQUE, QUATRE SAISONS--EVERYBODY!
SHE'S ONE OF THE MOST POWERFUL MAGES IN THE WHOLE WORLD!
NOW, THANKS TO YOU, *NONE* OF THEM ARE GETTING HER! THEY MIGHT ALL BECOME HER **ENEMIES** BECAUSE OF YOU!
AND THAT'S BAD.
IF THEY BECOME HER ENEMIES, SHE NEEDS SOMEONE POWERFUL ENOUGH TO PROTECT HER!
GISELLE SAID I'M SUPPOSED TO GET POWERFUL ENOUGH TO KILL HER.
WHY DOES SHE WANT ME TO DO THAT?
ACTUALLY... I'M SORRY. THAT WAS A BIT OF A LIE.

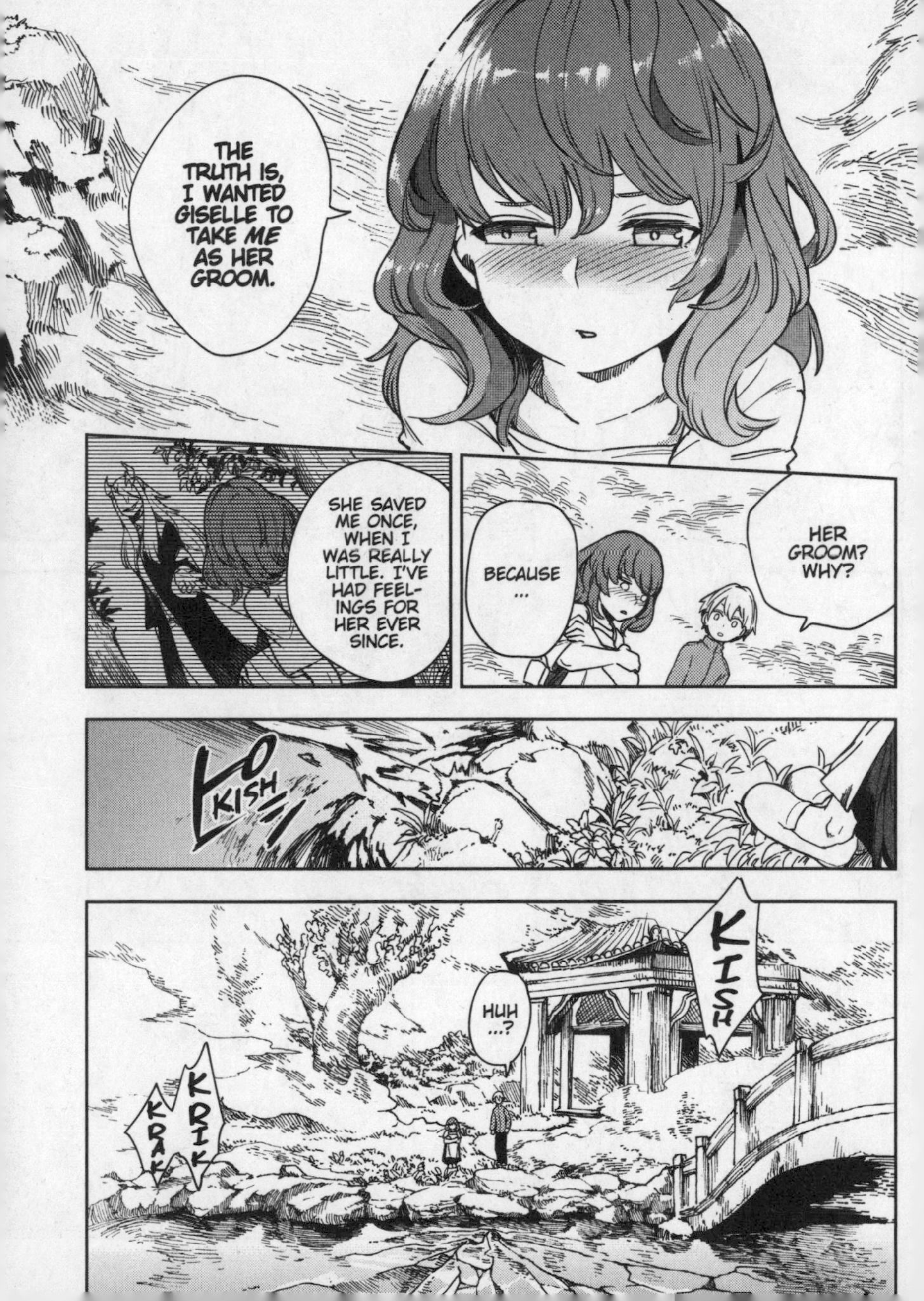
THE TRUTH IS, I WANTED GISELLE TO TAKE *ME* AS HER GROOM.
HER GROOM? WHY?
BECAUSE ...
SHE SAVED ME ONCE, WHEN I WAS REALLY LITTLE. I'VE HAD FEEL-INGS FOR HER EVER SINCE.
KISH
KISH
HUH ...?
KDRIK
KRAK

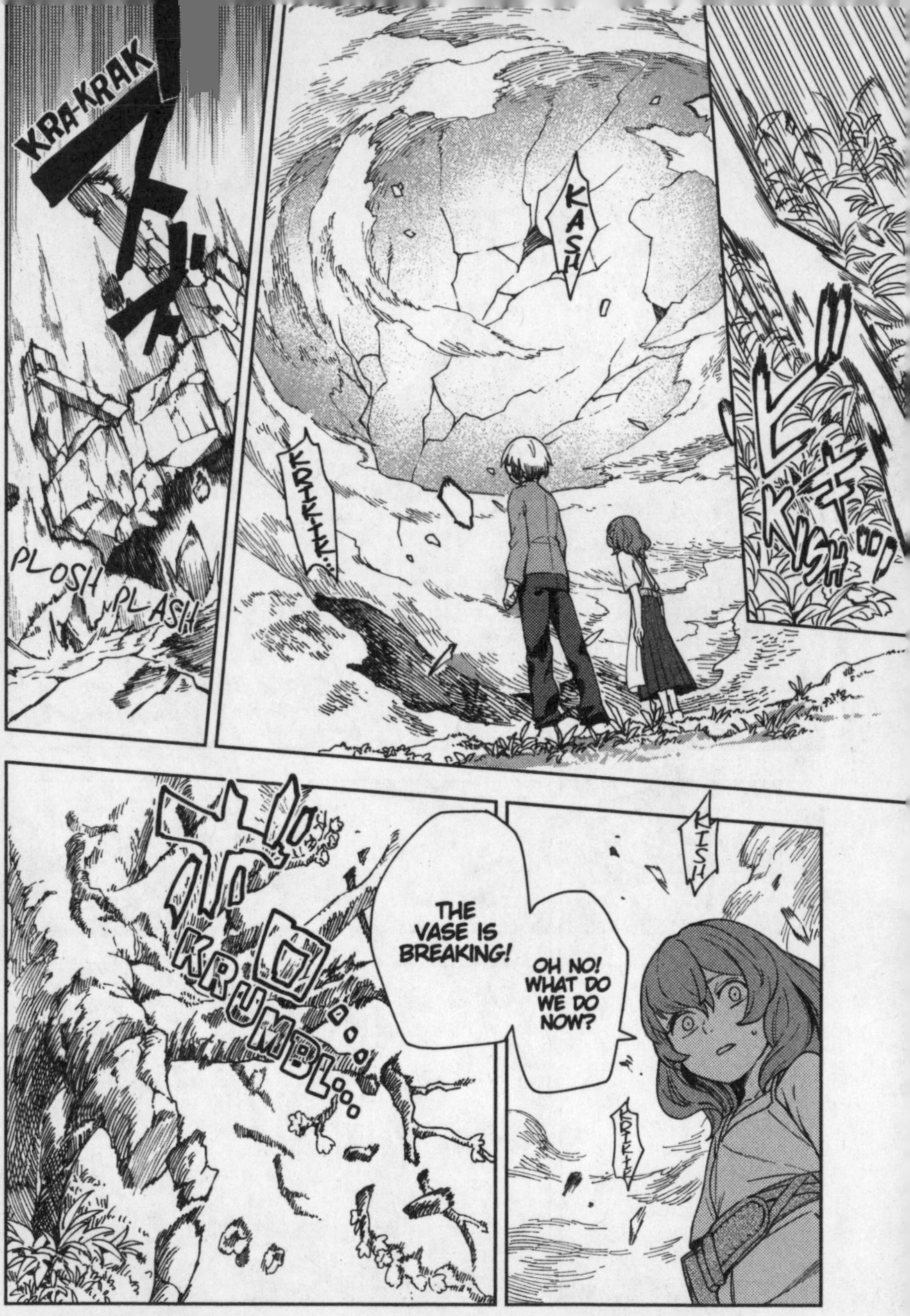
KYSH
KASH
KRIKKK...
KRA-KRAK
PLOSH
PLASH
KISH
THE VASE IS BREAKING!
OH NO! WHAT DO WE DO NOW?
KRIKK
KRUMBL...

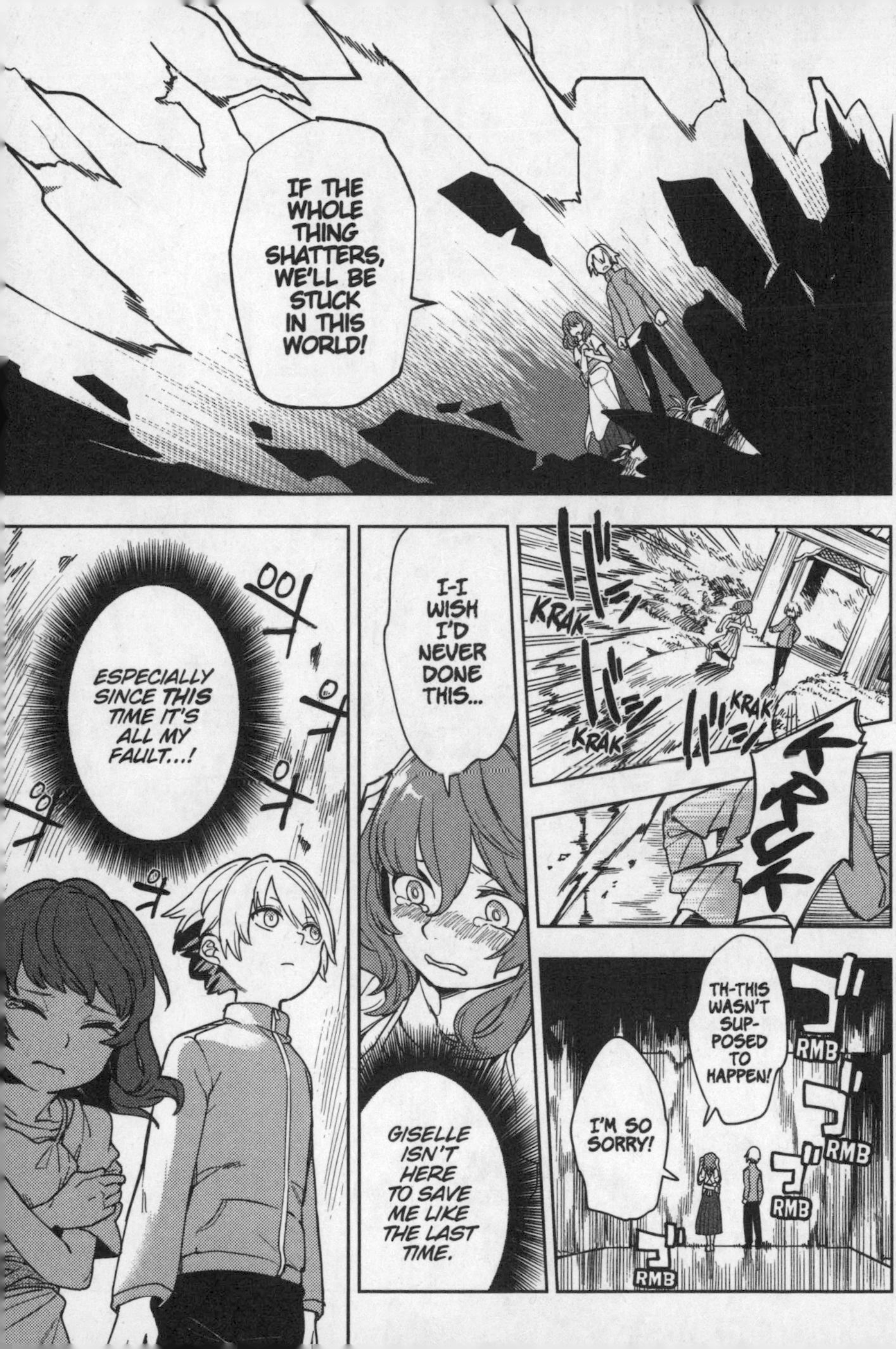
IF THE WHOLE THING SHATTERS, WE'LL BE STUCK IN THIS WORLD!
KRAK
KRAK
KRAK
TH-THIS WASN'T SUP-POSED TO HAPPEN!
I'M SO SORRY!
RMB
RMB
RMB
RMB
I-I WISH I'D NEVER DONE THIS...
GISELLE ISN'T HERE TO SAVE ME LIKE THE LAST TIME.
ESPECIALLY SINCE THIS TIME IT'S ALL MY FAULT...!

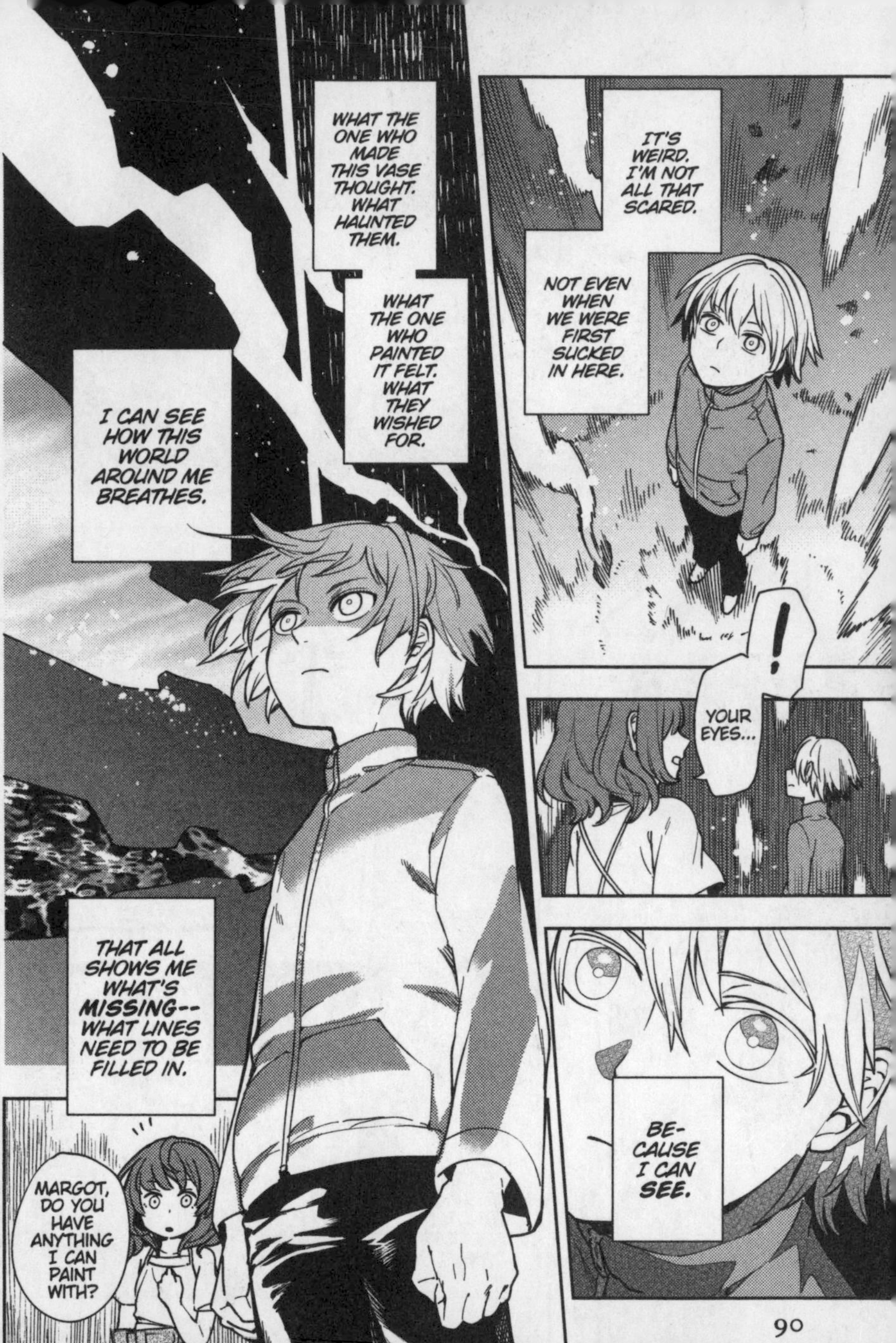
IT'S WEIRD. I'M NOT ALL THAT SCARED.
NOT EVEN WHEN WE WERE FIRST SUCKED IN HERE.
!
YOUR EYES...
BE-CAUSE I CAN SEE.
WHAT THE ONE WHO MADE THIS VASE THOUGHT. WHAT HAUNTED THEM.
WHAT THE ONE WHO PAINTED IT FELT. WHAT THEY WISHED FOR.
I CAN SEE HOW THIS WORLD AROUND ME BREATHES.
THAT ALL SHOWS ME WHAT'S MISSING-- WHAT LINES NEED TO BE FILLED IN.
MARGOT, DO YOU HAVE ANYTHING I CAN PAINT WITH?

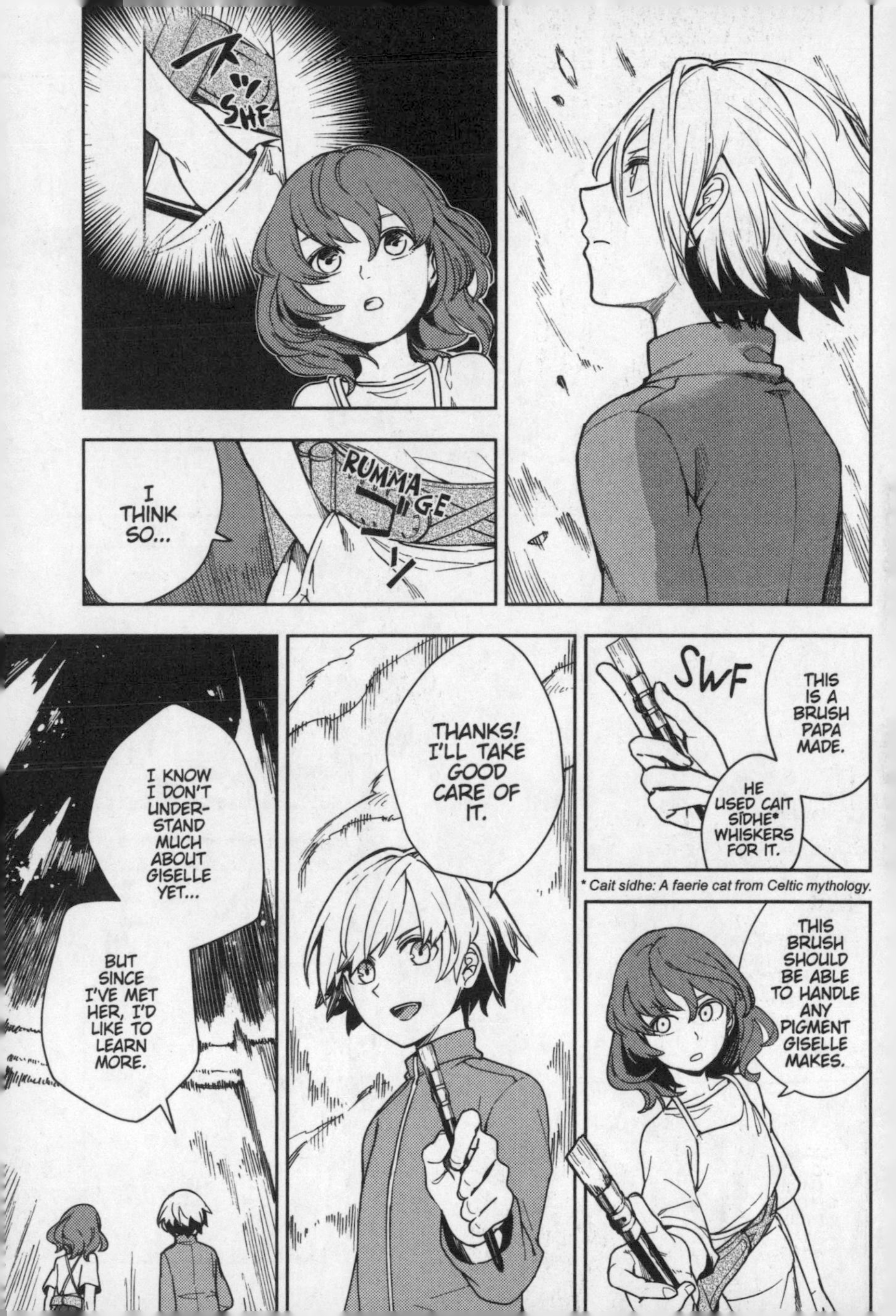
SHF
RUMMAGE
I THINK SO...
SWF
THIS IS A BRUSH PAPA MADE.
HE USED CAIT SÍDHE* WHISKERS FOR IT.
THIS BRUSH SHOULD BE ABLE TO HANDLE ANY PIGMENT GISELLE MAKES.
THANKS! I'LL TAKE GOOD CARE OF IT.
I KNOW I DON'T UNDERSTAND MUCH ABOUT GISELLE YET...
BUT SINCE I'VE MET HER, I'D LIKE TO LEARN MORE.

* *Cait sídhe: A faerie cat from Celtic mythology.*

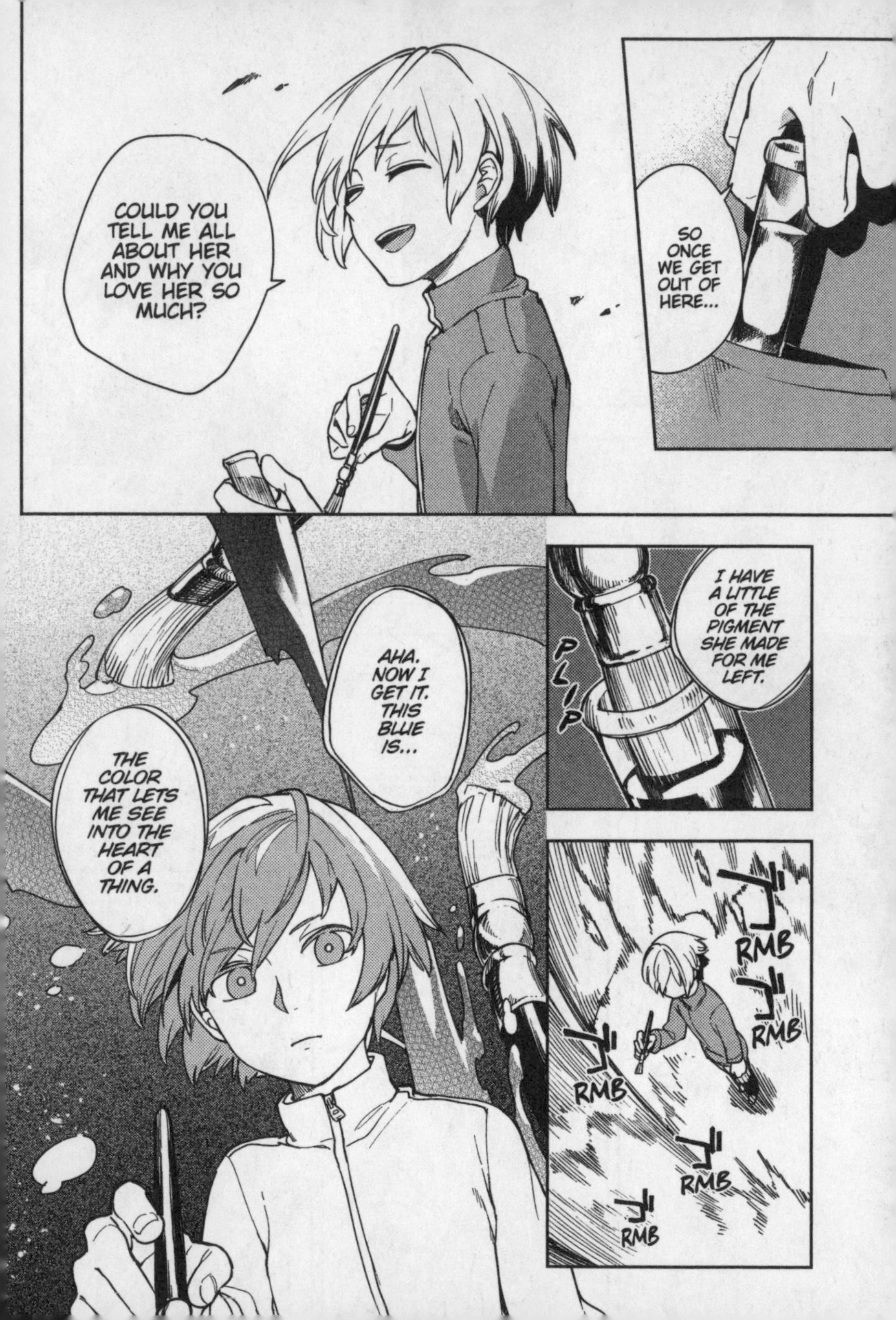
SO ONCE WE GET OUT OF HERE...
COULD YOU TELL ME ALL ABOUT HER AND WHY YOU LOVE HER SO MUCH?
I HAVE A LITTLE OF THE PIGMENT SHE MADE FOR ME LEFT.
PLIP
RMB
RMB
RMB
RMB
RMB
AHA. NOW I GET IT. THIS BLUE IS...
THE COLOR THAT LETS ME SEE INTO THE HEART OF A THING.

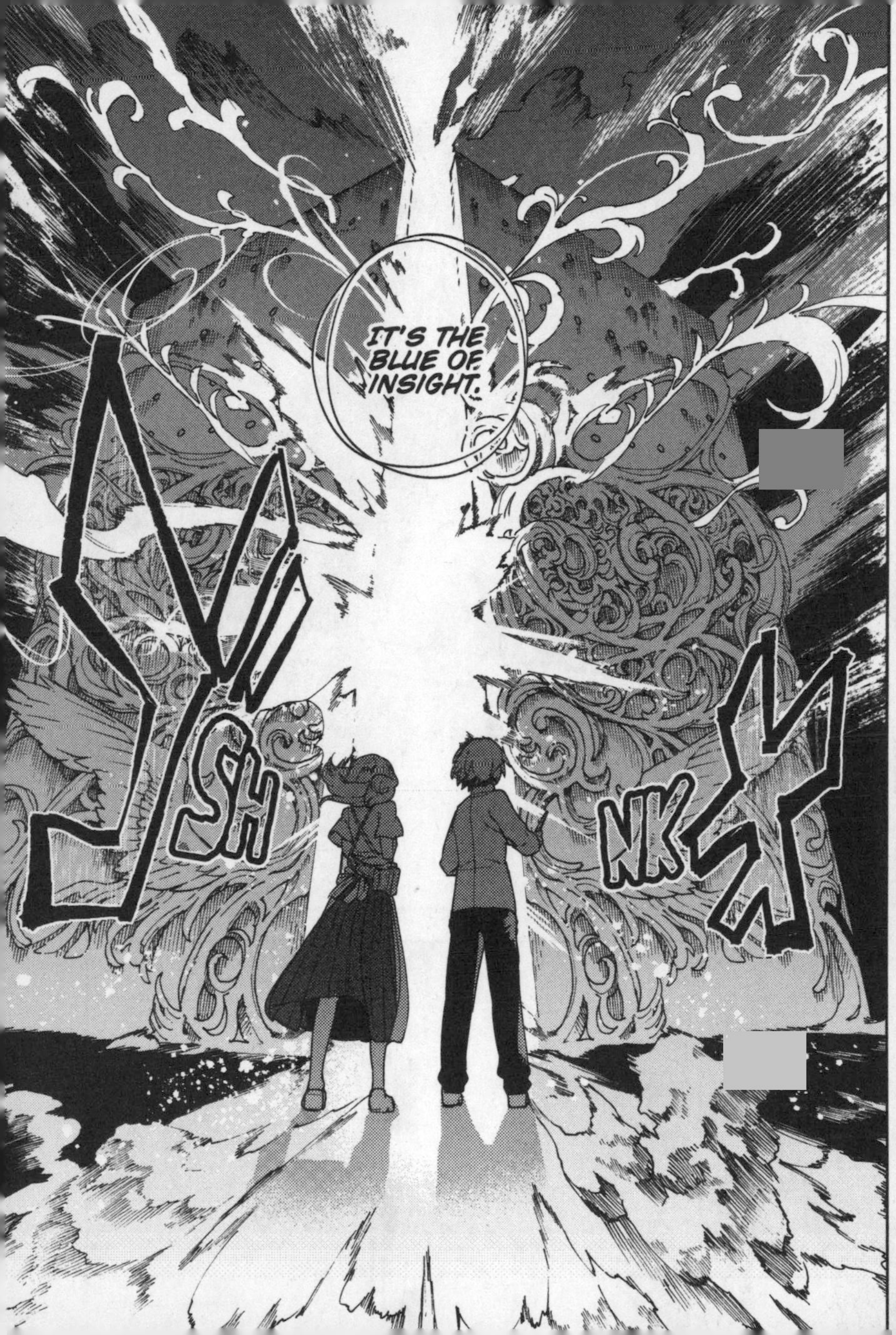
IT'S THE BLUE OF INSIGHT.
NK
SH

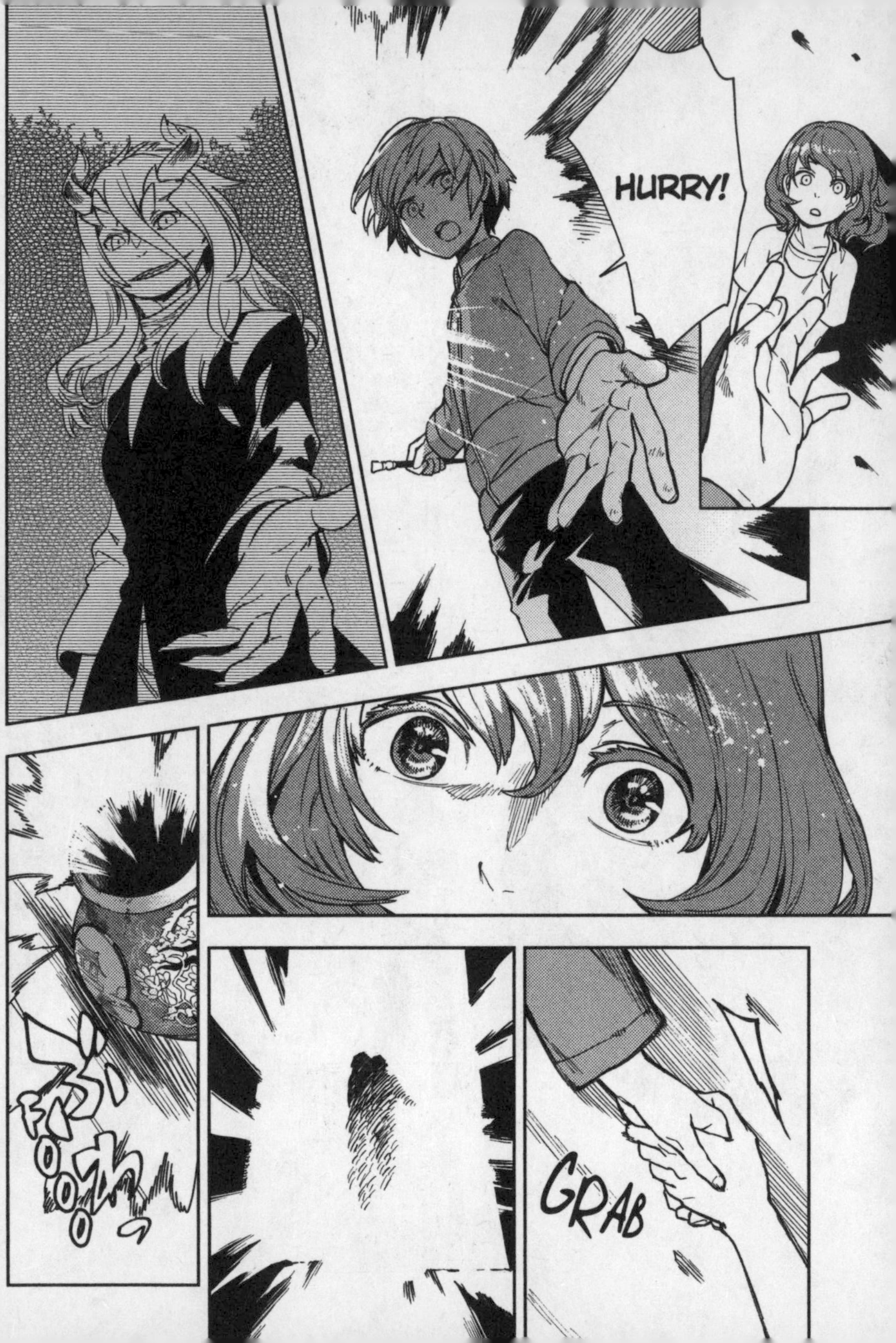
HURRY!
GRAB
FOOOO

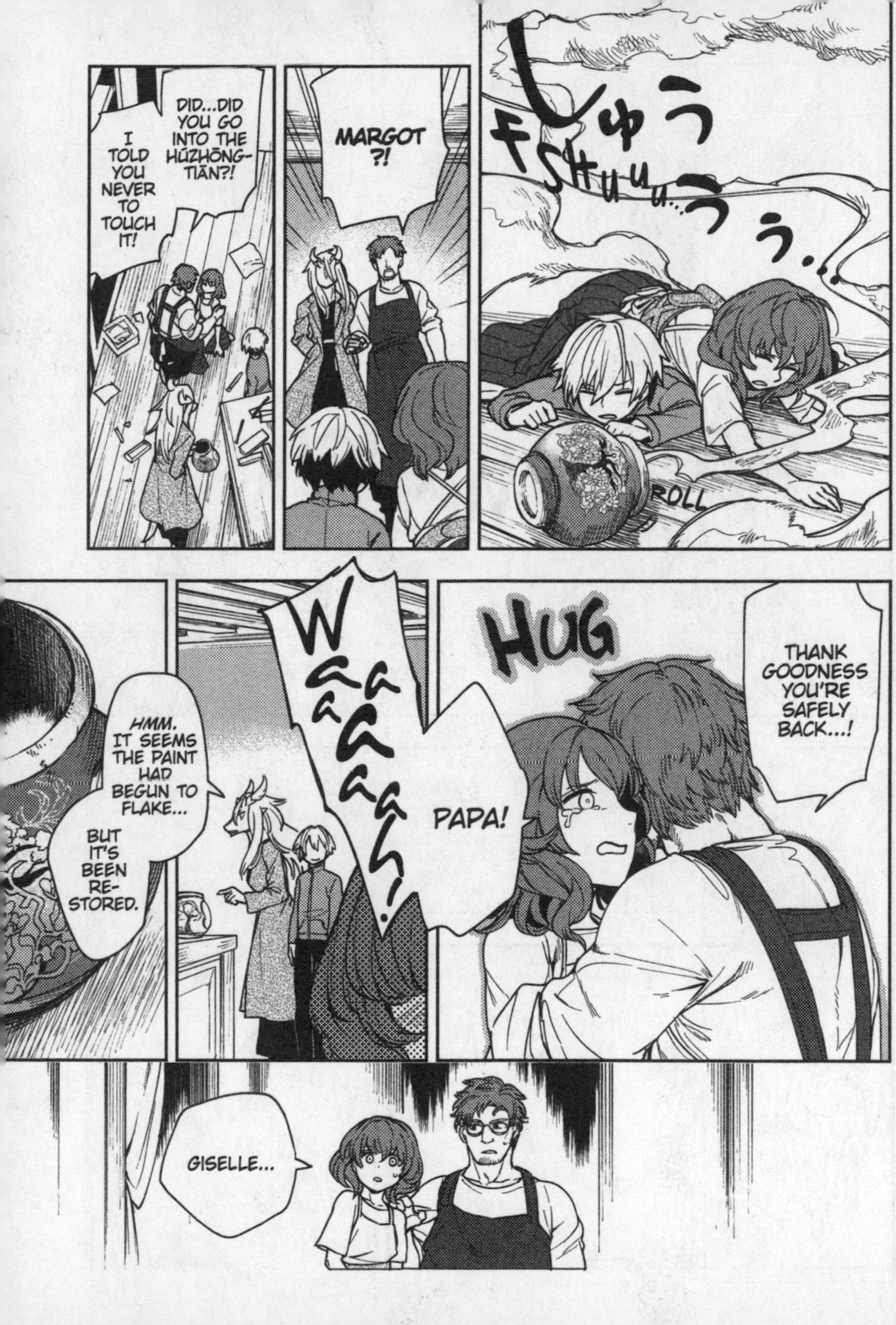
しゅう
FSHUuu...
うう...
ROLL
MARGOT?!
DID...DID YOU GO INTO THE HÚZHŌNG-TIĀN?!
I TOLD YOU NEVER TO TOUCH IT!
HUG
THANK GOODNESS YOU'RE SAFELY BACK...!
WAAAAAAH!
PAPA!
HMM. IT SEEMS THE PAINT HAD BEGUN TO FLAKE...
BUT IT'S BEEN RE-STORED.
GISELLE...

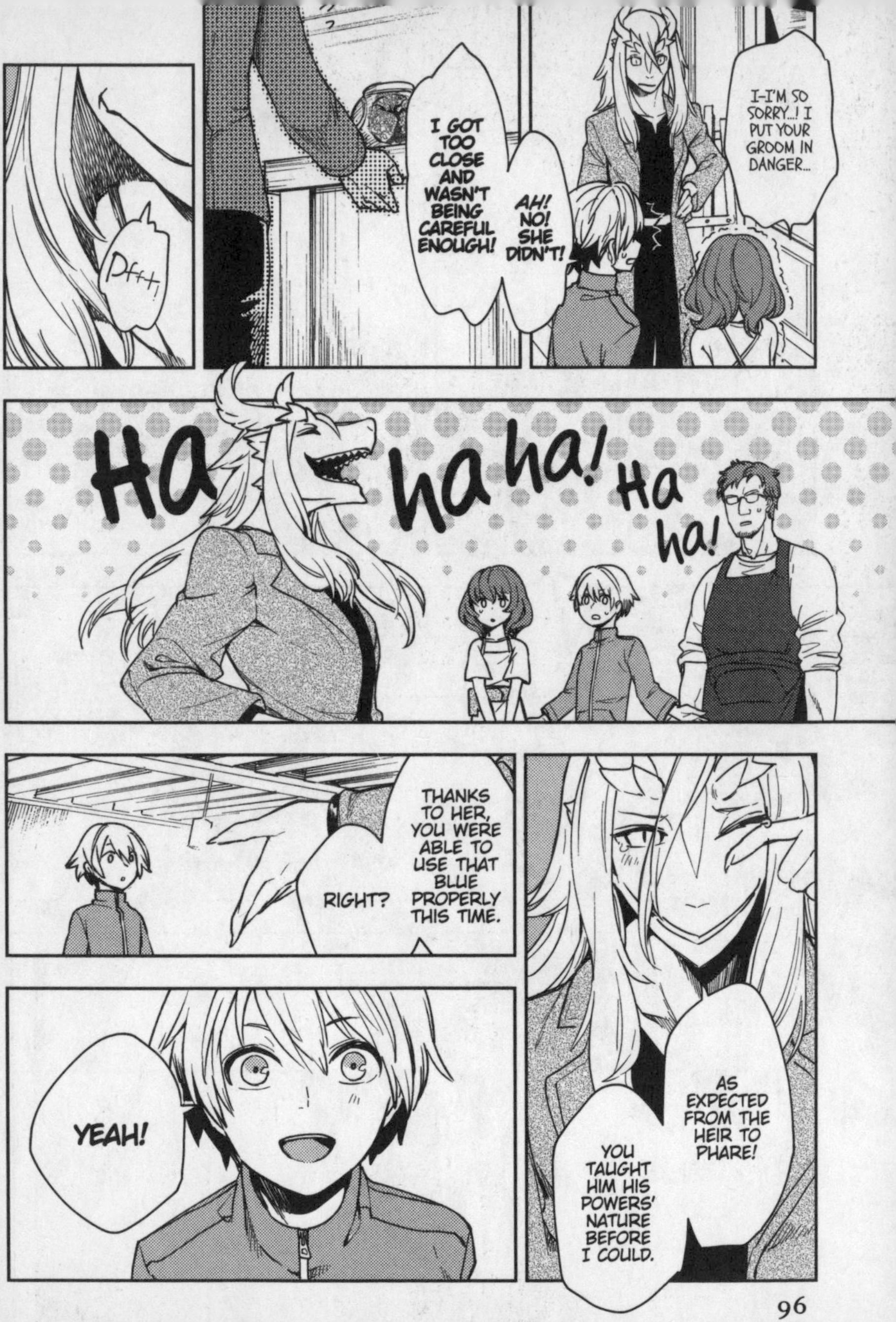

I-I'M SO SORRY...! I PUT YOUR GROOM IN DANGER...
AH! NO! SHE DIDN'T!
I GOT TOO CLOSE AND WASN'T BEING CAREFUL ENOUGH!
Pffft!
Ha haha! Ha ha!
AS EXPECTED FROM THE HEIR TO PHARE!
YOU TAUGHT HIM HIS POWERS' NATURE BEFORE I COULD.
THANKS TO HER, YOU WERE ABLE TO USE THAT BLUE PROPERLY THIS TIME.
RIGHT?
YEAH!

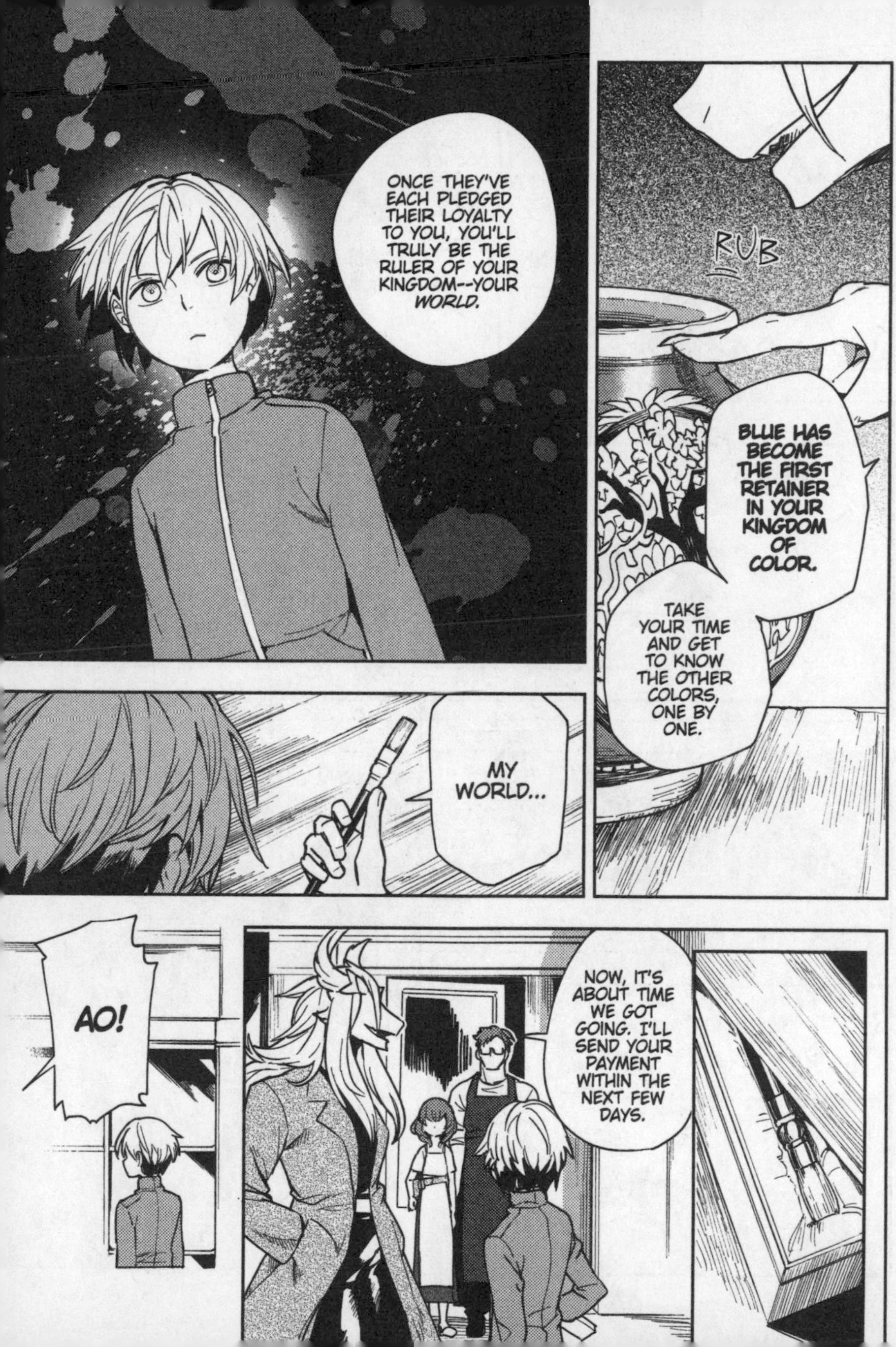
RUB
BLUE HAS BECOME THE FIRST RETAINER IN YOUR KINGDOM OF COLOR.
TAKE YOUR TIME AND GET TO KNOW THE OTHER COLORS, ONE BY ONE.
ONCE THEY'VE EACH PLEDGED THEIR LOYALTY TO YOU, YOU'LL TRULY BE THE RULER OF YOUR KINGDOM--YOUR *WORLD.*
MY WORLD...
NOW, IT'S ABOUT TIME WE GOT GOING. I'LL SEND YOUR PAYMENT WITHIN THE NEXT FEW DAYS.
AO!

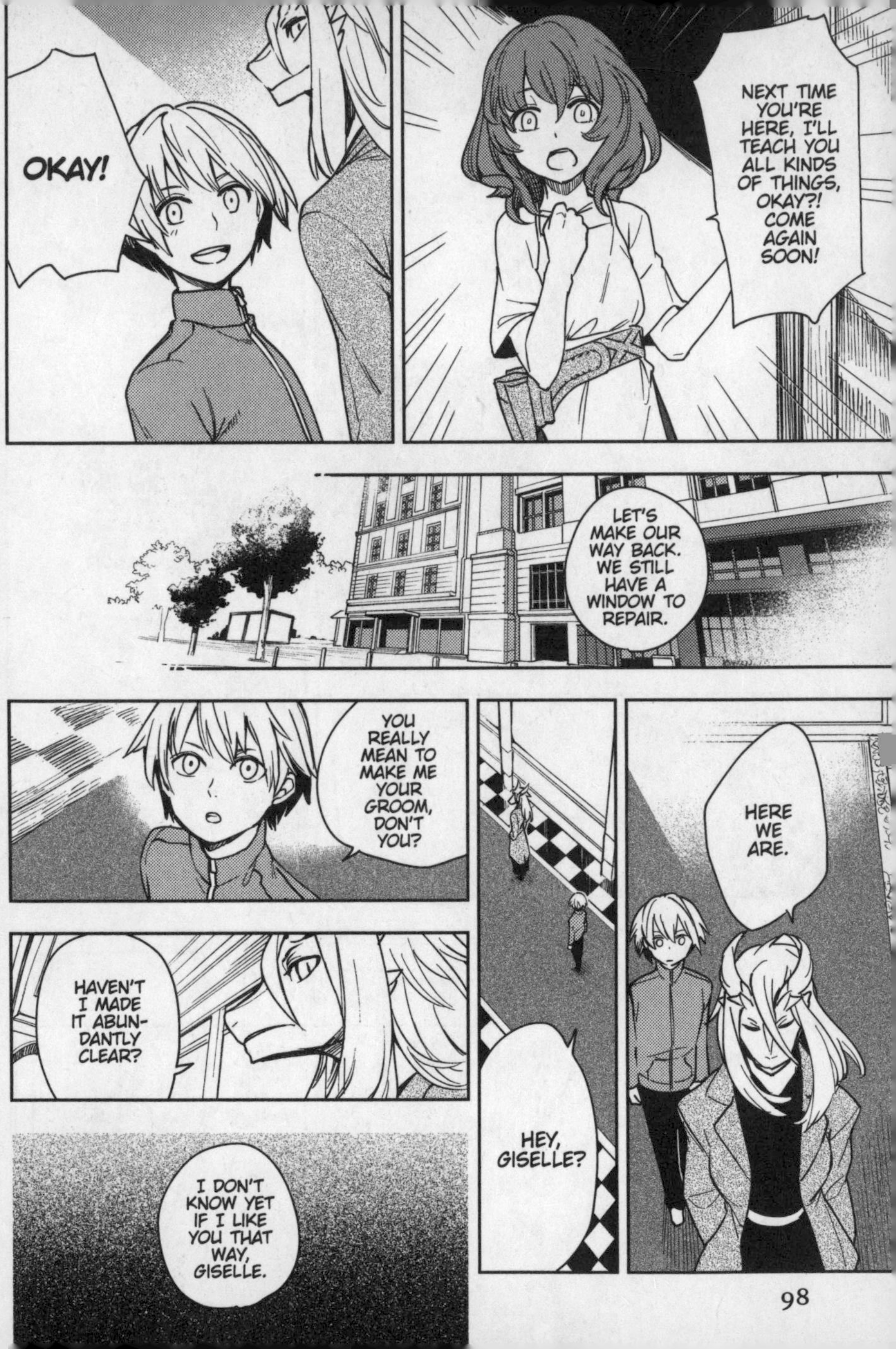
NEXT TIME YOU'RE HERE, I'LL TEACH YOU ALL KINDS OF THINGS, OKAY?! COME AGAIN SOON!
OKAY!
LET'S MAKE OUR WAY BACK. WE STILL HAVE A WINDOW TO REPAIR.
HERE WE ARE.
HEY, GISELLE?
YOU REALLY MEAN TO MAKE ME YOUR GROOM, DON'T YOU?
HAVEN'T I MADE IT ABUNDANTLY CLEAR?
I DON'T KNOW YET IF I LIKE YOU THAT WAY, GISELLE.

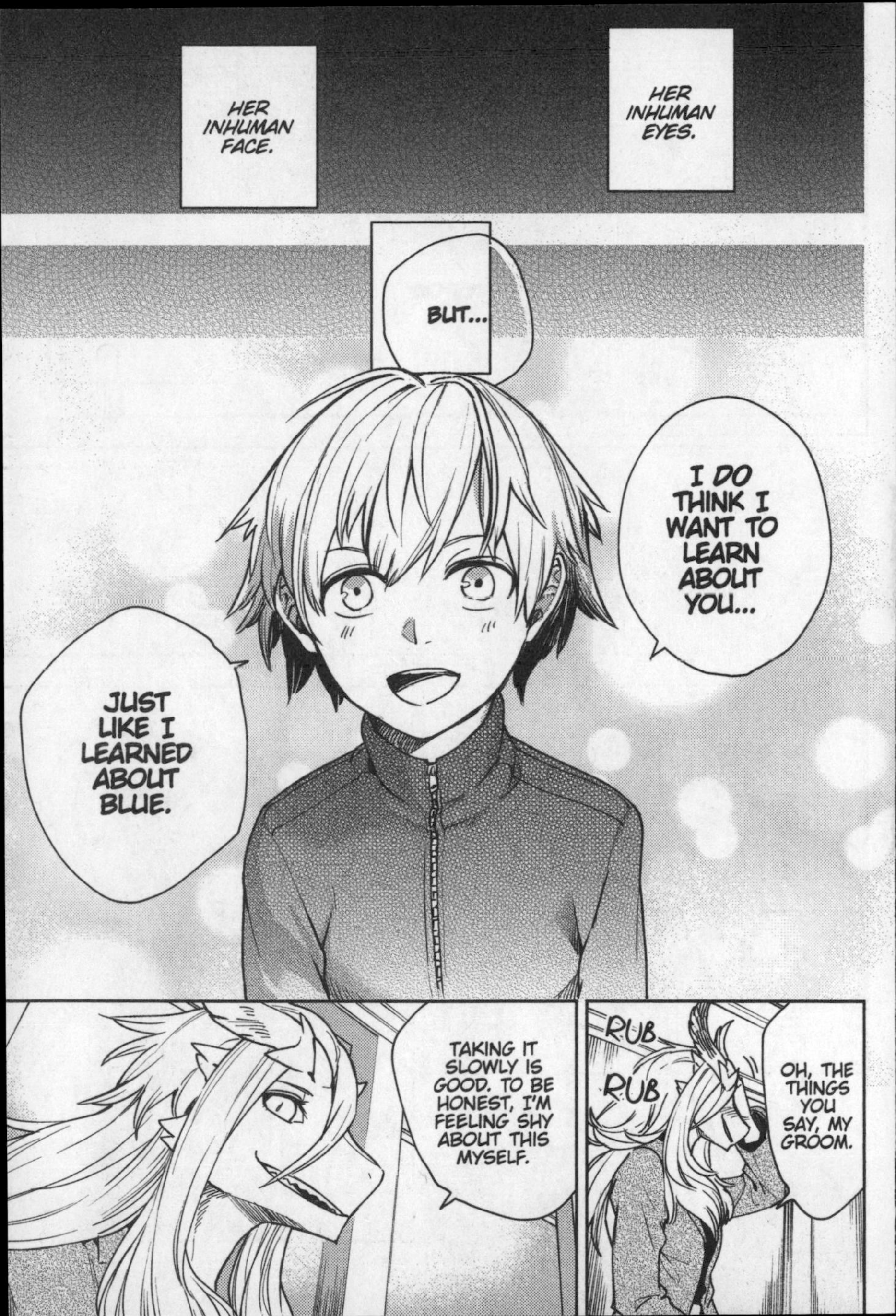
HER INHUMAN EYES.
HER INHUMAN FACE.
BUT...
I DO THINK I WANT TO LEARN ABOUT YOU...
JUST LIKE I LEARNED ABOUT BLUE.
RUB
RUB
OH, THE THINGS YOU SAY, MY GROOM.
TAKING IT SLOWLY IS GOOD. TO BE HONEST, I'M FEELING SHY ABOUT THIS MYSELF.

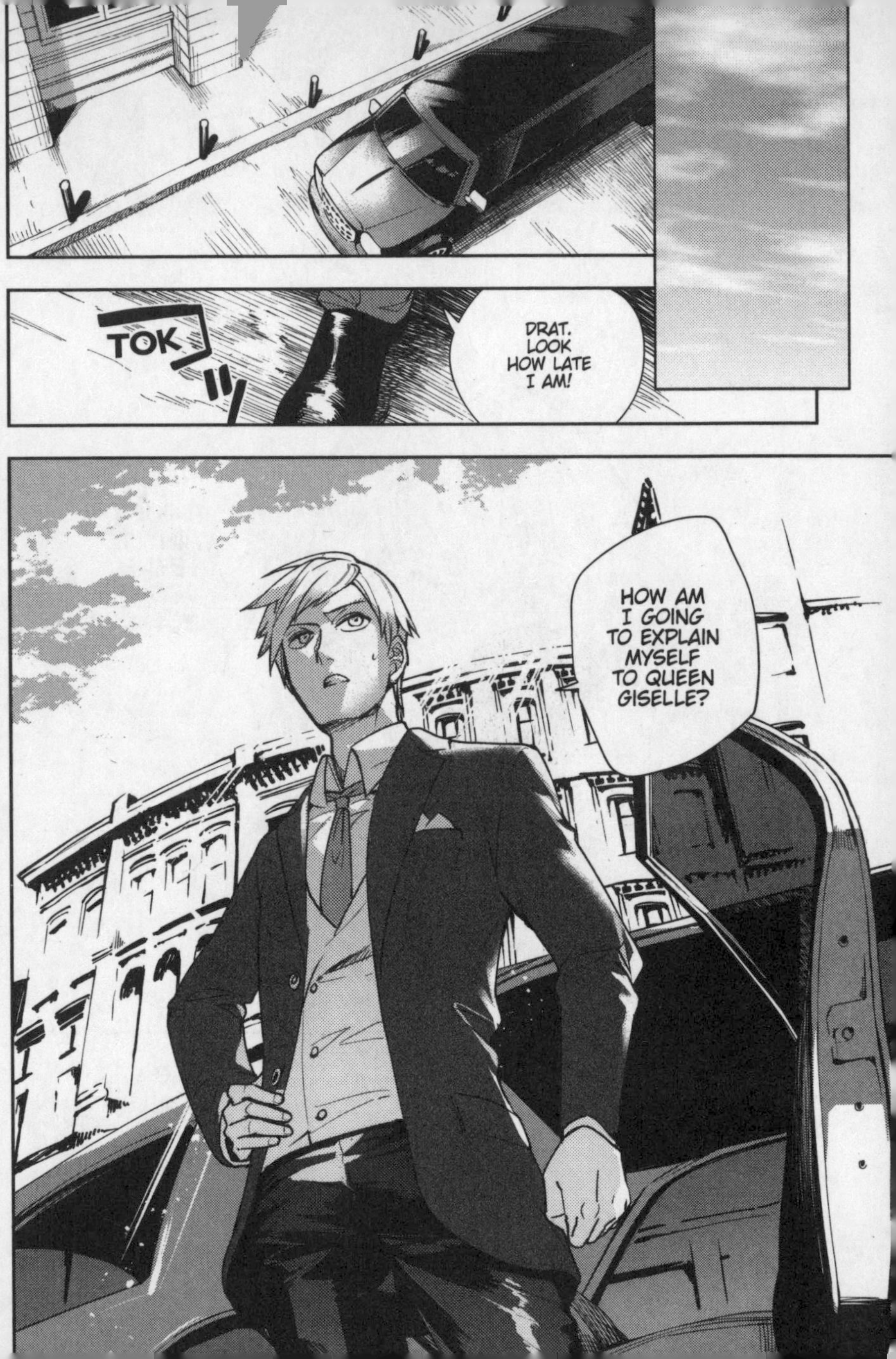
DRAT. LOOK HOW LATE I AM!
TOK
HOW AM I GOING TO EXPLAIN MYSELF TO QUEEN GISELLE?

The Ancient Magus' Bride

WIZARD's BLUE

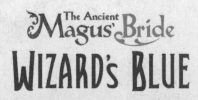

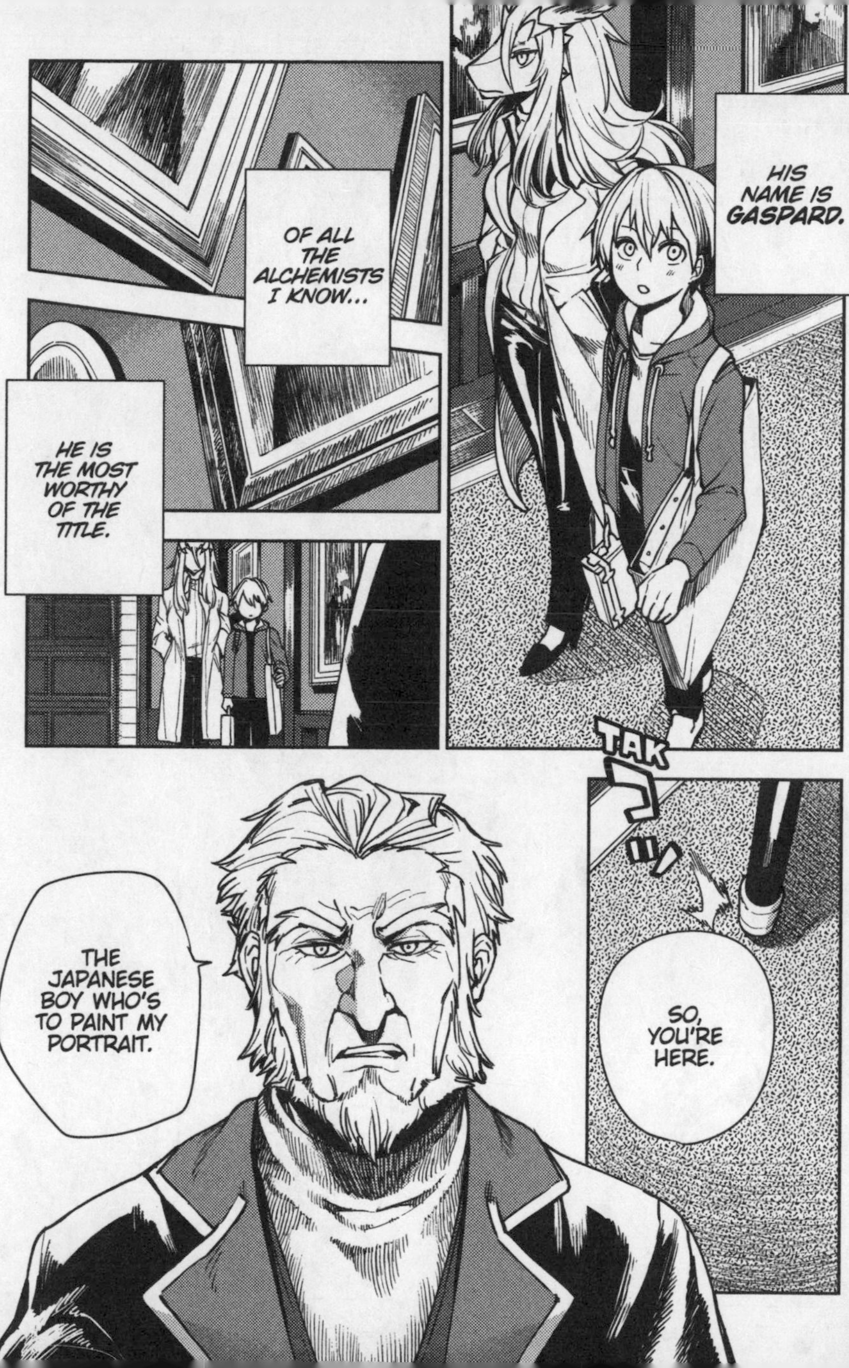
HIS NAME IS GASPARD.
OF ALL THE ALCHEMISTS I KNOW...
HE IS THE MOST WORTHY OF THE TITLE.
TAK
SO, YOU'RE HERE.
THE JAPANESE BOY WHO'S TO PAINT MY PORTRAIT.

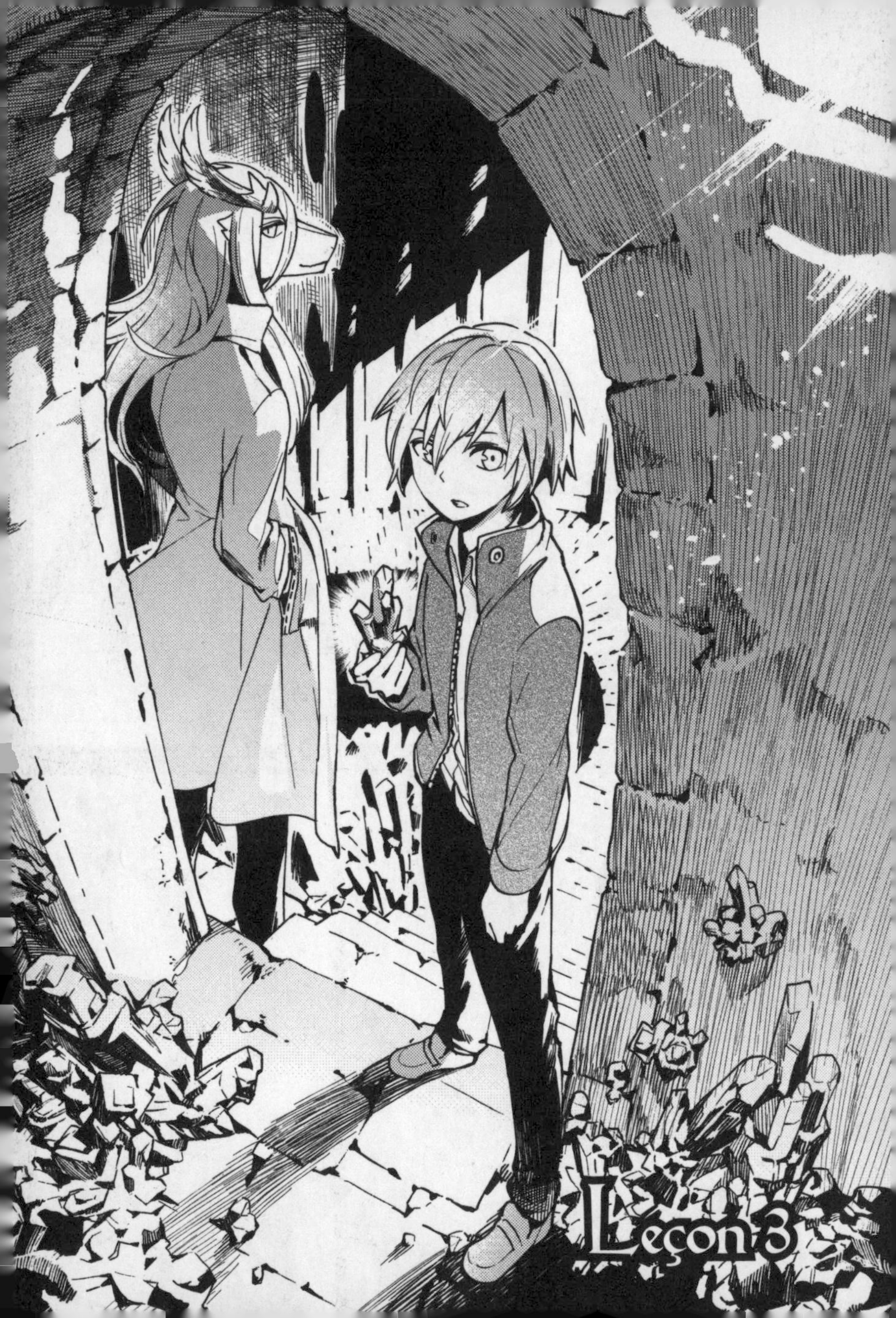
Leçon 3

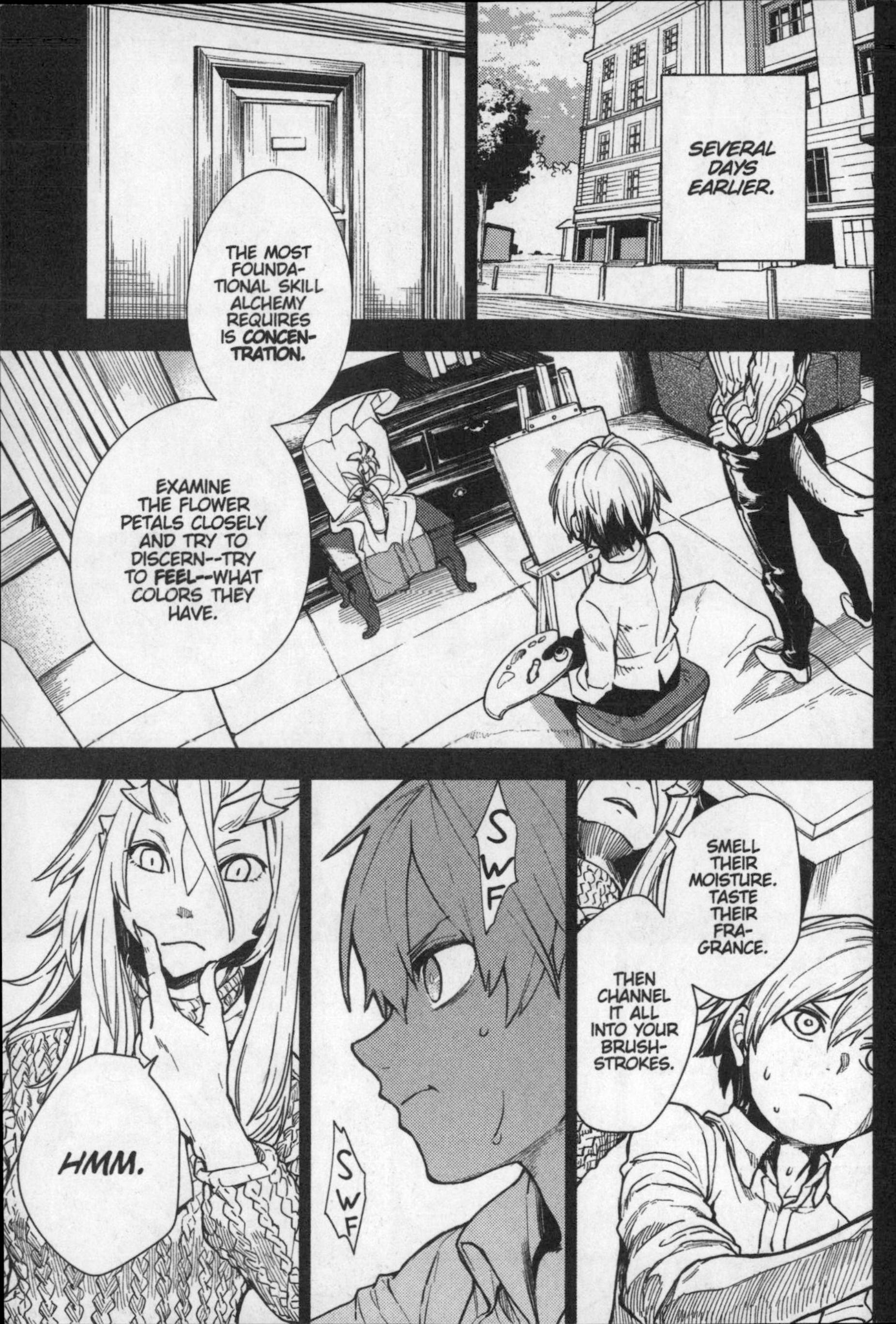

SEVERAL DAYS EARLIER.
THE MOST FOUNDATIONAL SKILL ALCHEMY REQUIRES IS CONCENTRATION.
EXAMINE THE FLOWER PETALS CLOSELY AND TRY TO DISCERN--TRY TO FEEL--WHAT COLORS THEY HAVE.
SMELL THEIR MOISTURE. TASTE THEIR FRAGRANCE.
THEN CHANNEL IT ALL INTO YOUR BRUSHSTROKES.
SWF
SWF
HMM.

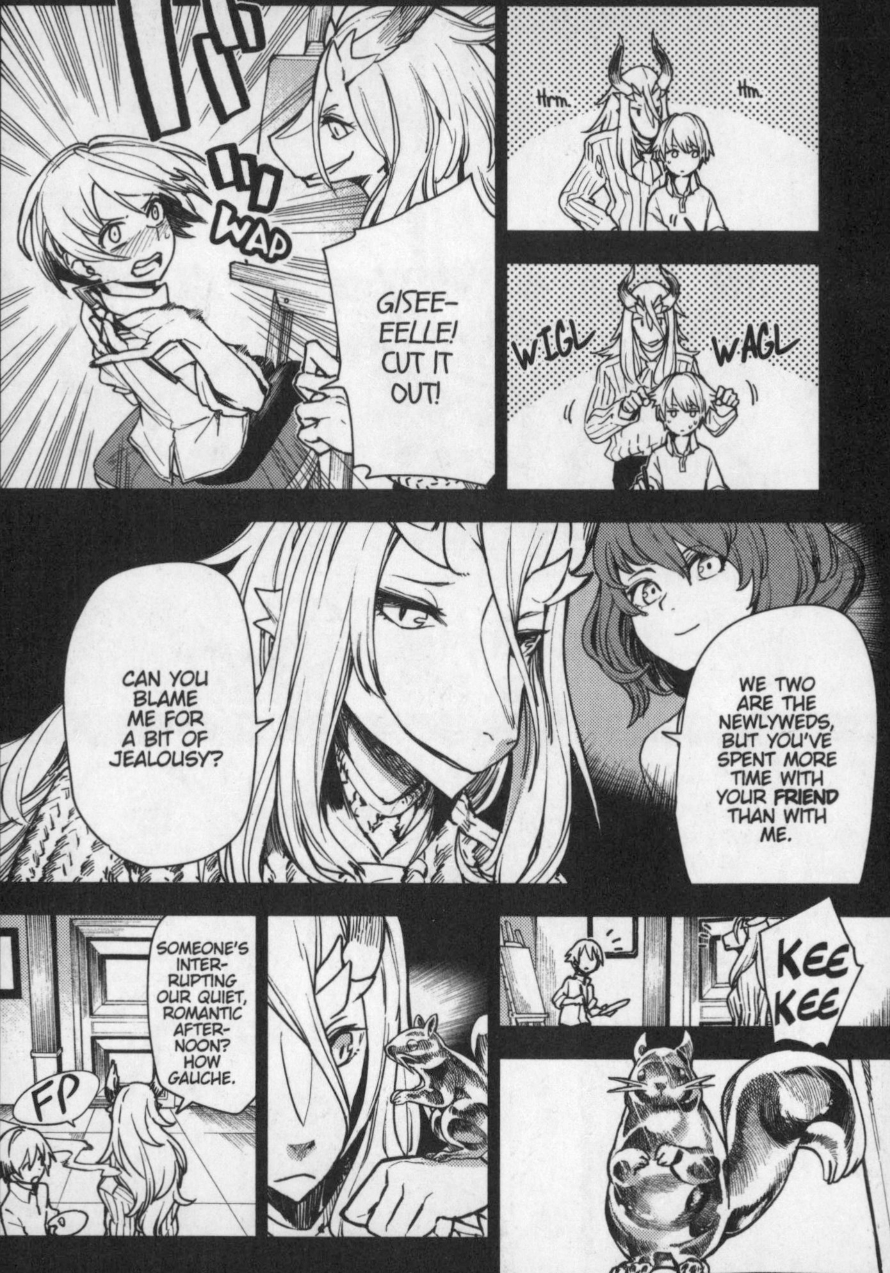
Hm.
Hrm.
WAGL
WIGL
GISEE-EELLE! CUT IT OUT!
WAP
WE TWO ARE THE NEWLYWEDS, BUT YOU'VE SPENT MORE TIME WITH YOUR **FRIEND** THAN WITH ME.
CAN YOU BLAME ME FOR A BIT OF JEALOUSY?
KEE KEE
SOMEONE'S INTER-RUPTING OUR QUIET, ROMANTIC AFTER-NOON? HOW GAUCHE.
FP

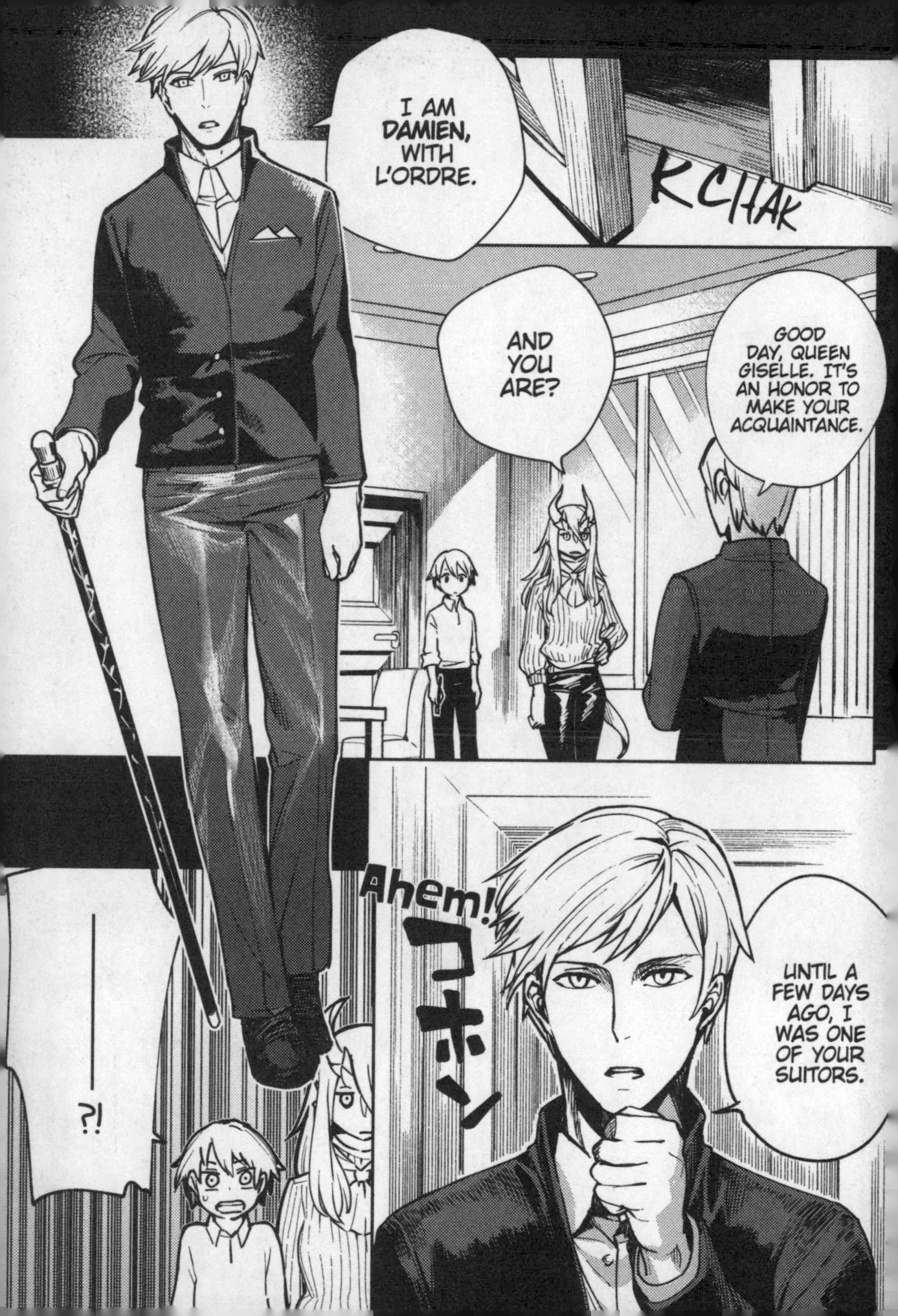
KCHAK
GOOD DAY, QUEEN GISELLE. IT'S AN HONOR TO MAKE YOUR ACQUAINTANCE.
AND YOU ARE?
UNTIL A FEW DAYS AGO, I WAS ONE OF YOUR SUITORS.
Ahem!
コホン
?!
I AM DAMIEN, WITH L'ORDRE.

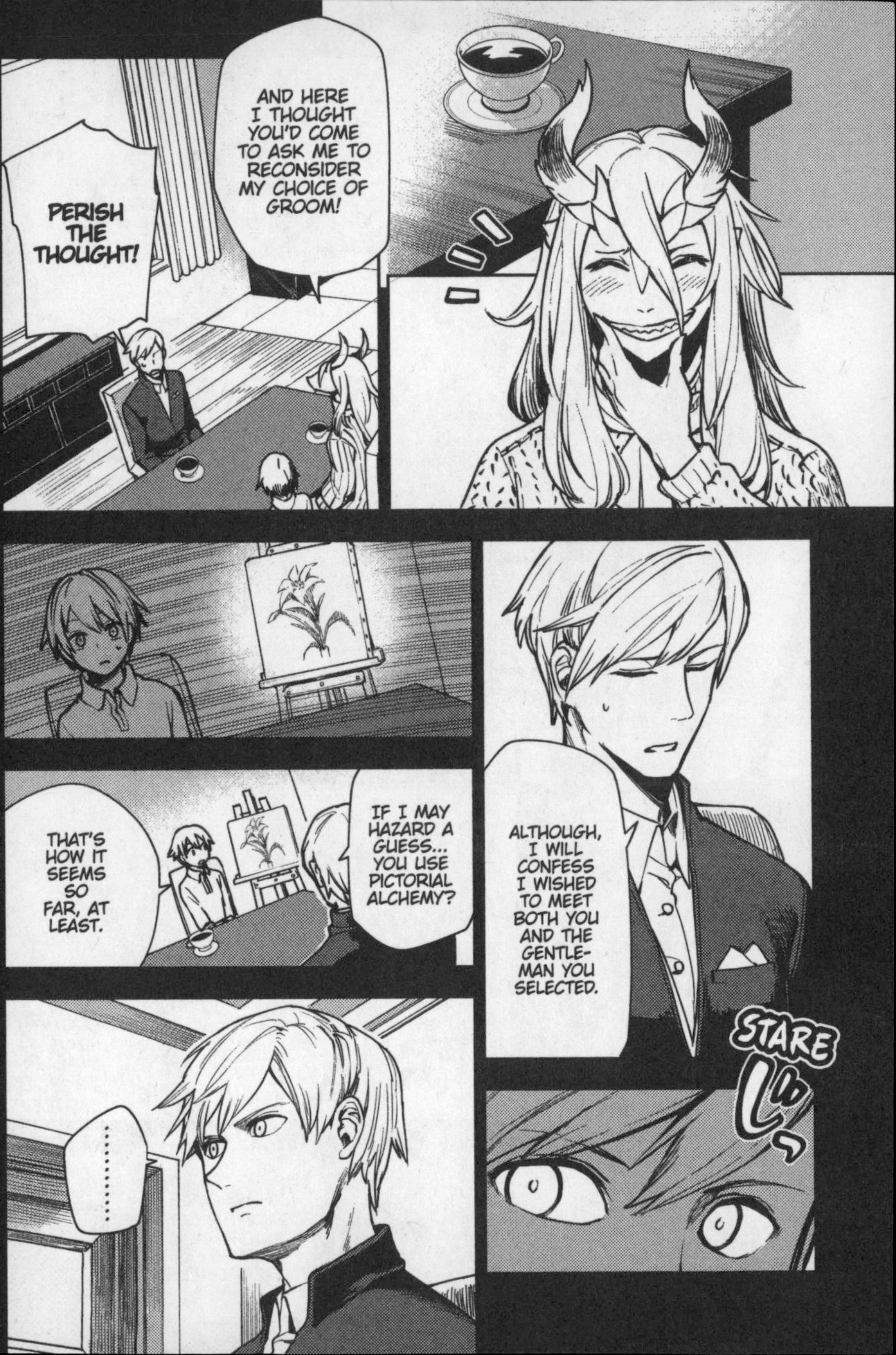
AND HERE I THOUGHT YOU'D COME TO ASK ME TO RECONSIDER MY CHOICE OF GROOM!
PERISH THE THOUGHT!
ALTHOUGH, I WILL CONFESS I WISHED TO MEET BOTH YOU AND THE GENTLE-MAN YOU SELECTED.
IF I MAY HAZARD A GUESS... YOU USE PICTORIAL ALCHEMY?
THAT'S HOW IT SEEMS SO FAR, AT LEAST.
STARE
......

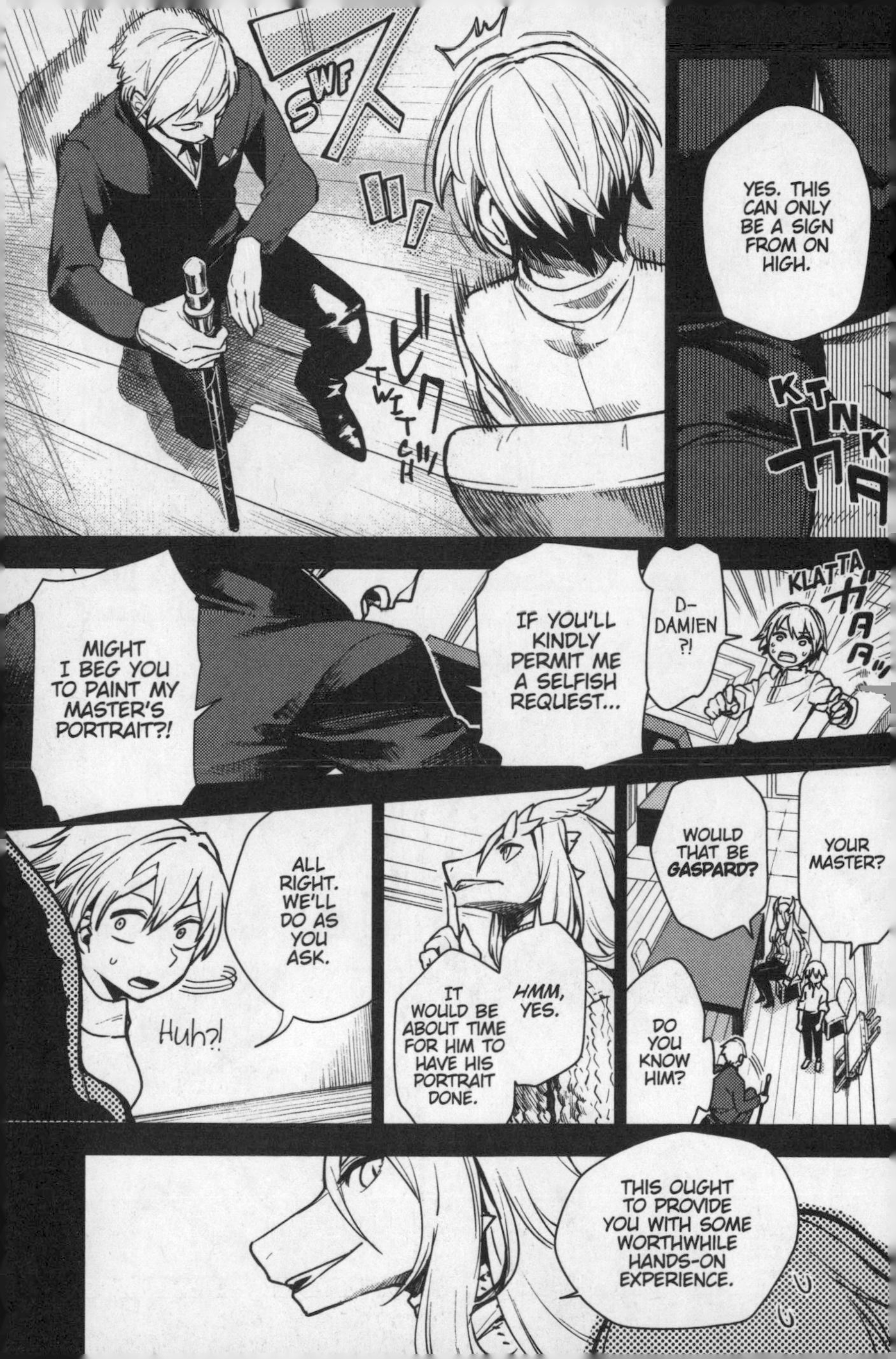
YES. THIS CAN ONLY BE A SIGN FROM ON HIGH.
KTNK
SWF
TWITCH
KLATTA
D-DAMIEN?!
IF YOU'LL KINDLY PERMIT ME A SELFISH REQUEST...
MIGHT I BEG YOU TO PAINT MY MASTER'S PORTRAIT?!
YOUR MASTER?
WOULD THAT BE **GASPARD?**
DO YOU KNOW HIM?
HMM, YES.
IT WOULD BE ABOUT TIME FOR HIM TO HAVE HIS PORTRAIT DONE.
ALL RIGHT. WE'LL DO AS YOU ASK.
Huh?!
THIS OUGHT TO PROVIDE YOU WITH SOME WORTHWHILE HANDS-ON EXPERIENCE.

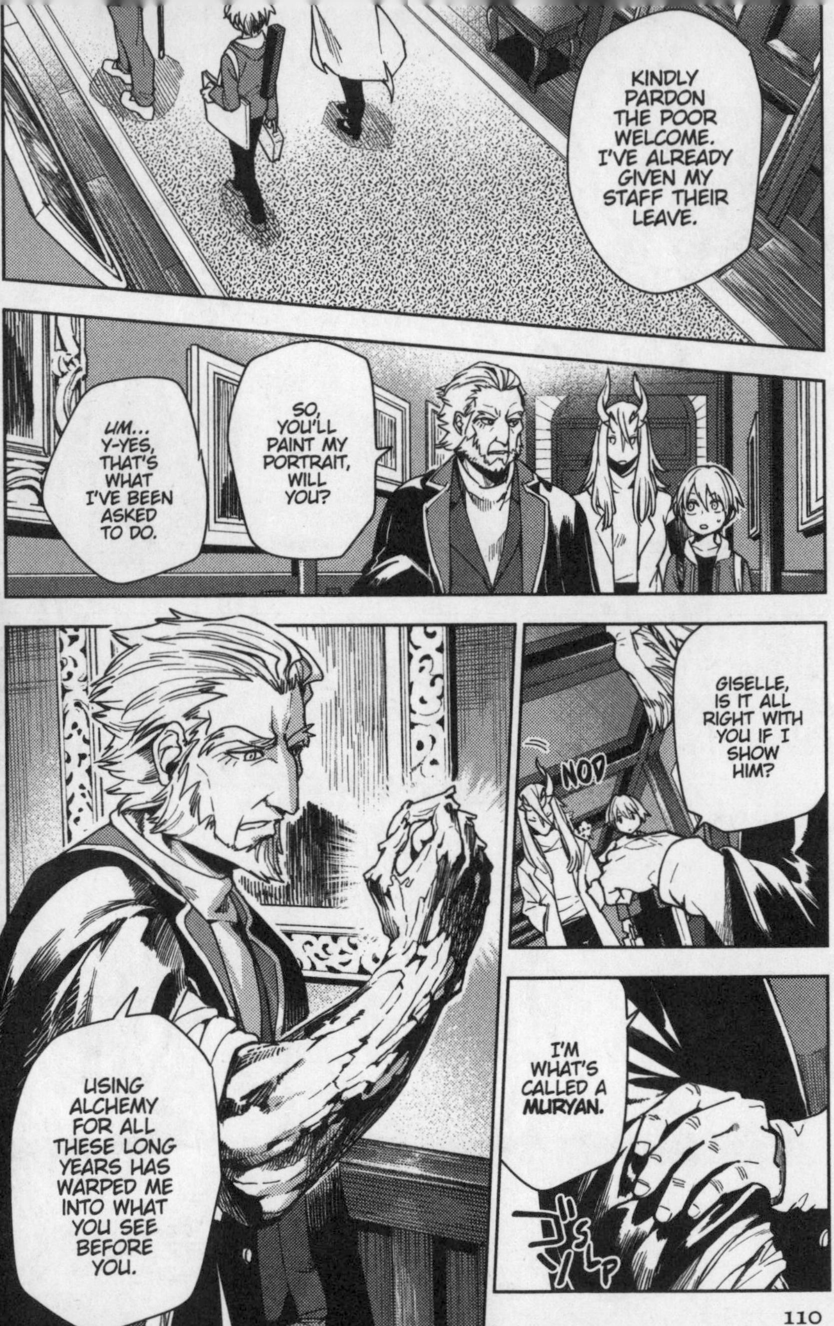
KINDLY PARDON THE POOR WELCOME. I'VE ALREADY GIVEN MY STAFF THEIR LEAVE.
SO, YOU'LL PAINT MY PORTRAIT, WILL YOU?
UM... Y-YES, THAT'S WHAT I'VE BEEN ASKED TO DO.
GISELLE, IS IT ALL RIGHT WITH YOU IF I SHOW HIM?
NOD
I'M WHAT'S CALLED A MURYAN.
SLP
USING ALCHEMY FOR ALL THESE LONG YEARS HAS WARPED ME INTO WHAT YOU SEE BEFORE YOU.

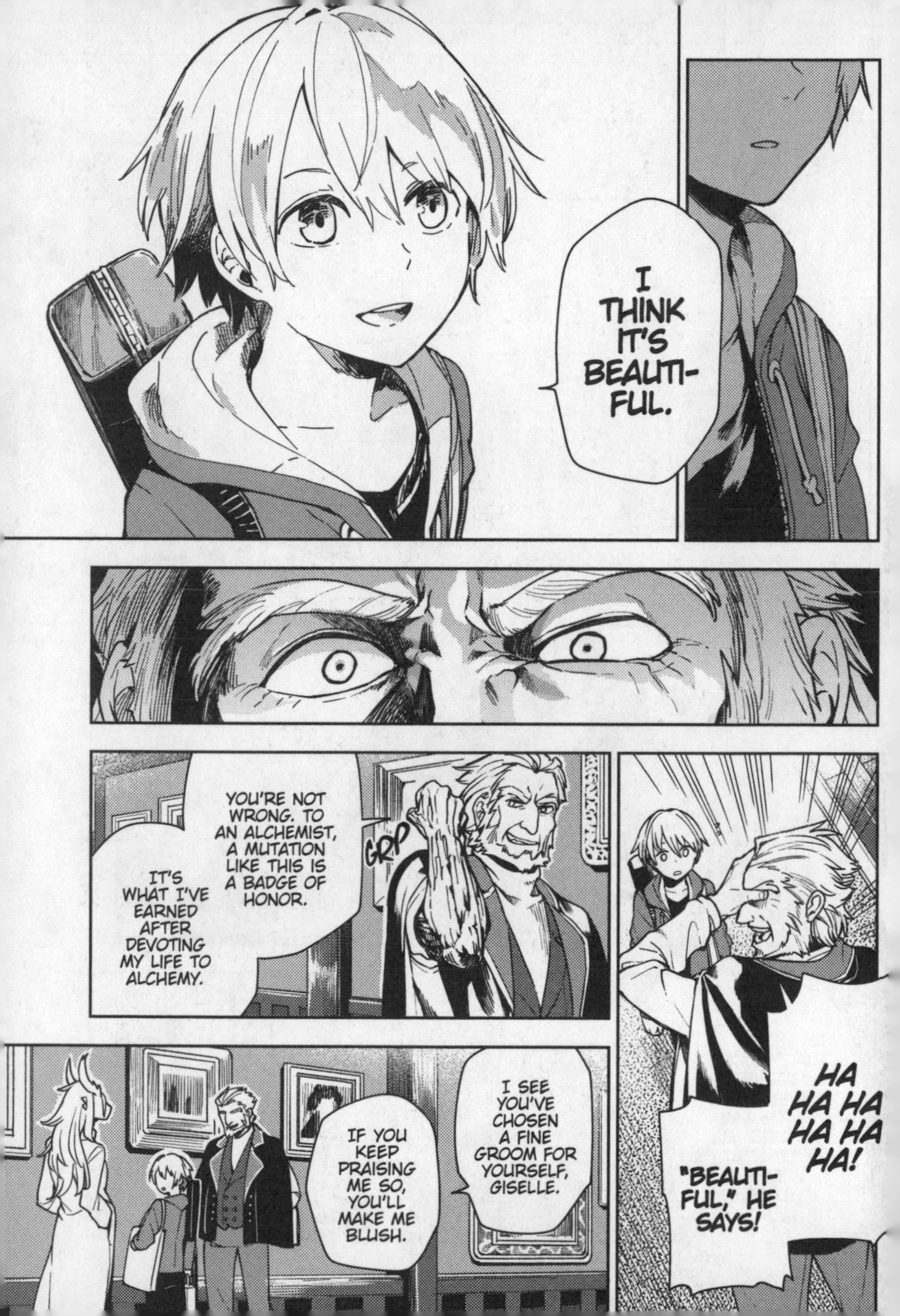
I THINK IT'S BEAUTIFUL.
HA HA HA HA HA HA!
"BEAUTIFUL," HE SAYS!
YOU'RE NOT WRONG. TO AN ALCHEMIST, A MUTATION LIKE THIS IS A BADGE OF HONOR.
GRP
IT'S WHAT I'VE EARNED AFTER DEVOTING MY LIFE TO ALCHEMY.
I SEE YOU'VE CHOSEN A FINE GROOM FOR YOURSELF, GISELLE.
IF YOU KEEP PRAISING ME SO, YOU'LL MAKE ME BLUSH.

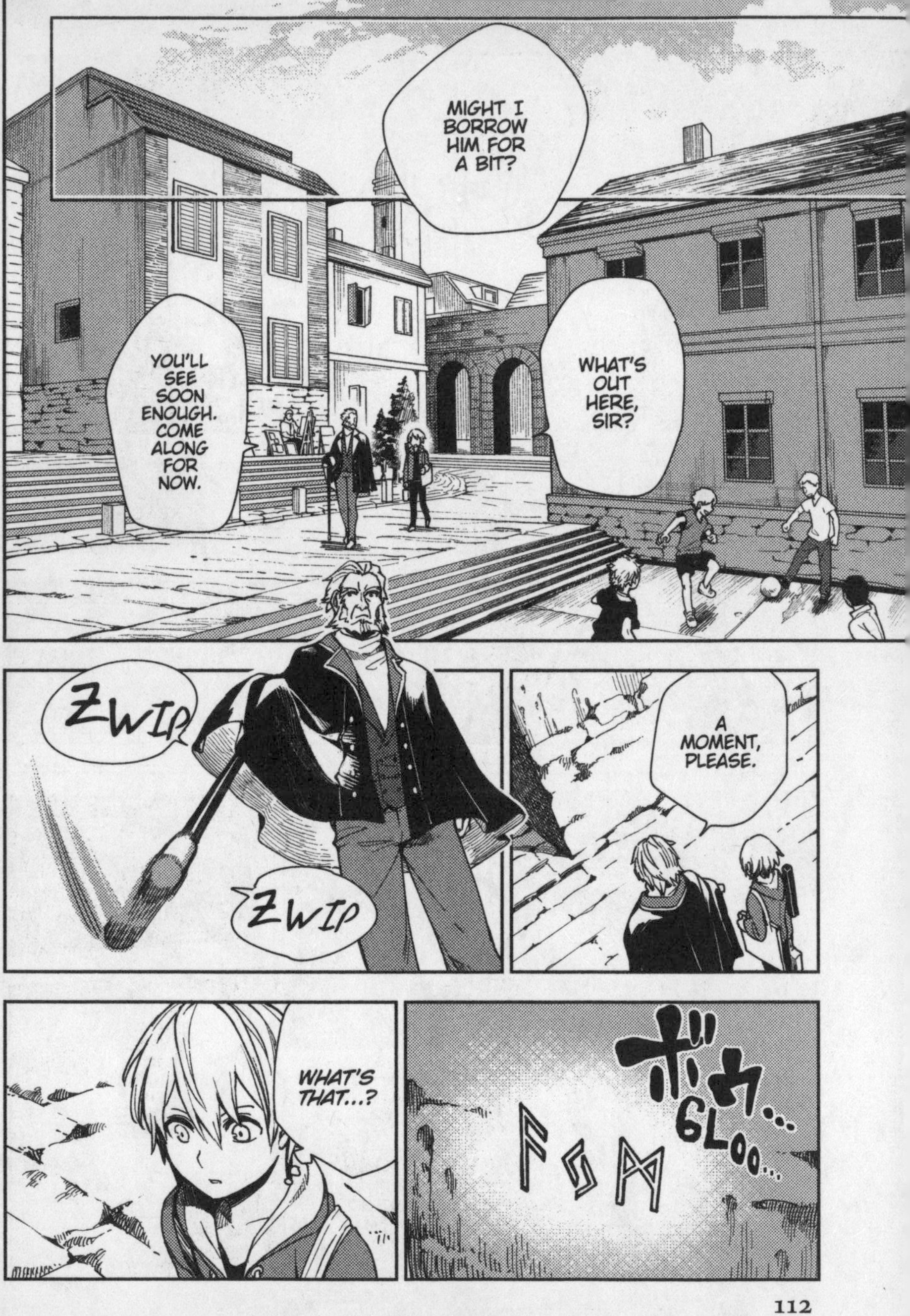
MIGHT I BORROW HIM FOR A BIT?
WHAT'S OUT HERE, SIR?
YOU'LL SEE SOON ENOUGH. COME ALONG FOR NOW.
A MOMENT, PLEASE.
ZWIP
ZWIP
ボウ…
GLOO…
WHAT'S THAT…?

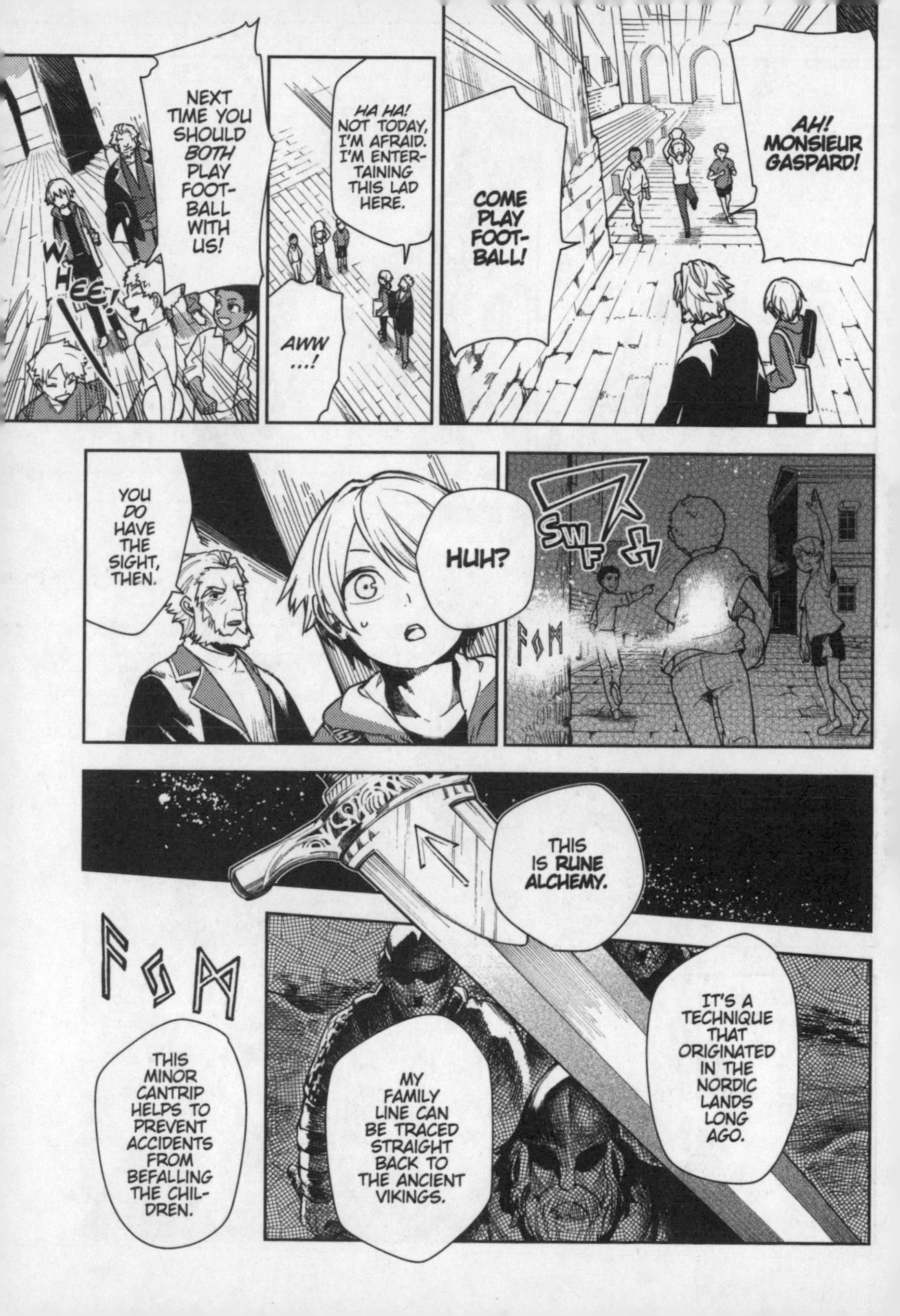
AH! MONSIEUR GASPARD!
COME PLAY FOOTBALL!
HA HA! NOT TODAY, I'M AFRAID. I'M ENTERTAINING THIS LAD HERE.
AWW...!
NEXT TIME YOU SHOULD BOTH PLAY FOOTBALL WITH US!
WHEE!
SWF
HUH?
YOU DO HAVE THE SIGHT, THEN.
THIS IS RUNE ALCHEMY.
IT'S A TECHNIQUE THAT ORIGINATED IN THE NORDIC LANDS LONG AGO.
MY FAMILY LINE CAN BE TRACED STRAIGHT BACK TO THE ANCIENT VIKINGS.
THIS MINOR CANTRIP HELPS TO PREVENT ACCIDENTS FROM BEFALLING THE CHILDREN.

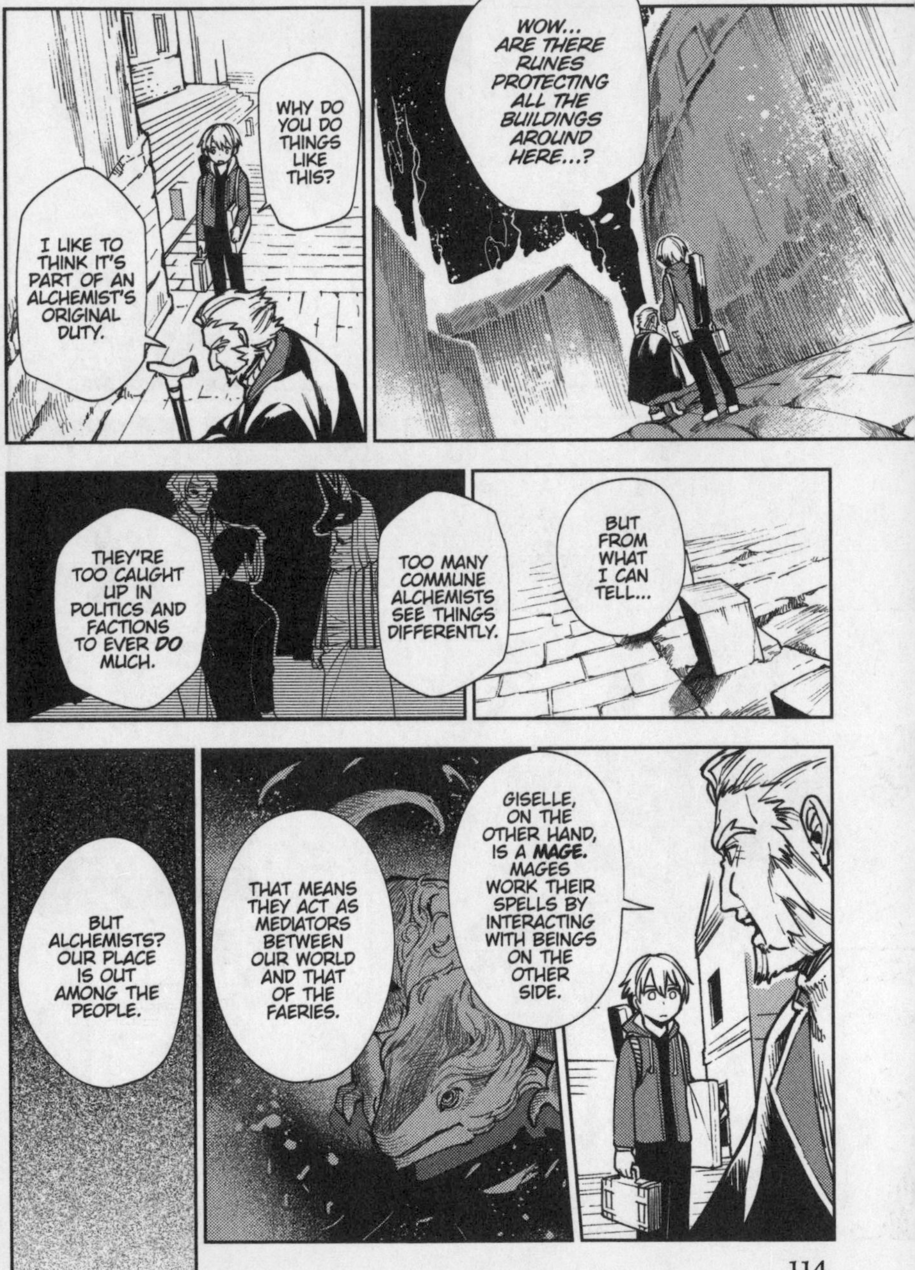
WOW... ARE THERE RUNES PROTECTING ALL THE BUILDINGS AROUND HERE...?
WHY DO YOU DO THINGS LIKE THIS?
I LIKE TO THINK IT'S PART OF AN ALCHEMIST'S ORIGINAL DUTY.
BUT FROM WHAT I CAN TELL...
TOO MANY COMMUNE ALCHEMISTS SEE THINGS DIFFERENTLY.
THEY'RE TOO CAUGHT UP IN POLITICS AND FACTIONS TO EVER DO MUCH.
GISELLE, ON THE OTHER HAND, IS A MAGE. MAGES WORK THEIR SPELLS BY INTERACTING WITH BEINGS ON THE OTHER SIDE.
THAT MEANS THEY ACT AS MEDIATORS BETWEEN OUR WORLD AND THAT OF THE FAERIES.
BUT ALCHEMISTS? OUR PLACE IS OUT AMONG THE PEOPLE.

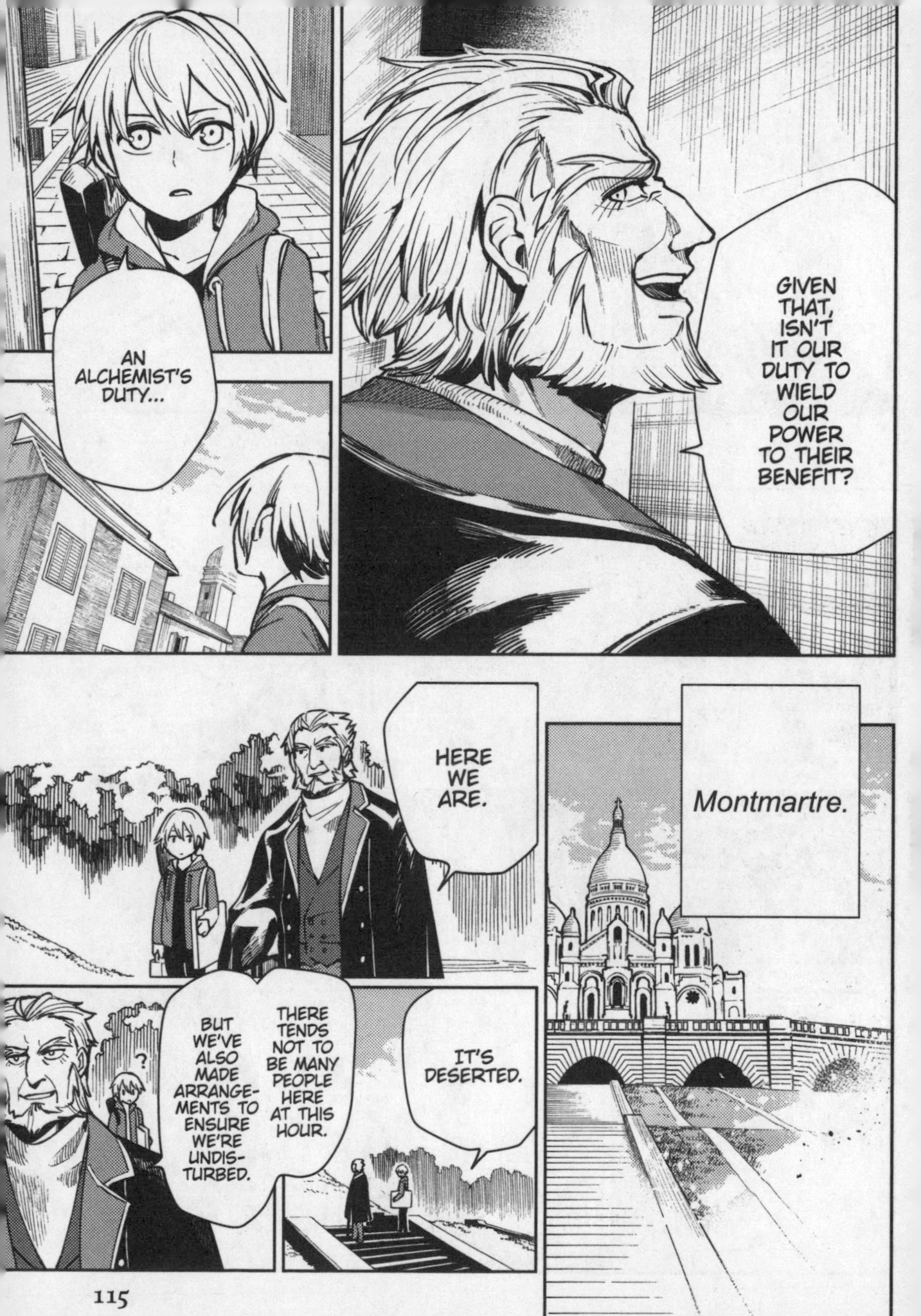
GIVEN THAT, ISN'T IT OUR DUTY TO WIELD OUR POWER TO THEIR BENEFIT?
AN ALCHEMIST'S DUTY...
Montmartre.
HERE WE ARE.
IT'S DESERTED.
THERE TENDS NOT TO BE MANY PEOPLE HERE AT THIS HOUR.
BUT WE'VE ALSO MADE ARRANGEMENTS TO ENSURE WE'RE UNDISTURBED.
?

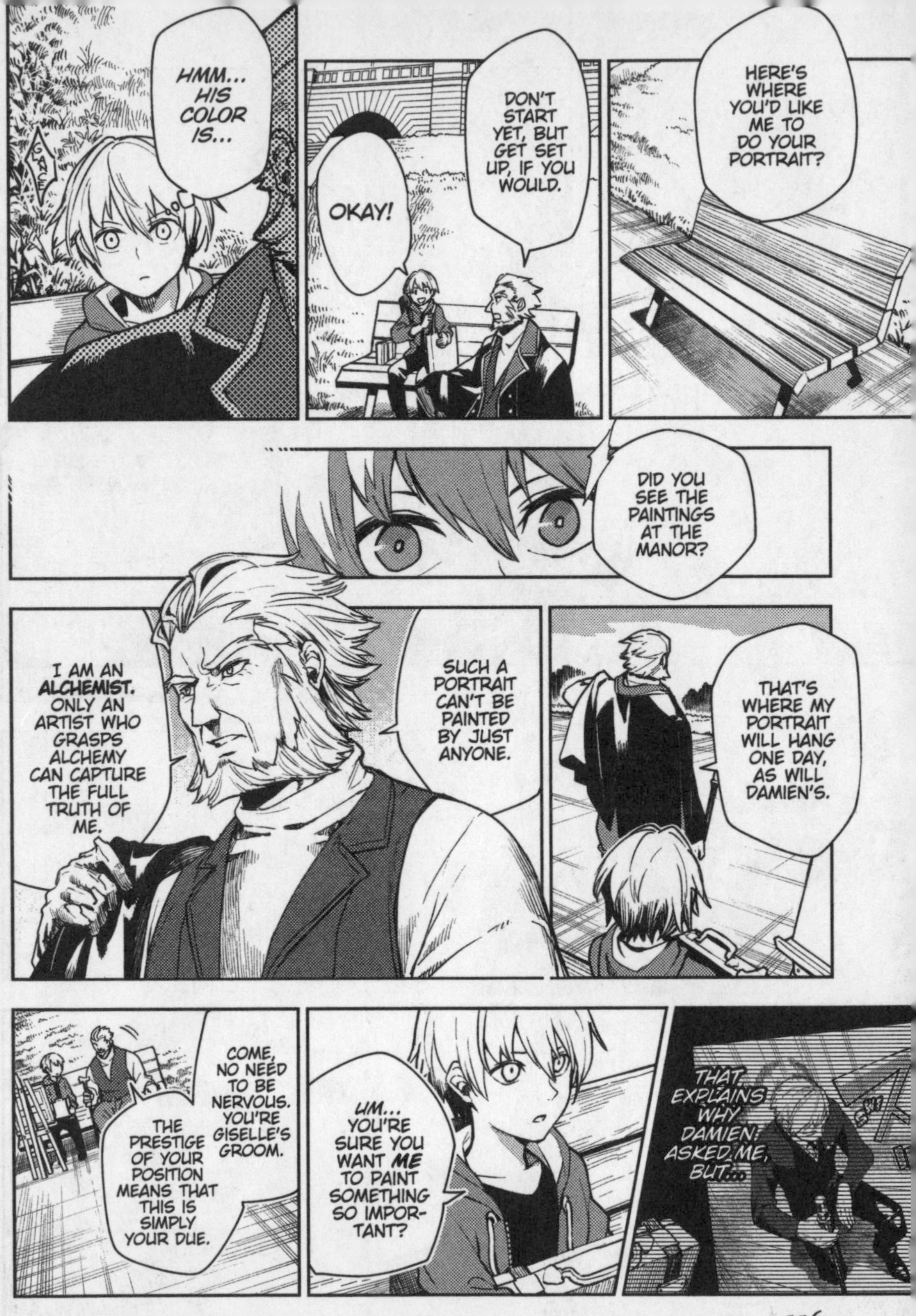
HERE'S WHERE YOU'D LIKE ME TO DO YOUR PORTRAIT?
DON'T START YET, BUT GET SET UP, IF YOU WOULD.
OKAY!
HMM... HIS COLOR IS...
GLANCE
DID YOU SEE THE PAINTINGS AT THE MANOR?
THAT'S WHERE MY PORTRAIT WILL HANG ONE DAY, AS WILL DAMIEN'S.
SUCH A PORTRAIT CAN'T BE PAINTED BY JUST ANYONE.
I AM AN **ALCHEMIST.** ONLY AN ARTIST WHO GRASPS ALCHEMY CAN CAPTURE THE FULL TRUTH OF ME.
THAT EXPLAINS WHY DAMIEN ASKED ME, BUT...
UM... YOU'RE SURE YOU WANT *ME* TO PAINT SOMETHING SO IMPORTANT?
COME, NO NEED TO BE NERVOUS. YOU'RE GISELLE'S GROOM.
THE PRESTIGE OF YOUR POSITION MEANS THAT THIS IS SIMPLY YOUR DUE.

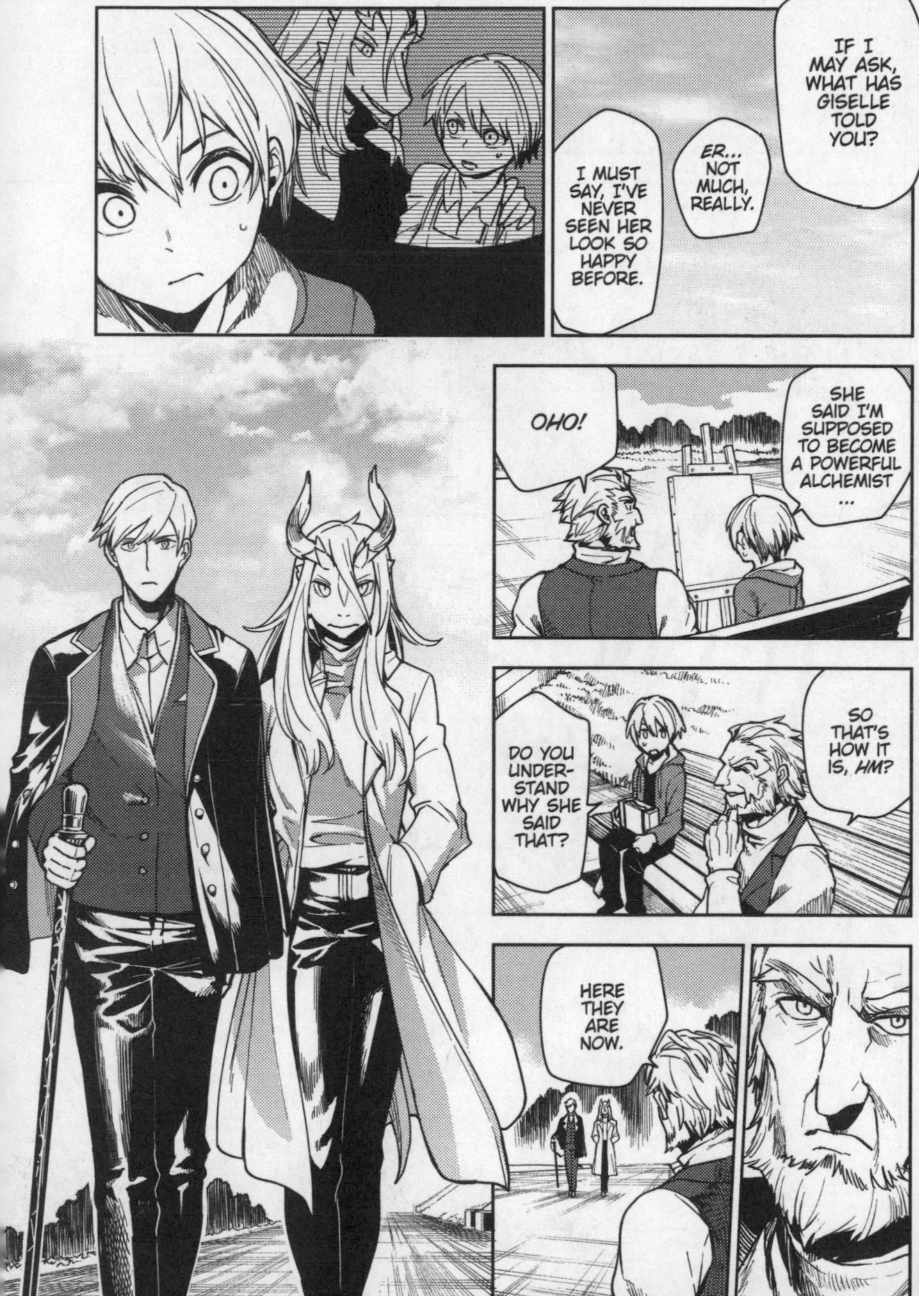
IF I MAY ASK, WHAT HAS GISELLE TOLD YOU?
ER... NOT MUCH, REALLY.
I MUST SAY, I'VE NEVER SEEN HER LOOK SO HAPPY BEFORE.
SHE SAID I'M SUPPOSED TO BECOME A POWERFUL ALCHEMIST...
OHO!
SO THAT'S HOW IT IS, HM?
DO YOU UNDERSTAND WHY SHE SAID THAT?
HERE THEY ARE NOW.

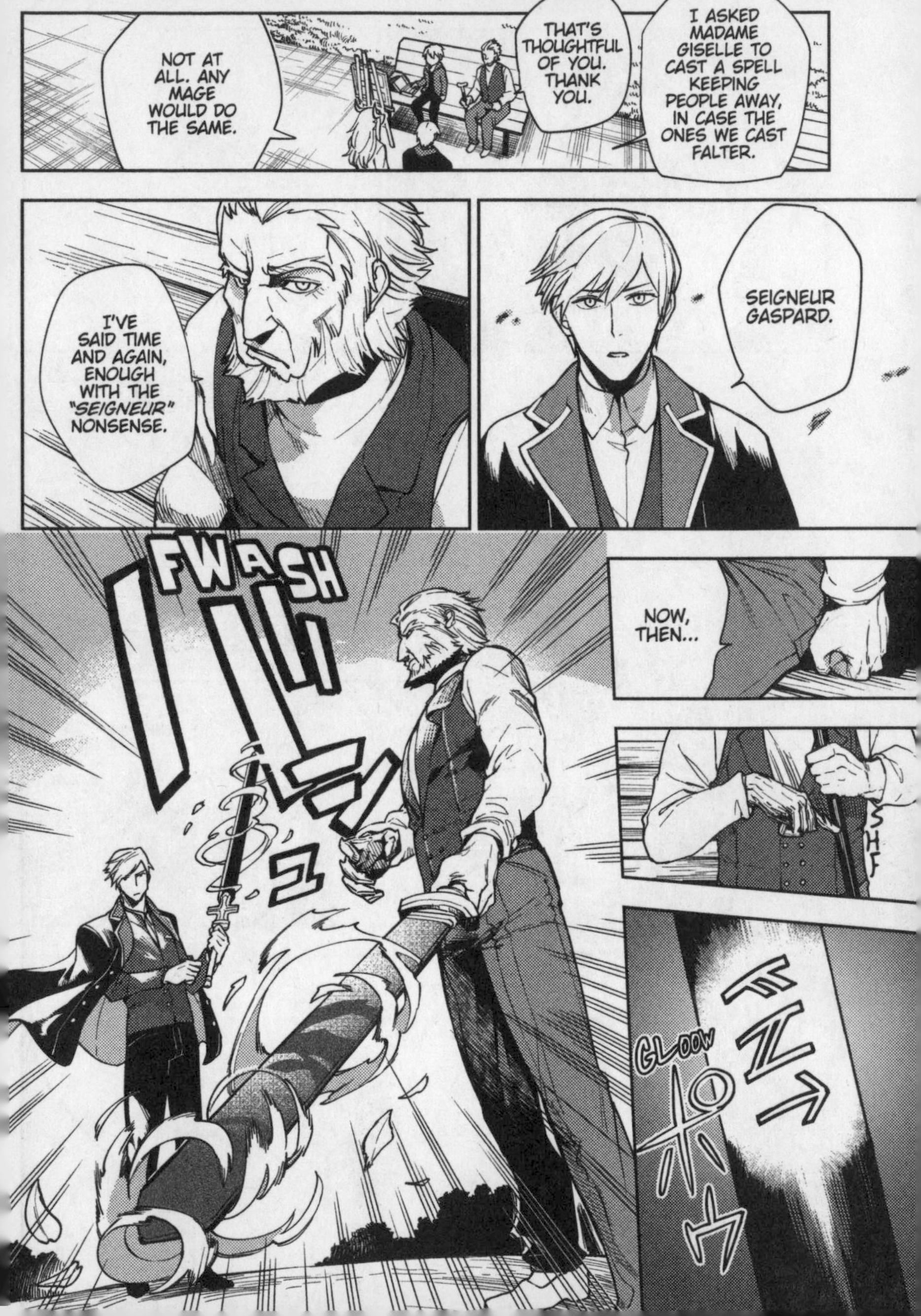
I ASKED MADAME GISELLE TO CAST A SPELL KEEPING PEOPLE AWAY, IN CASE THE ONES WE CAST FALTER.
THAT'S THOUGHTFUL OF YOU. THANK YOU.
NOT AT ALL. ANY MAGE WOULD DO THE SAME.
SEIGNEUR GASPARD.
I'VE SAID TIME AND AGAIN, ENOUGH WITH THE "SEIGNEUR" NONSENSE.
NOW, THEN...
SHF
GLOOW
FWASH

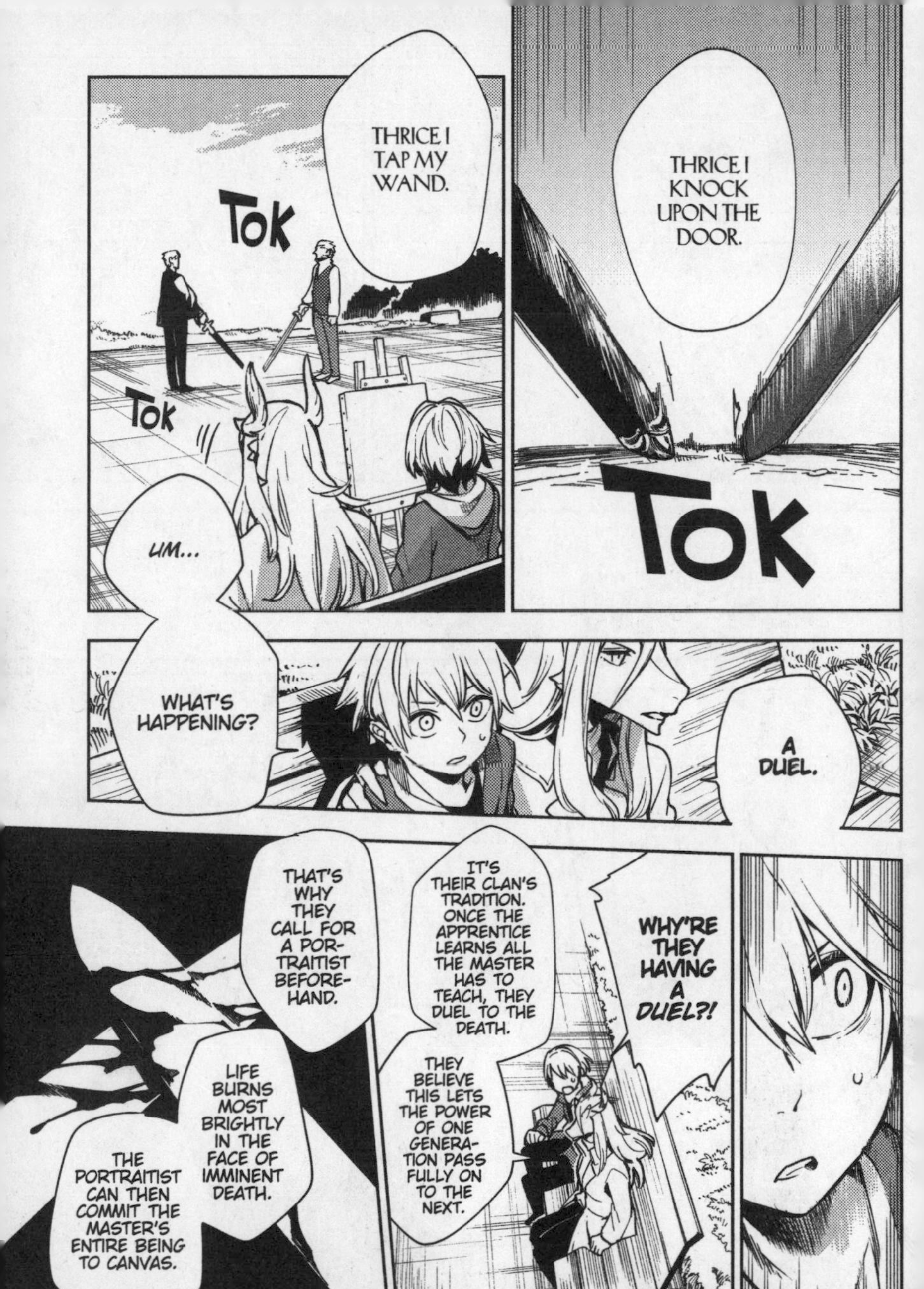
THRICE I KNOCK UPON THE DOOR.
TOK
THRICE I TAP MY WAND.
TOK
TOK
UM...
WHAT'S HAPPENING?
A DUEL.
WHY'RE THEY HAVING A DUEL?!
IT'S THEIR CLAN'S TRADITION. ONCE THE APPRENTICE LEARNS ALL THE MASTER HAS TO TEACH, THEY DUEL TO THE DEATH.
THEY BELIEVE THIS LETS THE POWER OF ONE GENERATION PASS FULLY ON TO THE NEXT.
THAT'S WHY THEY CALL FOR A PORTRAITIST BEFOREHAND.
LIFE BURNS MOST BRIGHTLY IN THE FACE OF IMMINENT DEATH.
THE PORTRAITIST CAN THEN COMMIT THE MASTER'S ENTIRE BEING TO CANVAS.

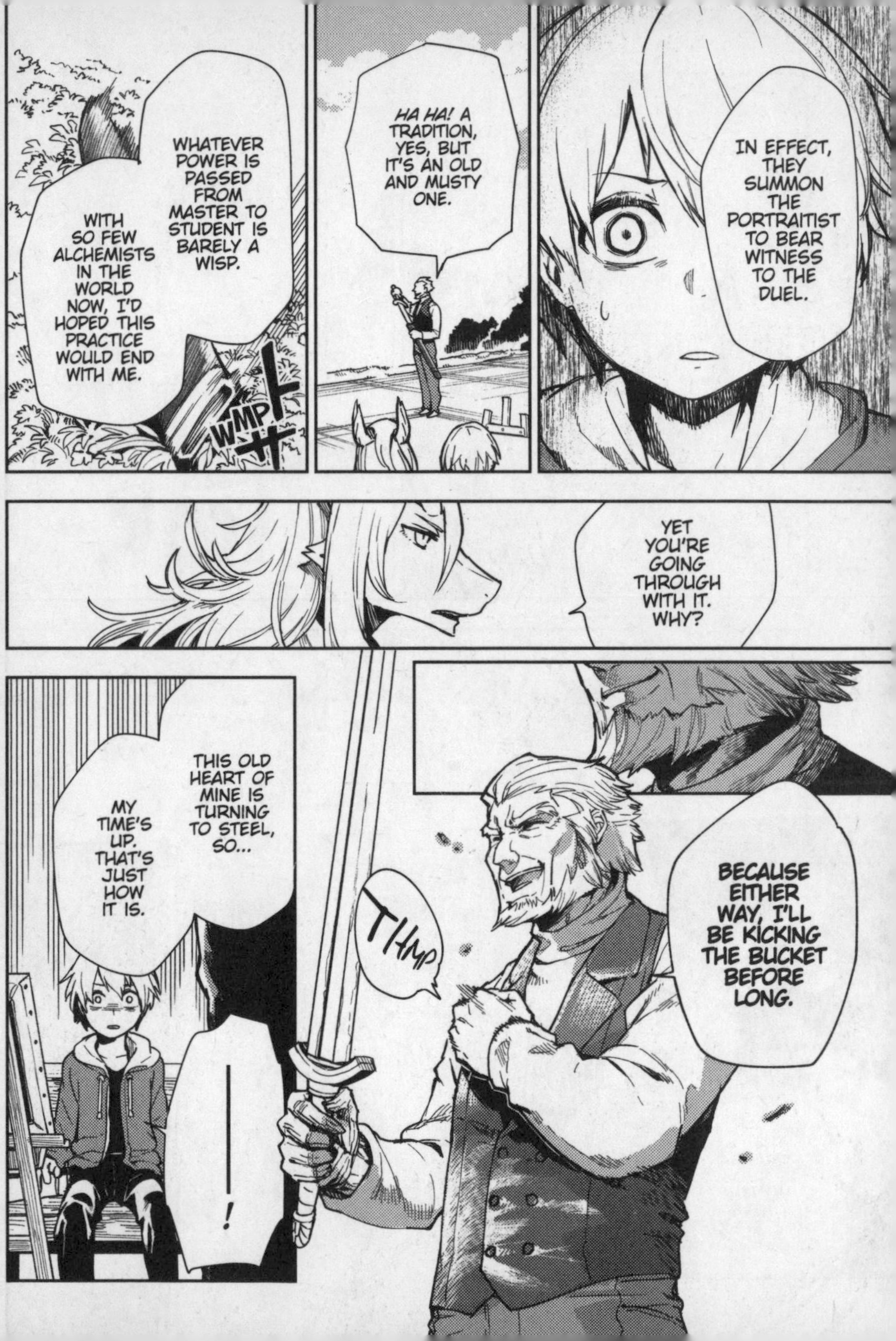
IN EFFECT, THEY SUMMON THE PORTRAITIST TO BEAR WITNESS TO THE DUEL.
HA HA! A TRADITION, YES, BUT IT'S AN OLD AND MUSTY ONE.
WHATEVER POWER IS PASSED FROM MASTER TO STUDENT IS BARELY A WISP.
WITH SO FEW ALCHEMISTS IN THE WORLD NOW, I'D HOPED THIS PRACTICE WOULD END WITH ME.
WMP
YET YOU'RE GOING THROUGH WITH IT. WHY?
BECAUSE EITHER WAY, I'LL BE KICKING THE BUCKET BEFORE LONG.
THMP
THIS OLD HEART OF MINE IS TURNING TO STEEL, SO...
MY TIME'S UP. THAT'S JUST HOW IT IS.
—!

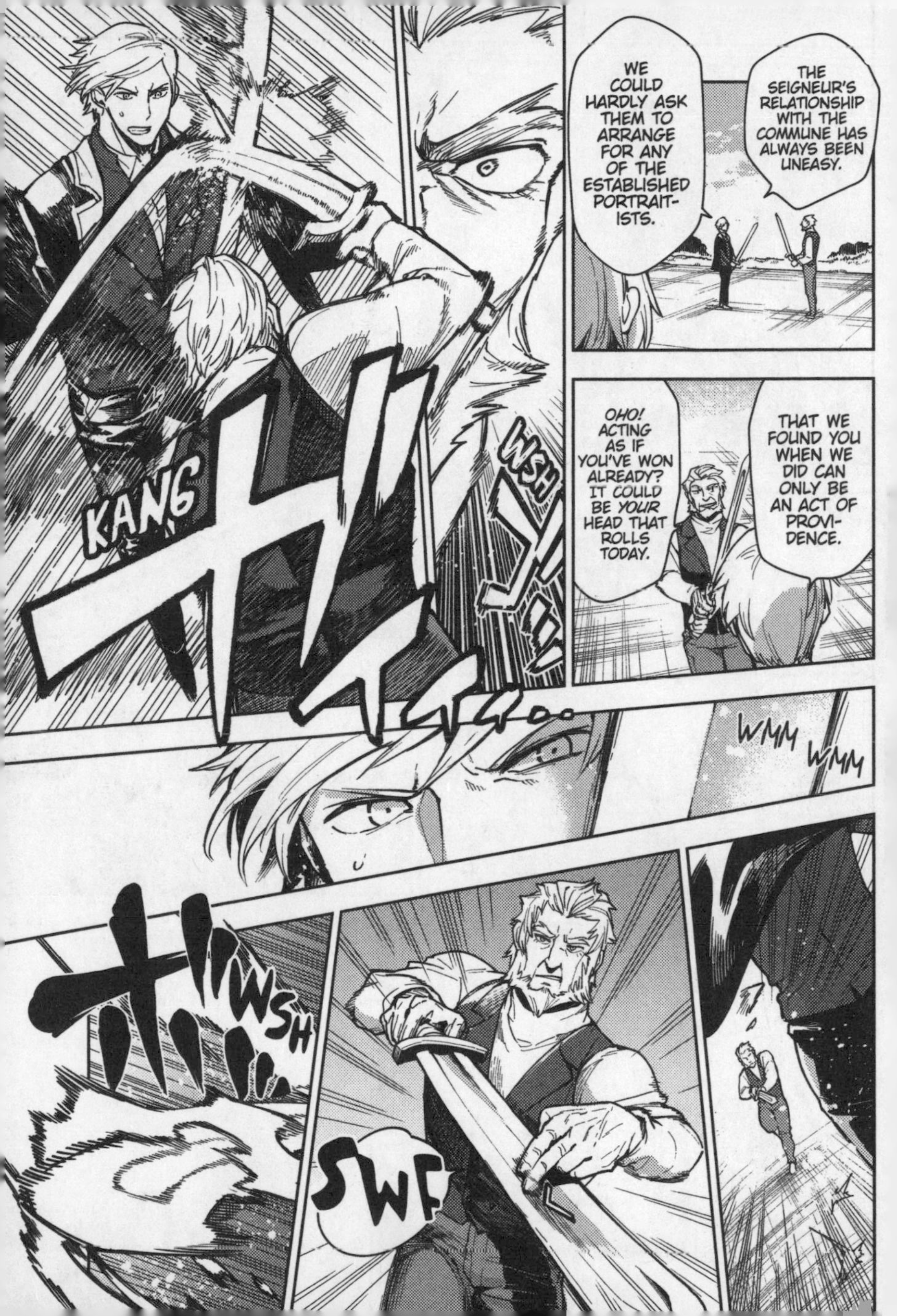
THE SEIGNEUR'S RELATIONSHIP WITH THE COMMUNE HAS ALWAYS BEEN UNEASY.
WE COULD HARDLY ASK THEM TO ARRANGE FOR ANY OF THE ESTABLISHED PORTRAIT-ISTS.
THAT WE FOUND YOU WHEN WE DID CAN ONLY BE AN ACT OF PROVI-DENCE.
OHO! ACTING AS IF YOU'VE WON ALREADY? IT COULD BE YOUR HEAD THAT ROLLS TODAY.
WSH
KANG
WMM WMM
SWF
WSH

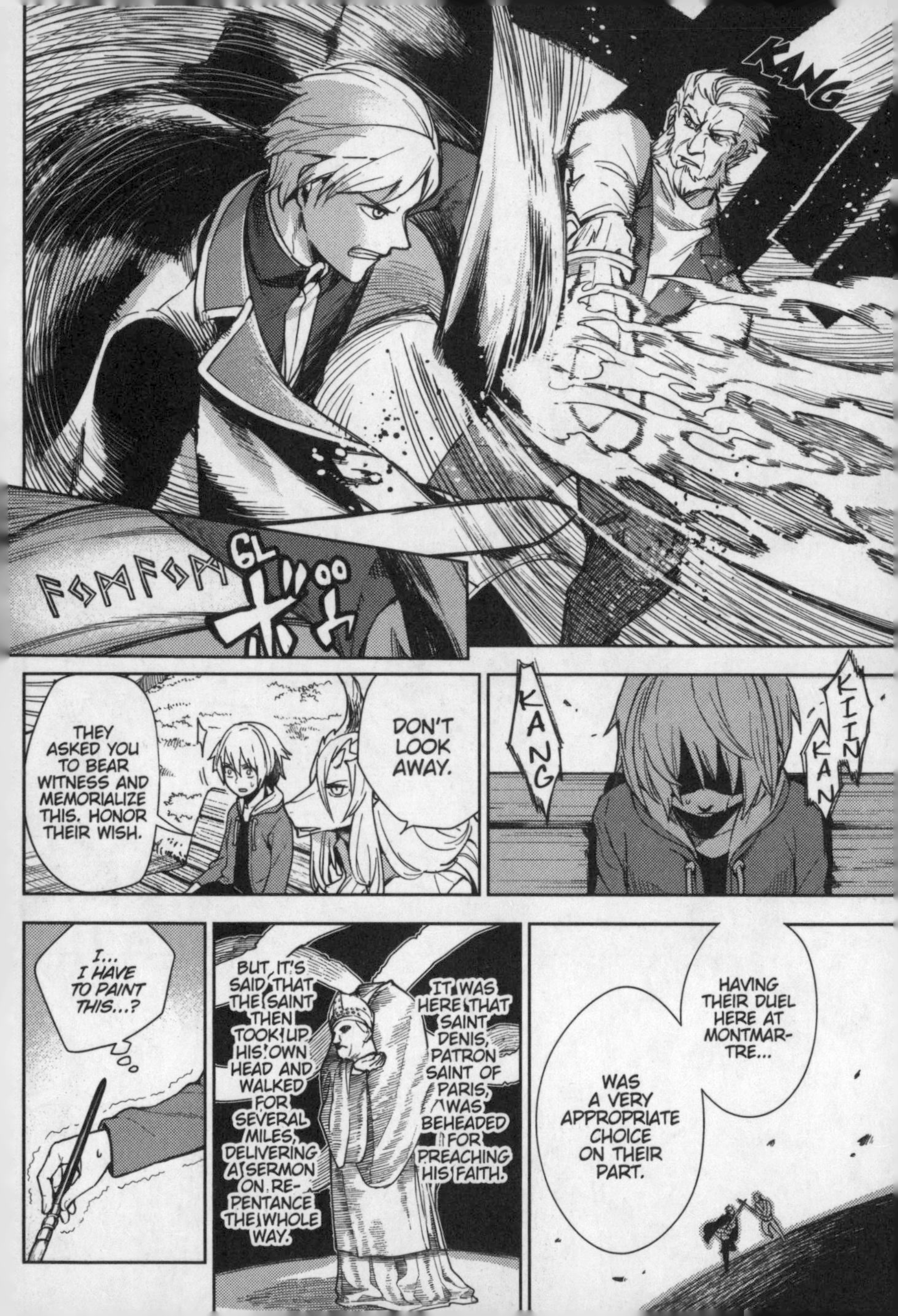
KANG
KIIIN
KAN
KAN
KANG
DON'T LOOK AWAY.
THEY ASKED YOU TO BEAR WITNESS AND MEMORIALIZE THIS. HONOR THEIR WISH.
HAVING THEIR DUEL HERE AT MONTMARTRE...
WAS A VERY APPROPRIATE CHOICE ON THEIR PART.
IT WAS HERE THAT SAINT DENIS, PATRON SAINT OF PARIS, WAS BEHEADED FOR PREACHING HIS FAITH.
BUT, IT'S SAID THAT THE SAINT THEN TOOK UP HIS OWN HEAD AND WALKED FOR SEVERAL MILES, DELIVERING A SERMON ON REPENTANCE THE WHOLE WAY.
I... I HAVE TO PAINT THIS...?

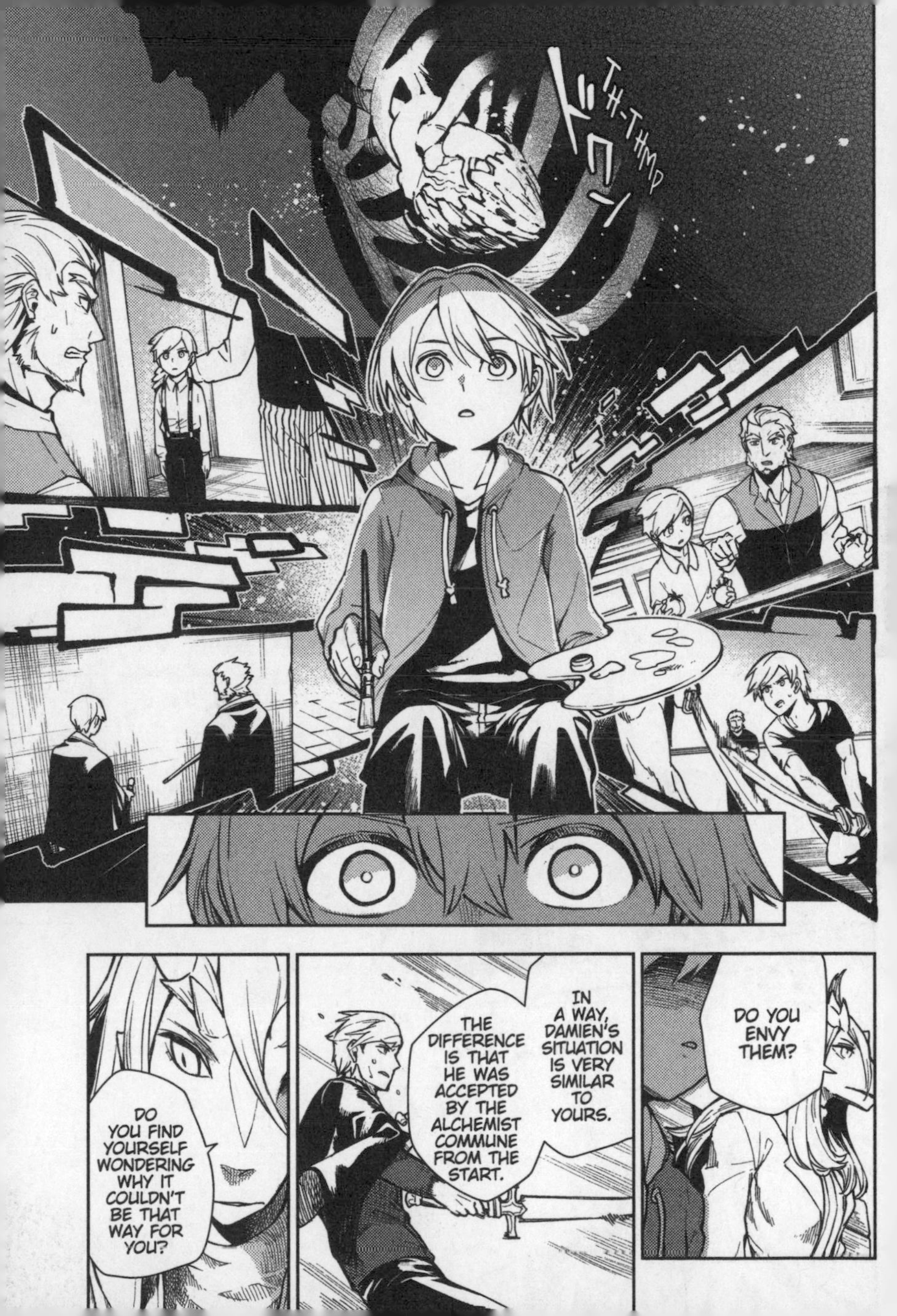
TH-THMP
DO YOU ENVY THEM?
IN A WAY, DAMIEN'S SITUATION IS VERY SIMILAR TO YOURS.
THE DIFFERENCE IS THAT HE WAS ACCEPTED BY THE ALCHEMIST COMMUNE FROM THE START.
DO YOU FIND YOURSELF WONDERING WHY IT COULDN'T BE THAT WAY FOR YOU?

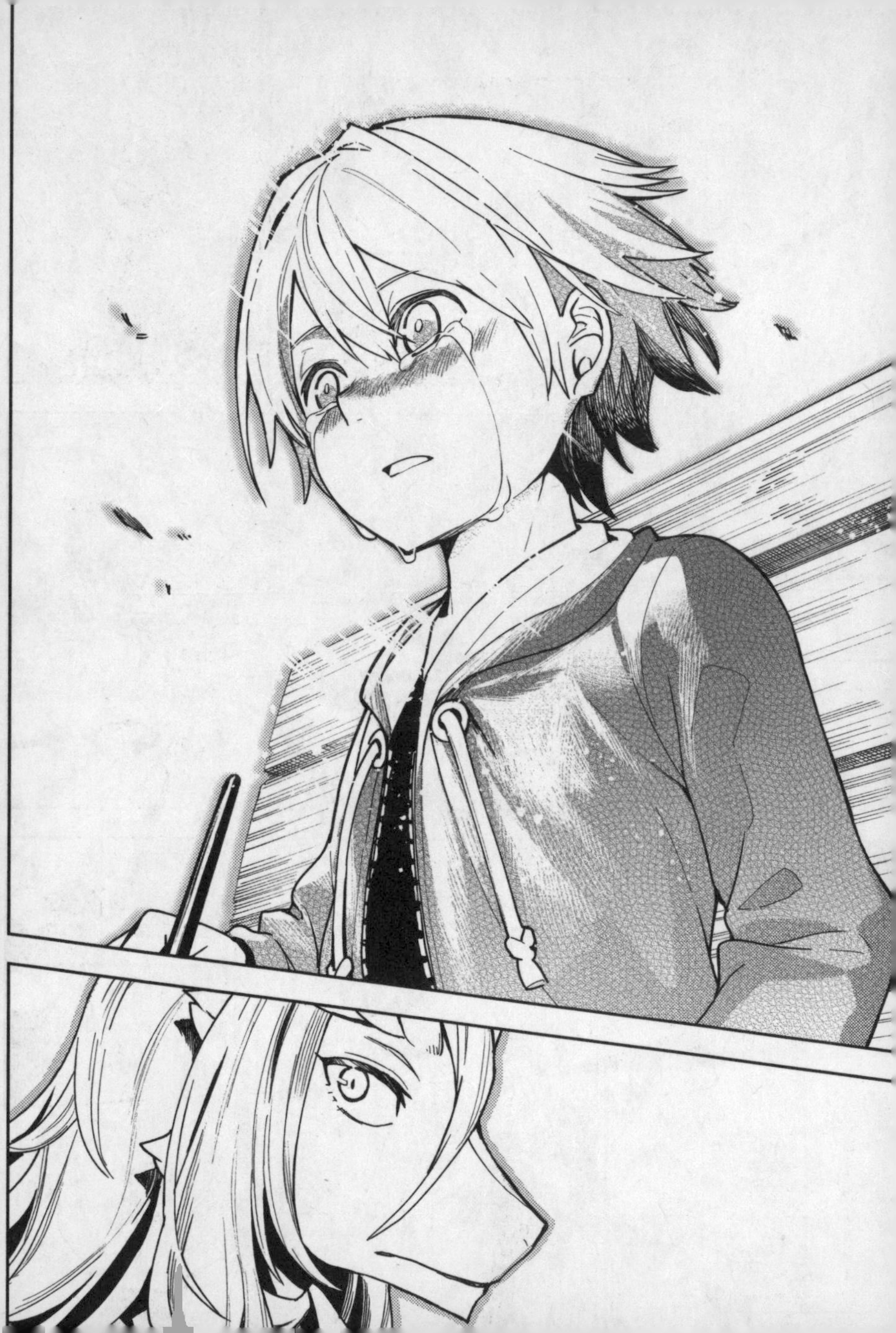

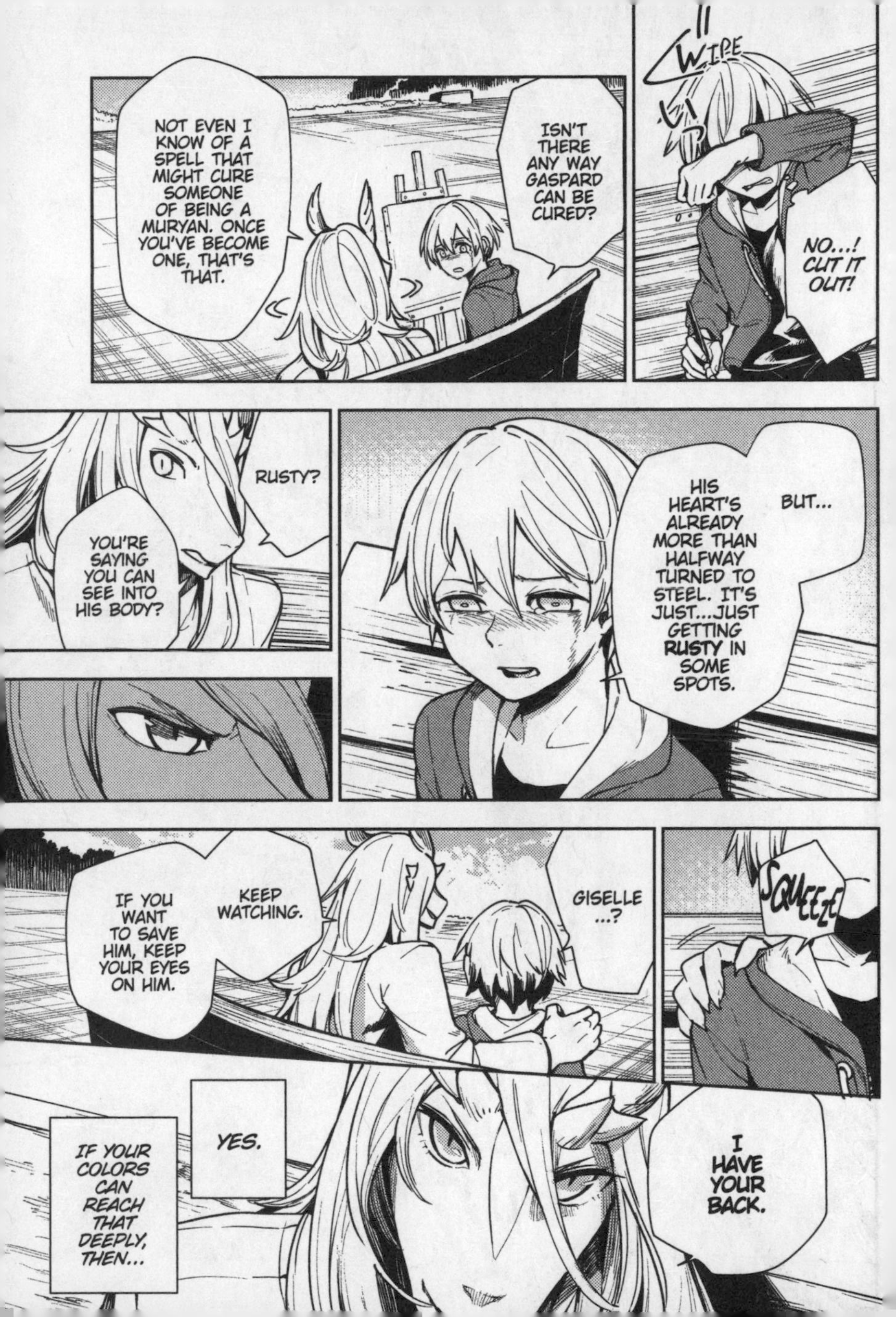
WIPE
NO...! CUT IT OUT!
ISN'T THERE ANY WAY GASPARD CAN BE CURED?
NOT EVEN I KNOW OF A SPELL THAT MIGHT CURE SOMEONE OF BEING A MURYAN. ONCE YOU'VE BECOME ONE, THAT'S THAT.
BUT...
HIS HEART'S ALREADY MORE THAN HALFWAY TURNED TO STEEL. IT'S JUST...JUST GETTING RUSTY IN SOME SPOTS.
RUSTY?
YOU'RE SAYING YOU CAN SEE INTO HIS BODY?
SQUEEZE
GISELLE ...?
KEEP WATCHING.
IF YOU WANT TO SAVE HIM, KEEP YOUR EYES ON HIM.
I HAVE YOUR BACK.
YES.
IF YOUR COLORS CAN REACH THAT DEEPLY, THEN...

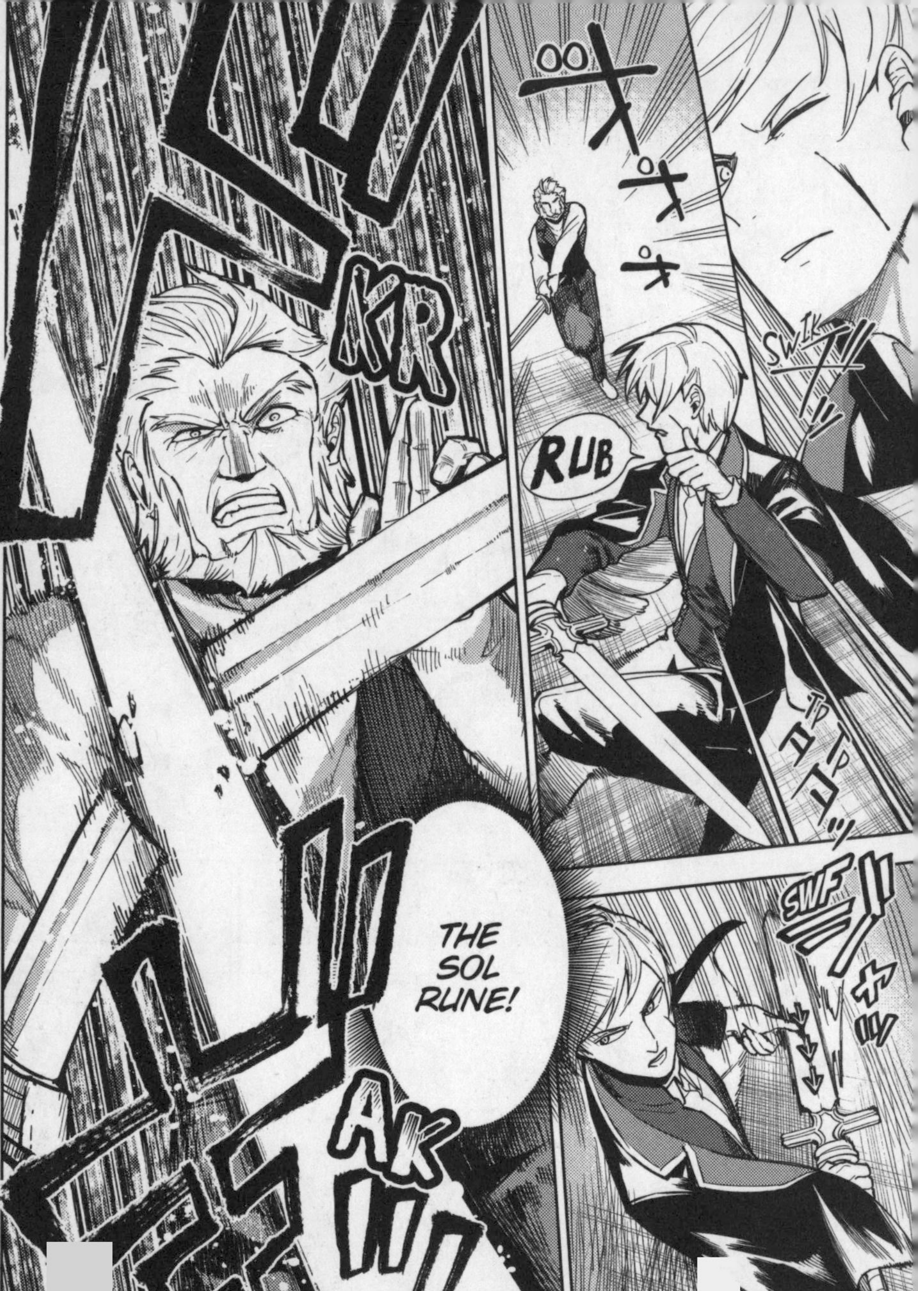
SWIK
RUB
TP TP
SWF
KR
THE SOL RUNE!
AK

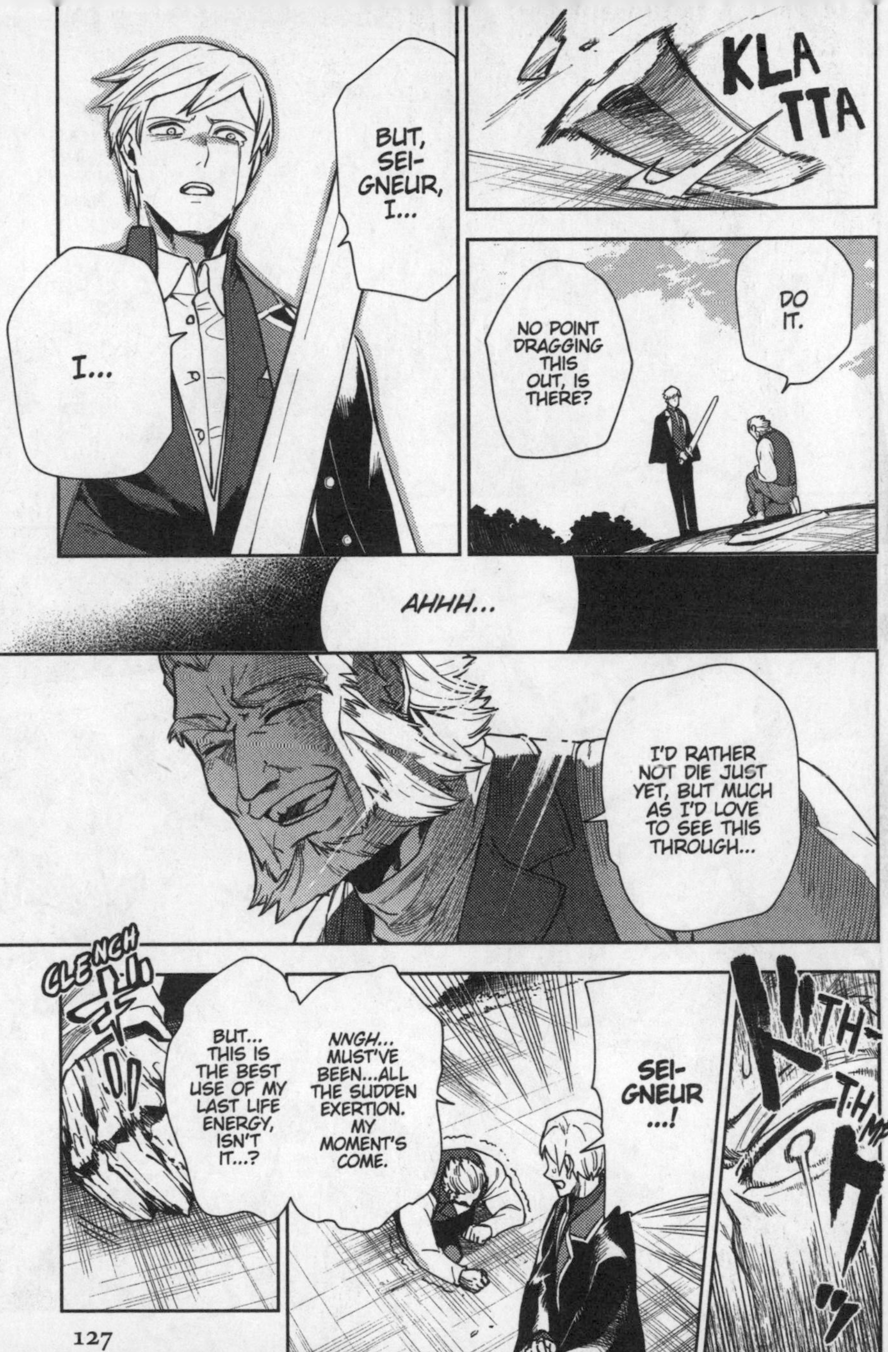
KLA TTA
DO IT.
NO POINT DRAGGING THIS OUT, IS THERE?
BUT, SEI-GNEUR, I...
I...
AHHH...
I'D RATHER NOT DIE JUST YET, BUT MUCH AS I'D LOVE TO SEE THIS THROUGH...
SEI-GNEUR...!
NNGH... MUST'VE BEEN...ALL THE SUDDEN EXERTION. MY MOMENT'S COME.
BUT... THIS IS THE BEST USE OF MY LAST LIFE ENERGY, ISN'T IT...?
CLENCH

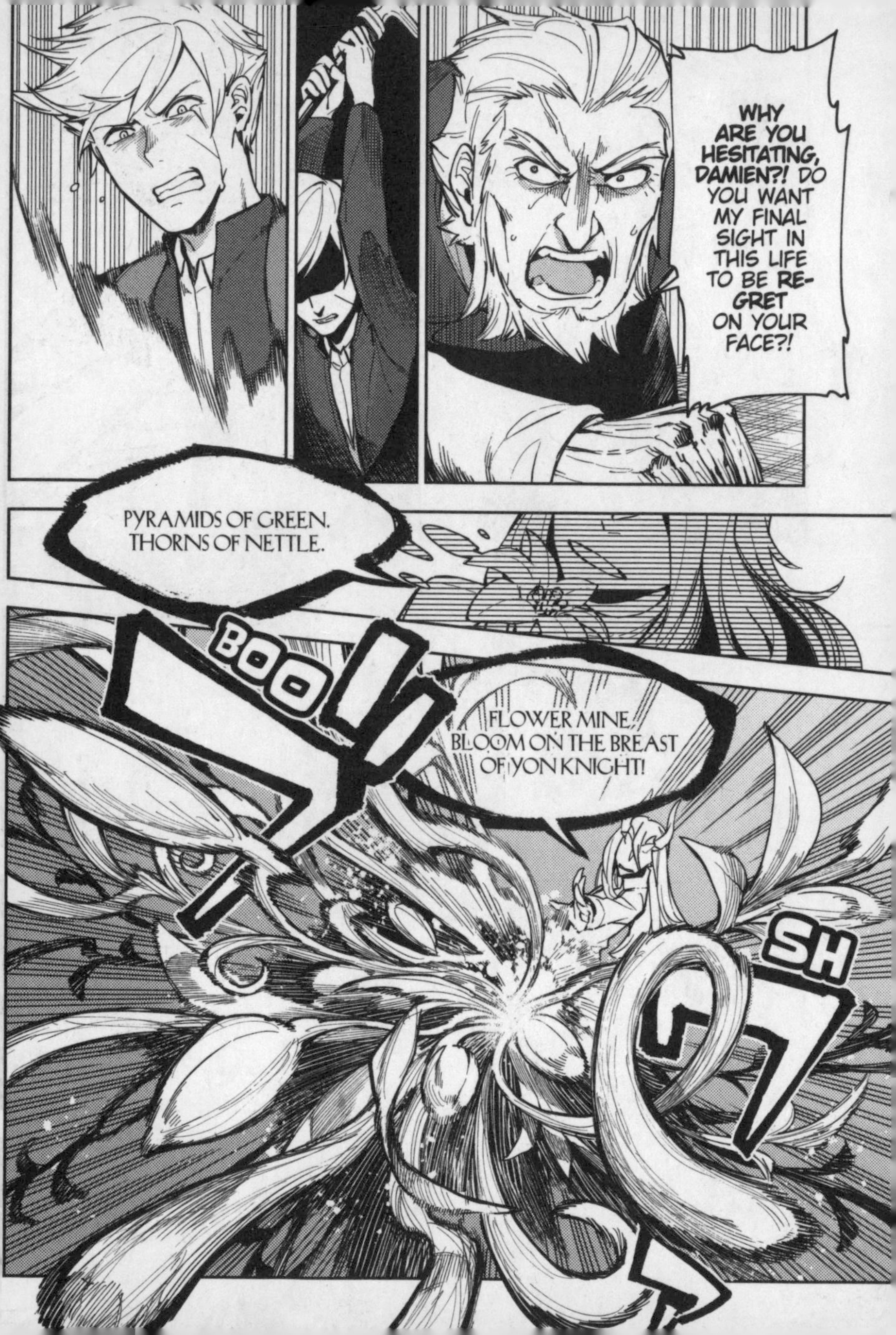
WHY ARE YOU HESITATING, DAMIEN?! DO YOU WANT MY FINAL SIGHT IN THIS LIFE TO BE RE-GRET ON YOUR FACE?!
PYRAMIDS OF GREEN. THORNS OF NETTLE.
BOOM
FLOWER MINE, BLOOM ON THE BREAST OF YON KNIGHT!
SHOO

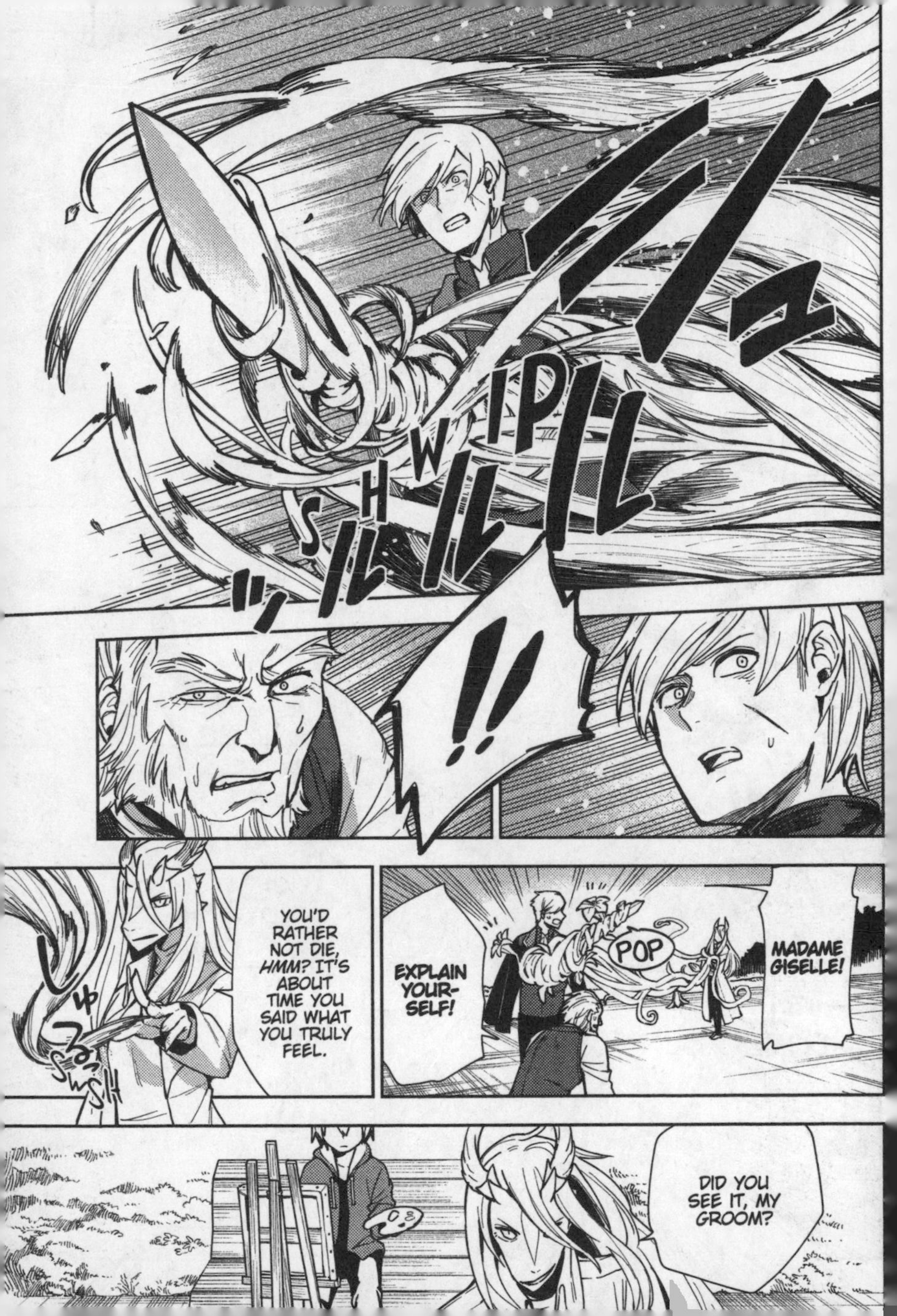
SHWIP
!!
MADAME GISELLE!
POP
EXPLAIN YOURSELF!
YOU'D RATHER NOT DIE, *HMM*? IT'S ABOUT TIME YOU SAID WHAT YOU TRULY FEEL.
SWISH
DID YOU SEE IT, MY GROOM?

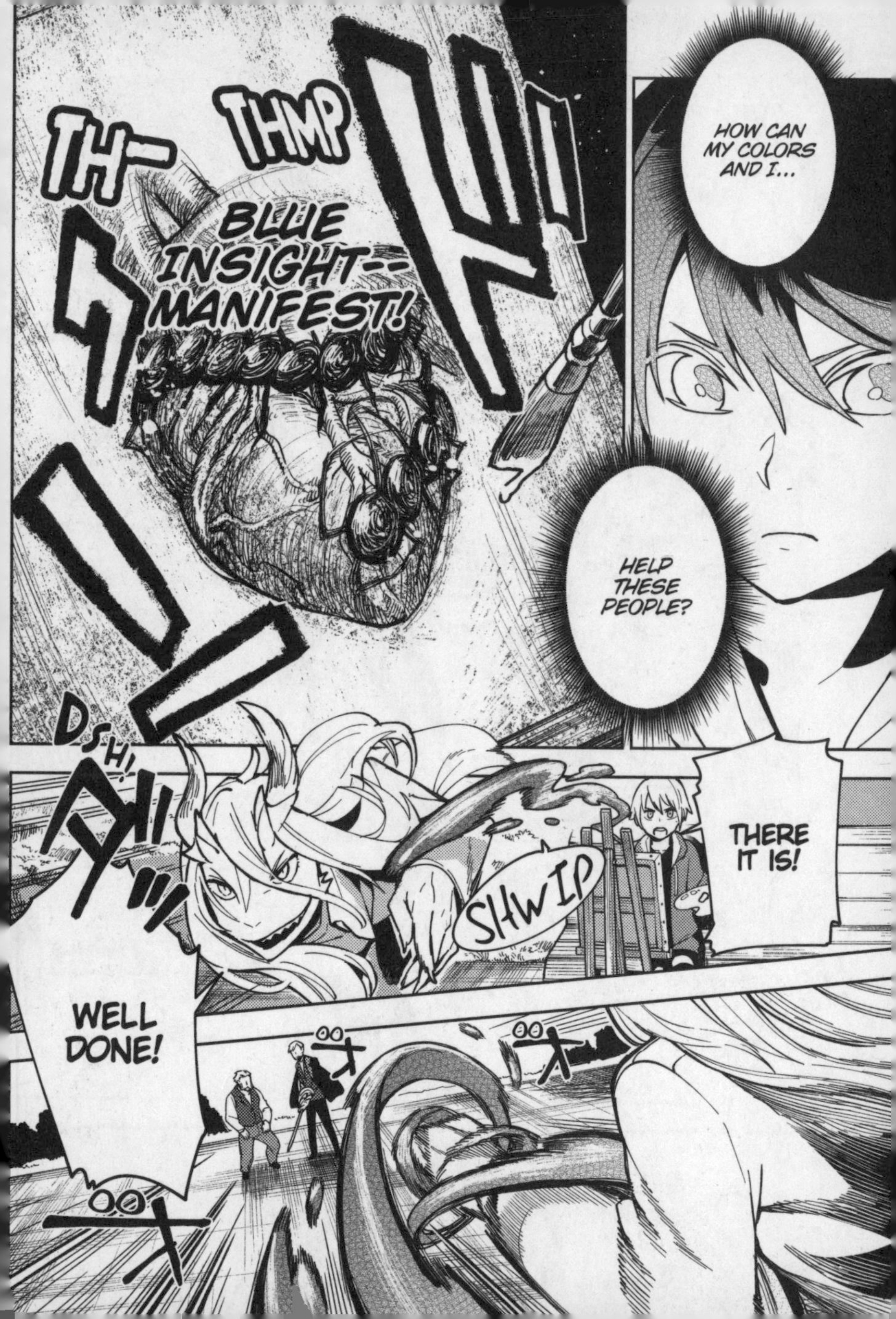

HOW CAN MY COLORS AND I...
HELP THESE PEOPLE?
TH- THMP
BLUE INSIGHT-- MANIFEST!
THERE IT IS!
SHWIP
DSHI
WELL DONE!

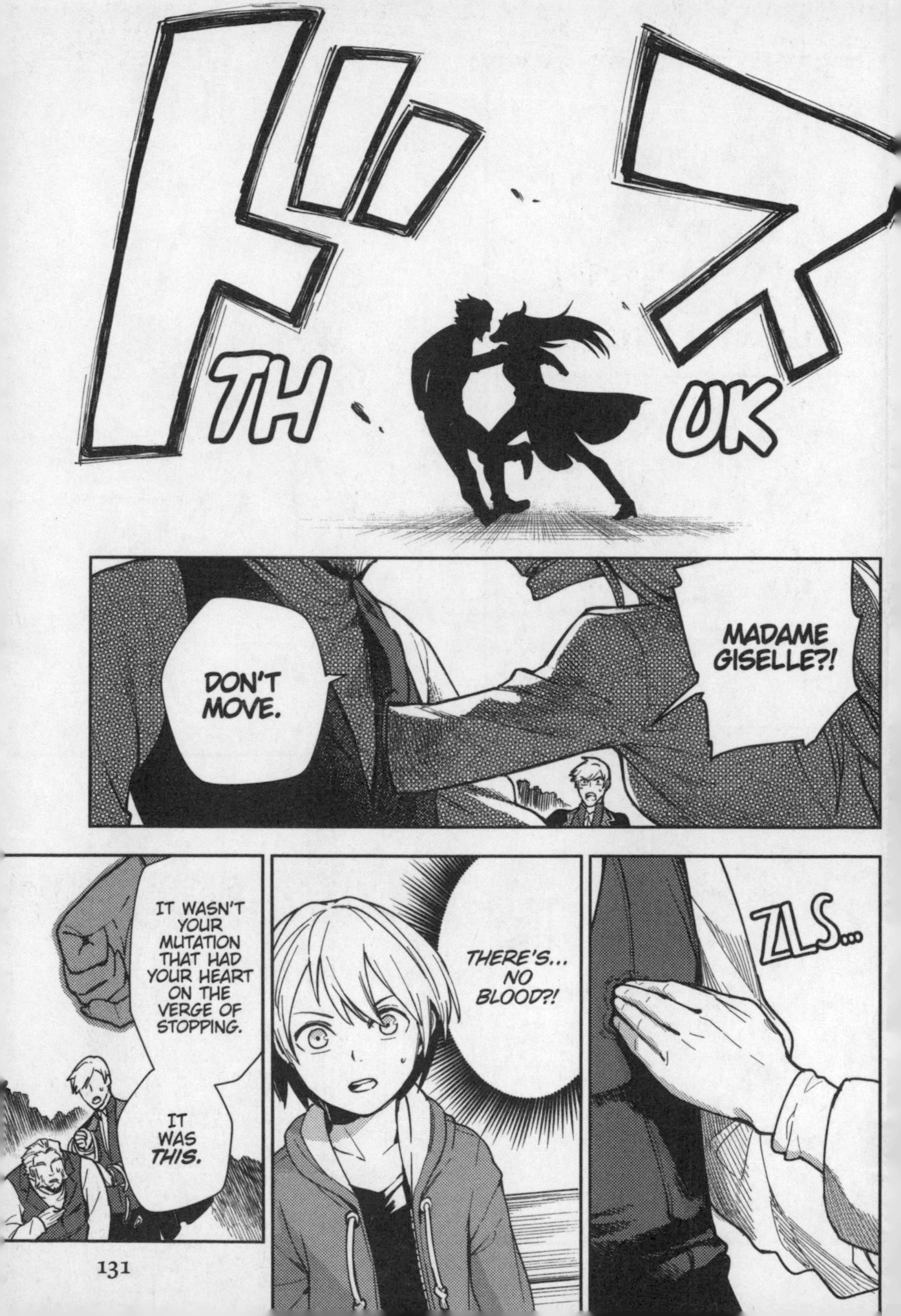
TH
UK
MADAME GISELLE?!
DON'T MOVE.
ZLS...
THERE'S... NO BLOOD?!
IT WASN'T YOUR MUTATION THAT HAD YOUR HEART ON THE VERGE OF STOPPING.
IT WAS *THIS.*

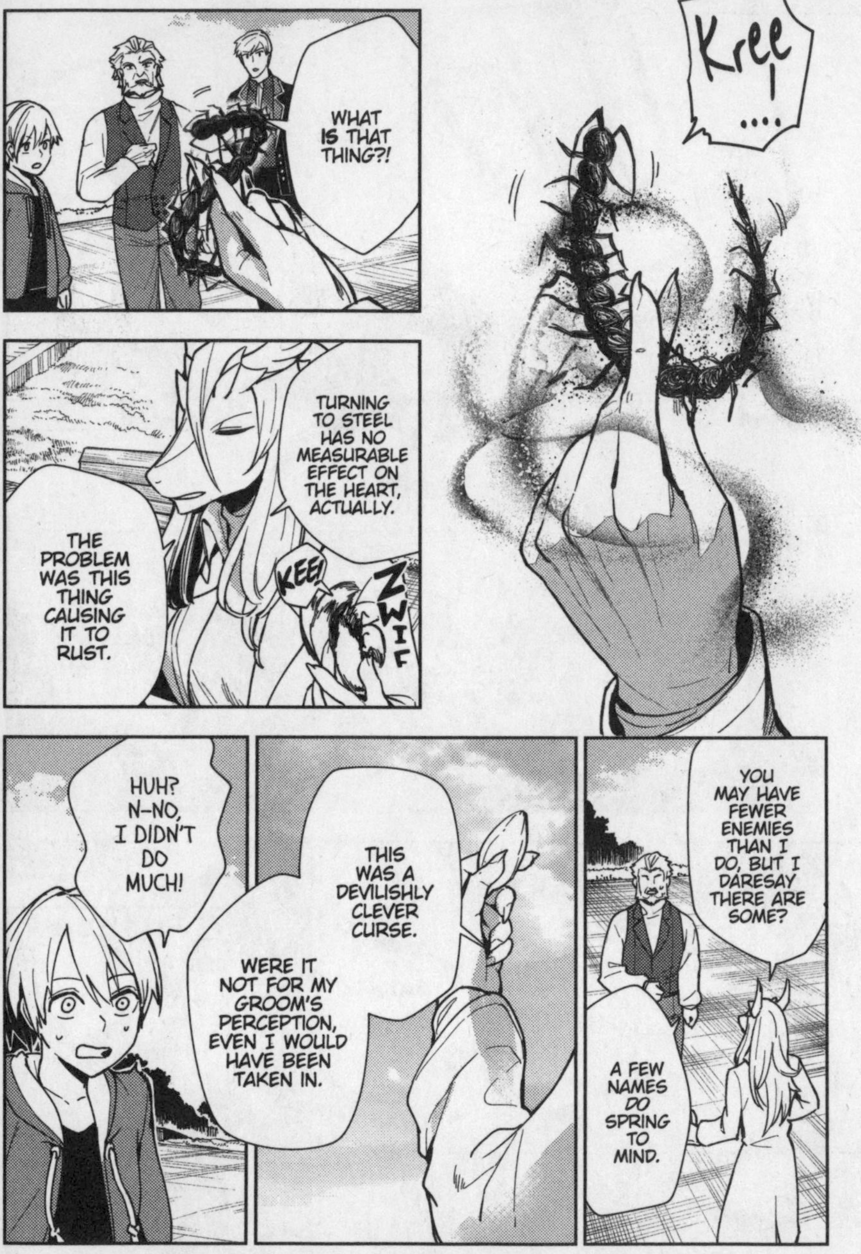
Kree....!
WHAT IS THAT THING?!
TURNING TO STEEL HAS NO MEASURABLE EFFECT ON THE HEART, ACTUALLY.
THE PROBLEM WAS THIS THING CAUSING IT TO RUST.
KEE!
ZWIF
YOU MAY HAVE FEWER ENEMIES THAN I DO, BUT I DARESAY THERE ARE SOME?
A FEW NAMES *DO* SPRING TO MIND.
THIS WAS A DEVILISHLY CLEVER CURSE.
WERE IT NOT FOR MY GROOM'S PERCEPTION, EVEN I WOULD HAVE BEEN TAKEN IN.
HUH? N-NO, I DIDN'T DO MUCH!

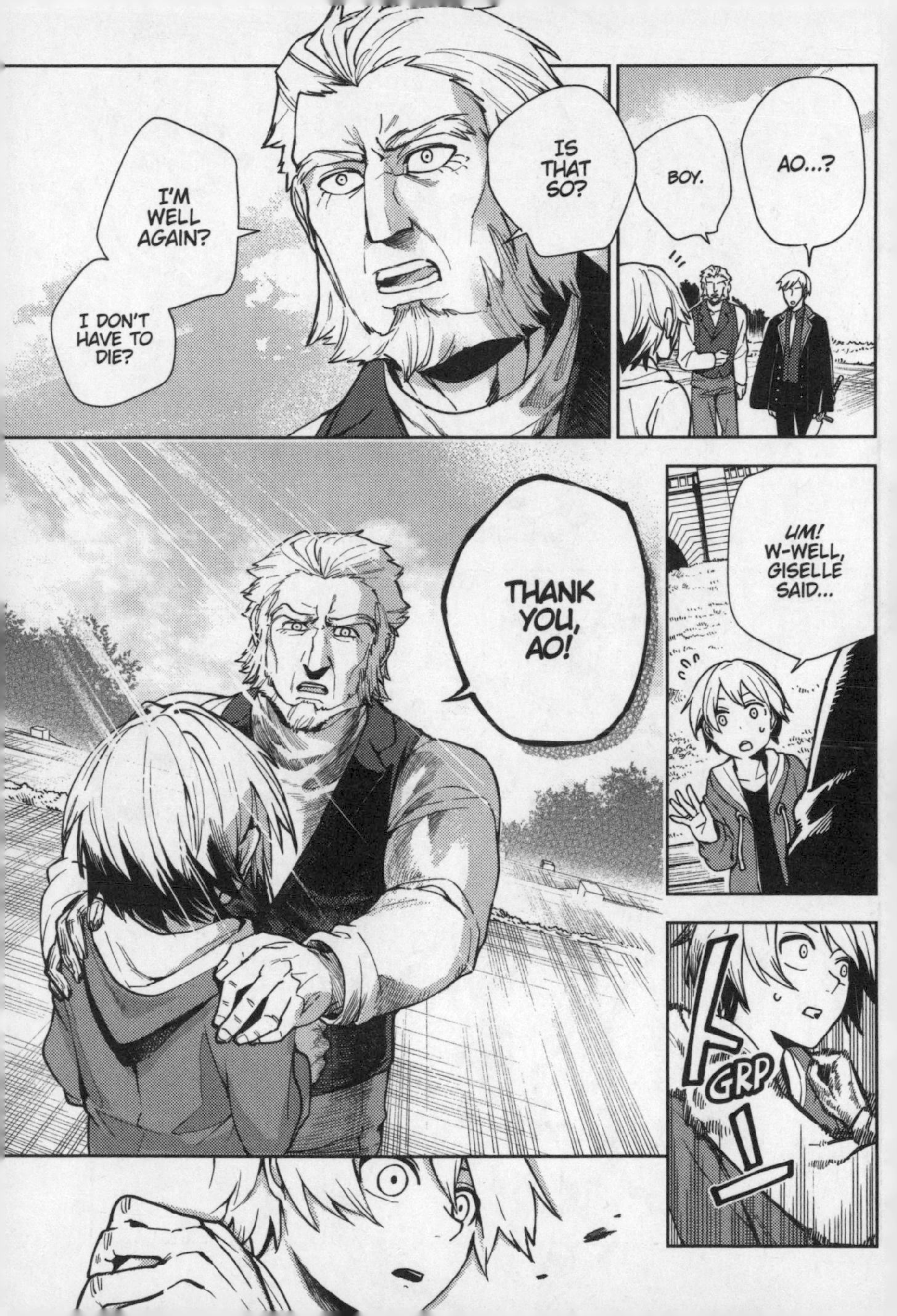
AO...?
BOY.
IS THAT SO?
I'M WELL AGAIN?
I DON'T HAVE TO DIE?
UM! W-WELL, GISELLE SAID...
GRP
THANK YOU, AO!

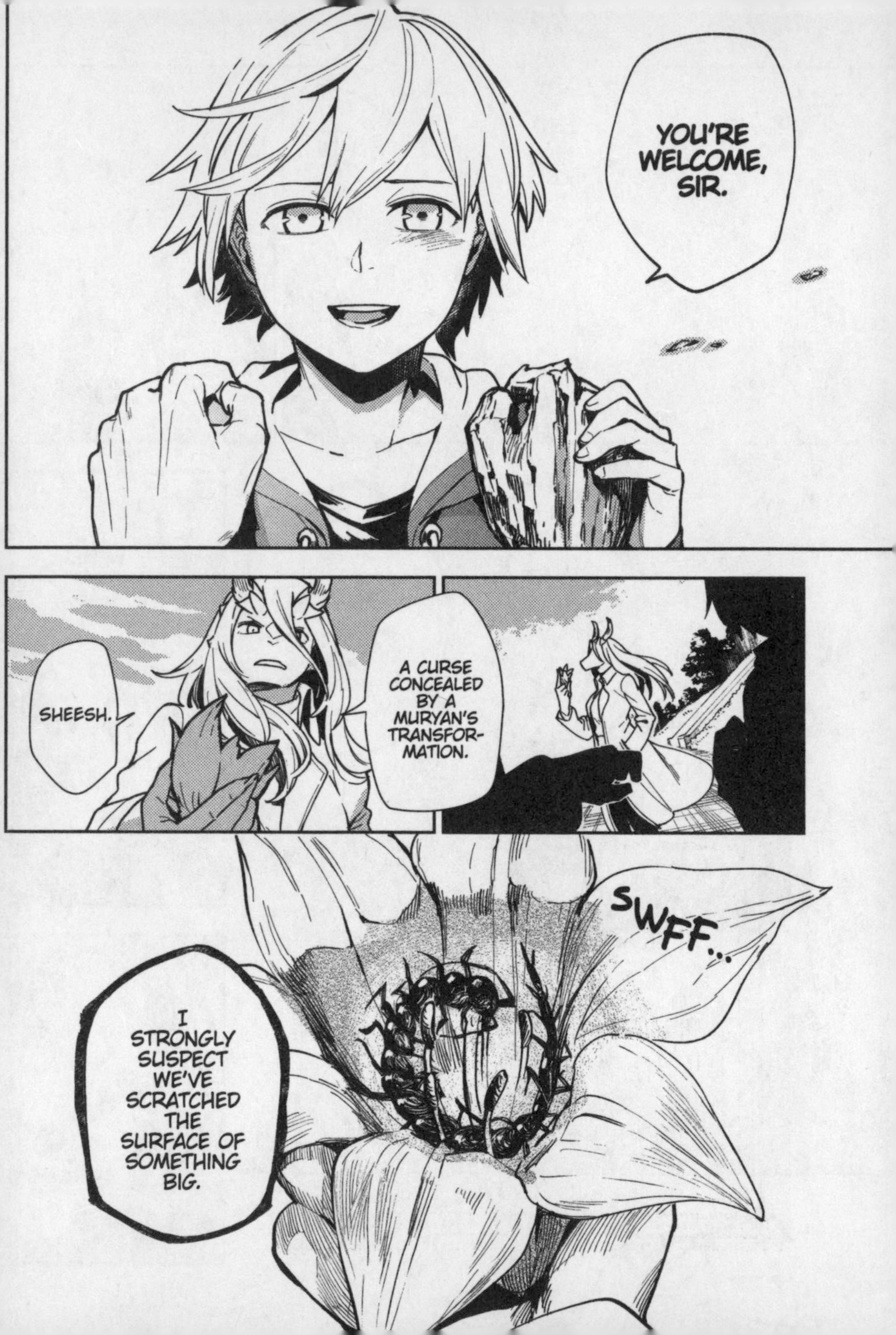
YOU'RE WELCOME, SIR.
A CURSE CONCEALED BY A MURYAN'S TRANSFORMATION.
SHEESH.
SWFF...
I STRONGLY SUSPECT WE'VE SCRATCHED THE SURFACE OF SOMETHING BIG.

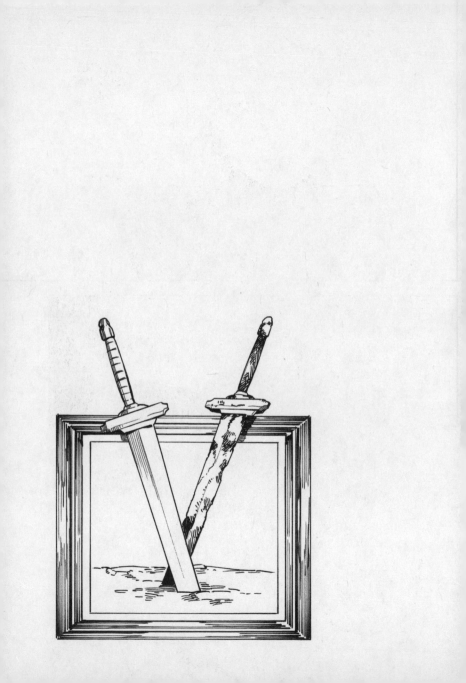

The Ancient Magus' Bride

WIZARD's BLUE

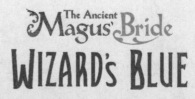

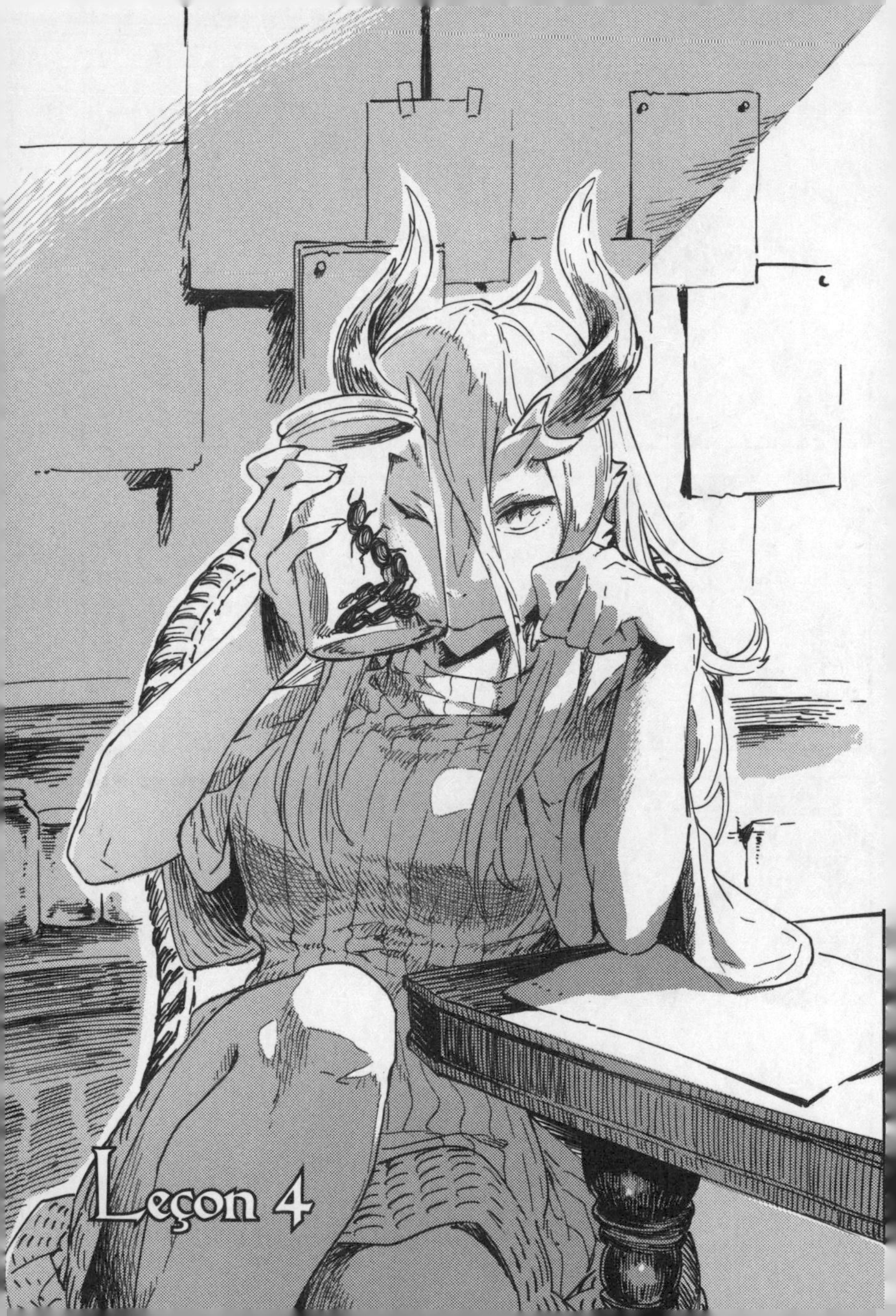
Leçon 4

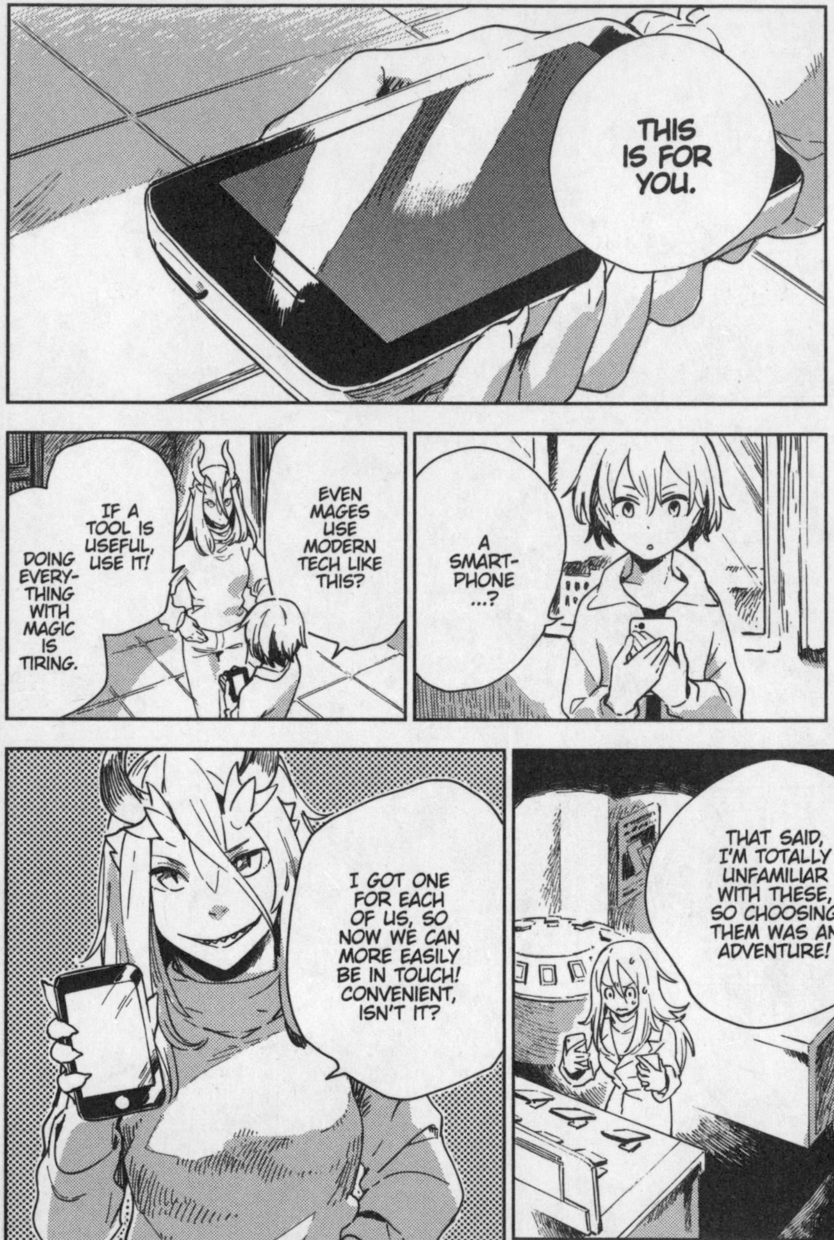
THIS IS FOR YOU.
A SMART-PHONE ...?
EVEN MAGES USE MODERN TECH LIKE THIS?
IF A TOOL IS USEFUL, USE IT!
DOING EVERY-THING WITH MAGIC IS TIRING.
THAT SAID, I'M TOTALLY UNFAMILIAR WITH THESE, SO CHOOSING THEM WAS AN ADVENTURE!
I GOT ONE FOR EACH OF US, SO NOW WE CAN MORE EASILY BE IN TOUCH! CONVENIENT, ISN'T IT?

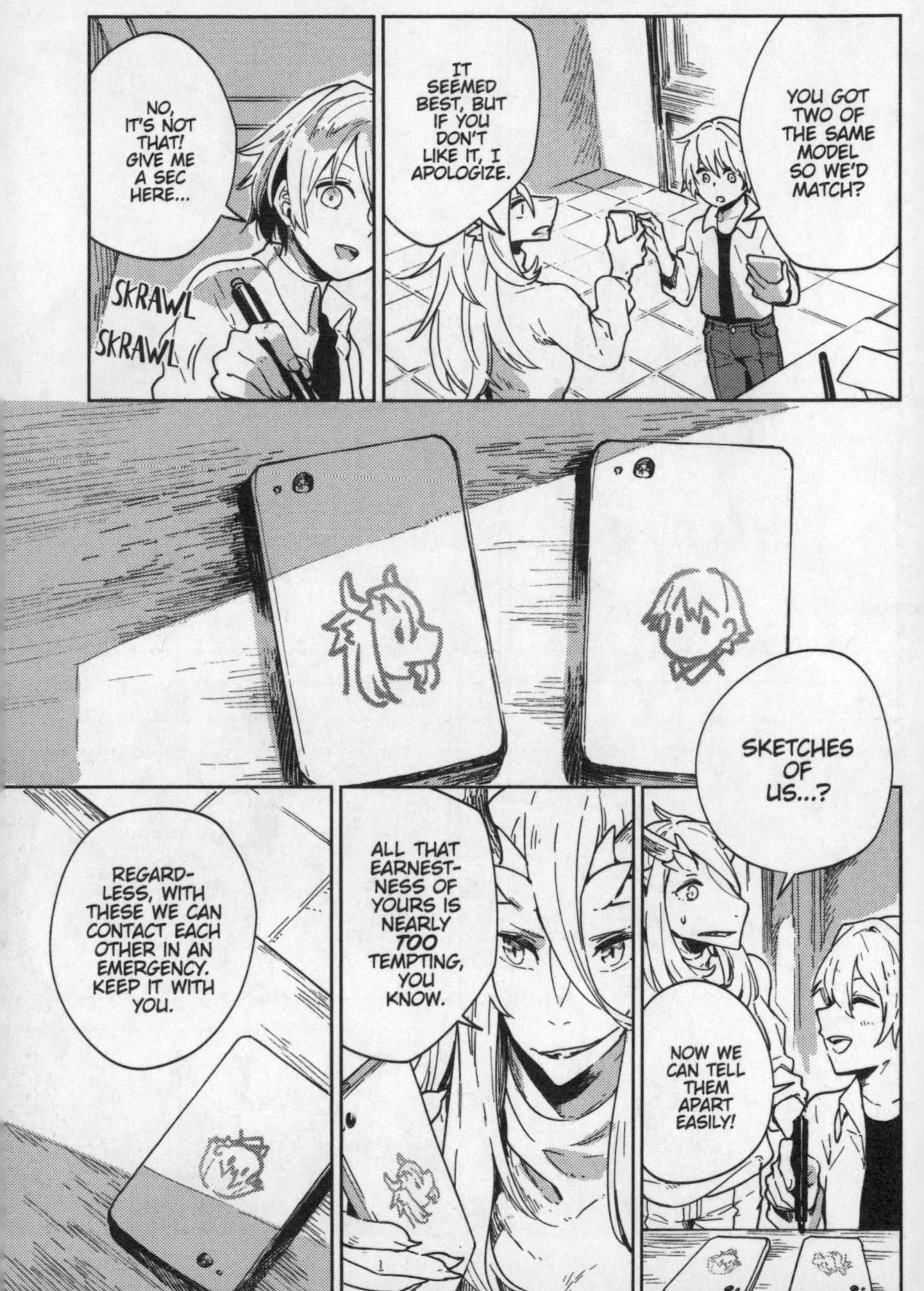
YOU GOT TWO OF THE SAME MODEL SO WE'D MATCH?
IT SEEMED BEST, BUT IF YOU DON'T LIKE IT, I APOLOGIZE.
NO, IT'S NOT THAT! GIVE ME A SEC HERE...
SKRAWL
SKRAWL
SKETCHES OF US...?
NOW WE CAN TELL THEM APART EASILY!
ALL THAT EARNEST-NESS OF YOURS IS NEARLY *TOO* TEMPTING, YOU KNOW.
REGARD-LESS, WITH THESE WE CAN CONTACT EACH OTHER IN AN EMERGENCY. KEEP IT WITH YOU.

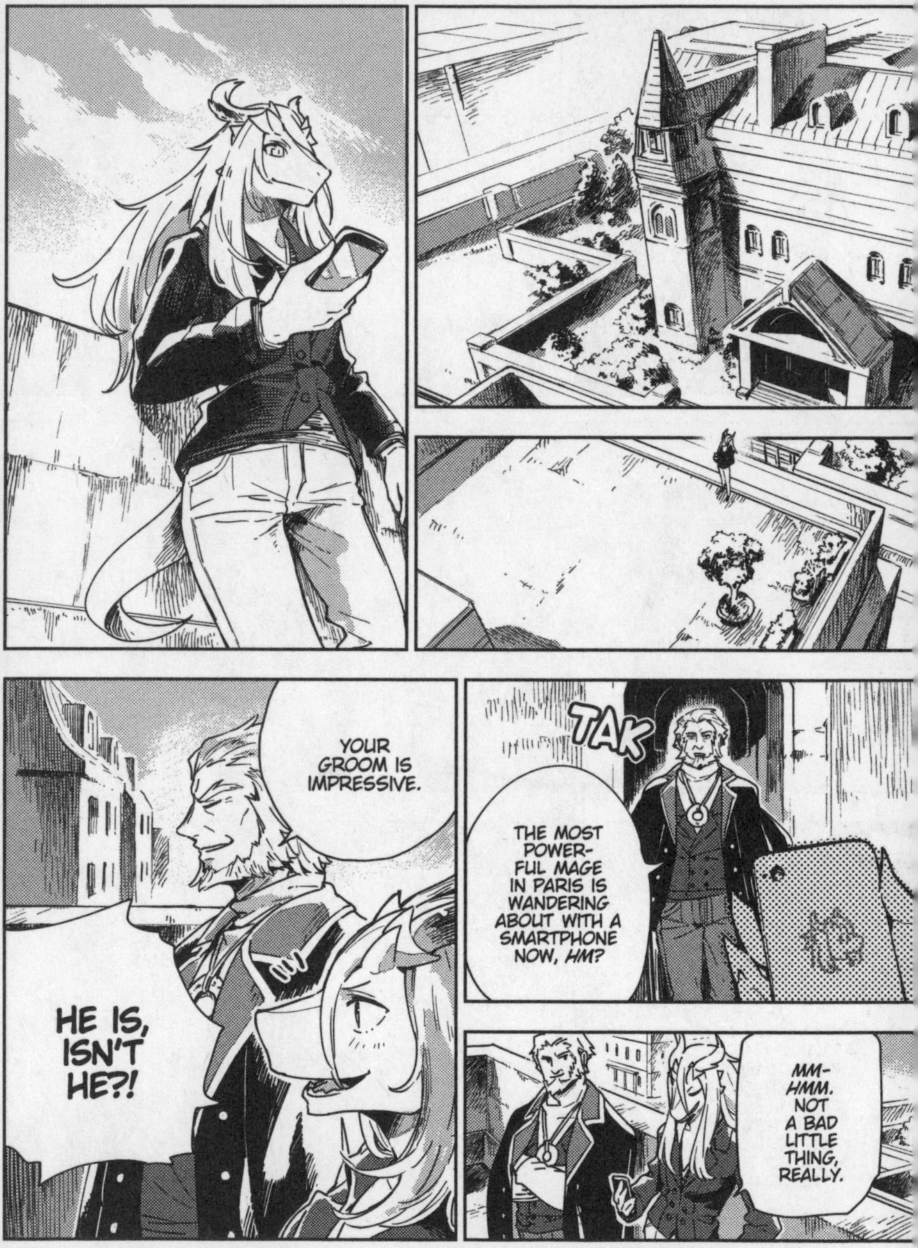
TAK
THE MOST POWER-FUL MAGE IN PARIS IS WANDERING ABOUT WITH A SMARTPHONE NOW, *HM*?
MM-HMM. NOT A BAD LITTLE THING, REALLY.
YOUR GROOM IS IMPRESSIVE.
HE IS, ISN'T HE?!

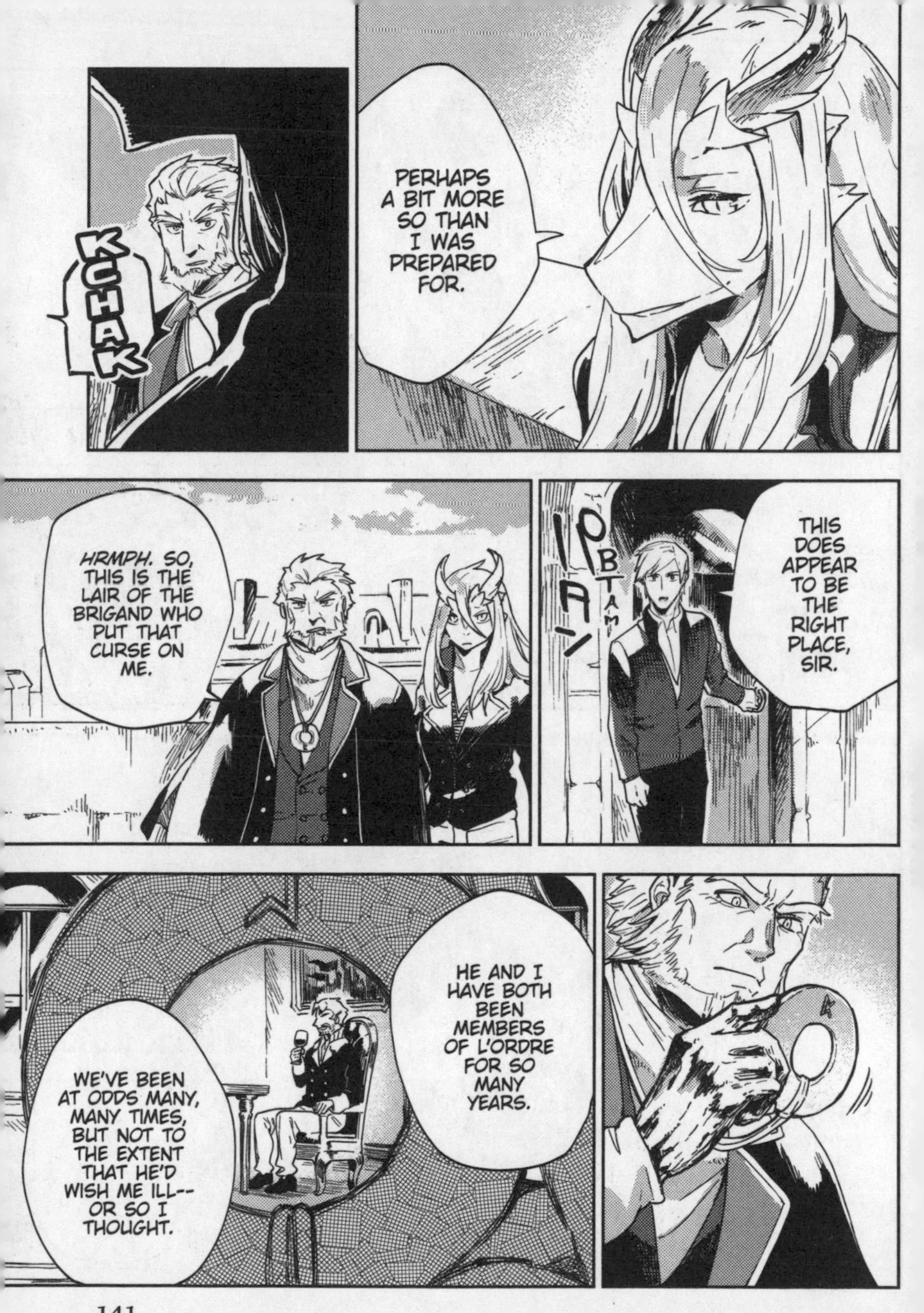
PERHAPS A BIT MORE SO THAN I WAS PREPARED FOR.
KCHAK
THIS DOES APPEAR TO BE THE RIGHT PLACE, SIR.
BTAM
HRMPH. SO, THIS IS THE LAIR OF THE BRIGAND WHO PUT THAT CURSE ON ME.
HE AND I HAVE BOTH BEEN MEMBERS OF L'ORDRE FOR SO MANY YEARS.
WE'VE BEEN AT ODDS MANY, MANY TIMES, BUT NOT TO THE EXTENT THAT HE'D WISH ME ILL-- OR SO I THOUGHT.

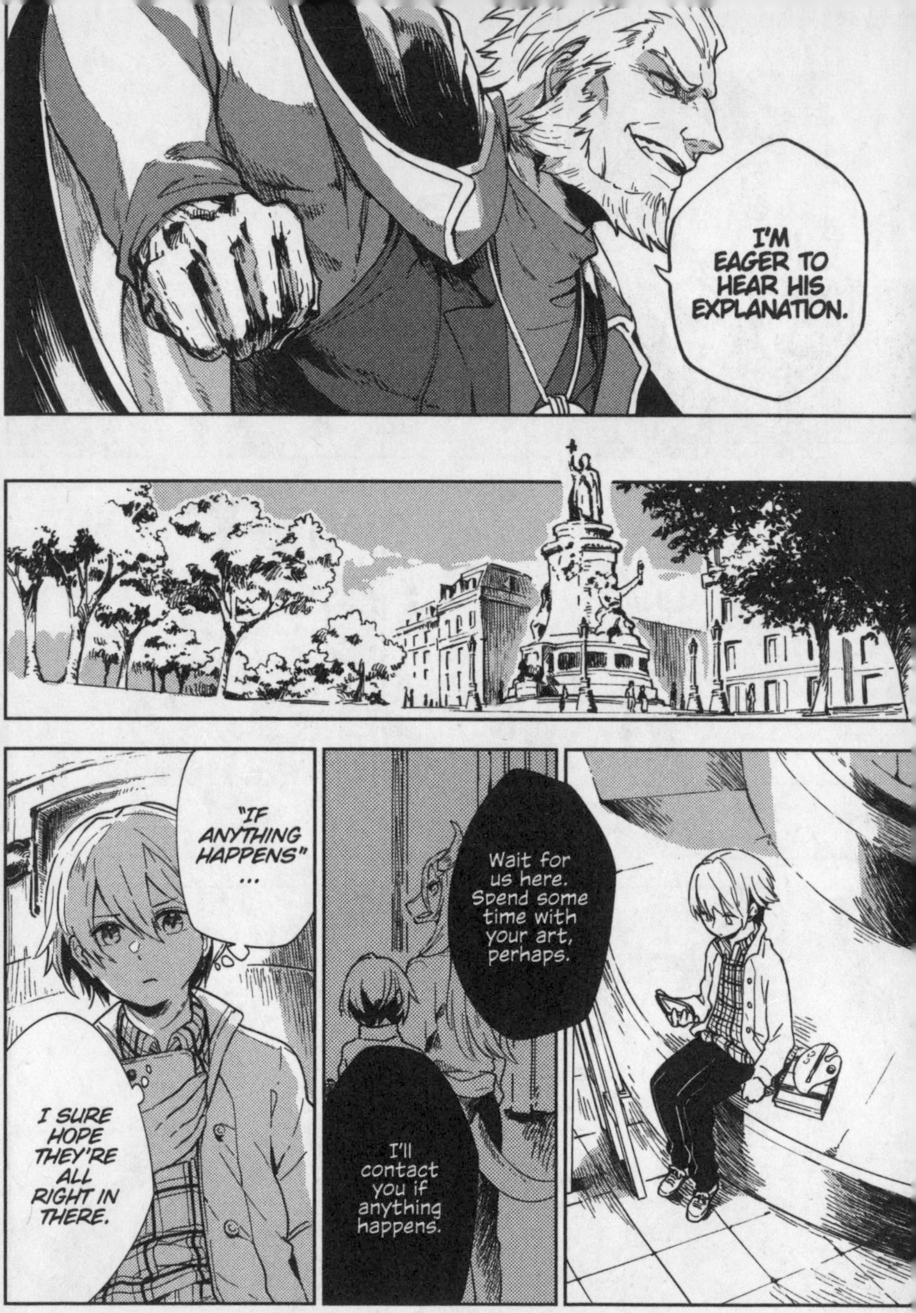
I'M EAGER TO HEAR HIS EXPLANATION.
Wait for us here. Spend some time with your art, perhaps.
I'll contact you if anything happens.
"IF ANYTHING HAPPENS" ...
I SURE HOPE THEY'RE ALL RIGHT IN THERE.

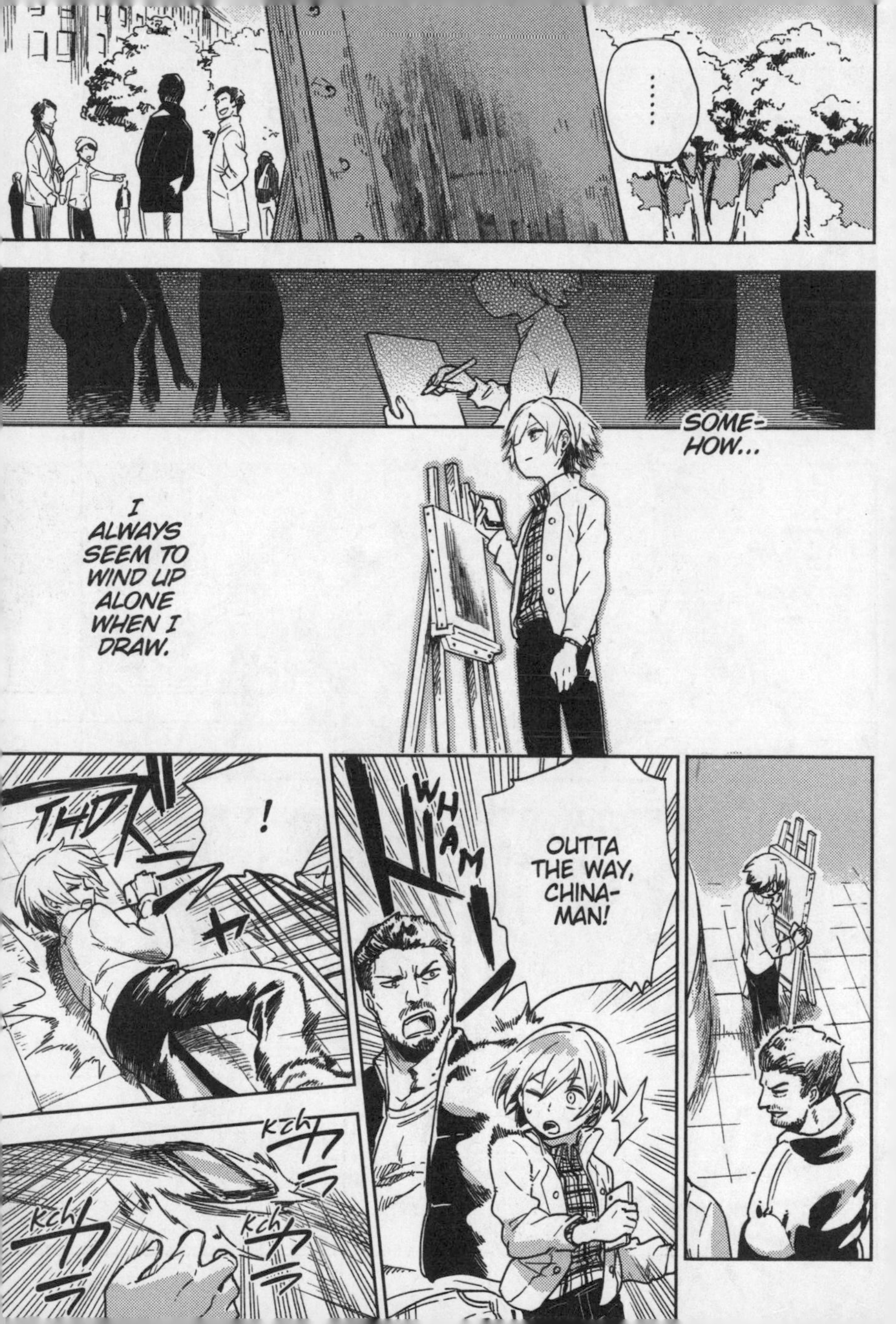

......
SOME-
HOW...
I
ALWAYS
SEEM TO
WIND UP
ALONE
WHEN I
DRAW.
WHAM
OUTTA
THE WAY,
CHINA-
MAN!
THD
!
KCH
KCH
KCH

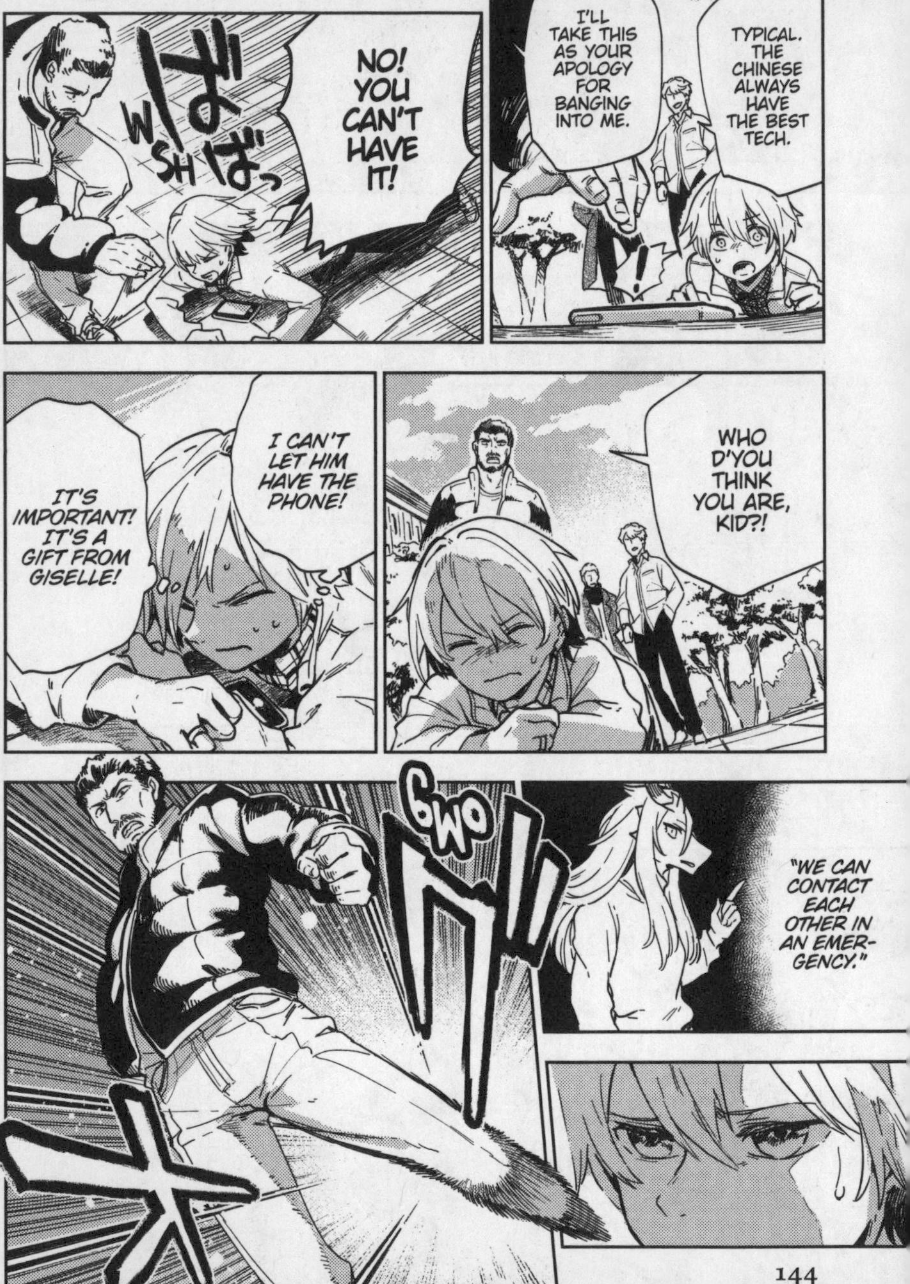
TYPICAL. THE CHINESE ALWAYS HAVE THE BEST TECH.
I'LL TAKE THIS AS YOUR APOLOGY FOR BANGING INTO ME.
NO! YOU CAN'T HAVE IT!
WHSH
WHO D'YOU THINK YOU ARE, KID?!
I CAN'T LET HIM HAVE THE PHONE!
IT'S IMPORTANT! IT'S A GIFT FROM GISELLE!
"WE CAN CONTACT EACH OTHER IN AN EMERGENCY."
GWO

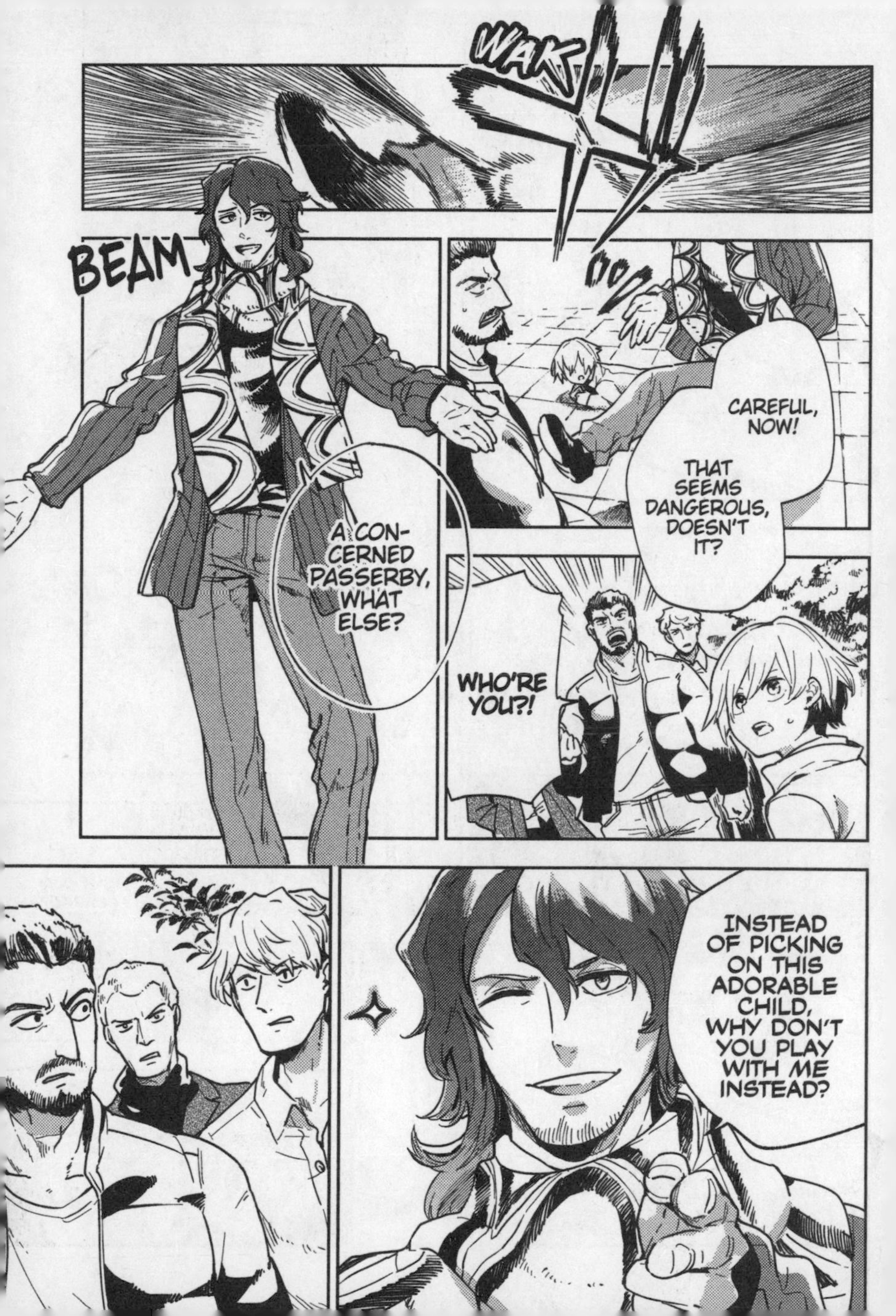
WAK
CAREFUL, NOW!
THAT SEEMS DANGEROUS, DOESN'T IT?
WHO'RE YOU?!
BEAM
A CONCERNED PASSERBY, WHAT ELSE?
INSTEAD OF PICKING ON THIS ADORABLE CHILD, WHY DON'T YOU PLAY WITH ME INSTEAD?

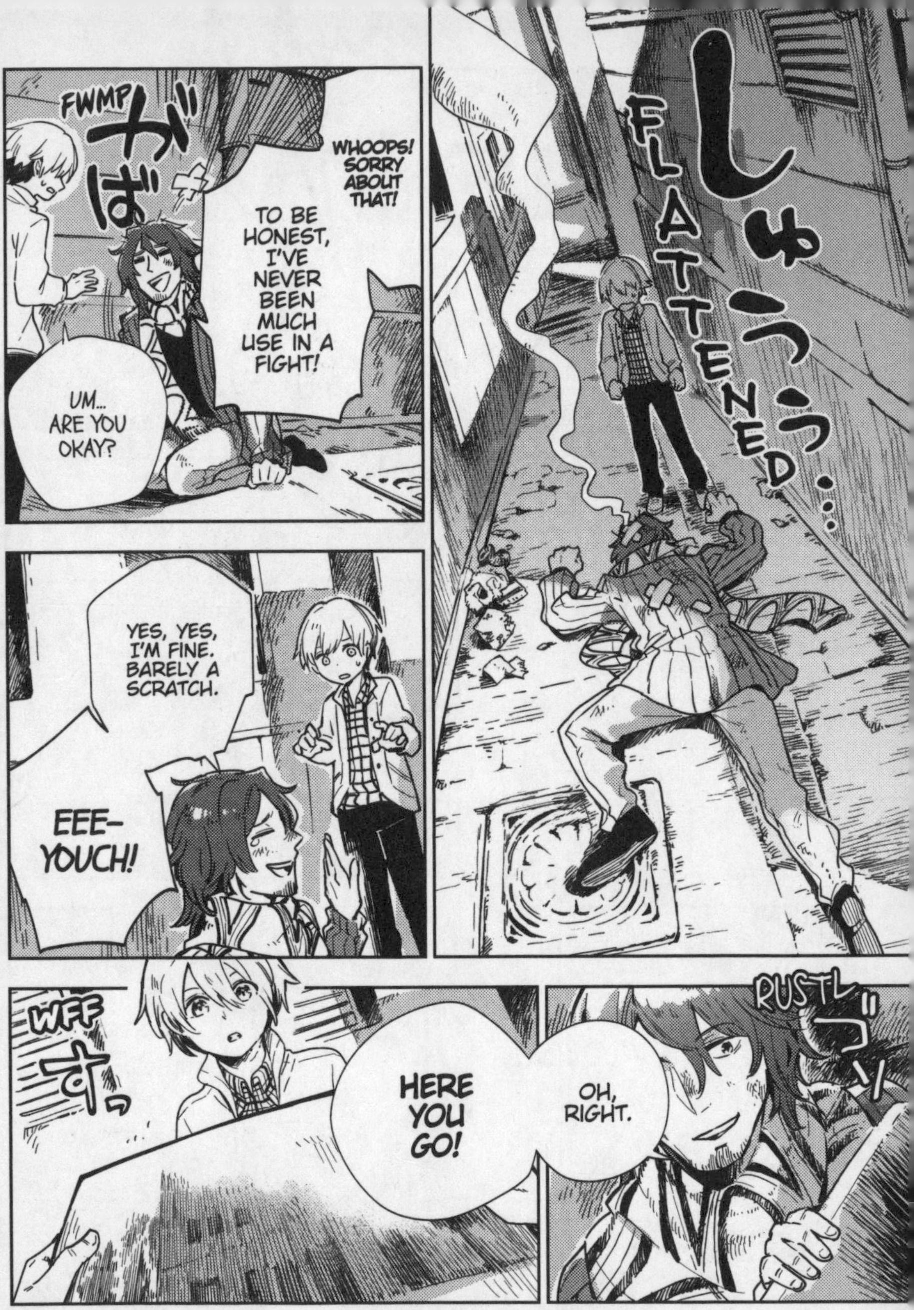
しゅううう
FLATTENED...
FWMP
がば
WHOOPS! SORRY ABOUT THAT!
TO BE HONEST, I'VE NEVER BEEN MUCH USE IN A FIGHT!
UM... ARE YOU OKAY?
YES, YES, I'M FINE. BARELY A SCRATCH.
EEE-YOUCH!
RUSTLE
ゴソ
OH, RIGHT.
HERE YOU GO!
WFF
すっ
...

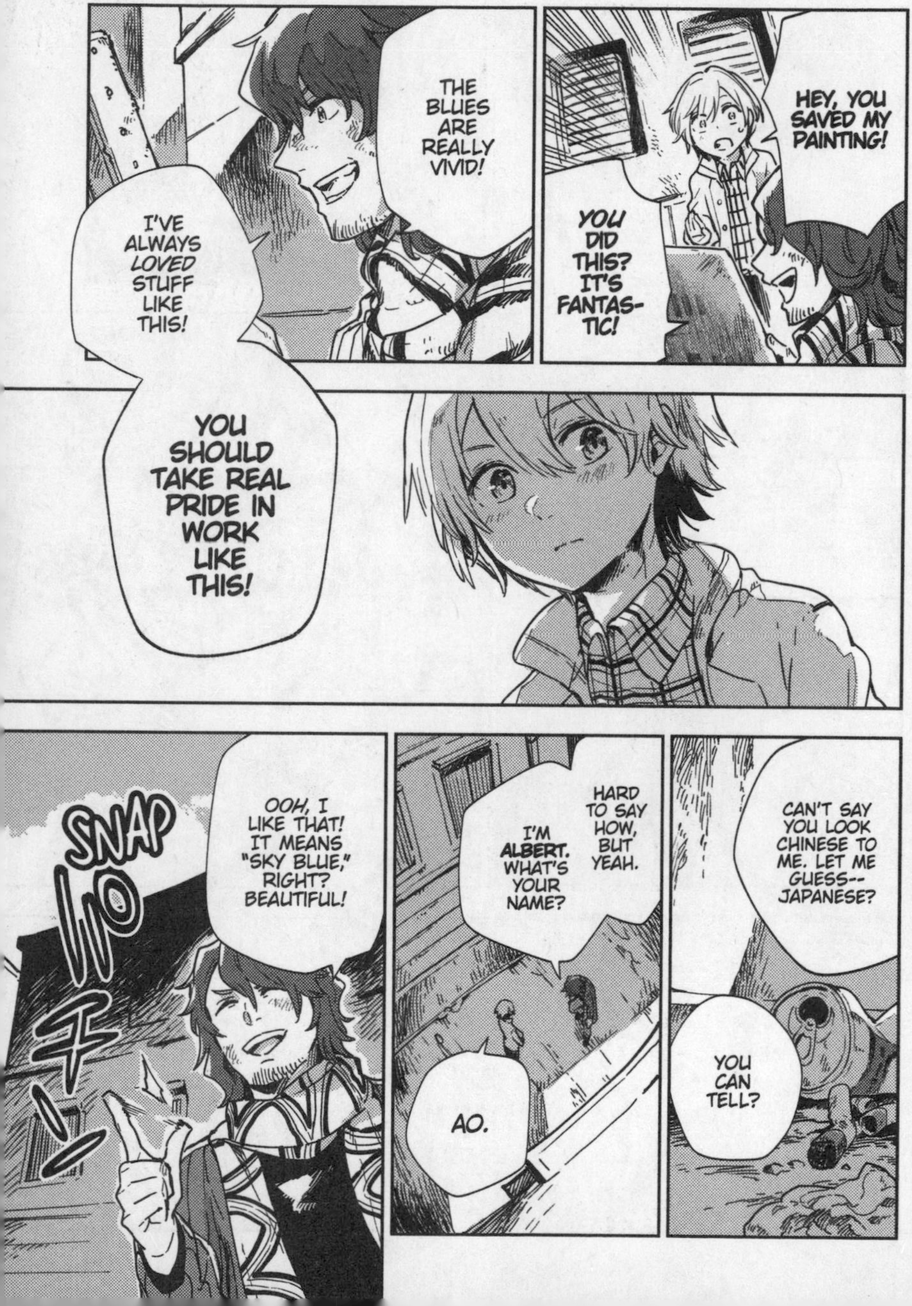
HEY, YOU SAVED MY PAINTING!
YOU DID THIS? IT'S FANTAS-TIC!
THE BLUES ARE REALLY VIVID!
I'VE ALWAYS LOVED STUFF LIKE THIS!
YOU SHOULD TAKE REAL PRIDE IN WORK LIKE THIS!
CAN'T SAY YOU LOOK CHINESE TO ME. LET ME GUESS--JAPANESE?
YOU CAN TELL?
HARD TO SAY HOW, BUT YEAH.
I'M ALBERT. WHAT'S YOUR NAME?
AO.
OOH, I LIKE THAT! IT MEANS "SKY BLUE," RIGHT? BEAUTIFUL!
SNAP

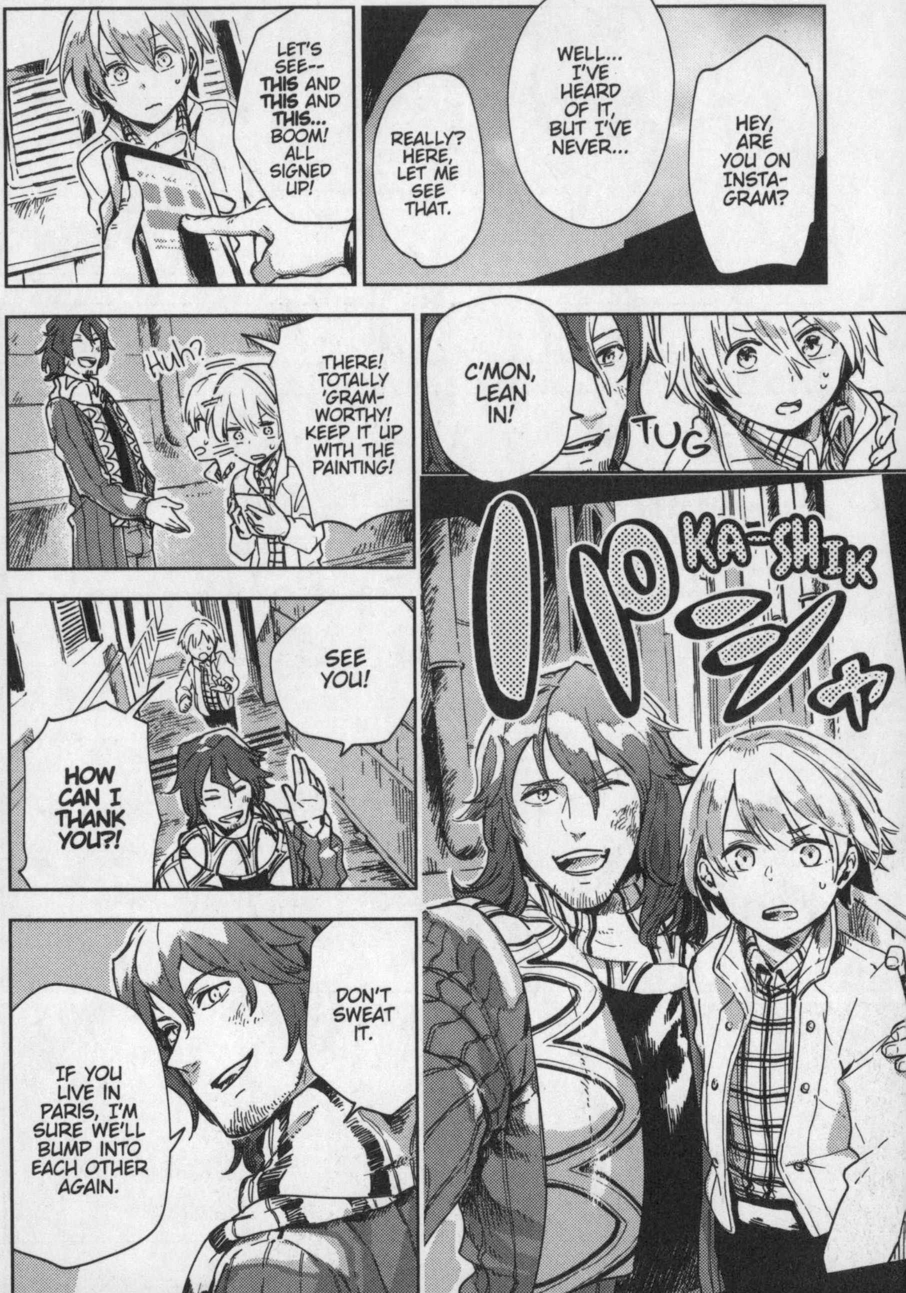
HEY, ARE YOU ON INSTA-GRAM?
WELL... I'VE HEARD OF IT, BUT I'VE NEVER...
REALLY? HERE, LET ME SEE THAT.
LET'S SEE-- THIS AND THIS AND THIS... BOOM! ALL SIGNED UP!
C'MON, LEAN IN!
TUG
KA-SHIK
THERE! TOTALLY 'GRAM-WORTHY! KEEP IT UP WITH THE PAINTING!
Huh?
SEE YOU!
HOW CAN I THANK YOU?!
DON'T SWEAT IT.
IF YOU LIVE IN PARIS, I'M SURE WE'LL BUMP INTO EACH OTHER AGAIN.

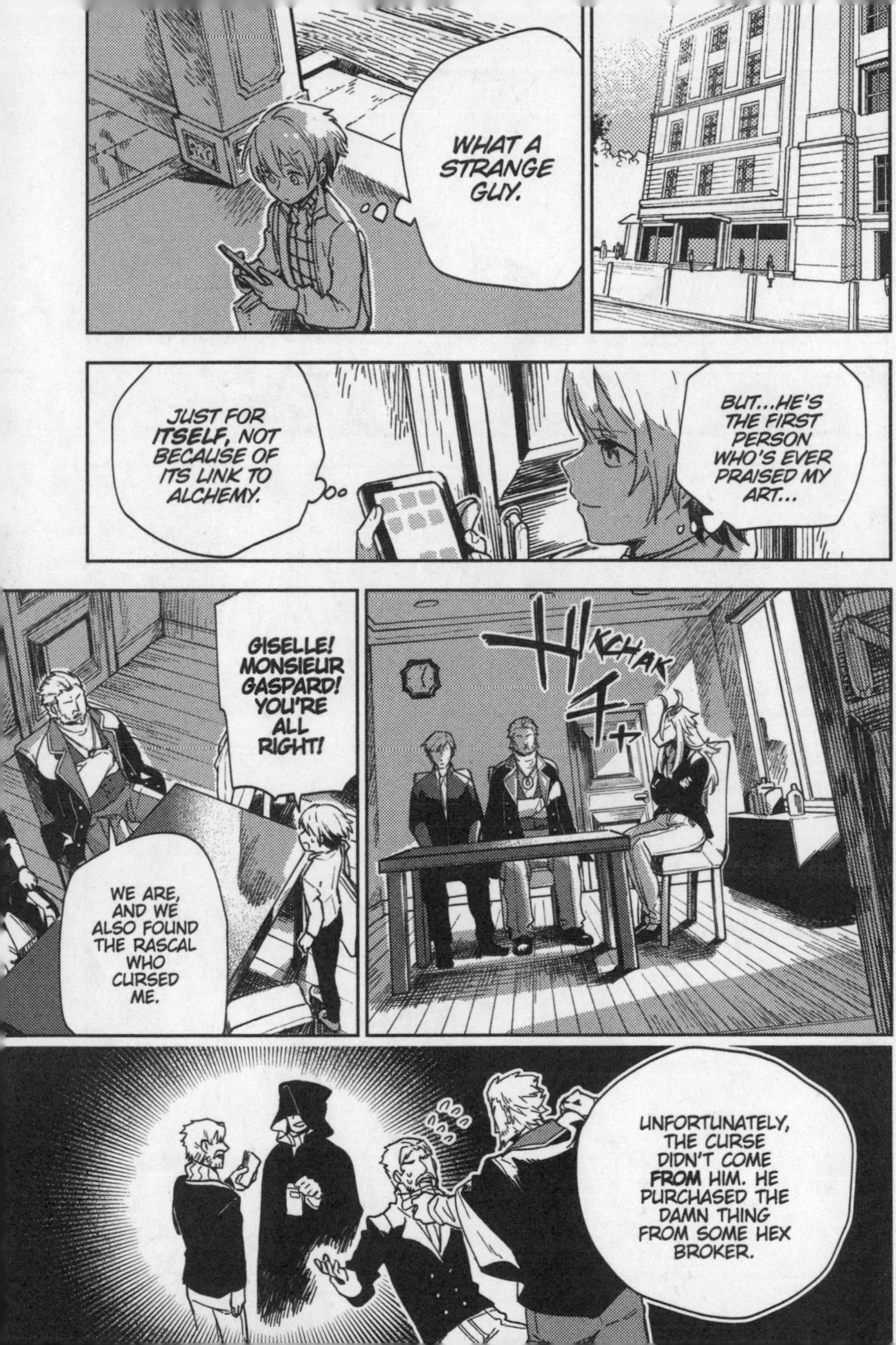
WHAT A STRANGE GUY.
BUT...HE'S THE FIRST PERSON WHO'S EVER PRAISED MY ART...
JUST FOR ITSELF, NOT BECAUSE OF ITS LINK TO ALCHEMY.
KCHAK
GISELLE! MONSIEUR GASPARD! YOU'RE ALL RIGHT!
WE ARE, AND WE ALSO FOUND THE RASCAL WHO CURSED ME.
UNFORTUNATELY, THE CURSE DIDN'T COME FROM HIM. HE PURCHASED THE DAMN THING FROM SOME HEX BROKER.

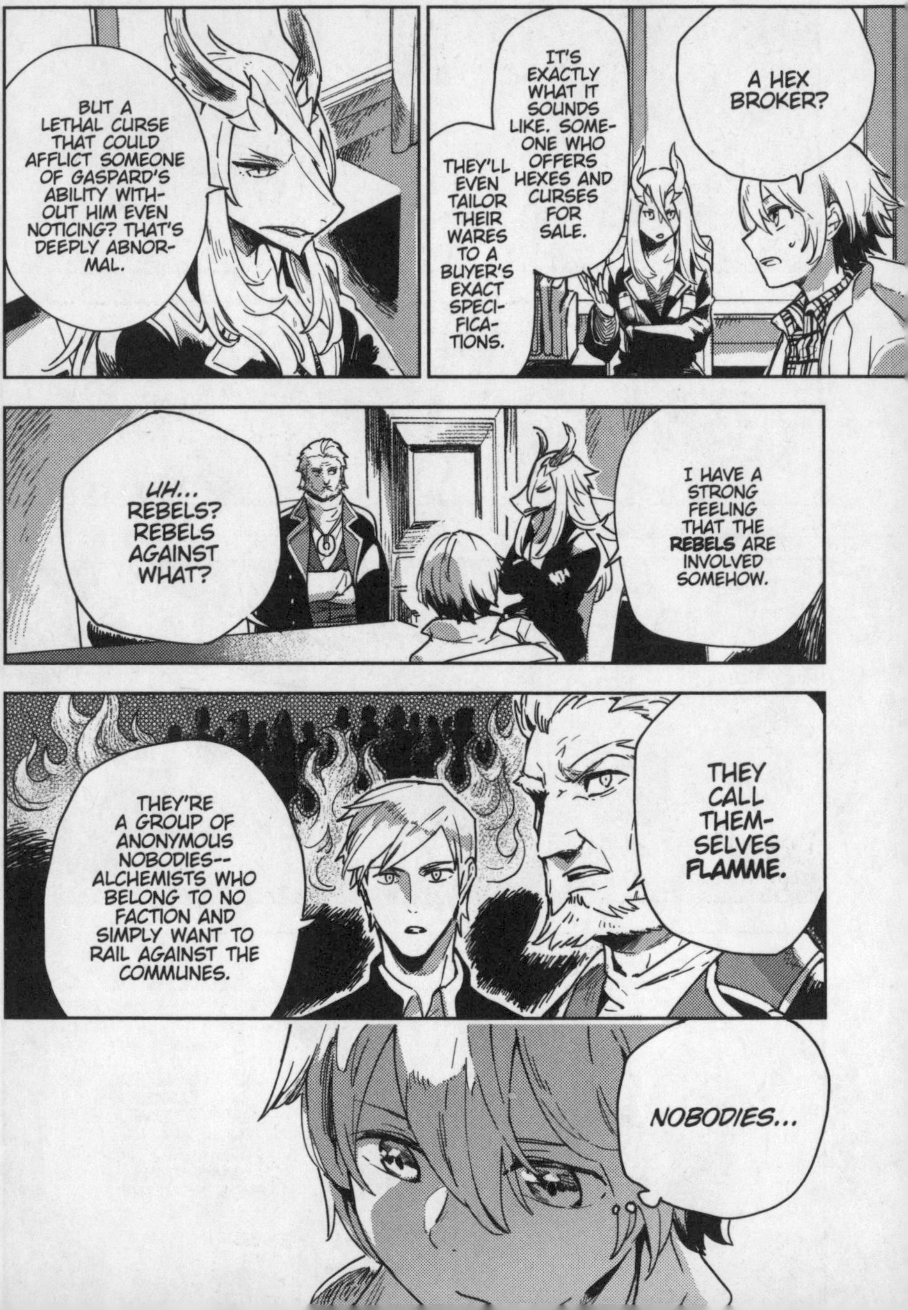
A HEX BROKER?
IT'S EXACTLY WHAT IT SOUNDS LIKE. SOMEONE WHO OFFERS HEXES AND CURSES FOR SALE.
THEY'LL EVEN TAILOR THEIR WARES TO A BUYER'S EXACT SPECIFICATIONS.
BUT A LETHAL CURSE THAT COULD AFFLICT SOMEONE OF GASPARD'S ABILITY WITHOUT HIM EVEN NOTICING? THAT'S DEEPLY ABNORMAL.
I HAVE A STRONG FEELING THAT THE REBELS ARE INVOLVED SOMEHOW.
UH... REBELS? REBELS AGAINST WHAT?
THEY CALL THEMSELVES FLAMME.
THEY'RE A GROUP OF ANONYMOUS NOBODIES--ALCHEMISTS WHO BELONG TO NO FACTION AND SIMPLY WANT TO RAIL AGAINST THE COMMUNES.
NOBODIES...

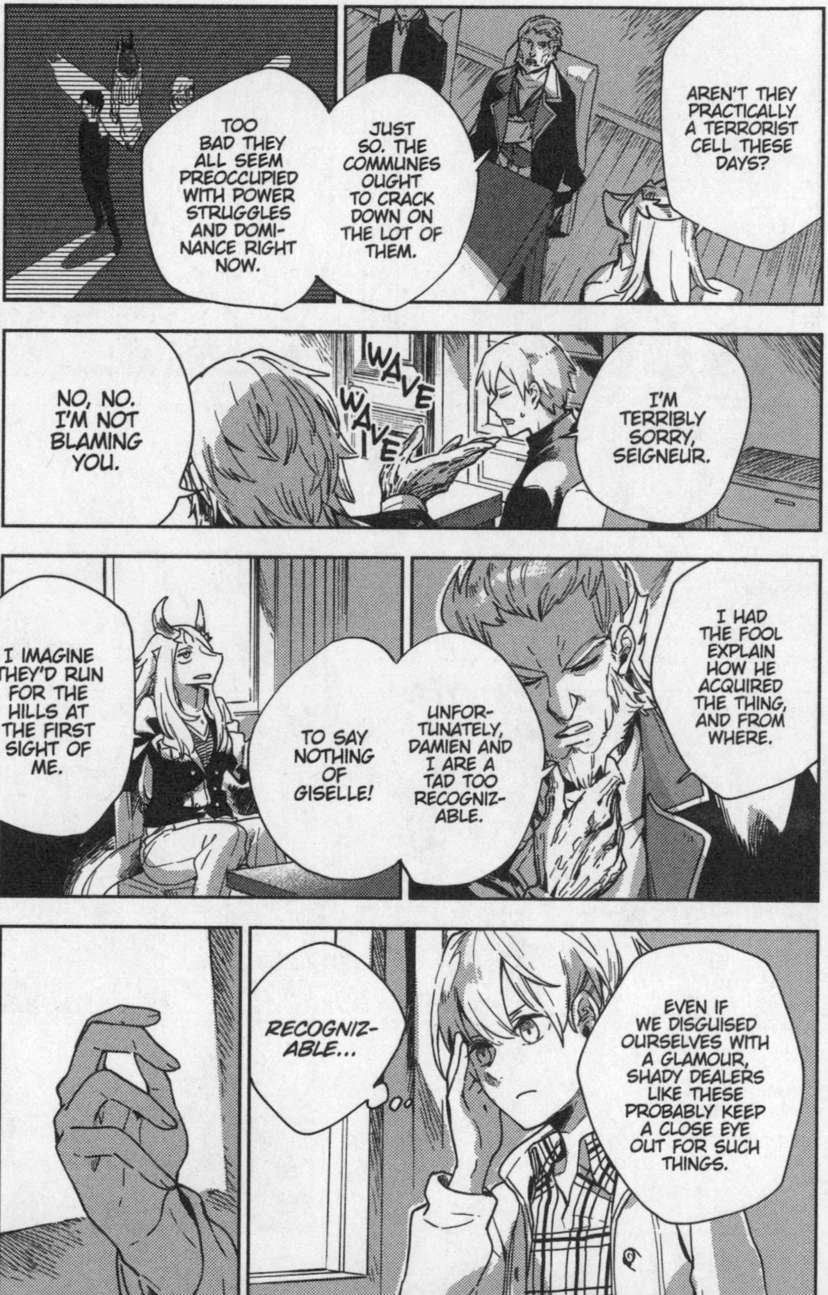
AREN'T THEY PRACTICALLY A TERRORIST CELL THESE DAYS?
JUST SO. THE COMMUNES OUGHT TO CRACK DOWN ON THE LOT OF THEM.
TOO BAD THEY ALL SEEM PREOCCUPIED WITH POWER STRUGGLES AND DOMINANCE RIGHT NOW.
I'M TERRIBLY SORRY, SEIGNEUR.
WAVE WAVE
NO, NO. I'M NOT BLAMING YOU.
I HAD THE FOOL EXPLAIN HOW HE ACQUIRED THE THING, AND FROM WHERE.
UNFORTUNATELY, DAMIEN AND I ARE A TAD TOO RECOGNIZABLE.
TO SAY NOTHING OF GISELLE!
I IMAGINE THEY'D RUN FOR THE HILLS AT THE FIRST SIGHT OF ME.
EVEN IF WE DISGUISED OURSELVES WITH A GLAMOUR, SHADY DEALERS LIKE THESE PROBABLY KEEP A CLOSE EYE OUT FOR SUCH THINGS.
RECOGNIZABLE...

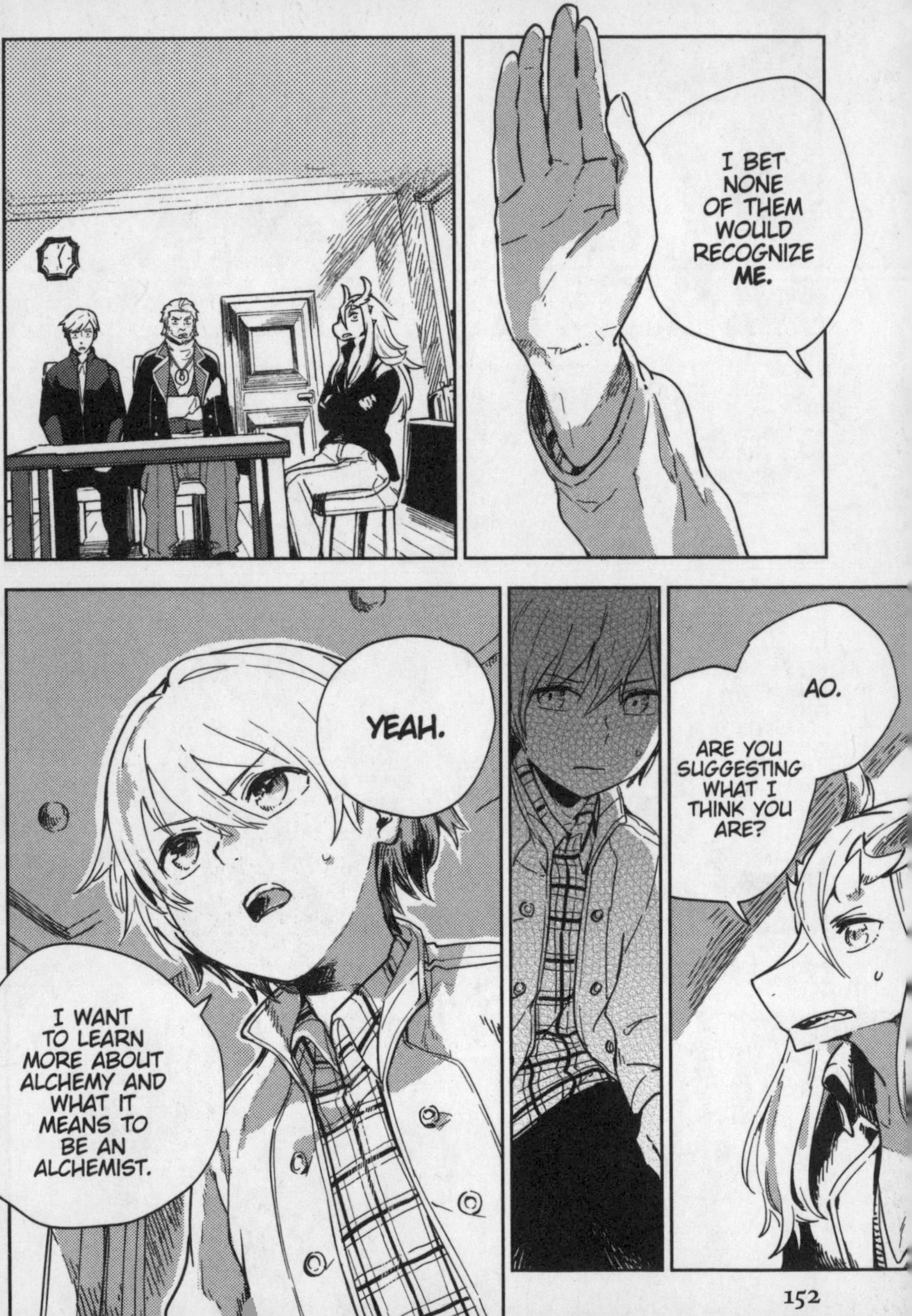
I BET NONE OF THEM WOULD RECOGNIZE ME.
AO.
ARE YOU SUGGESTING WHAT I THINK YOU ARE?
YEAH.
I WANT TO LEARN MORE ABOUT ALCHEMY AND WHAT IT MEANS TO BE AN ALCHEMIST.

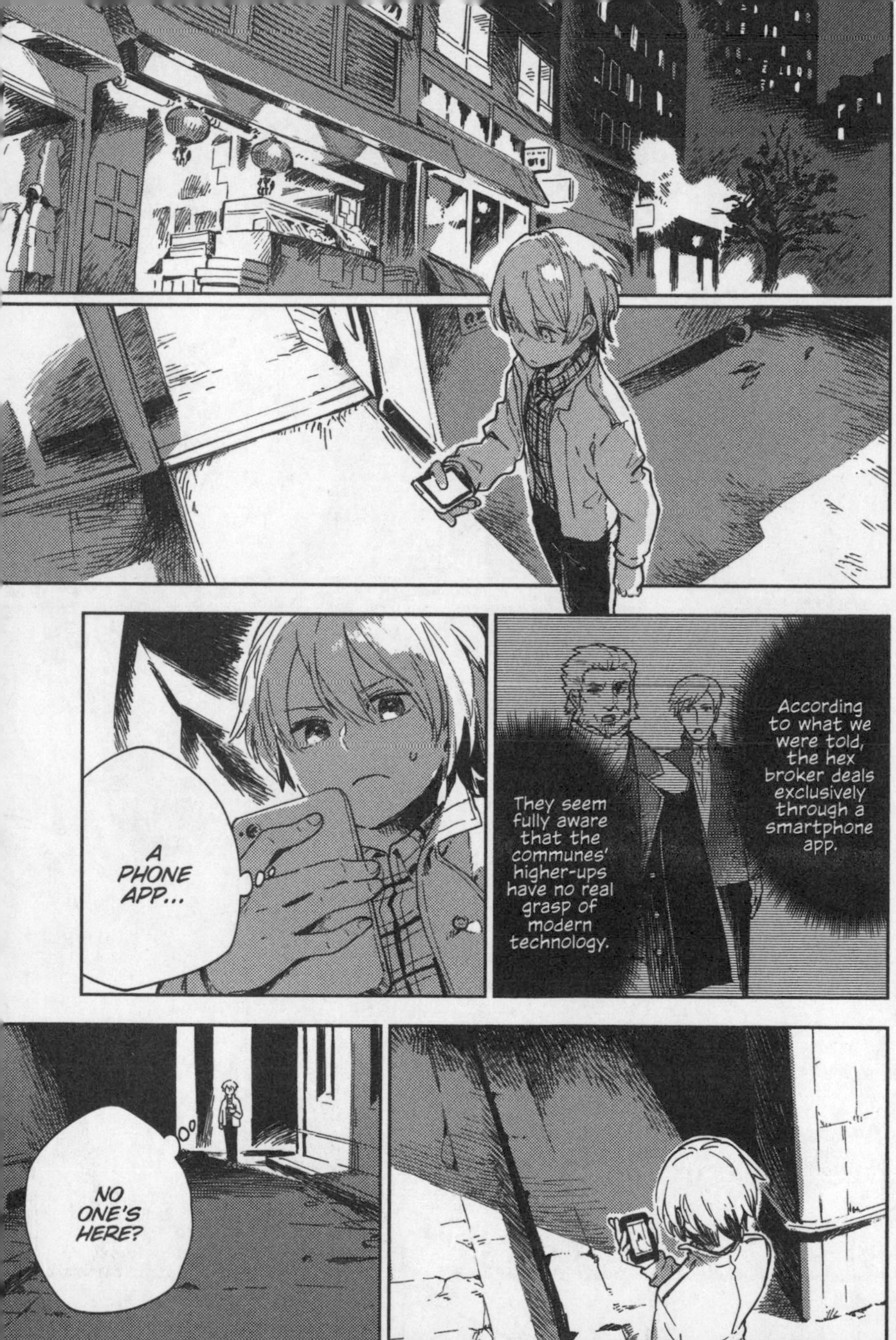

According to what we were told, the hex broker deals exclusively through a smartphone app.
They seem fully aware that the communes' higher-ups have no real grasp of modern technology.
A PHONE APP...
NO ONE'S HERE?

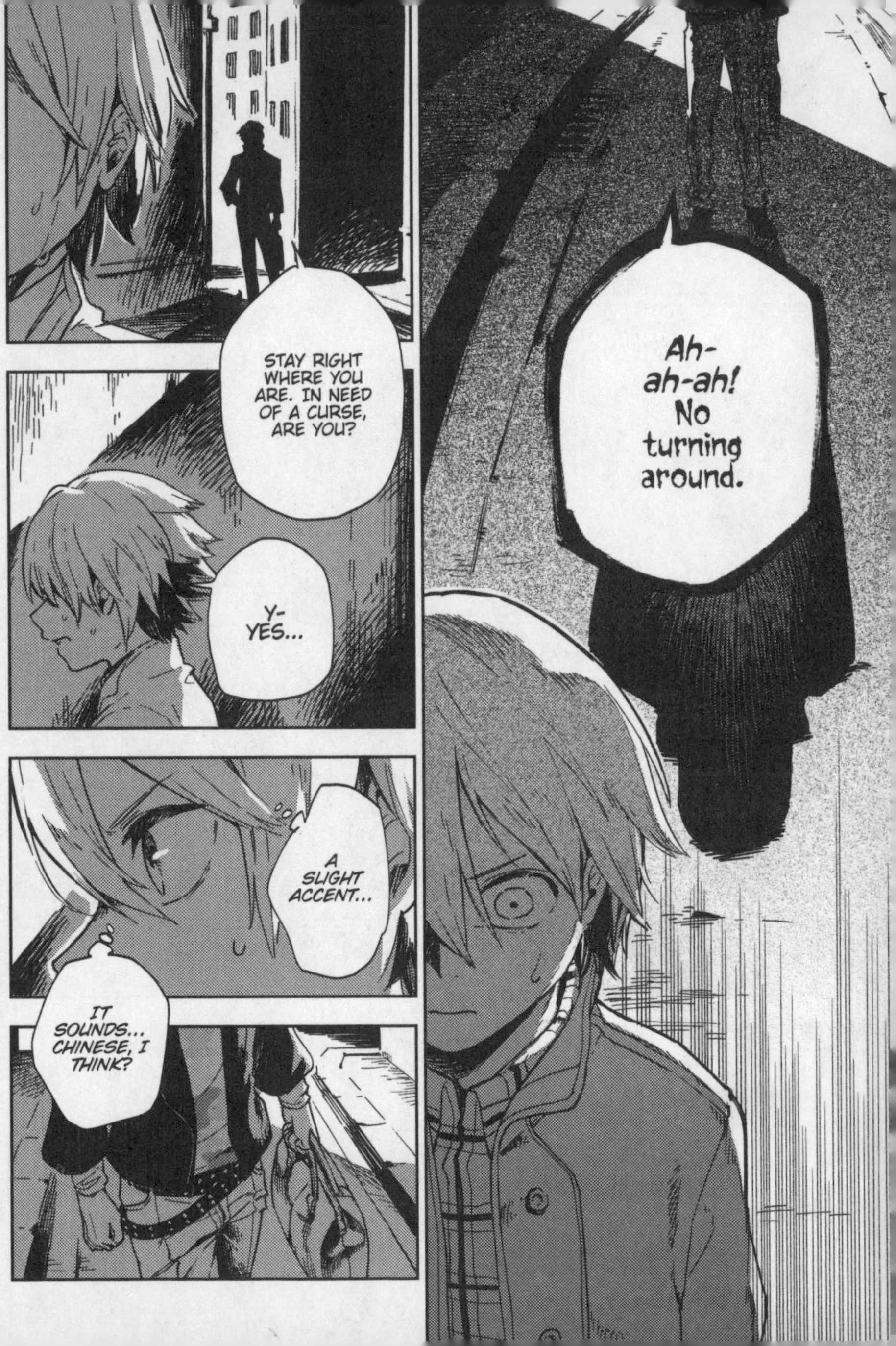
Ah-ah-ah! No turning around.
STAY RIGHT WHERE YOU ARE. IN NEED OF A CURSE, ARE YOU?
Y-YES...
A SLIGHT ACCENT...
IT SOUNDS... CHINESE, I THINK?

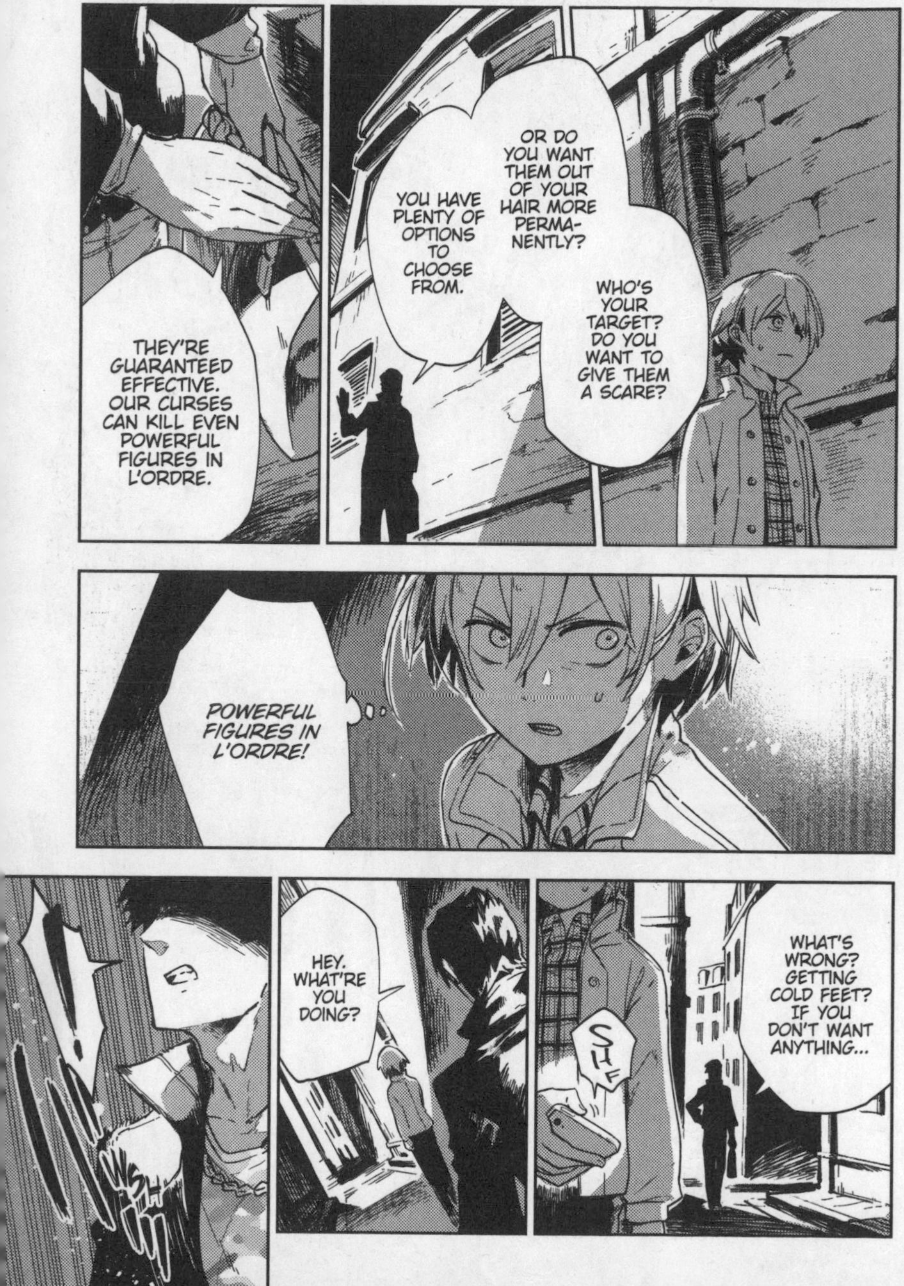

WHO'S YOUR TARGET? DO YOU WANT TO GIVE THEM A SCARE?
OR DO YOU WANT THEM OUT OF YOUR HAIR MORE PERMA-NENTLY?
YOU HAVE PLENTY OF OPTIONS TO CHOOSE FROM.
THEY'RE GUARANTEED EFFECTIVE. OUR CURSES CAN KILL EVEN POWERFUL FIGURES IN L'ORDRE.
POWERFUL FIGURES IN L'ORDRE!
WHAT'S WRONG? GETTING COLD FEET? IF YOU DON'T WANT ANYTHING...
SHF
HEY. WHAT'RE YOU DOING?
!
WSH

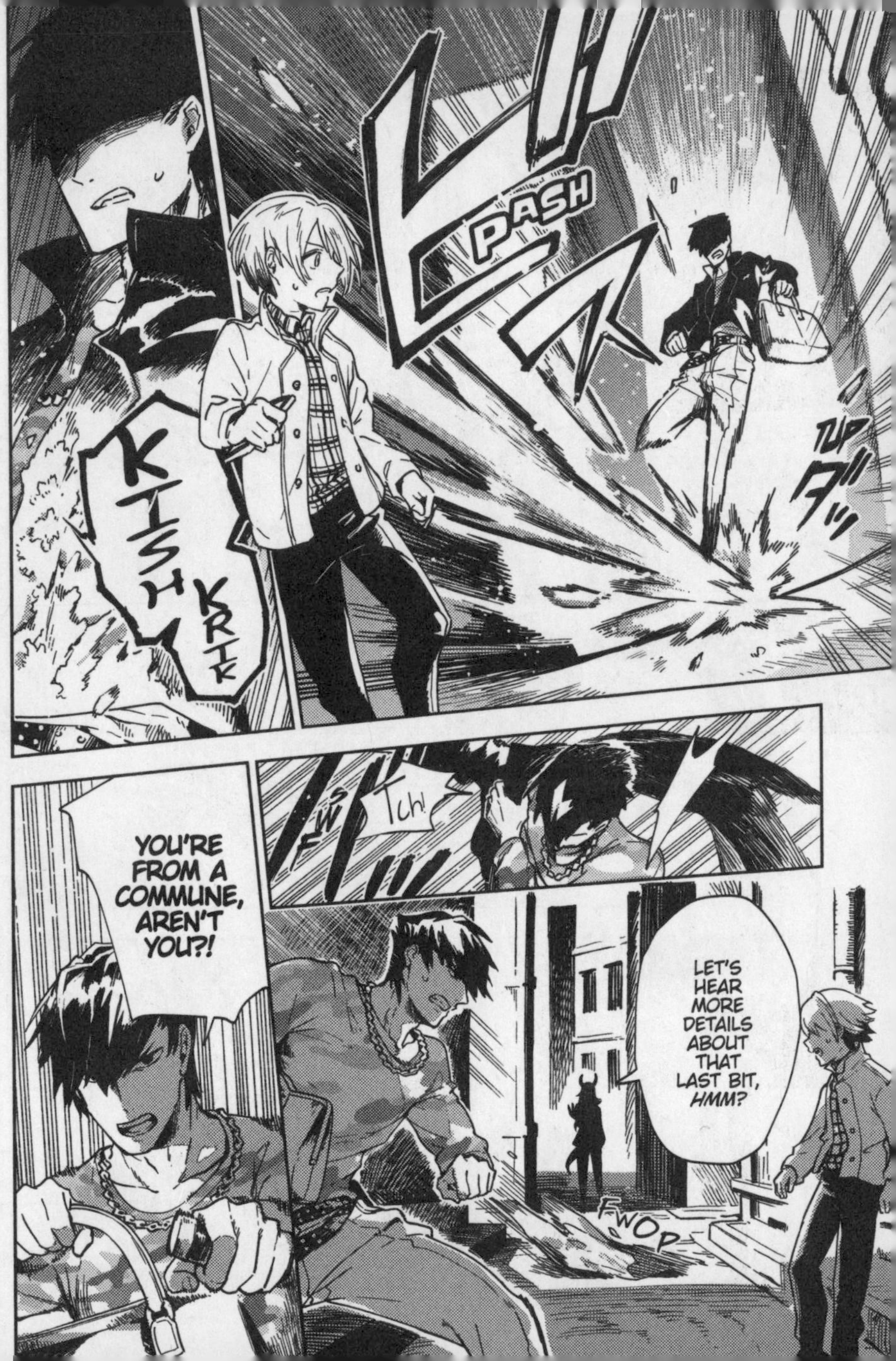
TUP
ダッ
PASH
KTISH
KRIK
FWS
Tch!
LET'S HEAR MORE DETAILS ABOUT THAT LAST BIT, HMM?
FWOP
YOU'RE FROM A COMMLINE, AREN'T YOU?!

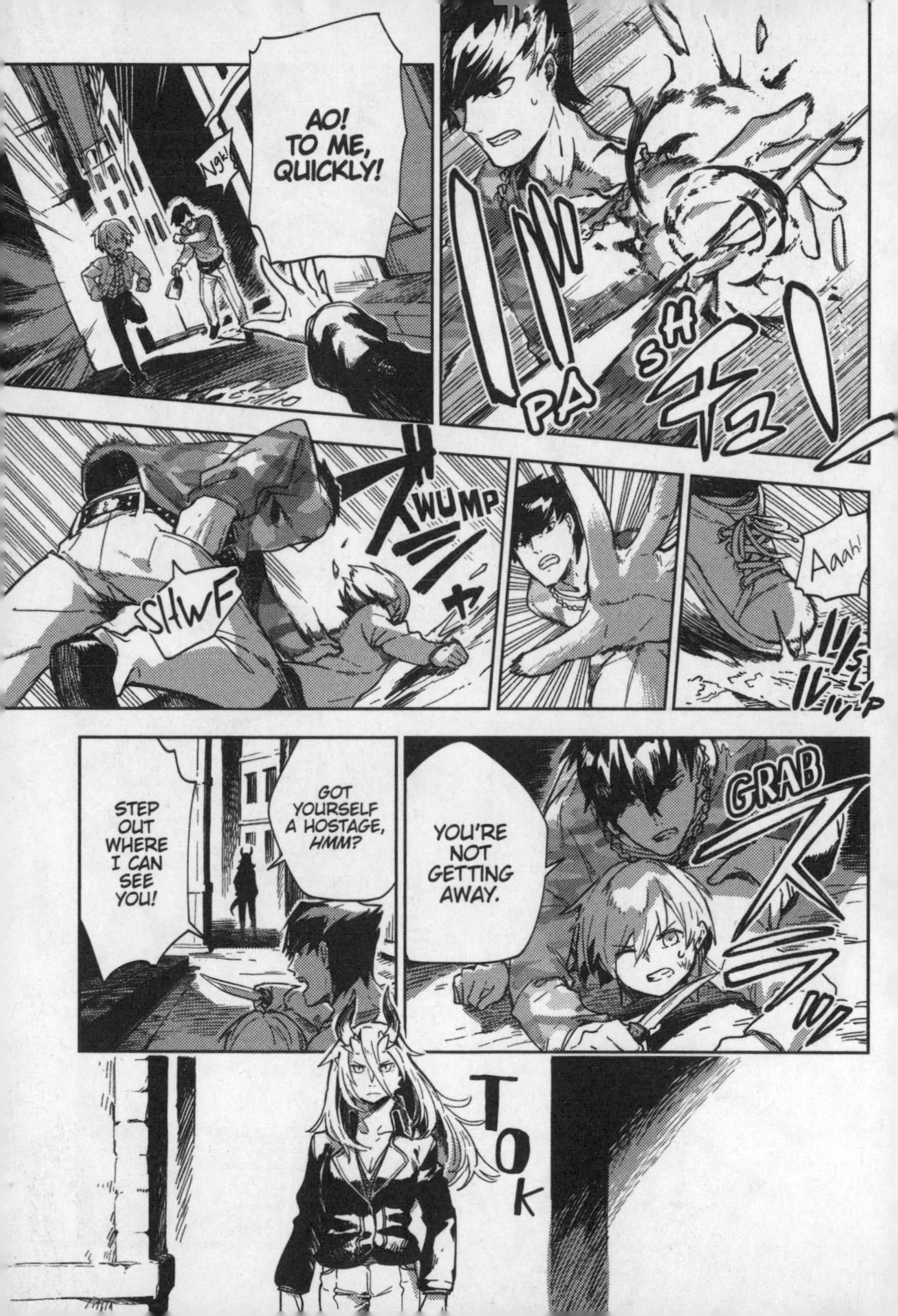
PA sH
AO! TO ME, QUICKLY!
Ngk!
Aaah!
SLIP
WUMP
SHWF
GRAB
YOU'RE NOT GETTING AWAY.
GOT YOURSELF A HOSTAGE, HMM?
STEP OUT WHERE I CAN SEE YOU!
TOK

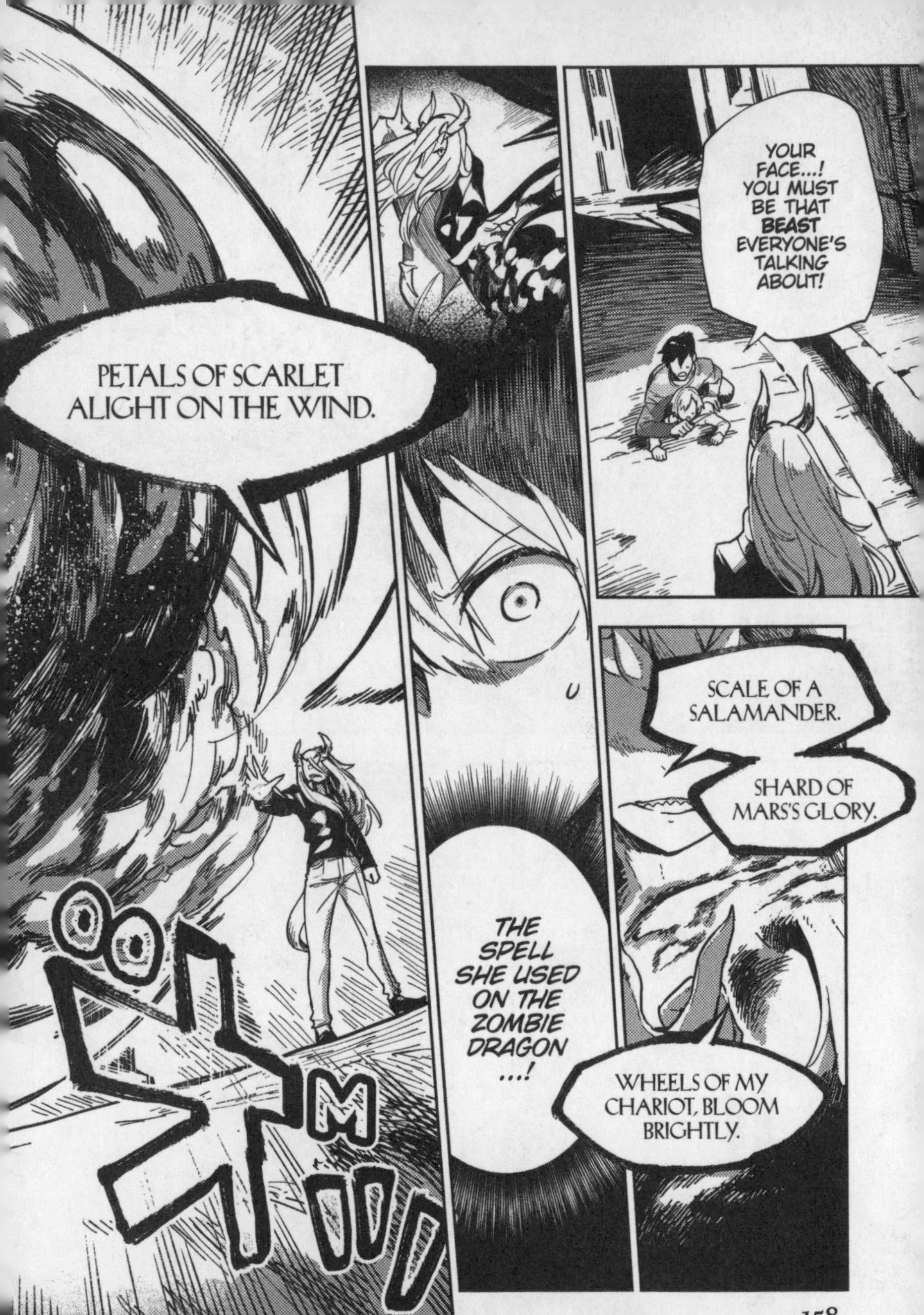
YOUR FACE...! YOU MUST BE THAT BEAST EVERYONE'S TALKING ABOUT!
SCALE OF A SALAMANDER.
SHARD OF MARS'S GLORY.
WHEELS OF MY CHARIOT, BLOOM BRIGHTLY.
THE SPELL SHE USED ON THE ZOMBIE DRAGON ...!
PETALS OF SCARLET ALIGHT ON THE WIND.

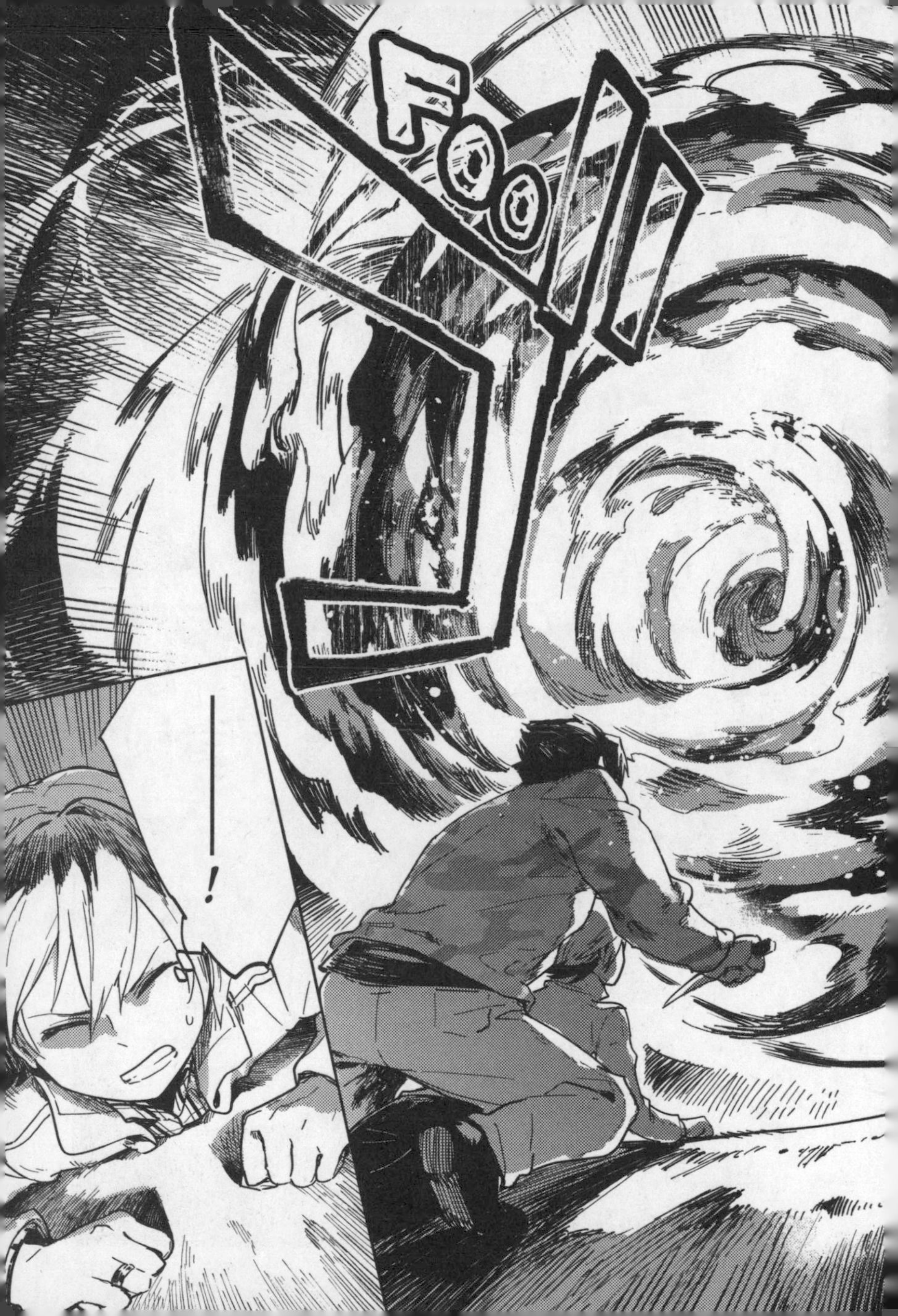
——!

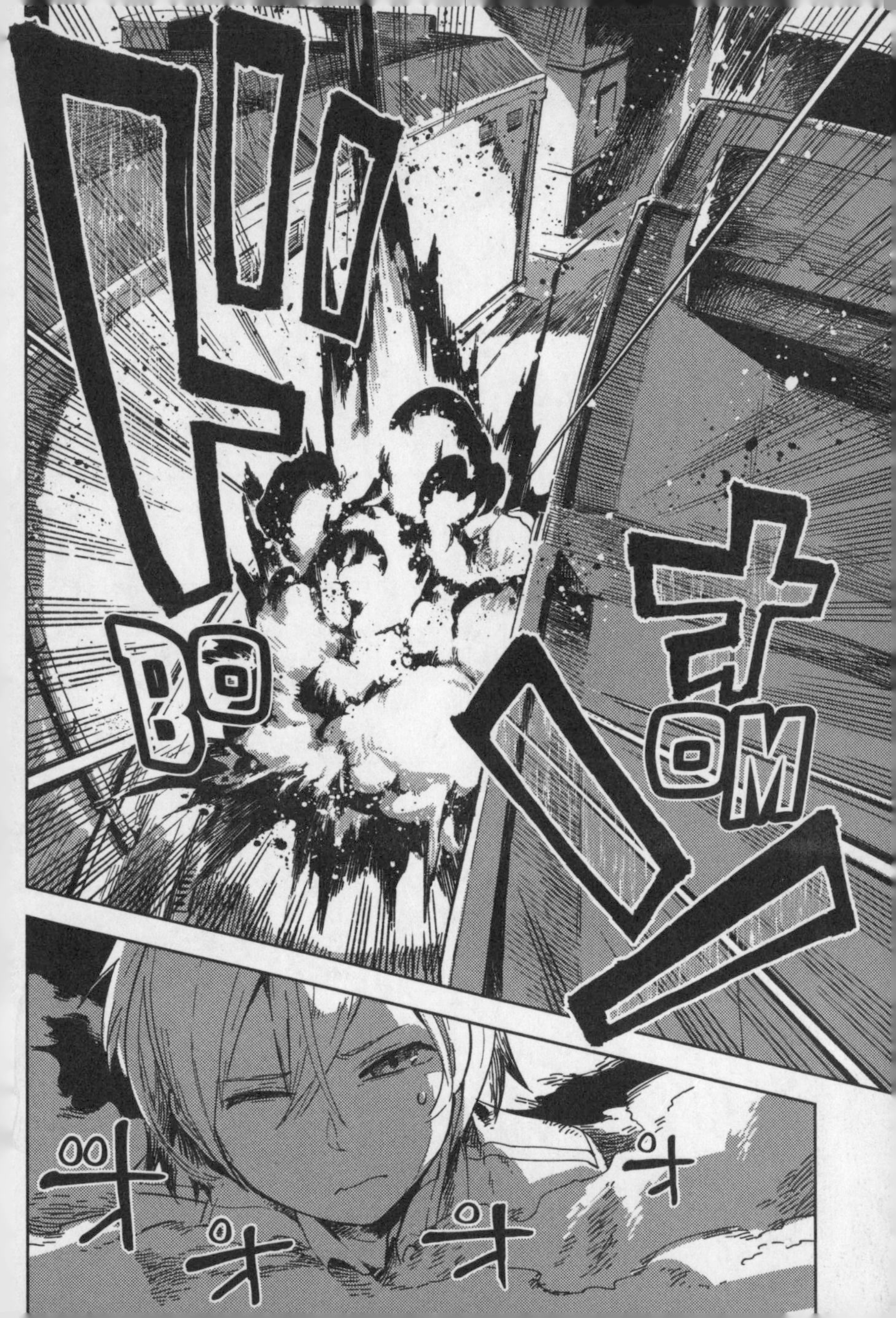
BOOM

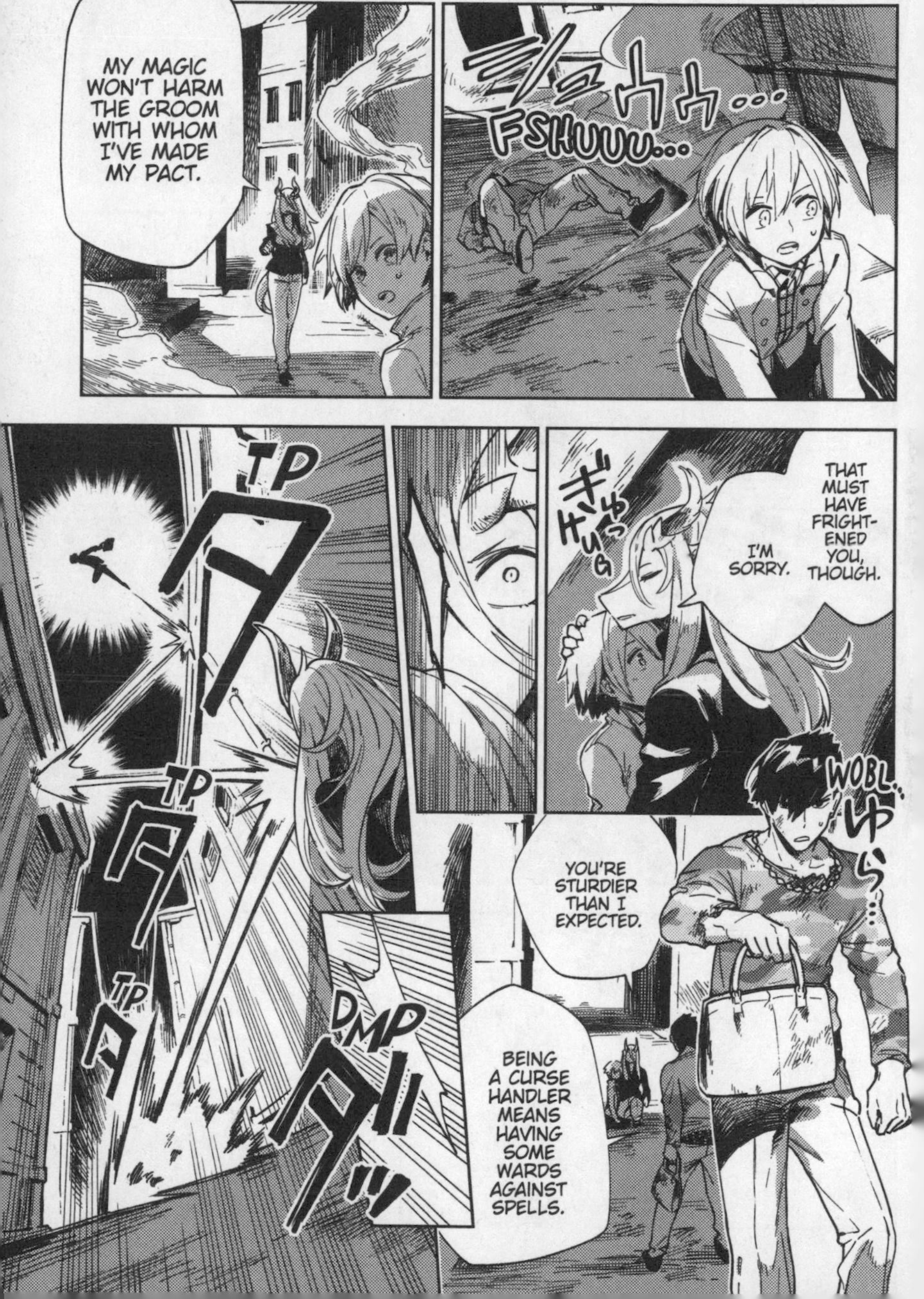

シュウウ…
FSHUUU...
MY MAGIC WON'T HARM THE GROOM WITH WHOM I'VE MADE MY PACT.
ぎゅっ
HUG
THAT MUST HAVE FRIGHTENED YOU, THOUGH.
I'M SORRY.
WOBL...
ゆら…
YOU'RE STURDIER THAN I EXPECTED.
BEING A CURSE HANDLER MEANS HAVING SOME WARDS AGAINST SPELLS.
DMP
ダッ
TP
タ
TP
タ
TP
タ

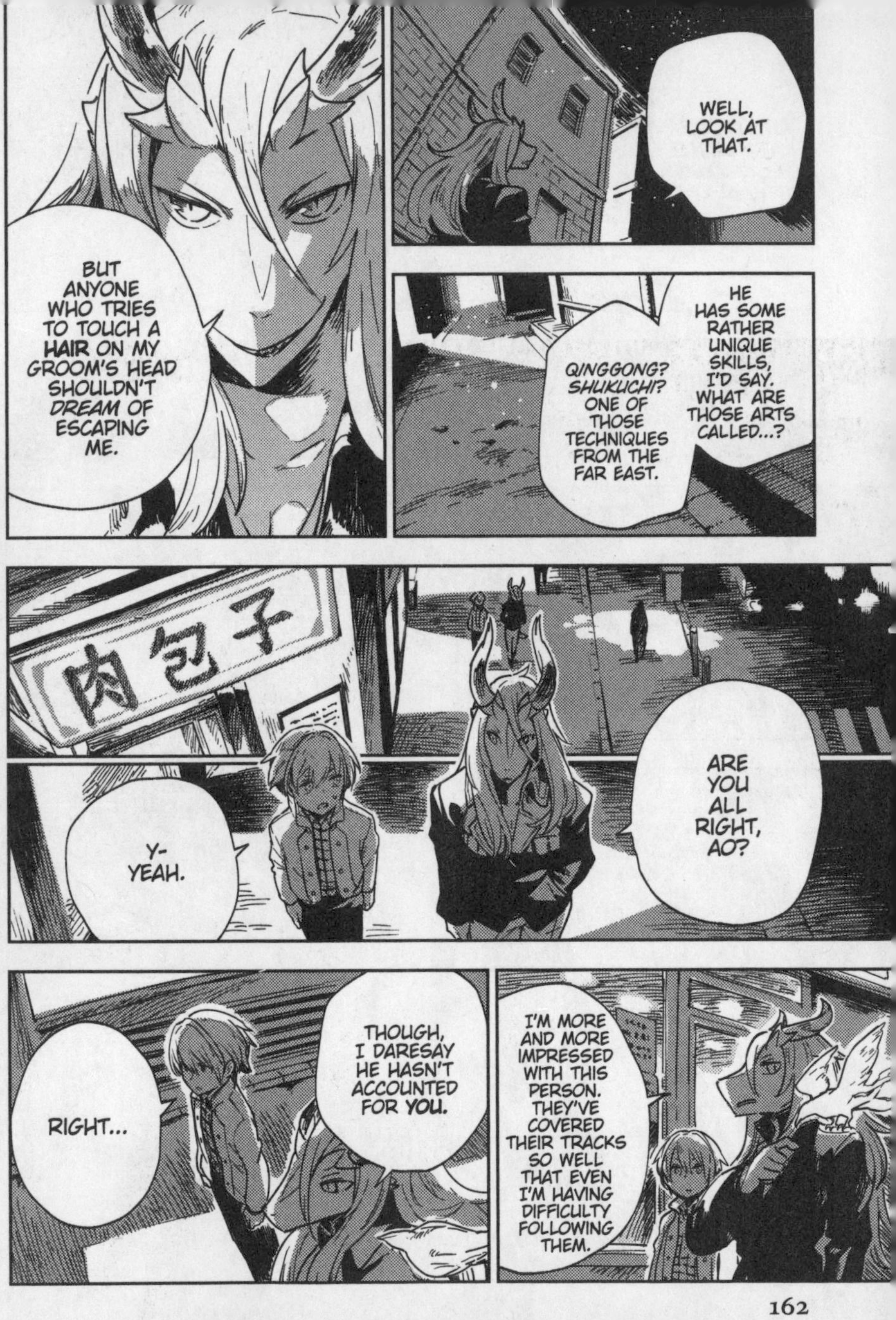
WELL, LOOK AT THAT.
HE HAS SOME RATHER UNIQUE SKILLS, I'D SAY. WHAT ARE THOSE ARTS CALLED...?
QINGGONG? SHUKUCHI? ONE OF THOSE TECHNIQUES FROM THE FAR EAST.
BUT ANYONE WHO TRIES TO TOUCH A HAIR ON MY GROOM'S HEAD SHOULDN'T DREAM OF ESCAPING ME.
肉包子
ARE YOU ALL RIGHT, AO?
Y-YEAH.
I'M MORE AND MORE IMPRESSED WITH THIS PERSON. THEY'VE COVERED THEIR TRACKS SO WELL THAT EVEN I'M HAVING DIFFICULTY FOLLOWING THEM.
THOUGH, I DARESAY HE HASN'T ACCOUNTED FOR YOU.
RIGHT...

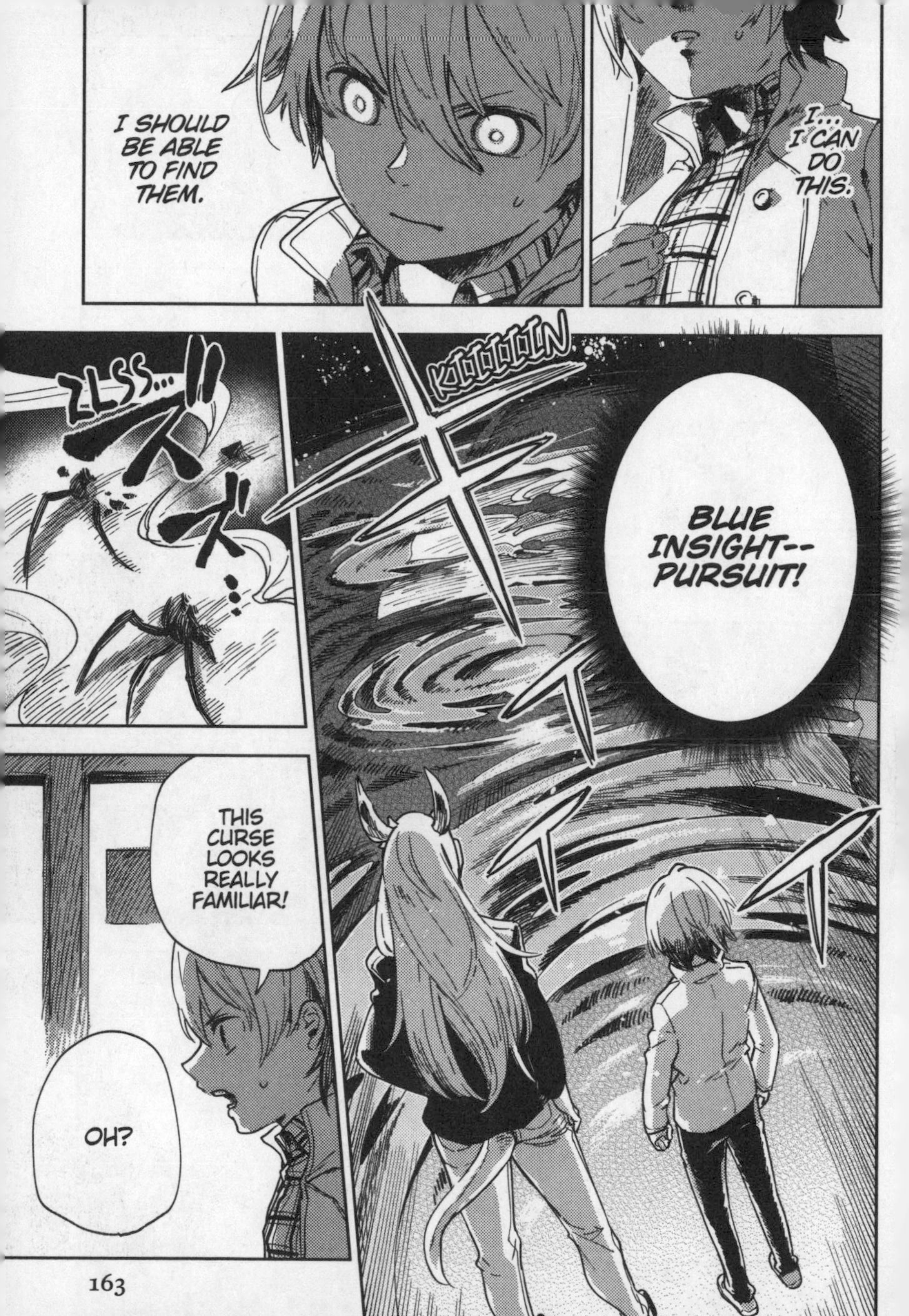
I... I CAN DO THIS.
I SHOULD BE ABLE TO FIND THEM.
KIIIIIIN
BLUE INSIGHT--PURSUIT!
ZLSS...!!
THIS CURSE LOOKS REALLY FAMILIAR!
OH?

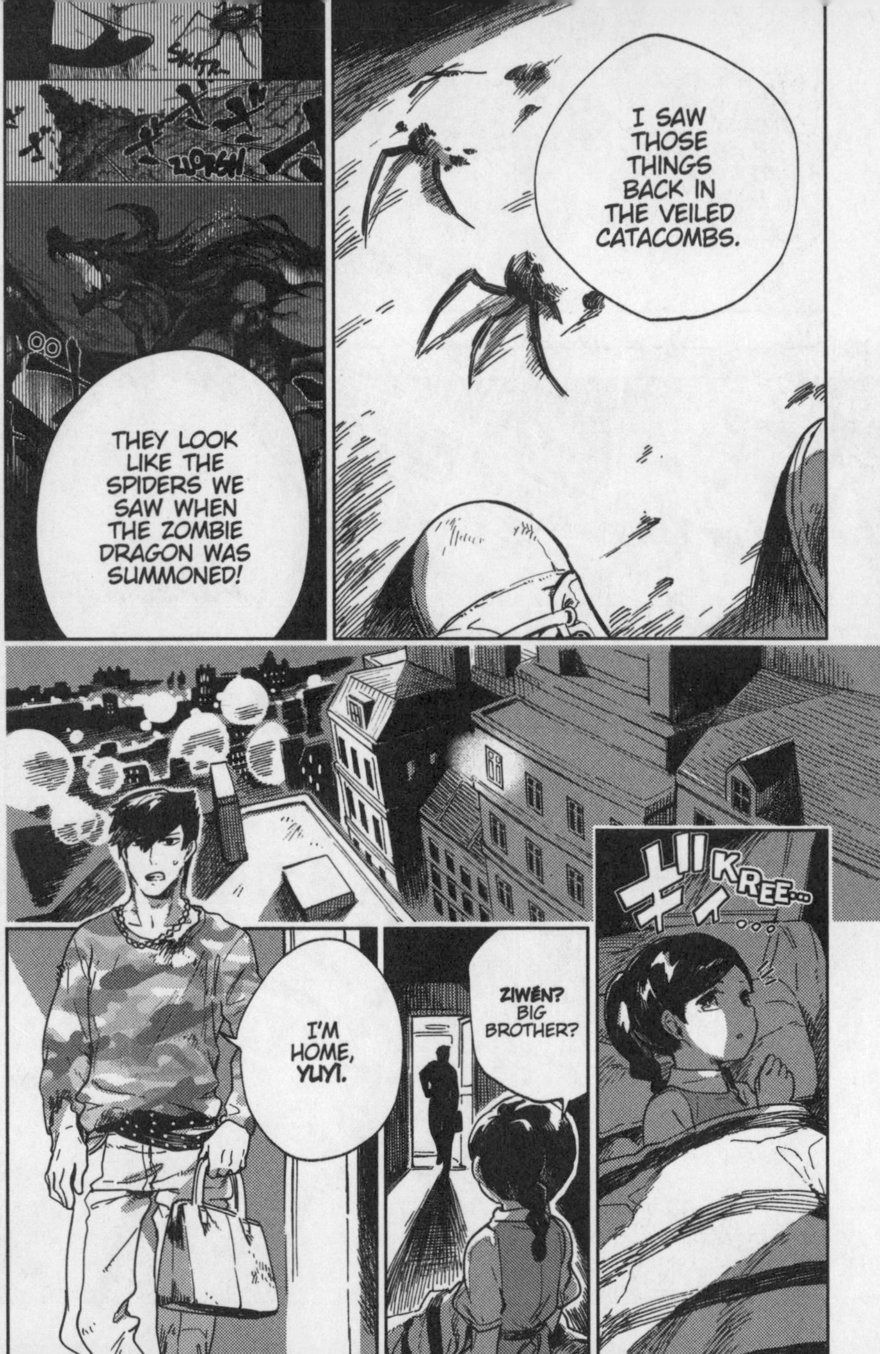
I SAW THOSE THINGS BACK IN THE VEILED CATACOMBS.
SKTTR...
ZLORGH
THEY LOOK LIKE THE SPIDERS WE SAW WHEN THE ZOMBIE DRAGON WAS SUMMONED!
KREE...
キィ…
ZIWEN? BIG BROTHER?
I'M HOME, YUYI.

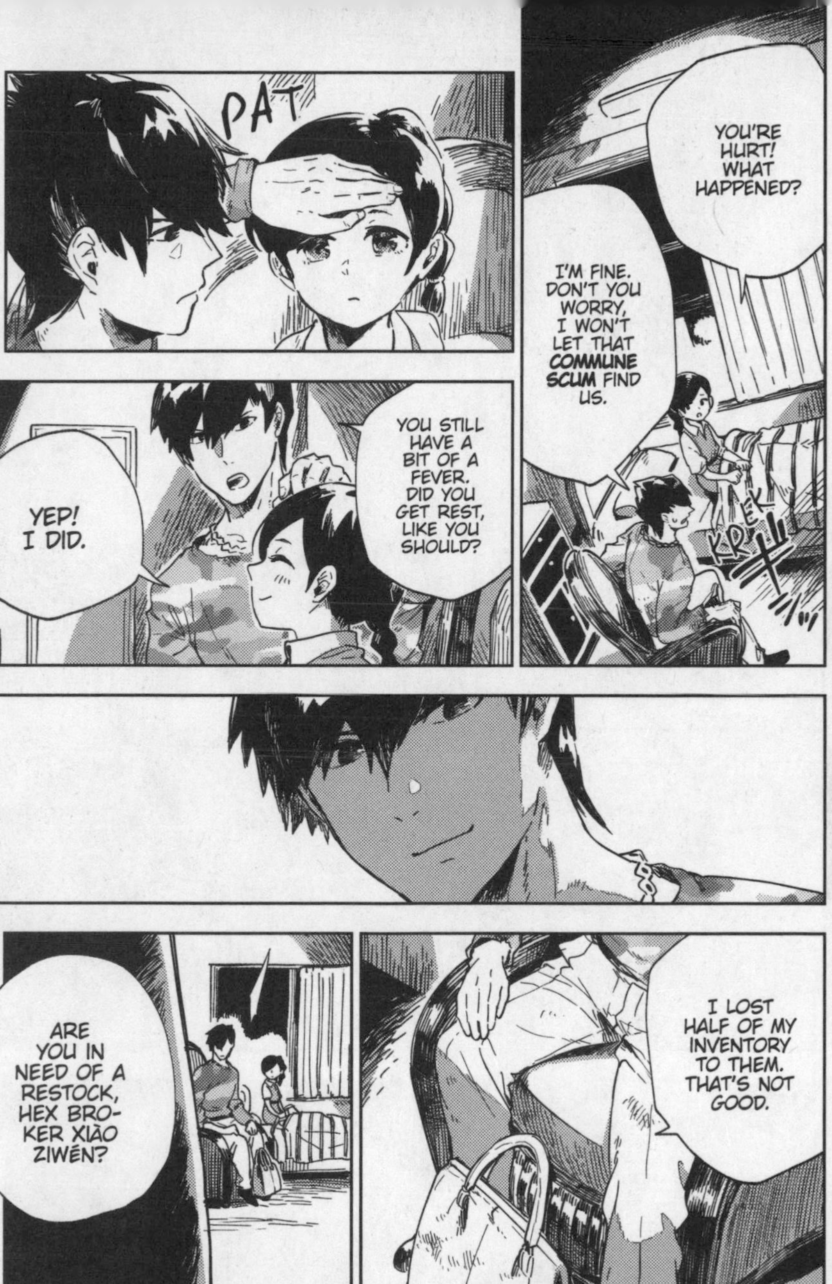
YOU'RE HURT! WHAT HAPPENED?
I'M FINE. DON'T YOU WORRY, I WON'T LET THAT **COMMUNE SCUM** FIND US.
KREK
PAT
YOU STILL HAVE A BIT OF A FEVER. DID YOU GET REST, LIKE YOU SHOULD?
YEP! I DID.
I LOST HALF OF MY INVENTORY TO THEM. THAT'S NOT GOOD.
ARE YOU IN NEED OF A RESTOCK, HEX BROKER XIÀO ZIWÉN?

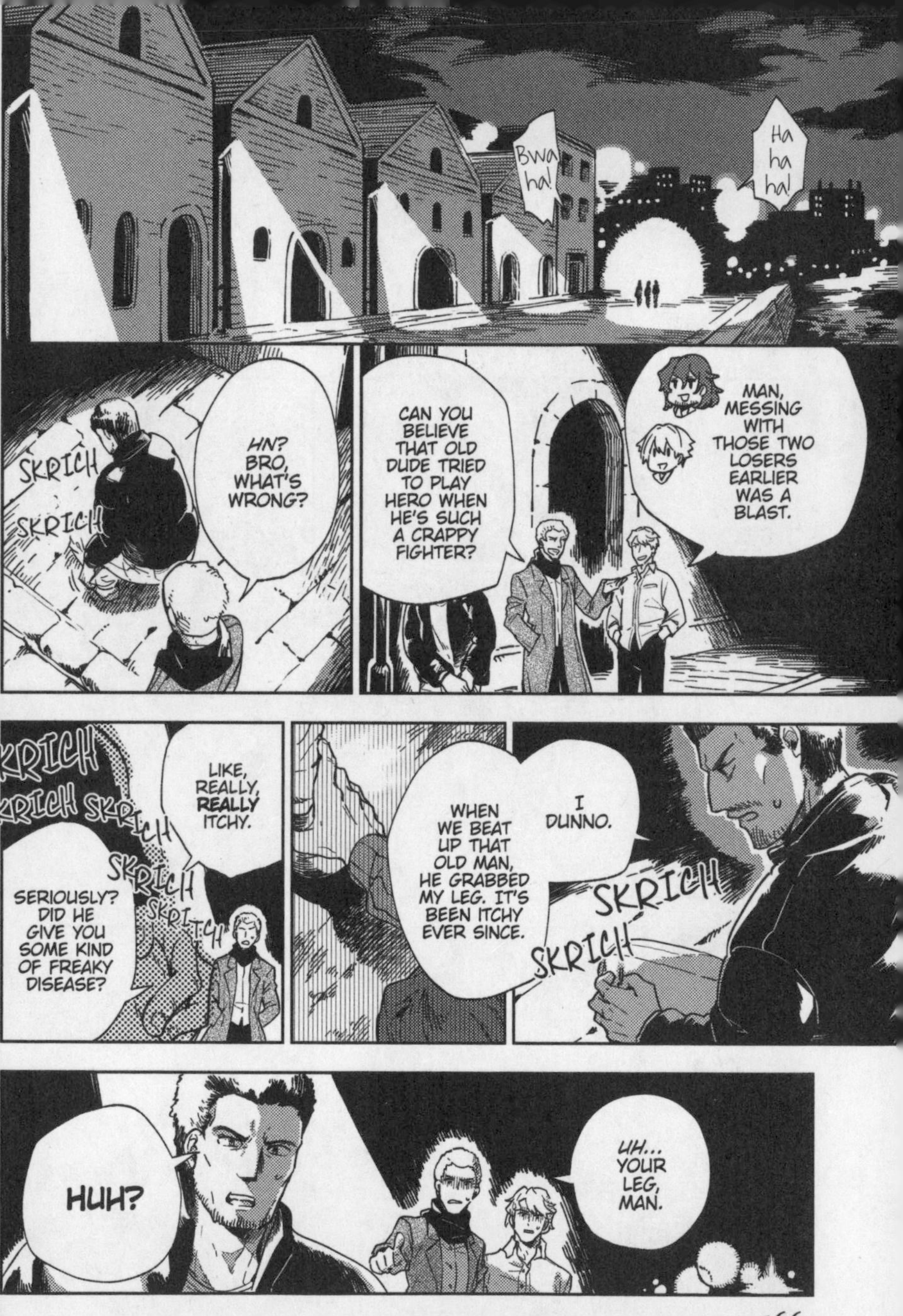
Ha ha ha!
Bwa ha ha!
MAN, MESSING WITH THOSE TWO LOSERS EARLIER WAS A BLAST.
CAN YOU BELIEVE THAT OLD DUDE TRIED TO PLAY HERO WHEN HE'S SUCH A CRAPPY FIGHTER?
HN? BRO, WHAT'S WRONG?
SKRICH
SKRICH
I DUNNO.
SKRICH
SKRICH
WHEN WE BEAT UP THAT OLD MAN, HE GRABBED MY LEG. IT'S BEEN ITCHY EVER SINCE.
LIKE, REALLY, **REALLY** ITCHY.
SKRICH
SKRICH SKRICH
SKRICH
SKRITCH
SERIOUSLY? DID HE GIVE YOU SOME KIND OF FREAKY DISEASE?
UH... YOUR LEG, MAN.
HUH?

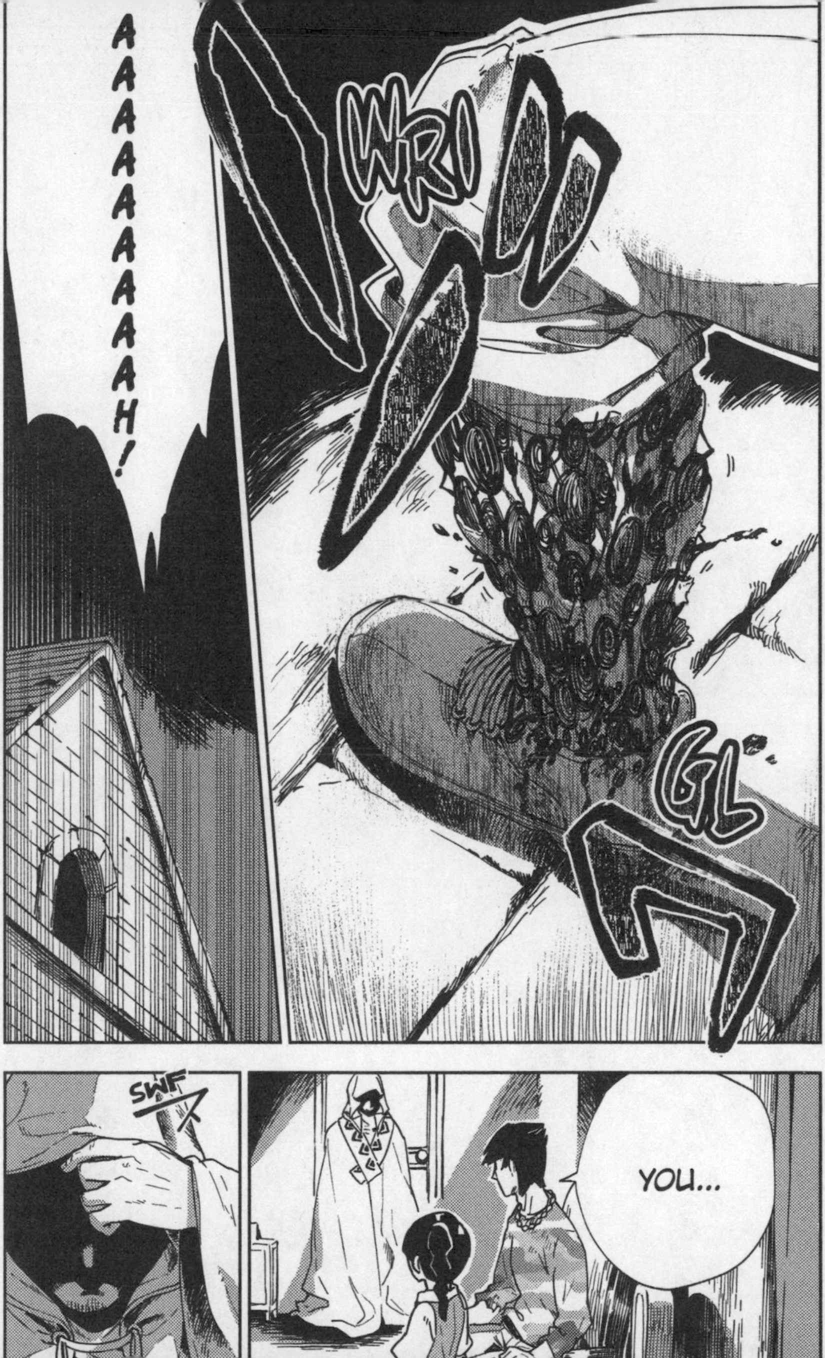
WRI
GL
AAAAAAAAAH!
YOU...
SWF

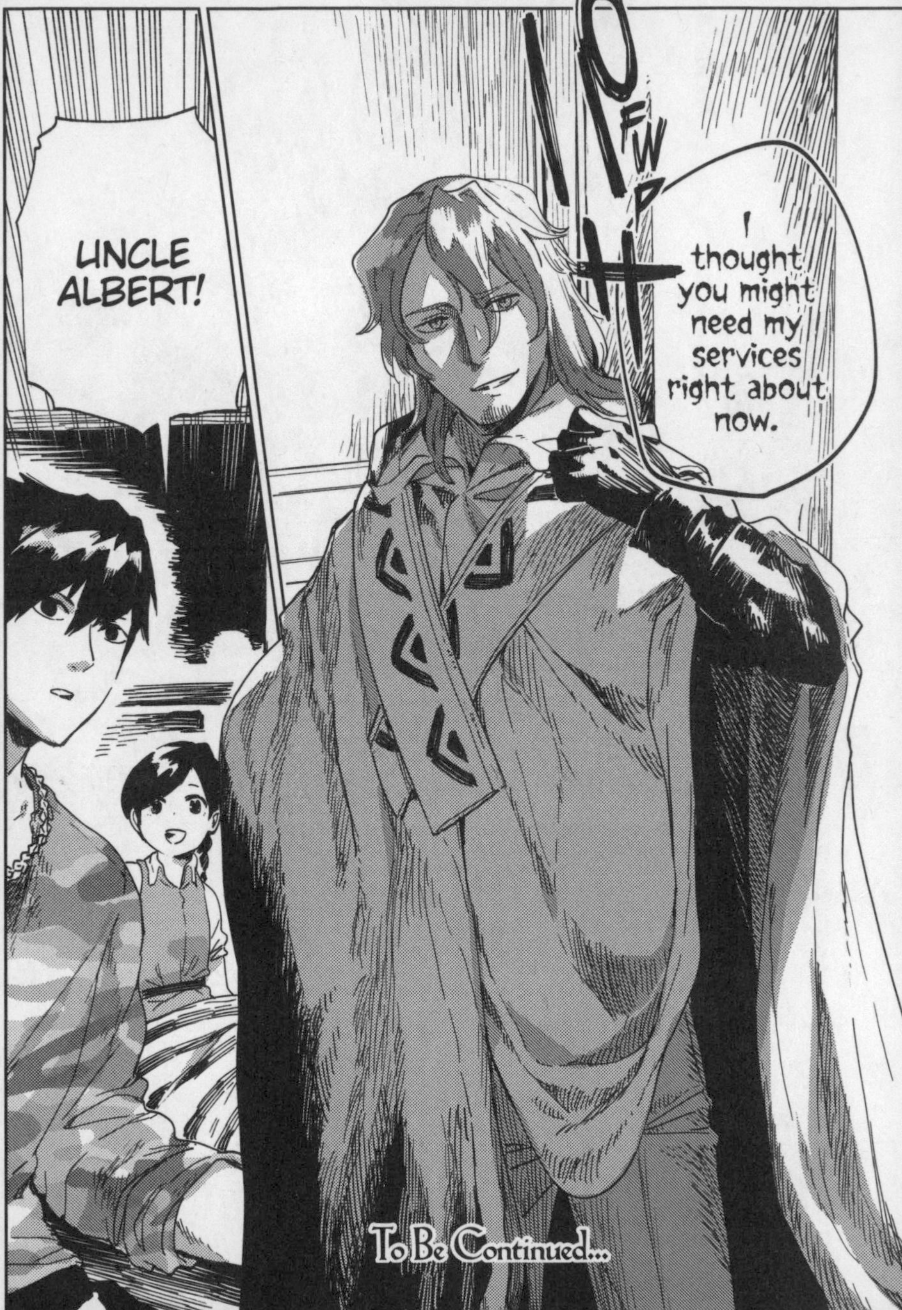
FWP
I thought you might need my services right about now.
UNCLE ALBERT!
To Be Continued...

The Ancient Magus' Bride

WIZARD's BLUE

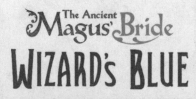

Bonus Four-Panel Manga

Security Measures

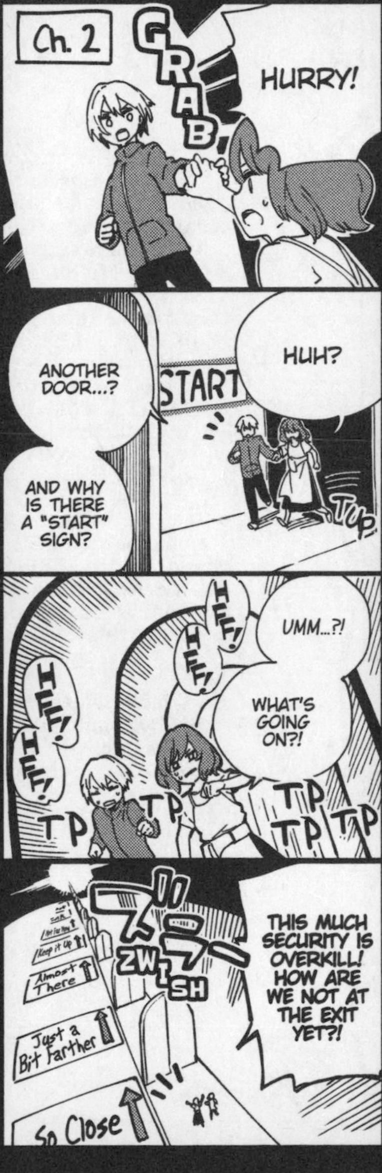
Ch. 2
GRAB
HURRY!
HUH?
ANOTHER DOOR...?
START
AND WHY IS THERE A "START" SIGN?
TUP
UMM...?!
HEF! HEF!
WHAT'S GOING ON?!
HEF! HEF! HEF!
TP TP TP TP TP
THIS MUCH SECURITY IS OVERKILL! HOW ARE WE NOT AT THE EXIT YET?!
ZWISH
Keep it Up
Almost There
Just a Bit Farther
So Close

You Dropped This

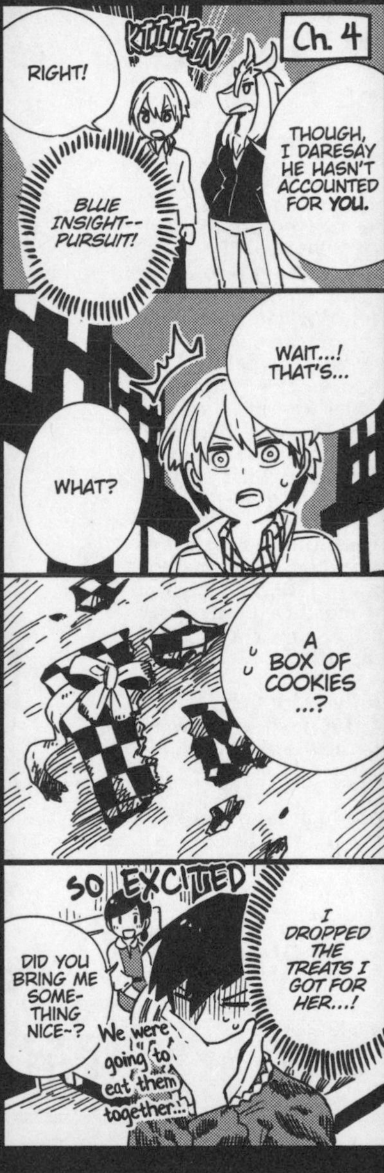
Ch. 4
KIIIIIN
THOUGH, I DARESAY HE HASN'T ACCOUNTED FOR YOU.
RIGHT!
BLUE INSIGHT--PURSUIT!
WAIT...! THAT'S...
WHAT?
A BOX OF COOKIES ...?
I DROPPED THE TREATS I GOT FOR HER...!
SO EXCITED
DID YOU BRING ME SOME-THING NICE~?
We were going to eat them together...

Afterword

Hi! I'm Makoto Sanda, the writer.
I've been given the honor of managing a
corner of the universe Kore Yamazaki-san
created. I'm no stranger to writing about magic
and alchemy, as I penned *The Case Files of
Lord El-Melloi II* (Kadokawa), *Rental Magica*
(Kadokawa), and others, but when I received
the official request for this story in the winter
of 2018, I was incredibly nervous. Several
months later, after two or three meetings, we
decided to flip the original work's "inhuman
monster x young human girl" dynamic on its
head—and thus Ao and Giselle were born. Of
course, it goes without saying that Isuo
Tsukumo-san's vibrant art provided quite
a bit of inspiration for them.

To me, being entrusted with another creator's
world is like adding a new color to my palette.
I hope Ao's pictorial alchemy will, in a similar
fashion, go on to add even more brilliant colors
to the intricate canvas that is the world of *The
Ancient Magus' Bride.*

As Giselle watches hopefully over him, Ao will
timidly, bashfully follow the path set before
his feet, slowly mastering new colors one by
one.

I hope that *Wizard's Blue,* which Isuo Tsukumo
and I have created together, will become a
precious and beloved color to you, too.

Penned while watching *The Case Files of Lord
El-Melloi II: {Rail Zeppelin} Grace Note.*

三田 誠
Sanda Makoto

Understanding Tsukumo in Five Panels or Less!

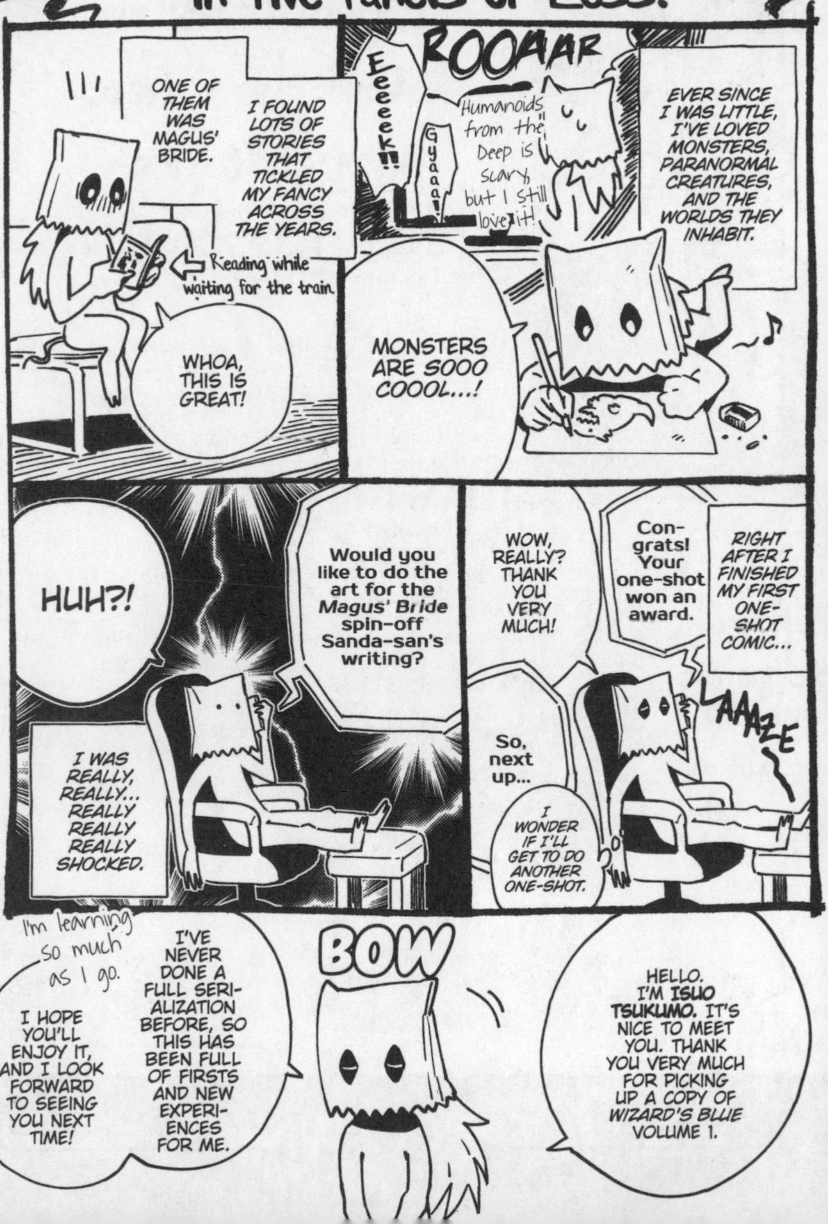
EVER SINCE I WAS LITTLE, I'VE LOVED MONSTERS, PARANORMAL CREATURES, AND THE WORLDS THEY INHABIT.
ROOAAAR
Humanoids from the Deep is scary, but I still love it!
Eeeeek!!
Gyaaa!
MONSTERS ARE SOOO COOOL...!
I FOUND LOTS OF STORIES THAT TICKLED MY FANCY ACROSS THE YEARS.
ONE OF THEM WAS MAGUS' BRIDE.
Reading while waiting for the train.
WHOA, THIS IS GREAT!
RIGHT AFTER I FINISHED MY FIRST ONE-SHOT COMIC...
Con-grats! Your one-shot won an award.
WOW, REALLY? THANK YOU VERY MUCH!
LAAAZE
So, next up...
I WONDER IF I'LL GET TO DO ANOTHER ONE-SHOT.
Would you like to do the art for the Magus' Bride spin-off Sanda-san's writing?
HUH?!
I WAS REALLY, REALLY... REALLY REALLY REALLY SHOCKED.
HELLO. I'M ISUO TSUKUMO. IT'S NICE TO MEET YOU. THANK YOU VERY MUCH FOR PICKING UP A COPY OF WIZARD'S BLUE VOLUME 1.
BOW
I'VE NEVER DONE A FULL SERI-ALIZATION BEFORE, SO THIS HAS BEEN FULL OF FIRSTS AND NEW EXPERI-ENCES FOR ME.
I'm learning so much as I go.
I HOPE YOU'LL ENJOY IT, AND I LOOK FORWARD TO SEEING YOU NEXT TIME!

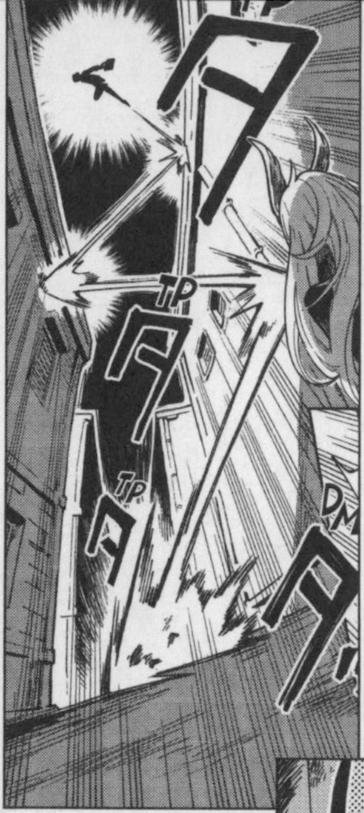
TP
TP
DM

Encounters are more than mere happenstance— they may be fate.

Ao and Giselle follow the tracks left by the mysterious hex broker...

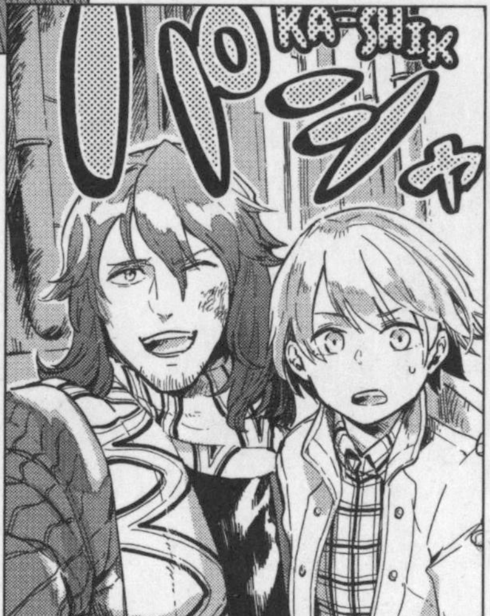
KA-SHIK

but what awaits them at the end of the trail...?

VOLUME 2 COMING SOON

Delve deeper into *The Ancient Magus' Bride* universe with *Wizard's Blue's* fresh take on the relationship between the human and the inhuman!

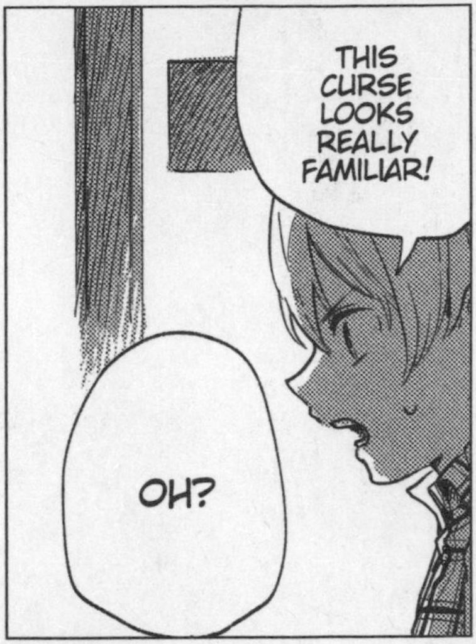
THIS CURSE LOOKS REALLY FAMILIAR!
OH?

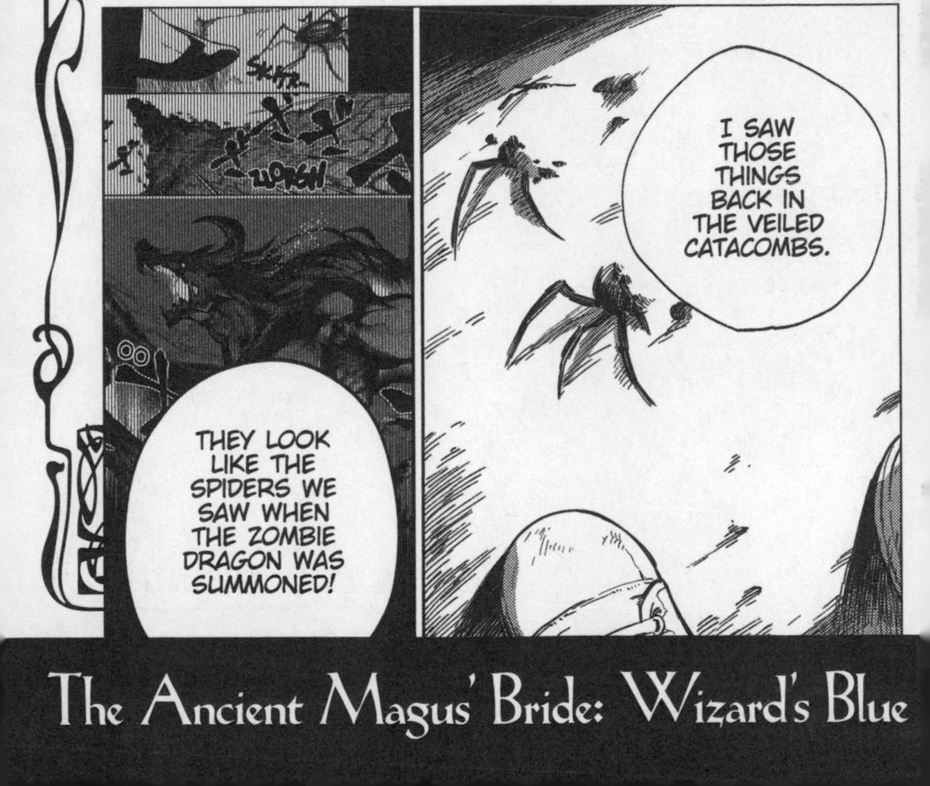
I SAW THOSE THINGS BACK IN THE VEILED CATACOMBS.
SKRR-
ZLORSH
THEY LOOK LIKE THE SPIDERS WE SAW WHEN THE ZOMBIE DRAGON WAS SUMMONED!

The Ancient Magus' Bride: Wizard's Blue

The Ancient Magus' Bride

WIZARD's BLUE

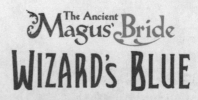

SEVEN SEAS ENTERTAINMENT PRESENTS

The Ancient Magus' Bride
WIZARD'S BLUE
VOLUME 1

story: MAKOTO SANDA   art: ISUO TSUKUMO   script supervisor: KORE YAMAZAKI

TRANSLATION
Adrienne Beck

ADAPTATION
Ysabet Reinhardt MacFarlane

LETTERING AND RETOUCH
Carolina Hernández Mendoza

COVER DESIGN
Nicky Lim
(LOGO) Kris Aubin

PROOFREADER
Janet Houck

EDITOR
Shanti Whitesides

PREPRESS TECHNICIAN
Rhiannon Rasmussen-Silverstein

PRODUCTION MANAGER
Lissa Pattillo

MANAGING EDITOR
Julie Davis

ASSOCIATE PUBLISHER
Adam Arnold

PUBLISHER
Jason DeAngelis

THE ANCIENT MAGUS' BRIDE PSA. 108 WIZARD'S BLUE VOL.1
© Kore Yamazaki 2019 © Isuo Tsukumo 2019 © Makoto Sanda 2019
Originally published in Japan in 2019 by MAG Garden Corporation, TOKYO.
English translation rights arranged through TOHAN CORPORATION, Tokyo.

Seven Seas press and purchase enquiries can be sent to Marketing Manager
Lianne Sentar at press@gomanga.com. Information regarding the distribution
and purchase of digital editions is available from Digital Manager CK Russell
at digital@gomanga.com.

Seven Seas and the Seven Seas logo are trademarks of
Seven Seas Entertainment. All rights reserved.

ISBN: 978-1-64505-839-7

Printed in Canada

First Printing: September 2020

10 9 8 7 6 5 4 3 2 1

FOLLOW US ONLINE: www.sevenseasentertainment.com

READING DIRECTIONS

This book reads from **right to left**, Japanese style.
If this is your first time reading manga, you start
reading from the top right panel on each page and
take it from there. If you get lost, just follow the
numbered diagram here. It may seem backwards at
first, but you'll get the hang of it! Have fun!!

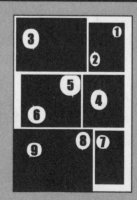